THE ENDS OF RESEARCH

EXPERIMENTAL FUTURES

technological lives, scientific arts, anthropological voices

A series edited by Michael M. J. Fischer and Joseph Dumit

TOM ÖZDEN-SCHILLING

The Ends of Research

Indigenous and Settler Science
after the War in the Woods

DUKE UNIVERSITY PRESS
Durham and London
2023

Printed in the United States of America on acid-free paper ∞
Project Editor: Liz Smith
Designed by A. Mattson Gallagher
Typeset in Untitled Serif and Fira Sans by
Westchester Publishing Services

Library of Congress Cataloging-in-Publication Data
Names: Özden-Schilling, Tom, [date] author.
Title: The ends of research : indigenous and settler science
after the War in the Woods / Tom Özden-Schilling.
Other titles: Experimental futures.
Description: Durham : Duke University Press, 2023. |
Series: Experimental futures | Includes bibliographical
references and index.
Identifiers: LCCN 2023008654 (print)
LCCN 2023008655 (ebook)
ISBN 9781478025535 (paperback)
ISBN 9781478020790 (hardcover)
ISBN 9781478027669 (ebook)
Subjects: LCSH: Anthropology—Canada. | Science—Canada. |
Technology—Canada. | BISAC: SOCIAL SCIENCE /
Anthropology / Cultural & Social | NATURE / Environmental
Conservation & Protection
Classification: LCC GN17.3.C2 O934 2023 (print) |
LCC GN17.3.C2 (ebook) | DDC 301.0971—dc23/eng/20230720
LC record available at https://lccn.loc.gov/2023008654
LC ebook record available at https://lccn.loc.gov/2023008655

Cover art: A 100-meter-wide right-of-way through Gitanyow
territory cleared for the Northwest Transmission Line.
Photo by author.

CONTENTS

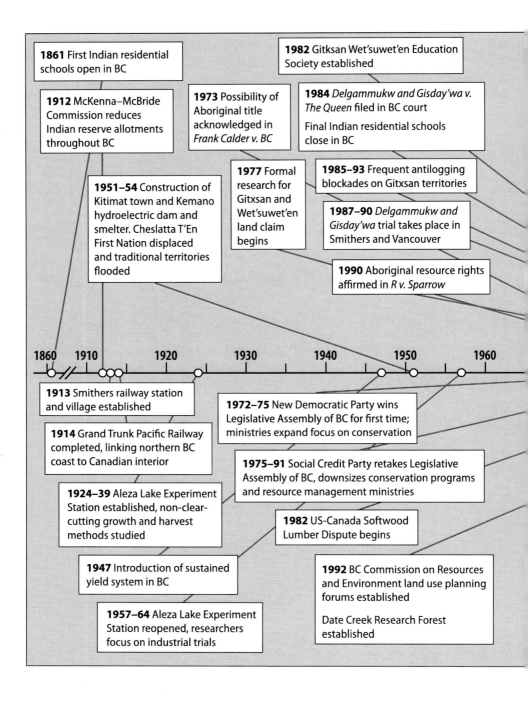

1861 First Indian residential schools open in BC

1982 Gitksan Wet'suwet'en Education Society established

1912 McKenna–McBride Commission reduces Indian reserve allotments throughout BC

1973 Possibility of Aboriginal title acknowledged in *Frank Calder v. BC*

1984 *Delgammukw and Gisday'wa v. The Queen* filed in BC court

Final Indian residential schools close in BC

1951–54 Construction of Kitimat town and Kemano hydroelectric dam and smelter. Cheslatta T'En First Nation displaced and traditional territories flooded

1977 Formal research for Gitxsan and Wet'suwet'en land claim begins

1985–93 Frequent antilogging blockades on Gitsxan territories

1987–90 *Delgammukw and Gisday'wa* trial takes place in Smithers and Vancouver

1990 Aboriginal resource rights affirmed in *R v. Sparrow*

1860　1910　　　1920　　　1930　　　1940　　　1950　　　1960

1913 Smithers railway station and village established

1972–75 New Democratic Party wins Legislative Assembly of BC for first time; ministries expand focus on conservation

1914 Grand Trunk Pacific Railway completed, linking northern BC coast to Canadian interior

1975–91 Social Credit Party retakes Legislative Assembly of BC, downsizes conservation programs and resource management ministries

1924–39 Aleza Lake Experiment Station established, non-clear-cutting growth and harvest methods studied

1982 US-Canada Softwood Lumber Dispute begins

1947 Introduction of sustained yield system in BC

1992 BC Commission on Resources and Environment land use planning forums established

Date Creek Research Forest established

1957–64 Aleza Lake Experiment Station reopened, researchers focus on industrial trials

1991 Initial *Delgamuukw* trial decision

2004 *Haida Nation v. BC* and *Taku River Tlingit v. BC* decisions affirm duty to consult

1993 Gitxsan Treaty Society established

BC Treaty Commission established

2010 Sixty-six BC First Nations sign Save the Fraser declaration protesting Enbridge pipeline

Unistot'en Camp established

1994–2004 Watershed Restoration Research program funds new research on biodiversity protection, ecological systems, and water quality

2012 Idle No More protests begin in BC

Gitanyow Hereditary Chiefs establish interim Recognition and Reconciliation Agreement with BC government; Lax'yip Land Use Plan goes into effect

1997 *Delgamuukw* federal appeal ends with precedents for oral histories, call for retrial

2014 *Tsilhqot'in* final decision, Supreme Court of Canada

2019–20 Wet'suwet'en land guardians protesting Coastal GasLink project arrested, checkpoints dismantled

1998 Nisga'a Final Agreement ratified

2018 Wet'suwet'en chief Wah Tah K'eght (Henry Alfred) dies

1970   1980   1990   2000   2010   2020

1993 Aleza Lake Research Forest reopened by University of Northern British Columbia

2004 Forests and Range Practices Act replaces Forest Practices Code as overarching BC forestry management policy

1998 Bulkley Land and Resource Management Plan finalized, first community land use plan accepted by BC government

2005 Campell government announces "New Relationship"

2006–16 Enbridge Northern Gateway pipeline project

2001–17 Moore Foundation establishes Wild Salmon Ecosystems Initiative; philanthropies displace provincial government as leading funders of research

2018 BC experiences worst forest fire season on record; 1.35 million hectares burned

2002–9 BC Forest Service Research Branch and numerous regional offices closed

A NOTE ON THE MAPS

As this book argues repeatedly, any cartographic object should be treated
with caution and care. This same warning applies to all of the maps displayed
in this book, all of which were composed by Nicholas O'Gara from a complex
array of sources. Lakes and rivers were downloaded from the US Geological
Survey's (USGS) "North America Rivers and Lakes" website (United States
Geological Survey 2022) and edited based on satellite photos from Google
Maps. Hillshade and roads are based on data from the USGS 3D Elevation
Program (United States Geological Survey 2021) and from the Government
of Canada's National Road Network GeoBase Series (Government of Canada
2022b), respectively. The locations of populated places were downloaded from
the Canadian Geographical Names Database (Government of Canada 2022a).
Data for the original boundaries of the Bulkley Land and Resource Management Plan area, which were in effect from 1998 until 2006, were downloaded
from the Government of British Columbia's "Bulkley Valley Sustainable
Resource Management Plan" website (Government of British Columbia, n.d.).
The borders of the Gitxsan and Wet'suwet'en traditional territories were georeferenced from images of the maps produced for the original *Delgamuukw
and Gisday'wa* trial (Gitxsan Watershed Authorities, 2004; Office of the
Wet'suwet'en, n.d.). The borders of the Gitanyow traditional territories are

based on the geographic information systems (GIS) shape files produced for the Gitanyow Lax'yip Land Use Plan (Gitanyow Hereditary Chiefs 2009).

The lines, points, and polygons depicted on these maps are meant to provide readers with visual heuristics for navigating the stories herein, but they are also meant to underline the diversity of the different kinds of claims that have been made on the landscapes of northwest British Columbia since the 1980s. Because the precise borders of the Gitxsan, Wet'suwet'en, and Gitanyow territorial claims have been subject to substantial legal debate and bureaucratic action, the boundaries of individual clan and house group territories for the three nations have been omitted. Readers should be aware, however, that all of these house group "boundaries" have longer and more established histories of recognition among Gitxsan, Wet'suwet'en, and Gitanyow people than the geo-bodies of any of the three First Nations as a whole (see Napoleon 2005; Thom 2009). Information on individual house groups is available on the maps and mapping resources cited above as well as in other documents cited throughout the following chapters.

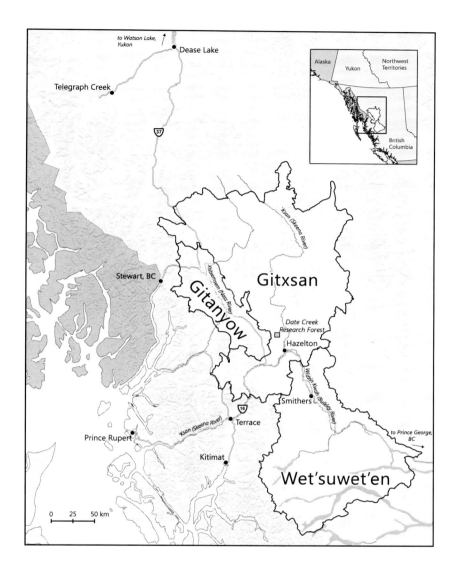

MAP 0.1 Map of Gitxsan, Gitanyow, and Wet'suwet'en territories and surrounding region in northwest British Columbia. For an explanation of the relative positions of the borders of these territories, see A Note on the Maps.

In the final days of September 1988, a small group of Gitxsan people block-aded a bridge outside Kispiox reserve village in northwest British Columbia, Canada.[1] No non–First Nations traffic—and especially no logging trucks—would be allowed to cross the sole bridge linking the northern reaches of the Gitxsan traditional territory to the rest of the province.[2] Within hours, four additional Gitxsan blockades were established nearby. By the next evening, logging truck drivers and White residents from neighboring towns had begun gathering on the other side of the bridge, and armed police officers were arriving as well. The people who organized the initial blockade later admitted that they had no idea how long the standoff might last (Glavin 1990). The impetus for blockades, though, had been building for years. Hearings had recently begun in *Delgamuukw and Gisday'wa v. The Queen*, a lawsuit asserting ownership over 58,000 square kilometers of land in the region that the chiefs of the Gitxsan and neighboring Wet'suwet'en First Nations had been preparing for over a decade.[3] Time and again during the original trial, Gitxsan and Wet'suwet'en claimants had asked the government of British Columbia to halt industrial logging on the contested territories until the question of land ownership could be resolved in court. North of Kispiox Bridge lay the valleys of the upper 'Ksan (Skeena River) and its tributaries, some of the few remaining forests in the rugged region yet to be subject to extensive clear-cutting. Repeatedly denied the opportunity to consult with the provincial government about the scale of these harvests or receive any royalties from subsequent sales, dozens of Gitxsan decided to halt the flow of timber away from their territories by themselves.

A few tense days after they began, the blockades were taken down. Almost immediately, however, political actors and journalists across North America began citing the confrontations as the Gitxsan First Nation's opening salvo in an antilogging revolution that had already come to span the entire Pacific coast (Glavin 1988; Campbell 1989). In the final decades of the twentieth century, more than one hundred blockades and other direct actions would eventually be carried out to protest the expansion of industrial logging in old-growth forests from Alaska to Northern California (Satterfield 2002). Among the myriad Indigenous and non-Indigenous groups to stage protests during this period, Gitxsan activists were perhaps the most prolific. Between 1988 and 1993, Gitxsan people organized dozens of road and railway blockades throughout northwest British Columbia (Blomley 1996). Some, like the blockade at Kispiox Bridge, lasted a few days. Others simply slowed the flow of passenger traffic, as Gitxsan men and women handed pamphlets to travelers driving on highways through their reserves. A handful of blockades stretched on for months, and temporarily prevented timber harvesters from accessing enormous regions of forested land. To many outside observers, the Gitxsan blockades transcended immediate questions over the ownership of particular territories. Rather, the conflicts extended and exemplified a continent-spanning battle over "nature" writ large: a northern front for the "War in the Woods" (Braun 2002).

This is not a book about blockades. To most Gitxsan activists, the headline-grabbing confrontations of the 1980s were simply continuations of long-running forms of resistance against colonial power—routine practices that had been heightened to keep concrete sovereignty demands visible while their chiefs were cross-examined in court (Galois 2007; A. Mills 2005; Monet and Skanu'u 1992; Sterritt 1989).[4] In the decades since, however, some Gitxsan have incorporated these labors of resistance into new technical initiatives and knowledge-making projects where they have encountered other kinds of activists—activists with different understandings of resistance, different concepts of survival, and different ideas about how the futures of the region's forests ought to unfold.

This book is about knowledge-making labor undertaken after direct conflict on the land. It is about how this labor, and the epistemic encounters this labor engendered, eventually came to define the lives of the scientists and other researchers—both White and First Nations—who built lives in northwest British Columbia in the wake of the original War in the Woods. Yet it is also about the elusiveness of resolution, and the effects of conflict and yearning on individuals. The following chapters are about people whose investments in long-term ecological experiments and other technical projects, and whose senses of place and purpose, have become entangled in unending, ever-changing debates over the ways knowledge might legitimate political action.

Many of the watershed restoration and land defense projects established in northwest British Columbia at the end of the twentieth century are well known among conservationists around the world. In the first years after Gitxsan-led campaigns against resource extraction first came to be labeled as part of a Pacific coast–spanning "war," locally organized land use planning forums, forest growth experiments, and First Nations–led technical training and digital countermapping programs brought international attention and hundreds of aspiring researchers to northwest British Columbia. With a handful of the many First Nations researchers already living in the region, some of these new arrivals became internationally recognizable figures; several of their initiatives continue to be cited as groundbreaking achievements in global histories of ecological conservation and Indigenous activism. Almost immediately after most of these initiatives began, however, the government ministries that supported them radically shrank. New forest management policies swiftly reduced the authority of government scientists. Incipient First Nations treaty-making and development consultation processes stalled or unraveled. In the years since, most of the people who had hoped to devote their lives to these projects have had to reframe their research and their designs on power simply to make ends meet.

These trends are not unique to British Columbia. Throughout North America and in other settler colonial spaces across the world, landscapes surrounding protracted resource conflicts have played host to a wide range of experiments in science-based governance—a range of experiments that grew rapidly during the final years of the twentieth century (Nadasdy 2003; Whyte 2013; Z. Todd 2014; Neale and Vincent 2017; D. E. Powell 2018; Cattelino 2019; Liboiron 2021). Such experiments have been designed with many different goals in mind. In some, organizers have sought to mollify resistance to specific extractive projects by inviting skeptical residents into new participatory forums, or by attempting to depoliticize debates over the ecological effects of these projects through new configurations of technical media. In others, researchers have leveraged government and corporate funds made available in the name of "conflict resolution" to generate new tools for land-based activism. Regardless of their original aims, however, many of these experiments have found prolonged and unruly afterlives amid the uncertainties of government downsizing. Particularly in rural areas like northwest British Columbia, many of the White and Indigenous researchers who have invested time and meaning in these initiatives have seen their own roles as neighbors, experts, and kin change, as well. Yet together, these people and projects have persisted. By exploring how research and researchers have remade one another in the long shadow of the War in the Woods, this book raises new questions about the entangled afterlives of conflict and science-based governance. What part of a project, an expert identity, an aspiration, or collaborative relationship "survives" amid perpetual change?

Each of the following chapters focuses on a facet of rural researchers' social and professional "survival" that has been unsettled by government downsizing: prominent forestry scientists retiring without successors to carry on decades-long studies; First Nations capacity-building initiatives designed to train local cohorts of Indigenous technicians collapsing for want of funds; tense negotiations over the roles that corporate-funded data collection projects might play in the futures of collaborative activism. Treating these transitions as intimate processes of social reproduction, the book shows how new concepts of inheritance, nostalgia, resilience, and extinction have come into use among White and First Nations researchers who see the future health of the region's forests as interwoven with the continuance of their careers. Each chapter also examines specific planning documents, Indigenous territory maps, and other technical artifacts produced through these initiatives, and explores how such artifacts have served researchers as vehicles for surviving institutional restructuring. For many researchers, the relationships that have cohered around these artifacts have become crucial spaces for imagining futures beyond their transient institutional arrangements, beyond settler colonial extractivism, and beyond the War in the Woods. Taken together, these researchers' stories highlight the creative forms of labor required to sustain practices of inquiry when both landscapes and social formations are in flux.

To be clear: White and First Nations researchers have experienced government downsizing in different terms. Many have also articulated the meaning and stakes of continuance in different registers as well. Each of the following chapters, then, shows how specific research and documentary practices have persisted alongside particular modes of reflecting on these practices and narrativizing them within other accounts of individual and collective life. Part of the purpose of this book is to show how this twinned attention to acts and accounts of continuance might be useful in other anthropological studies of science and technology. Indigenous literary scholars have been refining similar frameworks for decades. Over the course of his career, Anishinaabe (Minnesota Chippewa Tribe, White Earth Reservation) author and literary theorist Gerald Vizenor developed the term "survivance" to describe the acts and modes of reflection through which Indigenous individuals negotiate the legacies of colonialism in their everyday lives. These practices and accounts are rarely heroic, Vizenor insists, but neither are they grim or despairing. Survivance is more than mere survival; like the figure of the shape-shifting bear that often emerges in Vizenor's literary work, survivance encompasses situated responses that can be simultaneously ironic, violent, and playful (see Vizenor 1990, 1994). As such, acts of survivance are often indirect in their effects. Like many of the long-term research practices described in the following pages, these acts are also replete with moral ambiguities and potential complicities. Throughout his scholarly and literary writings, Vizenor expresses a deep suspicion of totalizing answers to colonial violence and its myriad political and affective legacies. "The ironic fullness of original sin, shame, and stigmata want salvation, a singular solution to absence and certain victimry," he writes. "There is a crucial cultural distinction between monotheism, apocalypticism, natural reason, and native survivance" (2008, 18). Practitioners of survivance, Vizenor's writings make clear, know that the work of resistance is ongoing, and that it must be made to continue even as projects change form and individual practitioners depart.

This book is not about how experts and expert knowledge become implicated in resource politics, land disputes, or other engagements with power. Survivance, as I interpret it throughout the following chapters, is simply a method for making collaborative life in the face of continual disruptions. By focusing on White and First Nations researchers' attachments rather than on the rise and fall of specific institutions or projects, this book challenges prevailing anthropological approaches to expertise by asking how researchers' lives come to matter within rural histories of conservation and extractivism. This approach is particularly urgent in zones of Indigenous and settler colonial conflict, where understanding how individuals' lives and aspirations come to shape collective projects remains crucial to understanding how such projects reshape individual lives in turn, particularly as prevailing livelihood strategies and policy regimes undergo continual change. As I describe in the epilogue, the arrests of dozens of Wet'suwet'en antipipeline activists in northwest British Columbia in early 2020 initiated hundreds of Indigenous-led blockades that effectively shut down Canada's rail and maritime shipping infrastructures for nearly a month. Much like the earlier blockades against industrial forestry, the ways that contemporary activists articulate new challenges to extractivism will echo long past these initial moments of confrontation; some challenges will eventually be woven into the fabric of activists' lives. In the meantime, the stories that fill the following pages—stories about finding meaning in lives devoted to research—may yet offer clues about the kinds of challenges young activists might encounter as they persist with their work in the face of unceasing change.

ACKNOWLEDGMENTS

This book bears the fingerprints of hundreds of generous souls. Since first beginning ethnographic work in British Columbia in 2011, I have found a remarkably welcoming community there, particularly in and around the town of Smithers. Yvonne Lattie and her family, Bridie O'Brien, Neil J. Sterritt, Kenny Rabnett, Doug Donaldson, Amanda Follett, Phil Burton, Taylor Bachrach, Russell Collier, John Ridsdale, Daryl Hanson, Roger McMillan, Don Morgan, Rick Budhwa, and many others all helped me to find my bearings and get myself entangled in the joys and dramas that come with small-town life. Perhaps more than any other single individual, Richard Overstall helped to connect me with many of the people who became my primary interlocutors. Richard also helped to demystify the dense and complicated recent history of the Bulkley Valley for me during long, patient conversations. My first hosts in Smithers, Tracy and Bill McIntyre, emphatically made me part of their family throughout my time in the northwest, and helped me to feel like I had known them, their friends, and their neighbors for years. Darlene Vegh and her husband, Gary, as well as Dave Coates, Sybille Haussler, and Johanna Pfalz, have welcomed me back to the region multiple times, and have helped to turn the entire research and writing process into a sustained labor of love.

Elsewhere in British Columbia, I also enjoyed gracious welcomes and good conversation. In Prince George, Gail Fondahl, Staffan Lindgren, Kathy Lewis, Dezene Huber, and Greg Lowan-Trudeau helped me to expand and improve my project through productive and engaging correspondences. Ramona Rose and Kim Stathers were skillful and tireless guides of the Northern BC Archives; with Mike Jull and Harry Coates, Ramona and Kim welcomed me into the region's intellectual community and introduced me to numerous other interlocutors as I began to develop new projects. During my second period of fieldwork in Victoria, conversations with Christine Fletcher, Jim Goudie, Marvin Eng, and other forestry researchers provided a Rosetta Stone that helped me to unlock the meanings and insinuations of Victoria's particular dialects of ministry-speak. I am especially grateful to Marvin and to Marvin's wife, Christie Wishart Eng, for making sure that my time in the capital wasn't spent solely in interviews and office visits. Andrew Fall was similarly expansive and inclusive during my brief visit to his home on Lasqueti Island.

I have had the good fortune to share my work with a number of helpful readers and audiences. Paul Nadasdy, first as a discussant on a panel that Tyler McCreary and I organized for a meeting of the American Anthropological Association, and later as a generous reader of still-forming book chapters, has been crucial in pushing me to broaden my conceptualization of the project as a whole. Renya Ramirez, Michael Hathaway, Jessica Cattelino, and Hugh Gusterson also joined Paul and me for a workshop on the full manuscript, and each provided exhaustive and invaluable commentary— an especially notable gift considering the fact that the workshop took place (on Zoom, alas) during the first week of COVID-related shutdowns in the United States. Members of the Harvard Political Anthropology and Political Ecology Working Group were indispensable in helping me to rework early drafts; Delia Duong-Ba Wendel, Eve McGlynn, Jared McCormick, and the indefatigable Rachel Thompson were particularly generous with their time and feedback.

Outside Massachusetts, I received far-ranging and provocative feedback on different versions of chapters from thoughtful audiences at the Department of Geography at Florida State University; the Environmental Studies program at Tufts University; the Department of Anthropology at State University of New York in Oswego; the Department of Sociology and Anthropology at Bowdoin College; the Department of Anthropology at Macquarie University in Sydney, Australia; the Natural Resources and Environmental Studies Institute at the University of Northern British Columbia; the Science and Technology Studies Circle and, later, the Weatherhead Center for International Affairs at Harvard University; the Humanities Research Center at Rice University; the Department of Anthropology at Durham University; the Department of Sociology at Koç University; the Humanities, Arts, and Social Sciences faculty at the Singapore University of Technology and Design; the College of Environment and Natural Resource Management at Cần Thơ University in Vietnam; the Engineering, Design, and Society program at the Colorado School of Mines; the Department of Anthropology at the University of Wyoming; the Undergraduate Anthropology Club at the University of Arkansas at Little Rock; and the Department of Sociology and Anthropology at the National University of Singapore.

My debts on and off campus at MIT have become intricate enough to fill a phone book. Stephen Tapscott has been a stalwart friend, role model, and life coach since I first enrolled in his course, Modernist Poetry, in 2003. My cohort mates in the HASTS program, Emily (Xi) Lin, Canay Özden-Schilling, and Amah Edoh, and many of our fellow graduate students in the program struggled valiantly to make Cambridge both an intellectual community and a place of belonging and care. I am particularly grateful to Michaela Thompson, David Singerman, Marie Burks, Shreeharsh Kelkar, Peter Oviatt, Shira Smu'ely, Teasel Muir-Harmony, Ben Wilson, Rebecca Woods, Chihyung Jeong, Alma Steingart, Orkideh Bezrouhan, Nate Deshmukh-Towery, Ellan Spero, Reneé Blackburn, Lucas Müller, Emily Wanderer, Lisa Messeri, Michael Rossi, Candis Callison, Ashawari Chaudhuri, Amy Johnson, Clare Kim, Rijul Kochhar, Crystal Lee, Jia Hui Lee, Lan Li, Grace Kim, Beth Semel, Luisa Reis Castro, Alison Laurence, Mitali Thakor, Catarina Scaramelli, Nicole Labruto, and Shekhar Krishnan.

Thanks in part to a Social Science Research Council (SSRC) Dissertation Development Proposal Fellowship group called Mediated Futures organized by Arvind Rajagopal and William Mazzarella, my early attempts at drafts were seen by far more eyes and far better brains than I deserved. For nearly a decade, Bryce Peake, Eric Hirsch, Yana Stainova, Andrew Brandel, and Samuel Shearer have been some of my most diligent and thoughtful readers and friends. Together with Aslı Arpak, Leksa Lee, Julia Yezbick, and especially Lindsay Bell, Denielle Elliott, and Tyler McCreary, this group has contributed far more to the words and ideas spelled out here than I could have possibly deserved. In different settings, Megan Brown, Richard Daly, Bill Rankin, David Kneas, Josep Simon, Tim Neale, Vincent Duclos, Candis Callison, Robyn D'Avignon, Lyle Fearnley, Jennifer Hamilton, Warwick Anderson, Gabriella Soto-Laveaga, Daniella Bleichmar, Emma Kowal, Jessica Smith,

Chris Andersen, Kyle Powys Whyte, Joanna Radin, Ron Niezen, and Donna Goldstein have each greatly helped to improve my ideas as well. In addition to the generous support I received from the SSRC for preliminary fieldwork in British Columbia, summer research grants from the MIT International Science and Technology Initiative, the MIT Center for International Studies, and the Wenner-Gren Foundation (Dissertation Fieldwork Grant #8720) have all provided critical financial support for different stages of the project. Several people at Duke University Press also deserve big thanks for somehow making the overall book publication process into a genuinely enjoyable experience. I am particularly grateful to Ken Wissoker for his support and guidance during the review process, and to Ryan Kendall and Liz Smith for their skill and patience in guiding me through the production process.

During my time as a graduate student, faculty in the Departments of History and Anthropology, and the Science, Technology, and Society (HASTS) Program at MIT were instrumental in helping me to develop this project. I am particularly grateful to Jeff Ravel, Susan Silbey, David Jones, Natasha Schüll, Amy Moran-Thomas, Jean Jackson, Jim Howe, Elizabeth Wood, Anne McCants, Craig Wilder, Robin Scheffler, Will Derringer, Hannah Shell, Clapperton Chakanetsa Mavhunga, Ros Williams, and Lerna Ekmekçioğlu. I am permanently indebted to Harriet Ritvo for exposing me to the engrossing world of environmental history (and, by extension, environmental anthropology). Heather Paxson and Stefan Helmreich's influence on my trajectory in HASTS (and beyond) has been profound, given the measureless time and energy they have both poured into helping me think about how to assemble intellectual projects into a satisfying academic life. Other staff at MIT, including Bianca Singletary, Paree Pinkney, Judy Spitzer, Amberly Steward, Randyn Miller, and Carolyn Carlson provided help and encouragement at key junctures. Karen Gardner patiently helped me to navigate the myriad hurdles that frame student life at the institute, and like all HASTS graduate students, I cannot imagine how I would have completed my PhD without her.

Other mentors have invested tremendous care into my project and my development as a scholar. David Kaiser was the first professor to help me explore a single passionate interest—scientific visualization and simulation—in detail and depth. Julie Cruikshank became my first friend in British Columbia shortly after I arrived in Vancouver for fieldwork. The generosity and intelligence she shared with me during our periodic conversations and correspondences energized every step of my project, particularly during my first months in the northwest, when I still wasn't sure what I was looking for. Christine Walley helped shape my project goals and fieldwork strategies for years before I knew what conceptualizing a research topic truly meant. Mike Fischer and Susann Wilkinson have shared their curiosities, discoveries, experiences, and life events with me in a way that has made me feel like a part of their family, and I look forward to learning with them for decades to come.

Before I began my doctoral training as an anthropologist, Naomi Kohen, Jessica Shu, Matt Brooks, Greg Sanz, Chris Kelty, Colin Koopman, Ronald Gronsky, Daryl Chrzan, and Paul Rabinow and his "labinar" group at Berkeley all offered wisdom and encouragement that gave me the confidence I needed to transition away from my career in engineering. As I was concluding my PhD years later, I found another warmly supportive community at Tufts University, and then yet another as a postdoctoral fellow in the Canada Program at Harvard. At Harvard, Krishna Pendakur, Pierre Bélanger, Paul May, Michèle Lamont, Matthew Liebmann, Ted Gilman, Phil Deloria, Wade Campbell, Gillian Osborne, and Laura Martin each helped me to approach my research with fresh eyes, while Helen Clayton and Sarah Banse also helped me to situate myself in the Weatherhead Center and to make the most of my brief time at the university. I am also particularly indebted to the students who took the course Technology and Politics in Native North America with me at Harvard, many of whom proved to be fantastically engaged interlocutors. With these students, Shelly Long and Jason Packineau at the Harvard University Native American Program gave me a sense of belonging at the university that I would not have been able to achieve on my own. Cedric Woods at the Institute for New England Native American Studies at UMass Boston enacted a similar kind of welcome that helped me to feel more at home in the region as a whole.

As a member of the Department of Anthropology at Johns Hopkins University, I benefited from vigorous intellectual conversations with my colleagues, including Alessandro Angelini, Michael Degani, Clara Han, Niloofar Haeri, Anand Pandian, Deborah Poole, and Veena Das. Naveeda Khan provided crucial feedback on multiple drafts of several chapters and greatly helped me to clarify the aims of the book as a whole. I am also indebted to numerous graduate students in the department, particularly Paul Kohlbry, Grégoire Hervouet-Zeiber, Arpan Roy, Sumin Myung, Tom Thornton, Kunal Joshi, Sarah Roth, Heba Islam, and Zeynel Gül. Outside the Department of Anthropology, I have been fortunate to have developed a wide network of friends, many of whom have actively engaged with my research and pushed me in unexpected directions. Casey Lurtz, Erica Schoenberger, Yulia Frumer, Jeremy Greene, Bill Leslie, Sasha White, Elizabeth O'Brien, Graham Mooney, Joris Mercelis, Elanor Taylor, Rebecca Kelly, Meryl Lauer,

Scot Miller, Carsten Prasse, Tal Linzen, Yumi Kim, Christy Thornton, Becquer Seguín, Megan Avolio, Anicia Timberlake, François Furstenburg, and many others helped to create an ideal intellectual environment for developing this book and for beginning new projects. Elsewhere in Baltimore, Nicole Fabricant, Ruth Tolson, Patrick Connolly, Steve Perzan, Emily Billo, James Lynch, John Heltman, Maggie Epps, Jess Goddard, Nick LaPorta, Nicole Aranda, Chas Philips, Alisha Wolf, and Sarah Federman also helped me to expand the boundaries of my social and intellectual communities. Sadly, Nick O'Gara came to Baltimore only after I left, but he nevertheless played a crucial role in the production of the book by creating all of the maps included here. I am grateful to Nick for his skill and patience during that process.

Since moving to Singapore on Christmas Eve 2020, I have had the great fortune to find yet another community of smart, kind people, many of whom generously engaged with my work during the final revisions for this book. I thank in particular Hallam Stevens, Ben Cashore, Monamie Bhadra, V. Chitra, Elliott Prasse-Freeman, Emily Chua, George Radics, Jennifer Estes, Nathan Green, Zach Howlett, Ting Hui Lau, Jiat Hwee Chang, Greg Clancey, Tim Bunnel, Erica Larsen, Stuart Strange, Sulfikar Amir, Patrick De Oliveira, Haesoo Park, Fiona Williamson, and Ksenia Tatarchenko. I am grateful to all of them for making me feel so welcome in Singapore, particularly as I prepare to join the Singaporean academic community long-term.

My family also deserves thanks for the roles they have played in this project. My brother, Greg Schilling; my sisters, Tess Fonseca and Trina Arling; my niece Hannah; my brother-in-law, Steve Arling; and my sister-in-law, Wendy Fonseca have all heard me ramble about this project for hours on end, and have each offered key sounding boards at different stages in the writing process. My mother- and father-in-law, Aytül and Ercan Özden, hosted me during our now-regular summer visits to Turkey, where much of this book was written. My mom, Gail Schilling, remains the first writer I ever admired, and I am grateful to her for accompanying me on the emotional rollercoaster of the writing process.

My deepest gratitude is reserved for my wife and partner, Canay Özden-Schilling. For more than twelve years, she has lived with the problems and practicalities of this project as much as I have, and sometimes more. She took time away from her own work to stand watch with me, for weeks on end, as my dad began dying of lung cancer midway through my fieldwork. In happier times, Canay spent a month with me in British Columbia and Yukon, and over Skype from Pittsburgh and Cambridge, she helped me think through each one of the obstacles I encountered and the ideas I dreamed up while I worked up there. Together with our son, Leo—who was born in the early stages of writing this book, and who has now accompanied me to the field multiple times!—Canay has inspired me to try to do good and useful things with my time on earth. I'm proud to call her my primary interlocutor and best friend, and I feel privileged to be able to dedicate this book to her.

Several of the following chapters contain revised versions of material that has previously been published elsewhere. Brief selections of chapter 1 and the introduction originally appeared as an article in the *Journal for the Anthropology of North America* (Özden-Schilling 2019a); portions of chapter 4 were published as an article in *Anthropological Quarterly* (Özden-Schilling 2019b); and portions of chapter 5 were published as an article in *American Anthropologist* (Özden-Schilling 2022).

Introduction

"Who won the War in the Woods?" For ten long seconds, my words hung in the air. Our pickup truck was still a few minutes from reaching the maze of rutted logging roads that would take us the final twelve kilometers to the Date Creek Research Forest, where we would spend yet another day measuring trees. Like many early morning trips we had taken up to the research forest that summer in 2013, the three other researchers in the truck with me had spent much of the drive staring out their windows, slowly willing themselves awake. Kristen, a soil scientist-cum-ecologist, and Sanjit, a computer modeling specialist, were employed by an independent research center in the town of Smithers, a small mountain town that served as northwest British Columbia's administrative center.[1] Dennis, the driver of the truck, was a senior research scientist with the BC Forest Service and had been conducting experiments on tree growth and species succession in Date

Creek for more than two decades. Individually, each of the three maintained their own experiments throughout the region's vast forests, but they still periodically helped each other gather field measurements on long-term projects, particularly at the height of summer, when the light lasted for nearly eighteen hours each day.

Spending long summer days in the company of collaborating researchers, I slowly came to appreciate the productive effects of two different kinds of shared silence. As we worked together to identify, count, and measure trees in the field while navigating densely packed undergrowth, we learned each other's habits through repetitive physical acts, even as we often went many minutes at a time without speaking. During our hours on the road to and from field sites, meanwhile, the views alone discouraged idle chatter. As we drove north toward Date Creek each morning, the Bulkley River roared alongside the highway, the aspen groves crowding its banks giving way to dense spans of hemlock, pine, and western red cedar as the long, wide Bulkley Valley sloped northward before beginning to curve toward the west. The peaks of the Coast Mountains rose and fell on all sides, first Hudson Bay Mountain and the Babine Range as we pulled away from Smithers on the Trans-Canada Highway, then the towering walls of Rocher Déboulé as we crossed the Bulkley River on a slender suspension bridge, high above Hagwilget Canyon. Slowly, I was beginning to learn older names for these places as well. Ts'edeek'aay and Widzin Kwah on the Wet'suwet'en territories. Stegyawden and 'Ksan on the Gitxsan territories. Along the walls of each valley, bright green swaths of second-growth forest betrayed the locations of sprawling clear-cuts from the 1970s and '80s, before laws restricted the maximum size of new cutblocks in the region to sixty hectares each (Beese et al. 2019). To tourists who traversed the region in search of hiking trails or places to fish, the valleys might have appeared to be filled with unbroken forests. As I came to know more residents of the region who had joined anti-clear-cutting blockades decades earlier, I grew accustomed to hearing these juvenile tree stands described as "fading scars."

"The War in the Woods," I was often told, was a historical term. To many of the environmental scientists I had come to know in Smithers, the phrase described an earlier era, when confrontations between Gitxsan and Wet'suwuet'en First Nations activists and the logging companies that harvested timber on their territories regularly shut down the Trans-Canada Highway and the railway that ran alongside it. Most described what they knew of the blockades through reference to *Delgamuukw and Gisday'wa v. The Queen*, a precedent-setting land claim that Gitxsan and Wet'suwet'en chiefs had filed together in 1984. Among the Euro-Canadian scientists who had made their homes in northwest British Columbia since the beginning of the twenty-first century, I typically heard the *Delgamuukw and Gisday'wa* trials and the blockades of the 1980s and '90s framed in epochal terms, as one chapter—albeit a critical one—in a celebrated chronicle of regional activism. With other interlocutors, though, references to specific moments from the blockades drifted into everyday talk. A few days after I had attended a rodeo in the Kispiox Valley, a Gitxsan friend casually mentioned that the bridge that I had crossed on my way there had been the site of one of the first major standoffs between police and Gitxsan activists. Her brother, she remembered, had been one of the first Gitxsan to arrive at the bridge, before White loggers began arriving with guns.

Like many researchers who had come to call Smithers home during the 1980s and '90s, Dennis had developed much of his career in the shadow of the War in the Woods. He had secured the original funding for the research forest at the height of the blockades, during a spate of new provincial government initiatives designed to support research on alternatives to industrial forest harvesting techniques. He had assembled the original plan for his experiments at Date Creek in conversation with the Gitxsan chiefs whose territories converged there, and he had had periodic conversations with the same chiefs and their successors in the decades since. Dennis's wife, Pauline, a botanist, had even served as an expert witness on behalf of the Gitxsan during the *Delgamuukw and Gisday'wa* trials. The couple had spent most of their lives in Smithers, hunting for grants and research contracts while cultivating collaborations with other scientists living nearby. The labor of building continuous careers in the region had thickened their ties with people and places there, albeit in ways that sometimes proved difficult to describe. Occasionally on our morning drives, Dennis would point out specific features of the landscape—the site of an abandoned Forest Service experiment; a hiking trail he had explored years earlier with his daughter. He always chose his words carefully before answering my questions about the memories and experiences he had accumulated in the region, but he always came up with an answer. When I asked him who had "won" the War in the Woods, though, he simply smiled and glanced toward the back seat of the truck, where Kristen and Sanjit sat quietly.

Kristen and Sanjit returned Dennis's gaze: they were waiting for him to answer too. "I guess nobody really won," Dennis offered after a long pause. "It was an awfully long time ago." Another minute of silence passed. Over the course of the summer, Kristen had occasionally followed my ponderous questions with her own questions for Dennis. Which Gitxsan chiefs had been most interested in selective logging when Dennis first established the research forest? How might we format the data we were gathering that summer to make it easier to share with other researchers, including the growing contingent of botanists who were coming to Date Creek to study how climate change affected specific plant species? What had it been like to tour the forest with politicians, when the blockades were making international news? Over the decades, Dennis had recruited an idiosyncratic cast of collaborators to help him keep up with his long-term experiments at Date Creek and elsewhere throughout the region. It was Kristen, though, whom Dennis hoped that the BC Forest Service might hire to take over his position when he retired in a few years. Like me, she was curious about how Dennis's life had informed his work, and vice versa. Far more attentive to her mentor's quiet demeanor, though, she also seemed to know when to let certain topics rest.

As the pickup began the long climb to the research forest in the foothills of the Kispiox Range, Kristen finally spoke up. "But blockades are still happening." Dennis nodded silently, and kept his eyes on the road. Throughout the morning, on signs nailed to fence posts and telephone poles, we had seen dozens of messages denouncing a proposed liquid natural gas pipeline set to bisect the Gitxsan and neighboring Gitanyow territories. South of Smithers, members of the Unist'ot'en Clan of the Wet'suwet'en First Nation had already been running a camp and checkpoint for several years to prevent surveyors working for yet another proposed pipeline from performing technical work on their territories (Spice 2018; McCreary and Turner 2018). Marches were still being organized in Smithers and neighboring towns in concert with the Idle No More movement, a wave of Indigenous-led protests originally organized in response to proposed rollbacks in environmental assessment procedures that had begun sweeping through Canada the previous winter.[2] As we waited for Dennis to share his thoughts about how these earlier conflicts might be informing the present, though, he began talking about the other experiments he hoped we could check on later in the summer, once the main tree measurement survey was complete. It had been five years since he had last gathered data on wind damage within Date Creek, he remarked, and he hoped to revisit the study before snow began falling in September. As the truck fell silent again, Dennis insisted that he hadn't forgotten my question. "I'll keep thinking while we're out in the field today," he promised. "But I'm not sure how much more there is to say."

Slowing down as we approached the turnoff for the logging road that would take us to the research forest, Dennis reached down for his CB radio to let the Forest Service dispatcher know that we had left the highway before tuning the radio onto a local frequency. For the next half hour, we would listen for warnings of oncoming logging trucks descending south from new cutblocks farther north along the Skeena River. Bracing myself against the dashboard as the pickup lurched from the asphalt road onto gravel, I caught a glimpse of the steel girders of Kispiox Bridge, just a few dozen meters away.

Six years later, in 2019, I found myself in a house on another gravel road high above the Skeena River, ten kilometers away from Date Creek. Darlene Vegh, a Gitxsan and Gitanyow woman, was listening for logging trucks too. "That's the third one this morning," she grumbled as another rumbled past. "It's too late for them to be going up there. The ground is too soft." We tried to focus on the map she had just unfolded atop her kitchen table, but the distraction lingered. Early March used to be part of the regular logging season, she reminded me, but spring had begun coming earlier, and much more suddenly, since she and her husband had built their house in the Kispiox foothills in the early 1990s. The previous week, the temperature had hovered at 30°C below zero. Today it was plus 15°C. Two-meter-tall piles of plowed snow lining the sides of Vegh's driveway seemed to be melting before our eyes. "Those guys are probably coming from those new cutblocks near Kispiox Peak," she surmised as we returned our attention to the map. "They must be desperate if they're going so high up in the mountains to find wood, eh? Maybe we ought to drive up there this afternoon to check it out."

At the height of the War in the Woods, inspecting harvesting plans and confronting loggers on the Gitxsan traditional territories had been Vegh's full-time job. She had been a founding member of the Gitxsan Strategic Watershed Analysis Team, or SWAT, and had helped to design and implement the first procedures for government-mandated negotiations between logging companies and the Gitxsan *huwilp*, or house groups, whose chiefs had been claimants in the *Delgamuukw and Gisday'wa* trials. She and her SWAT colleagues had been early proponents of computer-based geographic information systems (GIS) mapping and had worked actively to turn the trail mapping and land cover data they gathered for the consultation process into a new infrastructure for Gitxsan-led research. The most famous artifact of SWAT's work was something I often saw printed on posters throughout the region: an exquisitely detailed digital map of the Gitxsan territories. On the paper printout of the map we examined that morning in March, hundreds of

Gitxsan place-names adjoined the Euro-Canadian names of towns, peaks, and rivers throughout the region. When I had first met Vegh in 2013, the layers of data that made up the map had already been serving as a foundation for the work of Gitxsan planners and politicians for over a decade. Vegh herself had worked from these layers whenever she assembled studies for individual house groups, as well as earlier in her career, when she worked for the Gitxsan First Nation writ large.

Six years earlier, Vegh had invited me to join her on a mapping project to inspect an alternative route for a proposed natural gas pipeline set to cross Gitanyow territory—her last professional field project, as it turned out, before she retired. The modest mapping project had been paid for by the TransCanada Pipeline (TCP) Corporation (now TCP Energy), the developers of another pipeline project south of the Gitanyow territories that had inspired Wet'suwet'en land defenders to establish checkpoints to block TransCanada employees and contractors from entering their territories (see epilogue). Keeping track of ecological changes on the land and pursuing other long-term stewardship and teaching goals through developer-funded contract work had exposed Vegh to new kinds of tensions between activists, elders, and other political leaders, she had reflected at the time, but her earlier projects carried complex complicities too. As we met at her home in 2019 to discuss the reception of her report on the Gitanyow project and to catch up on what had happened in our lives since, our conversations veered between stories about previous mapping expeditions and musings about new conflicts percolating nearby. Earlier in the week, she and her husband had driven up the road to bring food to a group of Gitxsan who had been running a small antilogging blockade throughout the winter. The previous chief of the territories in question, Vegh remembered, had been a vocal supporter of SWAT's projects in the 1990s. Revisiting the same territories as a recent retiree, though, had reminded her how much of SWAT's work had been left unfinished after the group's funding had disappeared.

First Nations mappers and scientists were supposed to have been saviors, Vegh reflected, but she still wasn't sure what their work had meant. "It feels like a lot of us were finally getting recognized as experts right when the government stopped caring about science." When I suggested that the status of research and researchers in the region might change if a new War in the Woods were to erupt, Vegh looked out the window and smiled. "Maybe you're right. It'd be funny if journalists start calling it that again," she sighed.[3] "It's pretty obvious to the folks who live up here that the conflicts never really stopped." In the meantime, though, she hoped younger mapmakers would take over tracking changes on the territories, even if they, too, could never know for certain what the legacy of their labors would be.

A War's Ends

Throughout the second half of the twentieth century, individual researchers and their respective institutions played diverse and sometimes contradictory roles in narrative accounts of forestry conflicts. To many Canadian and American commentators, the surging visibility of First Nations sovereignty demands and the increasingly confrontational tactics of White conservationists throughout coastal forests during the 1980s and '90s were symptoms of a global shift in extractivism. The conflicts that arose around old-growth forests, a diverse range of critics argued, were the direct consequence of "sustained yield" forestry planning: a massive, coordinated approach to clear-cutting and replanting trees (Braun 2002; Hayter 2003; Prudham 2005). Introduced to British Columbia by the BC Forest Service in 1947, the government researchers who designed the sustained yield system sought to replace the diverse range of planting and harvesting programs that had been developed there over the first half of the twentieth century with a simplified regimen, one capable of bringing the province's entire landbase into a single harvesting schedule (Orchard 1953; Prudham 2007). Shortly after the introduction of timber sale harvesting licenses in 1967 allowed licensees to consolidate cutting rights into larger and longer-term contracts, the dozens of independent operators that had previously constituted the industry were quickly consolidated into a handful of massive firms. By the 1970s, the subsequent expansion of the sustained yield system had helped to turn British Columbia into the largest single exporter in the Pacific Rim timber trade.[4] As the United States, British Columbia's largest export market, began imposing tariffs on BC lumber in the early 1980s, the need to find even cheaper sources of wood drove logging companies ever farther north, and ever deeper into old-growth forests.[5]

If the work of conventional forestry scientists and planners had led the province into the War in the Woods, a rising class of provincial politicians charged a new generation of researchers with devising a way out. In September 1991, three years after the initial Gitxsan blockade at Kispiox Bridge, the New Democratic Party (NDP) won control of the Legislative Assembly of British Columbia for the first time in nearly two decades. Promising to address the spiraling tensions surrounding First Nations land claims and industrial logging in old-growth forests, newly elected premier Mike Harcourt initiated far-ranging land use and governance reforms. Within a year, NDP appointees had reorganized the BC Ministry of Forests and increased its administrative control over commercial timber harvests. By the middle of the decade, the Harcourt government had begun establishing "community-based" land use planning forums in towns throughout the province, and substantially expanded the total land area protected within the provincial park system (Tollefson 1998; Giesbrecht 2003). In areas of the province where anti-clear-cutting protesters had been especially active, the provincial government empowered its Forest Service and Ministry of Environment to establish new research forests to study selective tree harvesting methods and watershed restoration processes (Davis 2009). At all levels of forest policy and administration, NDP officials promised, scientific researchers and original research would play crucial roles in mediating future conflicts.

Whether or not their members participated directly in any blockades, many First Nations experienced the War in the Woods as a period of rapid bureaucratization. In 1993, the Harcourt government formed a centralized commission for negotiating treaties in the hopes of discouraging other First Nations from pursuing their land title claims through provincial courts. By the middle of the decade, nearly half of the 203 federally recognized Indian band governments in the province had applied for government loans to begin their own treaty research (BC Treaty Commission 2021). Meanwhile, the BC Forest Service and other provincial government ministries began formalizing new consultation procedures for logging companies, mine operators, and other resource developers working on land subject to treaty claims. For First Nations groups like the Gitxsan that vested decision-making power in clans, house groups, and other hereditary institutions rather than in the federally administered band government system, the pressure to participate in treaty negotiations compelled them to establish entirely new bureaucratic institutions. By the end of the 1990s, the Gitxsan Treaty Society (GTS) had expanded beyond its initial role as representative for the more than eighty house groups of the Gitxsan First Nation officially participating in the treaty process.[6] As chiefs and researchers who had participated in the first *Delgamuukw and Gisday'wa* trial were regrouping for a provincial and a later federal appeal, the GTS established its own forestry consultation office, mapping division, and development corporation (Barry 2012). Rather than relying on Euro-Canadian experts to staff these new offices, however, the GTS joined dozens of other First Nations throughout the province in pressuring the provincial government to support their efforts to train their own experts (Ryan 2005). If future Gitxsan encounters with the state were to depend on the authority of science, Gitxsan leaders argued, then the Gitxsan would need their own researchers leading the way.

Almost as soon as they had begun, nearly all of the research-based governance and capacity-building initiatives established during the War in the Woods were radically scaled back. In 2001, the BC Liberal Party won control of the Legislative Assembly of British Columbia. Gordon Campbell, a Liberal member of the Legislative Assembly (MLA) who had actively campaigned against any negotiations with First Nations groups over land claims and had even launched an unsuccessful lawsuit against the recently completed Nisga'a Final Agreement, was elevated to the position of premier. Accusing First Nations litigants and other negotiating parties of damaging the province's rapidly expanding resource economy, the Campbell government launched a province-wide referendum seeking to undermine the BC Treaty Commission (BCTC) and absolve provincial ministries of their duties to negotiate with First Nations over proposed developments (Rossiter and Wood 2005).[7] Further insisting that the rising power of conservationists both within and outside the government had created an unfriendly climate for logging companies, Campbell also began dramatically downsizing all of the provincial government's resource management ministries.[8] Within months, the central Research Branch of the BC Forest Service, one of the most prestigious government-run forestry science centers in the world, began closing down, as most of its researchers were either laid off or reassigned to other Forest Service divisions. By the year's end, more than two-thirds of the satellite Forest Service offices throughout the province had been closed as well. As the new government began dismantling the research and capacity-building initiatives begun by the NDP, financial support for the salaries and research expenses of newly trained First Nations experts disappeared as well.

Hundreds of individual researchers' lives and careers were unmoored as the new century began. To some distanced observers, however, the progressive tenor of NDP-authored policy experiments seemed to be reestablishing itself almost as quickly as it had been swept aside. By the middle of the decade, the outright hostility that characterized the BC Liberal Party's rise to power had been softened through a range of conciliatory gestures. Perhaps wary of the negative publicity that his antagonism toward First Nations land claims would create as Vancouver prepared to host the 2010 Winter Olympics, Gordon Campbell dramatically shifted his stance on treaty-making and consultation during his second term as premier, and even vocally challenged the Stephen Harper–led Conservative federal government for disrupting provincial efforts to negotiate new agreements (Wood and Rossiter 2011). During the early years of the BC Liberal government's so-called New Relationship, Campbell's engagements with the BC Assembly of First Nations and other province-wide First Nations governing councils were further propelled by the premier's sober reckoning with decisions by the Supreme Court of Canada chastising the provincial government's failure to consult the Haida and Taku River Tlingit First Nations over proposed forestry and mining projects on their claimed territories (Olynyk 2005).[9]

Over time, the economic landscape of conservation-oriented research shifted as well, and new sources of support emerged. To some of the scientists I later interviewed at BC Forest Service headquarters in Victoria, the dramatic shifts initiated by the BC Liberal Party in the early 2000s were merely part of a longer cycle of institutional reorganization. Many of their colleagues in the capital city were regularly shifting between government and industry jobs during the period, they reminded me, and other federal and provincial initiatives designed to support First Nations job training and capacity building, particularly in the mining industry, emerged not long after the War in the Woods–era programs were canceled. By the end of the decade, conservation NGOs and other civil society groups supported by private philanthropies were already outpacing the BC government as the most significant funders of environmental research in the province (see chapter 5).

By the time Campbell's vaunted New Relationship and the rise of private research funding had begun to impact the work of many of my interlocutors in northwest British Columbia, their lives and aspirations had already changed. For researchers and activists working to transform the knowledge and relationships they had built through direct action protests into more durable infrastructures for governance, the temporalities of institutional restructuring manifest not as predictable cycles, but as sudden strains on their interpersonal bonds. These strains affected White and First Nations researchers in starkly different ways. After the regional Forest Service office in Smithers was closed in 2002, many government researchers were reassigned to new positions in the provincial capital. Others simply quit or lost their positions and began working as contract-based researchers, joining the dozens of consultants already living in the region. As the Gitxsan-led technical training programs were canceled and budgets for consultation offices were scaled back in 2001, many Gitxsan either moved back into logging jobs or left the region in search of new work suitable for their burgeoning technical skills. For some Gitxsan, the relationships that they had begun to build with non-Indigenous environmental scientists began fading as nascent collaborative projects—initiatives for cataloging medicinal plants, joint studies of watershed restoration techniques, and a Gitxsan-run berry harvesting cooperative, among others—saw their funding suddenly disappear.[10]

In different ways, Darlene Vegh and Dennis both described the vast patchwork of clear-cuts that had carved up the forests of northwest British Columbia as a metaphor for the precariousness of rural life. They each shared stories with me about the many twists their lives had taken as the institutional connections that initially supported their careers had continually eroded and changed form. They described how the labor of maintaining long-term projects had changed their sense of dependence on other researchers, and eventually subdued their expectations that their own work would yield quick returns. In their musings about the possible futures of the region, they each lingered over apparent gaps—lost funding, rifts with former patrons, geographically dispersed colleagues and kin. Occasionally, the language of some of their most wistful reflections came directly from the research and governance initiatives that had given form to their earliest professional aspirations. "I thought that if I could help the land, I could help the people," Vegh reminisced shortly after we first met. She had picked up the memorable line, she admitted, from a textbook: an artifact from the Gitxsan Territorial Management course through which she had begun learning how to make maps in the early 1990s. The course had produced only one class of graduates before losing funding and closing down. In much the same way that Dennis had derived new senses of meaning from his own long-term experiments by cultivating relationships with unlikely collaborators, though, Vegh had learned to "help the people" in other ways. Even if the maps, databases, and other products of her work had yet to achieve many of the concrete objectives that had first drawn her into a life of research, she reasoned, these artifacts and the people she had come to know while producing them could outlive her, as long as she didn't stand in their way.

Science and Survival in the Shadow of Conflict

In the closing years of the twentieth century, the government of British Columbia spent tens of millions of dollars attempting to establish new kinds of bureaucratic offices, outdoor laboratories, and technical training programs throughout its sprawling northern forests in the hopes that research and researchers might mollify future conflicts there. Many of the researchers who began building their careers through these processes actively positioned their projects to enroll residents into emergent governance processes and to underscore their own sense of investment in the region itself. Yet to what ends have these investments obtained as the work of institution building has been abandoned by a shrinking state? What kinds of relationships endure as waves of technocracy crest and retreat? What new relationships emerge?

Many scholars have described the refashioning of forested landscapes as the production of new kinds of subjects and new kinds of space (N. Smith 1984; Sivaramakrishnan 1999; T. M. Li 2014). Whether by reifying specific imaginaries of nature and culture (Braun 2002), naturalizing new systems of centralized management and extraction (Scott 1998; Prudham 2005), or translating conservation idioms into new mechanisms of discipline (Jacoby 2001; Agrawal 2005; Kosek 2006; West 2006), scientists and other technical experts have long been treated as indispensable to these processes. Yet the scientists themselves who apparently enact state control over forests and their communities maintain many different kinds of relationships with the institutions that fund their work. In the decades after World War II, dozens of forestry scientists from Europe, the United States, and Canada's metropolitan centers moved to regional BC Forest Service offices in Smithers, Prince George, and other emerging towns in northern British Columbia to help oversee the province-wide expansion of the sustained yield system. In memoirs published by the BC Forest Service, a few of these émigrés described their initial impressions of the region as if they were rugged explorers on a perilous adventure (see, e.g., Revel 2007). In the wake of the War in the Woods, new kinds of researchers were raised in and recruited to northwest British Columbia. New funding opportunities for watershed restoration research, expanded roles for conservationists within government-run resource management divisions, novel technical training initiatives for First Nations people, and proliferating bureaucratic tasks connected to treaty negotiations created hundreds of new jobs for environmental researchers and other experts across the region. A broad transition between technical frameworks for managing land, in other words, effected a profound demographic transition as well. Dozens of people already living in the area—many of them First Nations—began technical careers in order to fill these positions. Meanwhile, hundreds of other people—nearly all of them White—moved there in order to start or continue their careers in concert with these emergent initiatives. Over time, these arrivals helped further establish Smithers as a destination for young professionals and other "amenity migrants" (Chipeniuk 2004; Özden-Schilling 2019a). For Gitxsan people who had moved away from the region as young adults, however, the sudden emergence of technical jobs and training opportunities provided an additional impetus to return "home."

Many of the research and capacity-building projects begun in British Columbia during the 1990s had broad and ambitious horizons. Tracking generational changes in forest composition, like building new infrastructures for Indigenous-led research, demanded researchers who were willing to cultivate deep, long-term attachments to the locations of their work, and to conceptualize their own expertise as a product of place. Yet as the researchers themselves were keenly aware, the political projects that their work helped to underwrite had divergent aims and addressees. For the predominately Euro-Canadian researchers who pursued this work as employees of the BC Forest Service, as representatives of NGOs, or as independent researchers who funded their work through grants and commercial contracts, the sense of obligation they articulated around their research framed the forests of British Columbia as a consummate public resource. The vast majority—over 94 percent—of British Columbia's roughly 945,000 square kilometers of land is held by the provincial government as "Crown land," these researchers often reminded me.[11] Until very recently, most conservation-oriented research projects in the province had been funded by taxes on timber harvested from this same land (see chapter 5). Indeed, the fact that so much of BC's timber was logged on government-owned land formed the crux of the so-called Softwood Lumber Dispute, Canada's decades-long trade conflict with the United States (Zhang 2007). The proper stewardship of "public" forests, my non-Indigenous interlocutors routinely implied, was the duty of scientists working in the public interest—whether or not they had government jobs.

Whether in stories about their formative experiences as researchers, discussions of mapping practices, or speculations about future developments, Gitxsan and Gitanyow experts invariably framed their spaces of work through concrete obligations to specific house groups, family members, and representatives. As Darlene Vegh put it, "When I want to go into one of the [Gitxsan] house territories and make a map, I need to wait for the approval of the local chiefs, the [Gitxsan] Treaty Society, and the resource management group down at the band office. Those White guys can go in whenever they want, right? It's all just public land to them."[12] Individually, Vegh and other First Nations researchers described the sense of access and authority they felt over their traditional territories in deferential and circumspect tones. They also acknowledged that much of their work had become increasingly federated as relationships between traditional house group chiefs and bureaucratic officials had changed shape in recent decades due to constant changes in the ways that their institutions were recognized by the state (see Nadasdy 2017; McCreary and Turner 2018). Despite these transitions and tensions, however, individual researchers and the products of their research have continued to act as interfaces between life on the territories and the shifting terrain of Canadian law.

The ambivalent way that Canadian courts and bureaucratic organizations evaluate First Nations–produced technical data mirrors these institutions' deeply conflicted appraisals of other Indigenous engagements with land.[13] For nearly half a century after the federal reserve system was formally established in British Columbia and First Nations people were forcibly relocated to minute reserve villages throughout the province, First Nations groups were legally prohibited from pursuing legal action to reacquire control over the lands that had been stolen from them through the gazetting process. Even after the prohibition against organizing land claims was rescinded (along with prohibitions against potlatches and traditional feasts) through amendments to the federal Indian Act in 1951, First Nations people in British Columbia and elsewhere continued to be fined and arrested for using traditional fishing weirs and nets, harvesting trees and hunting without provincial licenses, and engaging in other subsistence practices. Many First Nations fishers and hunters active throughout the twentieth century, my Gitxsan interlocutors reminded me, were well aware that these rights had already been explicitly granted to them through the original Indian Act passed in 1876 (Kelm and Smith 2018). As the Nisga'a First Nation and other groups resumed their research on land claims following the midcentury amendments to the Indian Act, a growing range of settler audiences were forced to acknowledge these contradictions as well. In 1967, a Nisga'a hereditary chief named Frank Calder, who had already served for nearly two decades as an MLA of British Columbia, sued the government of British Columbia, asserting that the Nisga'a First Nation still owned their traditional territories along the Nass River, since they had never ceded these lands through a treaty. When the Supreme Court of Canada overturned the provincial courts' rejection of the suit six year later, the decision affirmed the prior existence of Aboriginal title. Since treaty-making in British Columbia had been halted with the signing of Treaty 8 in 1899, the *Calder* decision effectively signaled that nearly all of the land in British Columbia was subject to historical claims.

For First Nations people who were already engaged in institution-building work and land defense, the *Calder* decision immediately impacted their long-term goals and day-to-day lives. Gitxsan hereditary chiefs and other elders who had recently begun working with local Gitxsan artists to establish a museum and cultural center on the territories began hiring as research assistants young Gitxsan who were returning after completing their college degrees (Özden-Schilling 2020). Much like the technical capacity-building efforts that proliferated in the decades that followed, the land claims that these assistants eventually contributed to achieved mixed practical results. The federal appeal to the *Delgamuukw and Gisday'wa* case established precedents that enabled other First Nations to use oral histories and hereditary leaders as bases for making land claims of their own, and has been widely celebrated as an epochal transition in the global development of Indigenous engagements with settler law (Borrows 2002; Daly 2005). Yet the same decision also demurred on a technicality and failed to grant the Gitxsan territorial title, and instead invited them to return to court for a new trial—an invitation that, more than twenty years later, the claimants have yet to take up (Napoleon 2013).

Even as formal land title has remained elusive for nearly all First Nations claimants in British Columbia, practitioners of land defense have continually sought out new avenues for pursuing their work (Blackburn 2005). By the time Gitxsan and Wet'suwet'en hereditary chiefs initially submitted their joint land claim at the provincial courthouse in Smithers in 1984, other land claims researchers working elsewhere in British Columbia had been further energized by the explicit recognition of Aboriginal rights and land title in Section 35 of Canada's newly patriated constitution (Manuel and Derrickson 2015). One year before the initial provincial decision on the *Delgamuukw and Gisday'wa* claim was announced in 1991, land claims researchers and other people developing land defense strategies were encouraged yet again when the Supreme Court of Canada affirmed that Section 35 protected the fishing rights of Ronald Sparrow, a Musqueam man who had been arrested for using nets that were longer than those allowed by provincial law. By interpreting fishing and hunting as "inherent" Aboriginal rights, the *Sparrow* decision further asserted that it was up to provincial and federal authorities to prove that any future efforts to restrict Section 35–protected rights were legally justified, rather than leaving First Nations people to bear the burden of proof (Culhane 1998). A decade and a half later, the Supreme Court affirmed this distinction yet again when it agreed that the rights of the Haida Nation had been violated when a company harvesting tress on their claimed territories had transferred harvesting rights to another company without consulting the Haida (Weiss 2018).

My Gitxsan interlocutors knew the many legal decisions enframing Indigenous land rights in British Columbia, and occasionally cited them for me in painstaking detail. Yet when describing what empowered them to engage with their territories in meaningful ways—whether through data collection and direct action, or exploration and coexistence—most of these researchers referred less to Canadian law than to the persistent labor of their colleagues and kin (see Whyte 2018). While many different forms of jurisdiction had been recognized and reiterated through legal decisions and statutes, their comments reminded me, they still had to be enacted through the ongoing practice of activities like research and land defense (see Manuel and Derrickson 2015; Pasternak 2017). By underscoring how her work in the field was invariably shaped by shared, if amorphous, goals, Vegh quietly distanced herself from the emblems of prestige and political influence that served as currency in the networks that linked so many of the region's researchers to other professional worlds. Time and again as we discussed the possible impacts of the mapmaking and databasing work that she performed on behalf of specific house groups, she emphasized that the power to make decisions rested with the house groups alone. She had no wish to interfere with their deliberations, she insisted, but remained conscious of how the documents she produced might nevertheless turn vulnerable people and sensitive places into objects of study for others (see Tuhiwai Smith 1999). Vegh's reflections often conveyed a circumspect belief that she could not ameliorate these risks simply by investing her research with a generalized sense of pathos (see Million 2013; M. Murphy 2015). By keeping specific relationships in mind as she worked, though, she could enable others to keep working as well.

Who Won the War in the Woods?

More than three decades have passed since journalists and political actors began framing Gitxsan-led blockades as a branch of a broader War in the Woods. Another two decades have passed since most of the research and governance programs initiated during these conflicts were scaled back or abandoned by government funders. Yet despite the radically different understandings of justice and stewardship that enframe their technical work, White and First Nations researchers continue to find themselves and their research enrolled in debates over the war's ambiguous afterlives. The following chapters each offer routes for exploring the question I posed on the road to Date Creek. To repeat it here, with an additional provocation: Did scientists win the War in the Woods?

Most of my interlocutors were reluctant to claim that the conflicts over logging had ended in any decisive way, or that the period had produced any lasting beneficiaries. While the number of First Nations–led blockades declined in the late 1990s, most of the technical training and land use programs initiated by the Harcourt government were only marginally successful in achieving their original aims. As of 2021, only seven of the First Nations to begin the centralized treaty process have negotiated a final agreement (BC Treaty Commission 2021).[14] Many other First Nations have explicitly rejected the so-called land selection model utilized by the provincial negotiators and the underlying principle of federal extinguishment, a process whereby claimants must fully renounce their claims to their broader traditional territories prior to beginning negotiations in order for provincial authorities to potentially award them limited jurisdiction and royalty rights over minute portions of their original lands (Manuel and Derrickson 2015).[15] Meanwhile, new processes for consulting First Nations representatives for resource developments on claimed territories have engendered still more conflicts over jurisdiction and tremendous administrative strains for First Nations offices. Land and resource management plans have now been approved for nearly the entire province and have together led to the establishment of dozens of new provincial parks and other protected wilderness areas. Almost none of the new plans, however, involved substantial contributions from nonspecialist committees in the manner envisioned by the original developers of the format (see chapter 1).

Understood in terms of their transformative effects on land use laws and institutions, War in the Woods–era initiatives and reforms achieved mixed results. Yet by asking whether scientists—as individuals—"won" the war, this book examines a deep and abiding tension that such assessments have failed to address. How have the individual researchers enrolled into these conflicts been made responsible for securing different collective futures, and how have researchers' relationships with these collectives changed as the futures in question unraveled? Even as the Harcourt government hailed White and First Nations researchers as heroic mediators, environmental scientists working throughout British Columbia were personally accused by forestry-dependent residents of selfishly benefiting from the conflicts over clear-cut logging (Davis 2009; Parkins et al. 2016). The grants, field sites, and other resources that these researchers utilized to further their own careers, such critics complained in newspaper editorials and elsewhere, had come at the expense of families who had built their lives around logging jobs (Reed 2003; Satterfield 2002). For the meager handful of First Nations people to receive significant training from initiatives established during the period, accusations of unequal benefits went further still. Rather than using their skills to establish local institutional capacity, some critics argued, many of the graduates of these programs quickly "abandoned" their home communities to seek out better-paying jobs in urban centers (Cooke and O'Sullivan 2015; Hillier et al. 2020). The researchers who scrambled to continue their careers as supporting initiatives dissolved around them, these criticisms implied, had never really been committed to their collectives at all.

In order to understand how long-term research has come to matter to northwest British Columbia in the wake of the War in the Woods, the lives and trajectories of individual researchers must be considered in closer detail. Government downsizing has been a wrenching and disorienting experience for many of the people who built scientific careers during this era. Time and again, senior researchers presented the crumbling of technical infrastructures as scenes of personal loss. Data-driven land use plans abruptly disassembled after years in gestation. Field research training programs shut down after graduating but a handful of students. Long-term forestry experiments that fell into disuse after the scientists who managed them were reassigned to other sites. Despite becoming unmoored from their original institutions and projects, however, many of these researchers have continued to live in northwest British Columbia. For some, the maps, data sets, and other artifacts that their earlier projects produced have become increasingly crucial to their sense of belonging in the region, even as the political affordances of these artifacts have either attenuated or changed form as the region's institutional landscape has become more complex. The persistence of senior researchers and technical artifacts with connections to earlier conflicts over industrial forestry has also helped to draw new researchers to northwest British Columbia—researchers who often hope to build their own careers in concert with the region's celebrated legacy of activism. Yet as different generations of White and First Nations researchers articulate the value of their work amid this interplay of professional mobility and persistence, a critical question still lingers: How does the continuing "survival" of untethered research and researchers matter to the survival of other forms of life?

Making sense of how experts pursue new forms of belonging and meaning as their institutional attachments erode has become an urgent problem for anthropological studies of expertise. Historically, most of the individuals who populate academic treatments of technocratic power attract scholarly attention because of the ways that they carry out the directives of institutions, or because of how they "perform the state as unified, knowing, and beneficent" (Mathews 2011, 11; see also Mitchell 2002). Others are hailed primarily for resisting or subverting such plans (Scott 1985; Gibson-Graham 2006; Anand 2017). The majority of the individuals whose stories fill the following pages, though, fall into a third category: scientists and technicians whose institutional affiliations have shifted over time, or who have never held permanent positions with a single organization. By describing these people as *rural researchers*, I mean to underline this ambiguity. I include both city-based scientists whose infrequent, arduous journeys to places like northwest British Columbia helped to define these spaces as "remote" in the first place, as well as those who were born in these areas or eventually came to live in them year-round. The term also collapses a wide range of professional positions and affects: government-employed hydrologists who moonlight as consultants for conservation NGOs; managers of community forests who lecture school groups about the ecological pitfalls of clear-cutting; independent botanists who take pride in their work for community-run land planning boards; First Nations mapmakers who help dozens of different academic researchers conduct studies on traditional territories. By referring to all of these people as rural researchers, I primarily mean to signify the lingering ambitions that they have continued to invest in their shifting, uncertain roles. I also mean to underscore how these institutional uncertainties have engendered new strategies for performing expertise. Rather than attempting to project their authority by obscuring the failures of the institutions that originally funded their projects, rural researchers have increasingly called attention to the precarities they face to particularize new pleas for change.

As the following chapters show in detail, researchers' efforts to transcend the government attachments they accrued in the years after the War in the Woods reveal sharply divergent expectations of access to spaces of power. Many non-Indigenous researchers responded to the onset of government restructuring by designing new organizations to replace specific functions of government bodies where they had already enjoyed substantial careers. Following the closure of the Forest Service office in Smithers in 2002, for instance, Dennis's wife, Pauline, helped to found an independent research center, in part to facilitate the rescue of thousands of paper-based technical reports that had been stored at the former government office. Without a dedicated building and staff to manage the material generated by government-funded research, she and other scientists worried, decades' worth of archived field data would be lost as researchers dispersed and old reports were discarded.[16] For many Gitxsan, however, the blockades had led to some of their first substantial opportunities to work *with* the government of British Columbia. When the NDP rose to power and new capacity-building programs were radically expanded in the early 1990s, a few Gitxsan had already developed research experience helping to prepare paper maps, oral history transcriptions, and other documents for the original *Delgamuukw and Gisday'wa* trial (Sterritt et al. 1998; Marsden 2002; Daly 2005). Other Gitxsan had either been too young to participate in the trial, or had only begun to get involved in mapmaking projects after joining direct action protests when the trial was underway.

White and First Nations researchers' divergent experiences of downsizing have generated equally diverse strategies for adapting to new circumstances and attempting to regain power. Many of these strategies, my interlocutors acknowledged, had transformed their relationships throughout the region. Some Gitxsan researchers reflected on the conflicts that had driven them to break ties with former patrons, and the sense of estrangement they had felt while working to build up other, geographically dispersed networks (see chapter 2). Former government scientists living in Smithers, meanwhile, complained to me about the increasingly complicated funding mechanisms and collaborative arrangements required to keep long-term projects in motion, but nevertheless celebrated their newfound autonomy. At times, the ways that my Euro-Canadian interlocutors described the collapse of their old institutional orders seemed to signal a weary embrace of the neoliberal doxa that "all that is social could be otherwise" (Gershon 2011, 537).

And yet: something gets lost when we explain these transitions as merely the inexorable march of entrepreneurialism. The kinds of uncertainties that have accompanied government downsizing have not led most researchers who still live in the region to renounce the obligations they built up through their work. Many Euro-Canadian researchers described their experiences with downsizing to me as a heightened and rerouted sense of dependency. The contingency of each new job and funding arrangement reminded them that their aggregate labors were no longer encompassed within defined institutional positions and thus could not be easily "filled" after they moved on or retired. Far from eschewing these dilemmas by focusing on smaller projects and shorter timelines, many aging researchers have confronted downsizing's limits by displacing their earlier expectations for their work in the hopes that an attenuated version might somehow be saved.

Over time, I came to see small gestures of displacement suffused throughout my interlocutors' everyday lives. For most of these people, their reflections on the War in the Woods and its amorphous legacies did not end with laments, whether about the erosion of political institutions, the unraveling of social orders, or the forest-wide changes wrought by logging and climate change. Rather than ascribing these changes to a common trajectory, they troubled these narratives by investing seemingly dormant artifacts of their work with senses of latent potential. In subtle ways, both White and First Nations researchers found ways to remind me that these artifacts might outlive them, and called attention to other uncertainties beyond their control. Tended with interest and freed of expectation, the artifacts generated by rural research could get taken up later and put to new ends. It was in these kinds of displacements, rather than in the accumulation of knowledge or the perfection of theory, they suggested, where the futures of their work might reside.

Artifacts and Afterlives

By locating anxieties over collective survival at the center of contemporary rural research, this book aims to raise questions not typically applied to anthropological studies of expertise: How do technical artifacts facilitate the reproduction of social formations (including both traditional governance systems and communities of expertise), and how can the practices that artifacts engender reroute or refashion these processes? What happens to the relationships constituted through these practices after artifacts outlive the programs and policy regimes for which they were originally created? How has the persistence of technical artifacts impacted First Nations experts and their political goals differently from their non-Indigenous neighbors?

The following chapters show how maps, project reports, land use plans, and other artifacts of research eventually come to shape far more than the organization of resources and the application of power. Dislodged from their original scenes of application (Derrida 1988; see also Das 2007, 7), technical artifacts can also enact change simply by persisting over time, and "holding a place" for new relationships and forms of reason to emerge (Riles 2011, 172–76).[17] By continuing to anchor everyday research practices even as experiments end and policy regimes shift, some of these artifacts have also come to facilitate critical modes of relating and self-fashioning for the researchers navigating these changes (Fischer 2009, 197–214). The persistence of these attachments, historian William Rankin suggests, points to the need for "new categories . . . for analyzing science over the long[ue] durée" (2017, 353). Rankin himself offers two useful candidates: "When a celebrated and vibrant project becomes untethered from the network that

originally created it, it can transform into what I call a zombie project,"
Rankin explains, "with production being continued for new purposes by
different groups. Networks can likewise continue without shared commitment to a project, with a negative network of acrimony, criticism, and active
opposition remaining quite robust even as production splinters" (357–58).
Like the "state schemes" with which they are frequently, if unevenly, articulated, technoscientific networks and projects rarely simply succeed or
fail (Latour 1996; Li 2005). Taken up by individuals in the midst of their
own transitions, the artifacts of these ventures can also persist within other
forms of life (Haraway 1997; Dumit 2004; Fischer 2003).

In many ways, the tools of mapping and conservation research have
served their users as vehicles for both enacting and surviving institutional
restructuring. Unlike the technical artifacts analyzed in other treatments
of technopolitics, however, these tools do not necessarily serve to reorganize decision-making processes or facilitate direct enactments of political
authority (Mitchell 2002; see also Latour 1990). Rather, the marginalized
classification systems, territory maps, and planning documents I discuss in
the following chapters nevertheless profoundly shape rural researchers' real
and imagined connections to diverse spaces of power, from the hereditary
governing groups for which Gitxsan experts were enlisted as advocates, to
the centralized state bureaucracies that some settler scientists saw themselves leaving behind. These tools also offered their authors vehicles for
moving messages and meanings between groups whose members had previously communicated with each other and the world at large in substantially
different ways. Perhaps just as importantly, technical tools also occasionally
served as vehicles for the researchers themselves, by lending form to new
relationships and taking them elsewhere after patrons moved on.

The presence of government offices and personnel in northwest British Columbia has greatly diminished since the War in the Woods. Artifacts
of conservation and land claims research, however, have proliferated.
Throughout the region, references to technical documents and the circumstances of their production constantly filter into everyday conversation.
Dour BC Forest Service reports on future timber harvest levels; colorful
maps of watershed management areas, provincial parks, and Gitxsan and
Wet'suwet'en house group boundaries; newspaper editorials bemoaning
salmon population models or simulated projections of glaciers in retreat:
each kind of artifact offers either prompts for new complaints and assertions or details for ongoing chatter. By showing how the artifacts that pre-
cipitate these exchanges reposition researchers within the social worlds that

make up northwest British Columbia, however, I mean to draw a different set of coordinates between these researchers and the audiences of technical work. In subtle ways, the tools and documents produced in conjunction with long-term experiments and research-based governance initiatives have conditioned how researchers live and work in the northwest and how they imagine the region's histories. Over time, these artifacts have also come to shape how individual researchers articulate both their sense of the region's possible futures and their ideas for how their own work might help to bring these futures about. In addition to serving as props in cagey political performances that, as Andrew Mathews (2011, 3) argues, "affect how people believe or disbelieve in official knowledge about forests and about the state," the documents and maps of conservation research have increasingly served to reformat this authority by pointing to futures beyond the state as well.[18]

The researchers whose stories I share in the following pages often cited small, concrete things while explaining what had become of their institutional ties after government downsizing unmoored their careers. For Dennis, specific experiments and concepts that he developed through his work in the Date Creek Research Forest helped establish his reputation as a staunch critic of provincial forestry policy, even as they were taken up by other academic scientists around the world as tools for projecting the consequences of climate change (see Özden-Schilling 2021). Gitxsan researchers, meanwhile, sometimes described their research artifacts to me as reminders of unfulfilled promises—including promises that their earlier patrons had made to them, as well as promises that they and other experts had made to the members of specific house groups. Russell Collier, a Gitxsan man and GIS technician who helped Darlene Vegh to found SWAT in the mid-1990s, occasionally reminisced to me about the expensive computers and mapping software his office purchased with government grants. Not only were the computers critical to Russell's efforts to develop his own expertise and train young Gitxsan cartographers, he remembered, but they were also a sign that SWAT was becoming a "force to be reckoned with" in emergent contests with developers and the state (see chapter 2). After SWAT was disbanded several years later, though, the sight of the same computers gathering dust in the GTS office became for him and others a shorthand for institutional paralysis.

In critical ways, the persistence of technical artifacts produced in the wake of the War in the Woods has facilitated transfers of ideas and ambitions between different generations of researchers. This persistence, however, has also introduced new directions, possibilities, and uses. Dennis's data sets, like SWAT-produced maps, have been shared, inherited, and collaborated on by dozens of younger scientists, many of whom have been motivated by different understandings of the collective political projects for which these artifacts were originally developed. This is not to say that subsequent generations of researchers have simply taken up the artifacts of senior colleagues' work at random and applied them to different ends. The persistence of maps, data sets, and other tools of research has allowed senior researchers to practice strategic forms of deferral, as well, by providing platforms for facilitating technical collaboration during legal and political stalemates. More than three decades after the initial decision in the original *Delgamuukw and Gisday'wa* trial, Gitxsan researchers continue to rely on both old and new maps to cope with the loss of hundreds of historic trails and thousands of so-called culturally modified trees destroyed during the rapid expansion of clear-cutting on the Gitxsan territories in the 1970s and '80s (L. M. Johnson 2000).[19] Such trees, often several centuries old, had served generations of Gitxsan as trail markers and sources of bark products, and were thus of critical importance in proving historical use and occupancy in terms that Canadian courts would accept. As new generations of Gitxsan researchers build strategies for contesting pipelines and other emergent developments, the continuing loss of these trees and trails has increased their reliance on historical—and still accumulating—data sets to demonstrate the persistence of their engagement with the land.

In the two decades since the government of British Columbia began reducing its support for conservation research and First Nations technical capacity building, many of the collaborative relationships and governance experiments that White and First Nations researchers have assembled retain substantial paper trails and human links back to earlier, more centralized institutions.[20] Throughout the following chapters, I call attention to these material residues and to the aspirations of authority and legitimacy that still cling to them. Technocratic forms of conservationism, both the kinds that undergirded settler scientists' earliest calls for data-driven land use planning and the kinds that have come to influence many First Nations assertions of sovereignty in the decades since, were and still remain projects of collective transformation. The people with whom I worked found ways both explicit and indirect to remind me that their commitments to these projects had not faltered, even if the projects themselves have changed shape. The daily labor of confronting downsizing's limits shifted their sensibilities in other ways, however. By inscribing their anxieties about professional succession into conversations about the value of rural research writ large, many researchers struggling to stay in the northwest have unsettled precisely the kinds of technical assurances that their work was once meant to secure.

To talk of rural research as a problem of social reproduction means acknowledging bitter ironies. For decades, the governments of British Columbia and Canada have justified their interventions in First Nations communities by pointing to forms of continuity assumed to have broken down: collapsing governance relationships; disappearing languages and practices of land-based education and labor; ruptured transmissions of knowledge.[21] Indigenous scholars have repeatedly challenged these assumptions by calling attention to the myriad ways that tropes of Indigenous culture loss and disappearance are leveraged by state institutions to effect dispossession, environmental damage, and political marginalization (P. J. Deloria 2004; Blackhawk 2006; Callison 2020; Callison and Young 2020; Estes 2019; Hobart 2019; J. R. Smith 2021). As Dian Million (2013), Kyle Powys Whyte (2014, 2018), and others have shown in detail, many of these deployments have found their most pernicious impacts in misrepresenting the dynamic kin-based relations and labor through which critical knowledge-making projects have actually been sustained, including those that continue to support healing practices and collective responses to changing climates (see also Z. Todd 2014; Kolopenuk 2020). By examining how government institutions are struggling to reproduce themselves in Indigenous spaces, some scholars might justifiably argue, an incautious scholar could wind up contributing to these very erasures (see Coulthard 2014; V. Deloria 1988).[22]

Disentangling state justifications for technical capacity-building programs from these programs' ambiguous legacies and lived effects demands a new approach to the anthropology of science, particularly in settings of enduring colonial conflict. By recentering technoscientific practices and artifacts within the complex social worlds of the individual researchers enfolded into these conflicts, and by treating their formal institutional attachments as contingent, such an approach would refuse to treat technoscience solely as either telos or imposition (see Aporta and Higgs 2005; Medina, Da Costa Marques, and Holmes 2014; Mavhunga 2017). Particularly in zones of Indigenous and settler colonial conflict, a recentered understanding of technoscience would also enable scholars to more effectively track the ways individuals' lives and aspirations come to shape ostensibly collective projects, and how these projects reshape individual lives in turn.

As I show throughout the following chapters, White and First Nations researchers have been made responsible for securing collective futures in markedly different ways. For many of my interlocutors, these responsibilities were conveyed as a kind of inheritance. The ambitions invested in a long-term research site or a cherished planning document may be passed from senior Euro-Canadian researchers to younger collaborators as individual legacies—accomplishments to be developed as the latter see fit (see chapter 3). First Nations experts recruited to carry on precarious projects, however, often receive these inheritances as daunting demands. Reflecting to me on their experiences nearly two decades after the post–*Delgamuukw and Gisday'wa* period fell into disarray, Gitxsan cartographers remembered feeling compelled to view the sacrifices that they made for their work as inseparable from sovereignty's promise (see chapter 2). The primary vectors of their inheritance, in other words, were not data sets or research projects, but their identities as technical experts. Tethered to collective governance projects, though, these identities also discouraged some Gitxsan researchers from pursuing more flexible professional attachments as government support for Gitxsan-run initiatives began to dissolve.

Rather than challenging the grim depictions of endurance offered in so many ethnographic accounts of contemporary rural life, this book asks instead how certain problems of collective survival have come to be understood and administered to by some of the people entrusted with solving them. For many of these people, the shifts in practice that accompanied government downsizing carry their own threats of erasure. The people I call rural researchers have spent years cultivating new relationships and remediating old projects in response to these uncertainties. In the process, however, they have also had to navigate multiple different idioms of rupture. The death or succession of a chief; the retirement of a senior researcher; the cancellation of a policy or loss of a grant; the transformation of a patch of forest: each kind of change calls forth expert assurances that the futures of the entities in question will retain recognizable ties with their pasts. Each transition, in other words, demands a different mode of survivance (see Vizenor 1994).

In some ways, negotiating government downsizing has brought White and First Nations researchers closer together. All of my interlocutors have struggled to find funding to support their work and younger collaborators to carry it on. Numerous long-term projects begun after the War in the Woods have simply unraveled, leaving some of the people who invested in them with a lingering, sometimes bitter, sense of nostalgia (see chapters 1 and 2). Treating these processes as modes of succession and inheritance makes these attachments visible, but it also brings differences to the fore. Like most scientists, the ecologists and botanists I met in Smithers confronted new challenges with the tacit assumption that their disciplines were defined by transcendent theoretical commitments that would persist and develop, even if individual practitioners fell away or struggled to make ends meet. Gitxsan experts, meanwhile, confronted the assumptions of many government officials and White neighbors that their eventual assimilation by settler society and extractivist capitalism was only a matter of time. Both groups of researchers, then, have struggled to articulate what it would mean for their long-term research to "survive" as the institutions birthed amid the War in the Woods have continued to erode and transform. In the meantime, they still search for collective futures in which to invest their research, and for professional paths that will lead back to home.

Parallel Histories

This book is not about the strategic alliances that White and First Nations activists formed during the War in the Woods, or the labor that they and others have undertaken to keep these precarious partnerships intact in the decades since. Many rural researchers remain committed to the idea that a middle ground for negotiating settler colonialism's legacies might yet be built on the tenets of conservation science. Indeed, key land use policy changes and data-sharing infrastructures established across North America in recent decades have involved critical contributions from both White and First Nations researchers. As Larry Nesper (2002), Zoltán Grossman (2017), and others have shown, these engagements often help to bring entirely new subject positions and systems of value into being, and they often wholly deserve detailed studies their own. The ecology of institutions overseeing North America's forests is growing more fractured every year, and the roles that White and First Nations experts play within these institutions are becoming more complicated. The need for such analyses will only increase.

As a genre of anthropological writing, though, "conflict studies" carries distinct limits (see F. Li 2015). Beginning from sites of apparent conflict and compromise often leads ethnographic studies of Indigenous-settler engagements to implicitly reinforce prevailing assumptions about what ought to count as "collective life" in the first place. By looking for idiosyncratic practices of continuance, and by examining how new relationships and modes of belonging take shape around what Candis Callison (2014) calls "the communal facts of life," I seek instead in this book to understand how different conceptualizations of individual and collective life come into being within everyday spaces of research. This researcher-centered approach underscores a fundamental methodological challenge as well. As in so many other rural communities in western Canada, most of the First Nations people and Euro-Canadian settlers who reside alongside the Skeena River and its tributaries continue to live in virtual isolation from one another (Bell 2023; Dinwoodie 2002; Furniss 1999; L. A. Robertson 2005). Finding commonalities between each community's experiences and aspirations without overly dwelling on a few sites of direct engagement has occasionally required me to project potential points of intersection in spaces where actual dialogue is elusive.

The sense of isolation that many of my interlocutors expressed during our conversations underscored the awkward challenges I would soon come to face in attempting to represent these individuals' relationships with the institutions that were once their professional homes. More than four decades of land claims research, legal trials, treaty negotiations, and bureaucratic confrontations have left many Gitxsan experts exhausted and wary. Most had spent much of their professional lives serving as mediators between Gitxsan house groups and the Gitxsan bureaucratic institutions that emerged during the War in the Woods. They had also struggled to navigate an increasingly complex field of tensions linking these different bodies as treaty research and government policy introduced new ambiguities into their relationships with one another (Özden-Schilling 2020). As Val Napoleon (2005), a Cree legal scholar and longtime Gitxsan advocate, has argued, several long-standing fault lines were entangled with the original paper map produced for the original *Delgamuukw and Gisday'wa* trial, when trial researchers abridged Gitxsan claimants' depositions in a manner that caused one *wilp* (the singular name for a house group) to be left out of the completed map. During the trial as well as during subsequent treaty negotiations, Gitxsan representatives were also repeatedly told by government lawyers that any kind of participation in province-run research and planning projects could be interpreted as recognition of the state, and thus could be taken as grounds for abrogating their original claims (Napoleon 2001). As a consequence, questions about maps—including many of the digital maps that SWAT and other Gitxsan organizations had helped to assemble during the 1990s and early 2000s—are still often taken as questions about the legitimacy of the house groups and other traditional entities that the maps had been drawn to represent.

Echoes of decades-old frustrations reverberated through many of my conversations with Gitxsan researchers. Most of the tensions that preoccupied them during our time together, though, centered on emergent development disputes. As numerous locally active scholars and journalists have discussed at length, debt accrued through stalled treaty negotiations, and conflicting responses to new pipeline proposals have deepened existing rifts between some Gitxsan house groups and the GTS executives who still serve as the legal representatives of the entire Gitxsan *huwilp* (McCreary 2016; Jang 2017; Napoleon 2019). When a GTS executive made a unilateral agreement in 2011 allowing for the construction of a controversial pipeline through the Gitxsan territories, chiefs from roughly half of the Gitxsan house groups responded by staging a public blockade of GTS headquarters (Gitxsan Unity Movement 2012a).[23] The blockade had ended only a few months before I arrived in the region to begin my main period of fieldwork in early 2013, and lawsuits between the GTS and dissident house groups were still unfolding.[24]

The White scientists, technicians, and activists with whom I spent much of my time during this period often criticized the apparent "dysfunction" affecting Gitxsan-led bureaucratic institutions. Yet these same interlocutors also routinely decried the de facto segregation in place throughout rural British Columbia. Most of the board meetings and planning workshops I attended in Smithers began with an acknowledgment of the Wet'suwet'en First Nation, and the Gidimt'en Clan on whose territory the town itself was built. Many of the environmental scientists I came to know in the town, particularly younger people and midcareer professionals, were eager to detail their participation in community information sessions, teach-ins, and other First Nations–oriented outreach projects. They sometimes complained to me that they and other organizers of these events were relentless in their gestures of inclusiveness, but that these efforts were typically criticized or ignored by the First Nations groups they wished to recruit. Whenever local researchers or government scientists organized "community-wide" initiatives like land use plan amendments, risk assessments, or knowledge trusts, they invited representatives of the Office of the Wet'suwet'en or the Gitxsan Watershed Authority to participate in group discussions. As I eventually came to realize, however (and as numerous Indigenous scholars and their allies have long complained—see Nadasdy 2003; Whyte 2013), these invitations were typically extended only after the scope of a new plan or process had been agreed on and the terms of reference meant to structure ensuing discussions had already been spelled out. While a handful of individuals were deeply engaged in conversations and processes on both sides, White and First Nations technicians alike complained to me that their interactions with each other too often felt inconsequential.

In empirical terms, the dramatic decline in government support for independent research projects since the late 1990s and the cancellation of watershed restoration initiatives meant the near disappearance of opportunities for Smithers-based ecologists and Gitxsan and Wet'suwet'en mappers to apply for shared grants. As piecemeal jobs and research funds emerged elsewhere, erstwhile collaborators simply fell out of touch. Whenever I asked senior scientists and planners active in the region in the 1990s to reflect on their experiences working with First Nations mappers in the first years after the War in the Woods, most were far more blunt than their younger colleagues in their assessments of the disconnect that had developed in the years since. Some attributed the distance to other White activists' impatience with the land claims process. "'What are you going to do? Sit around and wait another thirty years? By then, there'd be no trees left!'" one planner sarcastically pantomimed, reenacting for me the logic espoused by many of her colleagues at the height of industrial logging's expansions in the region (see chapters 1 and 2). Others admitted that their timidity around "internal" disputes between house groups of the same First Nation had cast a pall over early collaborations, a state of unease that resurfaced whenever new collaborative endeavors were proposed. "We knew that that stuff was going on, but we knew that we couldn't delve into it, so we didn't," a longtime Smithers-based environmental planner admitted to me. "We just hoped it would all work out."

As I gradually came to know dozens of Smithers-based consultants and Gitxsan and Gitanyow mappers living throughout the region, I was struck by the professional isolation, even loneliness, that many of them had come to experience since their institutional identities began to transform in the early 2000s. My initial attempts to locate the authors of specific maps felt like a doomed quest to track professional nomads. Seeking out the institutions where new cartographic conventions had been established often led me to the websites of government divisions that had been dramatically reorganized or shut down since the maps in question were published, or to the rented office spaces of independent research groups surviving from grant to grant. During twelve months that I spent living in the northwest as well as during a series of one- to two-month-long visits spread out over the following eight years, I conducted interviews with over six dozen researchers and repeatedly accompanied several of them to collect data on forest growth experiments and other field-based trials. I also worked to make sense of the relationships they had articulated, however fleetingly, through the media they had produced earlier in their careers, a strategy that caused me to make repeated trips to other offices in southern and central British Columbia to meet former colleagues who had participated in earlier iterations of key projects.

Ultimately, the following chapters represent my attempt to treat Indigenous and non-Indigenous histories of research and institution building on their own terms. Read together, these twinned histories echo the feedback and dissonance of parallel debates conducted in adjacent spaces, yet often just out of earshot. The common characters linking the two sides thus frequently include research tools themselves: handheld Global Positioning System (GPS) devices; survey notebooks; digital map layers and elevation models; online data repositories; tree lists, whether as subjects of study, targets of extraction, or discrete monuments of ritualized modification. In many instances, these artifacts enabled researchers to coordinate key practices and sustain their relationships. Over time, as I argue in the following chapters, these artifacts also became objects of inheritance. They linked individual researchers across different generations, policy regimes, and settler-Indigenous divisions. For better or worse, it has been through these idiosyncratic transfers that the worlds of rural research have persisted. By holding open a place that future researchers might eventually come to inhabit, the artifacts of research have given ground to new collective dreams and ambitions even as the social worlds that make up the region remain in perpetual flux.

Chapter Outline

Each of the five following chapters details a process whereby researchers came to conceptualize "survival" in new terms. Chapter 1, "Nostalgia: Placing Histories in a Shrinking State," explores how forest ecologists and other environmental scientists living in Smithers articulated new senses of place and collectivity in the wake of government retreat. Rather than simply investing in new collaborative relationships, many of the scientists I met there—including dozens who arrived after downsizing had already begun—also articulated their work as contributing to a shared legacy of activism that they saw as defining the town's history. As I show, these nostalgic articulations have become increasingly crucial to rural researchers' efforts to define the meaning and boundaries of scientific communities in the absence of institutional structures. Contrary to prevailing images of technocratic expertise as an abstracting set of knowledge practices designed to place experts outside historical time (Ferguson 1990; Scott 1998; Mitchell 2002; see also Fabian 1983), I argue that rural researchers displaced by government restructuring have grown increasingly adept at "placing" their expertise in emergent genres of local history. In the process of articulating expertise to belonging, however, Smithers-based researchers have also helped to obscure the forms of mobility that continue to allow them and other Euro-Canadian researchers to live and work in the northwest—a place to which, unlike their First Nations neighbors, the majority of them first moved by choice.

Chapter 2, "Calling: The Returns of Gitxsan Research," traces the career arcs of two prominent Gitxsan mapmakers who first came to positions of power and visibility as the founding members of SWAT. The chapter follows their bifurcating careers after the collapse of a short-lived capacity-building program in the province drove many recently trained First Nations mapmakers away from their reserves in search of work. During the capacity-building era and throughout its aftermath, Gitxsan GIS experts negotiated expectations that their work would benefit their patrons and elders, and that they would devote their specialized labor to specific collective causes. Perhaps the biggest challenge faced by individual Gitxsan mapmakers, however, has been the expectation that they themselves would eventually come "home," and that they would help to redefine their nation's social worlds by connecting them to new technical networks. As they pondered how the artifacts of their work have been taken up by refashioned Gitxsan bureaucracies, some of them have struggled to reconcile the urgency of these demands with the estranging effects of displacement.

Both White and First Nations experts in northwest British Columbia saw their designs on influence and authority dramatically refashioned during the early years of the twenty-first century. The ways that these researchers reflected on the professional adaptations that they have made in the years since, however, caused them to frame their senses of obligation in markedly different ways. Particularly after the provincial government's promise of a New Relationship in 2005 brought new rhetorics of engagement into spaces and processes that elected officials had previously abandoned, the bonds that my interlocutors subsequently used their work to secure reflected shifting understandings about what kinds of shared futures they saw as possible. Chapter 3, "Inheritance: Replacement and Leave-Taking in a Research Forest," explores how Dennis, an aging forest ecologist, conceptualized the work of "passing on" the Date Creek Research Forest to a younger collaborator as the site began to decay. As the meanings of the partial cutting experiment that originally defined the forest diversified, both Dennis and Kristen, his prospective successor, have worked to position their work in Date Creek to highlight the provincial government's failure to manage its infrastructures along the temporal scales relevant to climate change. Like the Gitxsan house groups whose title claims to the land in question are still waiting to return to Canadian courts, the young woman entrusted with "inheriting" Date Creek is now learning to promote these multigenerational commitments as a new model of technical stewardship.

Chapter 4, "Consignment: Trails, Transects, and Territory without Guarantees," examines how new attachments and conceptualizations of stewardship have taken shape around flexible labor. With Darlene Vegh, I follow an ad hoc crew of temporary GIS mappers hired by the Gitanyow First Nation—a Gitxsan people with separate band governments, hereditary chiefs, and traditional territories from the neighboring Gitxsan First Nation—to map the route of a proposed pipeline through Gitanyow traditional territory. Focusing on the technical artifacts generated by transect mapping, an environmental mapping technique used to quantify objects of interest along a discrete linear path, the chapter examines how agile mapping and databasing practices have allowed Gitanyow and other Indigenous mappers to critique the geographical constraints of the provincial government's "land selection" model for negotiating new treaties with First Nations (namely, the demand that a First Nation renounce its claims over most of their traditional territory in exchange for broader jurisdictional powers over smaller areas). The chapter highlights the mundane and fragmentary nature of the practices through which contemporary forms of critique must be built—and, increasingly, deferred.

Chapter 5, "Resilience: Systems and Survival after Forestry's Ends," returns to Smithers to examine how some environmental scientists there have sought to imagine new forms for their work that would allow them to transcend their fears of further downsizing. In recent years, the concept of *resilience*—the idea that environmental systems and social forms can be designed to "bounce back" from disasters and other disruptive changes—has influenced a rapidly growing range of governance strategies in domains ranging from security planning and climate change mitigation to humanitarian aid. Among a number of Smithers-based scientists, resilience discourse and its associated initiatives have also reinvigorated their efforts to reconstitute an elusive sense of authority and power. To some senior researchers recruited to provide data and moral authority to one emergent policy initiative, however, the notion that translating laboriously accumulated field data into simplified risk models could ameliorate years of marginalization has only deepened their sense of estrangement. Chapter 5 shows how a handful of these researchers have sought to challenge the relativizing assumptions of resilience theory and the resignation of the people who promote it by defining the "survival" of rural research in more idiosyncratic and personal terms.

In a brief epilogue, I turn to the Wet'suwet'en territories near Smithers, and to a new kind of War in the Woods. During the decade since my first visits to northwest British Columbia, Gitxsan and Wet'suwet'en land defenders established additional checkpoints and blockades in response to a profusion of new pipeline projects and disagreements over logging privileges. As pipeline companies began seeking court injunctions to remove land defenders in 2018, my interlocutors foreboded, no one knew what would happen if Canadian police arrived at these sites in full force. In early 2020, the first major sweep of arrests at Wet'suwet'en-run territory checkpoints inspired a national wave of solidarity protests—perhaps the largest Indigenous-led uprisings in Canada since the original War in the Woods. Examining how some retrospective debates over failed consultation protocols have repositioned Wet'suwet'en researchers as potential saviors in the disputes, I speculate about how new generations of activists may see their own lives take shape around the elusive promises of rural research.

1

Nostalgia

Placing Histories in a Shrinking State

"We used to have fact-based decision-making. We now have decision-based fact-making." A murmur of laughter rippled across the room. Five minutes into his speech at the November summit, Nathan Cullen had earned the one-liner.[1] Looking out over the dozens of people crowded into the high-ceilinged gathering space of Northwest Community College (now Coast Mountain College), Cullen embodied the potent mix of political power and local legitimacy yearned for by so many of the scientists and activists sitting in the audience. Splitting the year between his modest bungalow a few blocks away from the basement apartment I rented in Smithers and his office in the House of Commons in Ottawa, Cullen's position as federal parliamentarian and opposition house leader made him a relatively frequent figure on the national political stage. His visibility was a source of pride for the Smither-eens who chatted with him at the weekly farmer's market, curried his input on environmental assessment panels, and planned social events with him at low-key summer festivals.[2]

Despite serving as the highest-ranking politician for one of the largest logging regions in the western hemisphere, the source of Cullen's popularity in the northwest was diffuse. Like other local politicians, his vocal support for conservation research and research-based governance programs had helped to temper the resentment felt by many Smithers-based researchers over the town's declining status as northwest British Columbia's administrative center. As government-run versions of these programs were continually scaled back or taken over by independent institutions, though, Cullen's role as the champion of rural expertise had grown more complex. Rallying crowds in the northwest increasingly meant drawing dramatic distinctions between the environmental scientists who often filled his audiences and the politicians who had apparently left them behind.

The way that Cullen and other politicians embraced the many researchers in the region made it easy to forget a demographic fact that blue-collar Smithereens pointed out to me all the time: few of the scientists who lived in Smithers had grown up in the rural north. Cullen himself, some scientists reminded me, had grown up in Toronto. This distinction was not necessarily a source of embarrassment. In private conversations, many of the researchers that I came to know shared their own tales about migrating to the region with no small amount of pride. Unlike many of their neighbors, they intoned, they had come to live in northwest British Columbia by choice. Throughout the months leading up to the summit, I had visited home offices around Smithers and the surrounding region, examining maps and sifting through computer databases and filing cabinets. Spending afternoons with botanists, wildlife biologists, and other environmental researchers, I shared in gossip and observed them as they went about their work. Some of my hosts shared long stories detailing their earlier lives and careers; many introduced me to their husbands and wives, who were often researchers as well. Whether I prompted them on the subject or not, all felt obliged to explain exactly how it was that they had wound up living in Smithers. Many had found a second home at the Bulkley Valley Research Centre (BVRC), an independent office established shortly after the regional Forest Service office in Smithers closed in 2002. In addition to conducting their own long-term research projects, BVRC affiliates actively encouraged other independent researchers to support one another by helping to connect them with public and private research grants. Periodically, the BVRC publicized these outreach initiatives through joint events with local politicians—events like the

FIGURE 1.1 Downtown Smithers, BC, with Ts'edeek'aay (Hudson Bay Mountain) in the background. Photo by author.

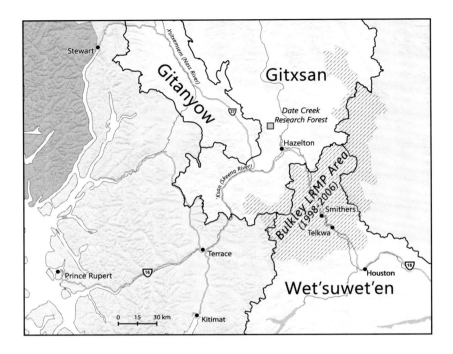

MAP 1.1 Map of Smithers, BC, and environs. Note the Bulkley Land and Resource Management Plan area, which overlaps substantially with the Wet'suwet'en traditional territory.

summit in November. If nothing else, a friend joked as we settled into our chairs before the first talk that morning, BVRC events usually offered a good pep rally for the many researchers in the centre's broad orbit. "It's nice to see folks and be reminded," she offered, "why so many of us are still here."

Throughout the summit, speakers acknowledged that 2013 had been a long year. After leading by as many as twenty points in province-wide polls in the weeks before the provincial elections in May, Cullen's New Democratic Party (NDP) had suffered a bewildering last-minute collapse, allowing the BC Liberal Party, their developmentalist opponents, to maintain control of the provincial government they had been leading for the past twelve years.[3] The proposed Enbridge Northern Gateway pipeline, at the time the most controversial of what would eventually become more than a dozen separate pipeline proposals set to bisect the region, had become such a contentious topic that the speakers half-jokingly forbade anyone in the crowd from mentioning the company by name. Numerous people in the audience had joined the Joint Review Panel of scientists and bureaucrats convened to canvass the province for popular input and assess the environmental impacts of the Enbridge proposal, only to have members of the Conservative Party–led federal government intervene in the assessment's final stages.[4] Even as Cullen and the other speakers who preceded him that morning gingerly avoided the topic of pipeline protests while passing around the microphone, the broad year-end portrait they painted for the region was replete with dispiriting numbers. The summer run of sockeye salmon had dropped to a record low throughout the surrounding Skeena River watershed, according to fisheries officials. Thousands of Gitxsan and Wet'suwet'en fishers who relied on their summer catch to fill their freezers for the winter, several speakers reminded the crowd, had been forced to buy most of their salmon that year from the Nisga'a First Nation in the neighboring Nass watershed.

As was often the case at small events in Smithers, Cullen shared the stage that morning with several other speakers whose positions put them in frequent contact with the town's scientists: the natural resources manager for the local Office of the Wet'suwet'en First Nation, the mayor of Smithers, and the provincial member of the Legislative Assembly (MLA) for the northwest's vast Stikine electoral district. The four men traded jokes about the dysfunction and melodrama making headlines around each other's legislative bodies. Like Cullen, the mayor and MLA were both members of the NDP, a growing social democratic political party that had overtaken the more centrist Liberals as Canada's party of Official Opposition in the federal elections of 2011.[5] Spanning each of the main jurisdictional scales of Canadian electoral politics, the three men stood as a reminder that the scientists of Smithers had a friend at each and every level where policy was being made, however marginal their positions in these spaces might be. In Smithers, with its bevy of displaced researchers and citizen activists, they were happy to hold court.

Most of the speakers worked in a few jokes to flag their awareness that they were preaching to the converted. As I scanned the predominantly White crowd, I saw dozens of scientists I had met throughout the year. A few hands were raised as the speeches drew to a close, but most people simply watched and listened. After a seemingly endless stream of public meetings focused on the Enbridge proposal that had taken up much of the summer and autumn, it seemed unlikely that anyone in the audience had come to the summit expecting to hear something new. As much as anything, though, Cullen told me afterward, the speakers simply aimed to keep the mounting sense of invisibility expressed by many of the town's scientists from devolving into despair. Decrying a recent spate of confrontations between NDP-backed climate scientists and federal Conservative politicians, Cullen cast Smithers itself as a heroic foe of the regimes in Ottawa and Victoria, and its residents as survivors of a hostile attitude toward scientists that had seemingly spread across Canada as a whole. "The rules are stacked right now," he declared, pacing the stage. "If you're a scientist, you are on trial right now, and you have to justify your very existence, and if you should have a voice in how we make decisions about what happens in the real world." If the state no longer cared for its experts, he wondered aloud, how were its experts supposed to care for the land?

For many researchers I had come to know in Smithers, the specter of state abandonment was inextricable from their sense of belonging in the northwest. It was also a common theme in their reflections on the region's histories. The first person to take the stage after a few brief introductory remarks from the organizers of the event and a welcoming prayer from a Wet'suwet'en official was Taylor Bachrach, a young web developer who was then serving as the mayor of Smithers, and who would eventually take over Cullen's post as federal parliamentarian six years later. Bachrach began the morning's first speech with a congratulatory overview of the town's forays into political and legal activism. Foreshadowing a theme that would arise time and again in other speeches as the morning wore on, Bachrach's invocation of the Bulkley Land and Resource Management Plan, or LRMP, presented the oft-cited document as a condensation of historical experience itself. "The Bulkley Valley has really led the way for so many decades when it comes to community-based resource management," Bachrach insisted. "There's a strong legacy of innovative governance systems and collaborative resource management systems . . . rising out of the conflict in the 1980s around forestry . . . and the establishment of the LRMP process and the Community Resources Board. I see so many people in this room who have sat on the Community Resources Board at different times." The products of this labor and the relationships established through it, Bachrach seemed to suggest, were precisely the things that a compassionate government should seek to protect.

During the time I had spent living in Smithers, these references had become a familiar refrain. One environmental lawyer remembered the beginning of the LRMP process in the early 1990s as a "high-water mark" for research-driven conservationism in the province. Taking initiative from the ongoing War in the Woods, as well as inspiration from new participatory mapping and conservation projects then emerging around the world (see Walley 2004; Hodgson and Schroeder 2002; Armitage, Berkes, and Doubleday 2007), the government had enlisted volunteers from rural communities to help map new conservation areas and landscape classification units across contested regions of the province. Few of the plans were actually completed by nonspecialist committees, and those that were ended up being dismantled shortly after the BC Liberal Party won the provincial government in 2001.[6] In one town, the community member elected committee leader had even been burned in effigy after negotiations fell apart (Booth and Halseth 2011). Following premier Gordon Campbell's reelection in 2004 and the initiation of the New Relationship with Campbell's second Liberal government, LRMP documents for other regions of the province were quietly completed by teams of government personnel working largely without community input. In Smithers, though, the original, enervated LRMP document and the process that had produced it remained a popular topic of conversation more than a decade after the original plan had fallen apart.

Throughout the summit, the mayor of Smithers and the three speakers who followed him drew direct links between the disparate researchers sitting in front of them and the volunteers who had originally begun drafting the LRMP nearly twenty years earlier. They hailed their audience members as the prospective authors of a regional history, the uniqueness of which stemmed directly from the region's remarkable density of researchers. In doing so, though, the four speakers also proffered a novel conceptualization of agency: a latent, intimately embedded sense of power befitting experts left waiting for their authority to return. Anchored in the LRMP and in the independent organizations that cited and celebrated the document, this sense of latent agency shaped many of my everyday interactions. Since arriving in Smithers, I had been routinely asked whether I had read the official LRMP document myself, sometimes even by residents who had arrived years after it had been written. Anyone could help to reanimate the document, their questions seemed to imply, so long as they were willing to work.

As my interlocutors liked to remind me, though, the returns for this work were elusive. Reflecting on both the drafting and substance of the document and the story of its later neglect, dozens of researchers and activists I met during the months leading up to the summit described their efforts to salvage the ambitions invested in the LRMP as a multifaceted and unending task. Even after the BC Liberal Party–led provincial government had begun to rebuild some of the conservation research offices and regulatory processes that they had abruptly abandoned at the turn of the century, the prospect of still more contractions and policy changes had only come to feel more acute. With so many scientific institutions in the province still at risk of closure or dramatic downsizing, some admitted, they were determined to convince other researchers moving to northwest British Columbia to develop new institutional spaces and collaborative relationships where they might fulfill the plan's original ambitions. In order to secure the region's futures, though, their reflections suggested, newcomers first had to embed themselves in its pasts.

Nostalgia for Technocracy

In public gatherings and intimate conversations, many of the researchers I encountered around Smithers reflected on their lives in northwest British Columbia as components of a shared history. Many had moved to the region in the twenty-first century, after government downsizing had already begun. Together, they had formed densely interwoven professional relationships through collaborative research projects, conservation initiatives, and other informal gatherings. Their arrivals augured other transitions as well. Over the two decades prior, the town of Smithers had transformed from a regional center for government experts into a rural destination for independent researchers and self-employed consultants. Many of these people readily acknowledged the contingencies that had shaped their convergence in the region and the uncertainties facing their futures there. When explaining what compelled them to remain in the Bulkley Valley throughout a seemingly endless series of institutional displacements, though, most invoked their own expertise as grounding an intrinsic sense of obligation. Regardless of how they had come to live in the forests of the northwest, they suggested, saving the region's damaged landscapes would invariably fall to scientists like themselves.

This chapter sets out to answer several questions. If researchers living in northwest BC have been "on trial" since the beginning of the twenty-first century, as their neighbor and federal representative provocatively insisted, how had they come to imagine their group as continuous in the first place, such that they could face a shared threat? How did the forms of professional mobility that allowed so many of them to move to the region by choice shape their subsequent sense of belonging there? And how are the senses of possibility emanating from these attachments articulated differently by researchers who are married to other researchers, and by other experts whose understandings of professional purpose are intimately tethered to securing work for others?

As much as Smithers scientists' assertions of collective belonging have marked the social milieus of the rural northwest, they have also placed equally strong demands on maps, planning models, and other material artifacts of knowledge production. These investments of meaning have become particularly salient amid the downsizing of government research, where land management plans and data archives at risk of being discarded have been taken up as objects of care by scientists struggling to stay in the region. Examining how these reciprocal remakings of mobile researchers and old research unfold over time, this chapter asks: How have particular documents and documentary practices been used to repair perceived ruptures in social continuity, and how have researchers' relationships to these documents transformed in the process? Foreshadowing questions I will take up in detail in subsequent chapters, I also periodically pause to reflect on the apparent arbitrariness of the ways White experts typically articulate their senses of place. If a common commitment to caring for documents can be used to legitimate assertions of belonging, how do environmental scientists weigh the claims of their neighbors, including First Nations experts whose obligations to land and kin have been placed on them since birth?

Among the many groups claiming attachments to the landscapes of rural British Columbia, the very language of "obligation" is itself contested terrain (Peyton 2017; Turkel 2007). As subsequent chapters make plain, generations of Gitanyow and Gitxsan men and women have devoted their lives to contesting the expropriation of their lands and resources. During the years I spent getting to know some of these people, some of them were still actively struggling to reconcile the labor they had spent on these projects with the new idioms of nationhood brought into circulation by land claims and treaty negotiations (Özden-Schilling 2020; Daly and Napoleon 2003; see also Nadasdy 2017). In such a deeply fraught setting, it may seem impertinent to ask readers to consider the senses of place and sociality cultivated by Euro-Canadian experts, particularly those who moved to the region when their careers were already well underway. At worst, by foregrounding how White researchers' senses of belonging have become threatened by government downsizing, the following stories might even be construed as a new form of "imperialist nostalgia" (Rosaldo 1989), one geared toward naturalizing the pretensions of experts by filiating them with events that transpired before they arrived.

As I aim to show in this chapter, the nostalgia of the researchers I met in Smithers evinces a subtler kind of complicity. Rather than performing pity for destroyed or disappeared others in the ways that Renato Rosaldo attributes to nostalgic agents of colonialism, conservation researchers' reflections on loss and belonging are more likely to signify attempts to make sense of their own experiences of displacement. Experts and their spouses, my interlocutors' comments suggested, had become estranged by government downsizing, devolution, and other processes of neoliberalization, just like everyone else. This is not to say that one should accept their claims at face value or attempt to commensurate them with other forms of suffering engendered by government withdrawal. In some ways, the laments that Smithers's scientists occasionally shared with me about the precariousness of their place in the region mirror the insecurities that Ann Laura Stoler (2016) discerns in the notes of marginal bureaucrats in the Dutch East Indies, each one struggling to maintain their authority within institutions always seemingly on the brink of collapse. For the scientists who moved to northwest British Columbia over the past three decades hoping to inaugurate a grand new project of research-based conservationism, though, their nostalgia signaled a sense of mourning for a political regime to which each of them hoped to contribute—a regime that never fully arrived.

In addition to projecting misgivings about the fragility of technocratic rule, the ways that environmental scientists have endured and reflected on the conditions of their work under government downsizing also evince a search for a coherent and meaningful life. At times, these reflections can help to reveal how professional identities and forms of life persist between changes in regime. Regardless of one's position in a social order, Svetlana Boym reminds us, negotiating these kinds of transitions is never a passive experience. Addressing the affective engagements of former Soviet subjects with their memories of life under socialism, Boym (2001) presents nostalgia as an ambivalent response to the demands of the present. "Nostalgia speaks in riddles and puzzles," she writes, "so one must face them in order not to become its next victim—or its next victimizer" (xvii). As I argue throughout this book, rural researchers have come to inhabit similarly bifurcated roles. Casting themselves as stewards of the region's forests by virtue of their commitments to conservation research, many of the researchers with whom I spent time in the northwest saw themselves simultaneously as rightful agents of government action as well as victims of government neglect.

Threaded through the everyday speech of alienated experts, nostalgia garners much of its productive potential by facilitating the expression of seemingly contradictory identities and positions. The manner in which this happens is often deceptively simple. For all its equivocations, nostalgia allows its bearers to enact change simply by calling attention to the passage of time. Time and again in Smithers, I observed scientists narrativize their research artifacts and professional paths as proof of their own persistence across regimes. By doing so, I argue, they leveraged other displaced researchers' nostalgia for the recent past as a constitutive force in the present, one that enabled many of them to lay claim to a sense of collectivity that otherwise might have been difficult to define. Nostalgic references to earlier technocratic forms also helped rural researchers assert a sense of separateness from the state in ways that reinforced their obligations to one another.

Strategic deployments of historical narratives serve more than ideology and statecraft, Boym reminds us: they are also critical to negotiating everyday life. "Nostalgia is not always about the past; it can be retrospective but also prospective," she writes. "Fantasies of the past determined by needs of the present have a direct impact on realities of the future. Consideration of the future makes us take responsibility for our nostalgic tales" (2001, xvi). Many of the processes I describe in this chapter might be understood as researchers' attempts to "take responsibility" for the past promises of research-driven governance. Often couching their assertions within proposals for new collaborative endeavors (see chapter 5), scientists living in northwest British Columbia decried the provincial government's abandonment of policy documents in order to show how their own continuing sense of commitment to these artifacts had engendered new domains of association. By the time the Campbell government's New Relationship–era policy reforms had begun to redirect provincial funds to conservation initiatives, many rural researchers had already learned to be wary of provincial entreaties and were busily investing their hopes and energies elsewhere (Wood and Rossiter 2011). The future of environmental governance had already been written, their complaints suggested; in order to bring it to fruition, rural researchers first had to hold on to the work that had already been done by others.

Asserting a sense of collectivity through marginalized documents can help individuals carry on through uncertainty and duress, but it can also tie new idioms of community to an elusive, aspirational tense. Explaining this divergence, Boym insists, demands a form of scholarship that is attentive to the practices informing these aspirations without subsuming them within structures of power. "To unearth the fragments of nostalgia," she writes, "one needs a dual archeology of memory and of place, and a dual history of illusions and actual practices" (2001, xviii). Such language is reminiscent of the way Lee Clarke (1999) defines "fantasy documents": meticulously crafted risk management and contingency plans prepared to describe how organizations ought to respond to nuclear explosions, oil spills, and other multifarious disasters. The instrumental value of such documents, Clarke argues, is often far surpassed by their symbolic affordances. Some "are little more than vague hopes for remote futures and have virtually no known connection with human capacity or will" (16), but nevertheless project a "remarkable . . . coherence of organizational coordination" (17). Indeed, the sense of faith that fantasy documents can help to secure, Clarke suggests, is crucial to the operation of organizational power writ large.

Fantasy documents offer useful analytics for explaining how organizations leverage the "surfeit of symbolism in everyday documents" (Clarke 1999, 13) to accumulate and maintain power. By offering tools for comparing bureaucratic documents to other forms of imaginative writing, Clarke's analysis can also shed light on how the effects of such symbolism might persist even after the attending organizational power has dissipated. Alexei Yurchak (2006) argues that the circulation and discussion of poems, satirical cartoons, and other media artifacts in the Soviet Union during the last decades of the regime helped to render its sudden collapse simultaneously shocking and unremarkable. "Many discovered that, unbeknownst to themselves, they had always been ready for it," Yurchak observes, "that they had always known that life in socialism was shaped through a curious paradox, that the system was always felt to be both stagnating and immutable, fragile and vigorous, bleak and full of promise" (4). The "explosion" of literary journals in the 1980s helped to promulgate "the use of binary categories to describe Soviet reality" (5), already a common practice in everyday conversation, Yurchak explains. The cultivation of deep attachments to transgressive documents estranged Soviet subjects from state discourse in ways that paradoxically helped to keep precarious dreamworlds intact (see Buck-Morss 2002). Over time, though, these attachments also came to offer people resources for articulating their aspirations within the new regime, and for narrating their experiences of transition.

Many of the scientists I met in Smithers explained their understanding of continuity to me by reflecting on the professional paths of specific individuals, including both their own "life histories" as well as the trajectories they discerned in the lives of their spouses and others. When I met Pauline in 2013, she had been working for more than three decades as a private forestry science consultant. Like a number of other Smithereens, however, the narrative arc of her professional career traced vectors through an ever-changing ecology of institutions. From our earliest conversations onward, Pauline explicitly, if somewhat bemusedly, presented the arc as defining a coherent path, albeit one that she had come to discern only retrospectively. An early internship as a botanist's field assistant along the nearby northwest coast followed by a graduate degree in the United States; a short stint as a researcher for the BC government, then decades as a contract-based scientist; an early role in drafting the region's first community land use plan, before cofounding an independent research center as a home for displaced scientists. Each role and position indexed a bounded institution and a moment in time. Taken together within Pauline's narration, though, they converged into a multilayered milieu. Narrating events from her own life to me alongside reflections on specific institutions that she herself had helped bring into being, Pauline implicitly defined the scientific life through the language of obligation. At each step, she shepherded the migration of memory between precarious institutional forms by saving old documents and cultivating relationships with other individual scientists. Her research had defined her relationship to the landscapes of British Columbia, yet it had also tethered her sense of self to the fulfillment of other scientists' aspirations as well.

Pauline's stories underline the paradoxical challenge of attempting to define an intellectual collective among rural scientists displaced by deregulation—an awkward task that has nevertheless come to carry a considerable sense of urgency. Since the turn of the twenty-first century, the provincial government's "dirt ministries"—an affectionate term that government staff members used to refer to the Ministry of Forests, the Ministry of Environment, the Ministry of Mines, and their later iterations—have continually shed research funds and personnel, both during periods of massive institutional restructuring as well as during initiatives purporting to bolster support for beleaguered regulatory processes (see McCarthy 2006). Throughout this period, cultivating legitimacy for new research-based policy proposals in the rural north has increasingly required individual researchers to project a distributed sense of authority by expressing solidarity with one another, even as they prepare for future displacements. Some, like Pauline, have thrown themselves into building independent research centers and other institutions less dependent on government grants. Even as they cautiously built relationships through these new groups, however, many of the researchers I came to know in Smithers also confronted the contingencies that bracketed their own professional lives by projecting a shared image of the past.

For people who have spent their lives building scientific careers, "the past" is invariably a multifaceted construction. As scholars such as Hans-Jörg Rheinberger (1993, 2010) and Michael Fischer (2009) show, narrating transitions within an individual career—the beginning of an experiment, a move to a new institution, the arrival of critical recognition for a previously marginal theory—requires scientists to account for their shifting modes of interconnection with other researchers and their own evolving senses of self (see Dumit 2004; Gusterson 2005; Traweek 1988). In reflections on the pasts of scientific work, what constitutes an "event" can also change in accordance with one's relationship to the technical objects involved (see Das 1995; Daston 2000). Pauline and others, for instance, often referred to specific policy changes as intimate betrayals, including in particular the shifts that led the BC Forest Service to close its regional office in Smithers and radically scale back its support for independent projects. "Everybody's flailing around," Pauline recalled. "Our jobs, our livelihoods, our sense of what we do in Smithers is coming apart, because government is not going to play a role in this stuff anymore."

Regardless of the affective registers in which they offered their reflections, the scientists I came to know throughout the region found ways of presenting their nostalgia as tethered to emergent concerns. Many of the specific government initiatives that threaded through my conversations around Smithers were treated simultaneously as ongoing processes and as painful memories, including in particular a series of laws introduced more than a decade earlier as part of a general provincial transition toward so-called results-based environmental management.[7] Dozens of former government researchers described experiencing the devolution of planning and regulatory roles to corporate developers as a kind of personal demotion. The Forest and Range Practices Act, assented to in November 2002, replaced state planners' prescriptions for where and how much to harvest with vague benchmarks authored by harvesting companies themselves, the broader effects of which often were difficult for assessors to measure or litigate against (see Stem et al. 2005).[8] With a steadily declining cohort of Forest Service researchers available to evaluate the plans of licensees even after the provincial government began promising in the mid-2000s to partially reverse its earlier personnel cuts, some researchers in Smithers lamented to me, even this meager auditing work was often left unfinished.

Policy failures, I was often reminded, had long been popular topics of conversation. Woven into researchers' stories about their lives and movements throughout the northwest, references to policies and funding programs offered a shorthand means for marking the duration personal commitments. As indices in everyday conversations among disparately positioned researchers, however, these references also lent form to an ethics of intervention. Time and again, I listened to my interlocutors in Smithers assail results-based management and the haphazard structuring of community-based planning initiatives as evidence that the provincial government could no longer be entrusted with the care of participatory forums, data, or even expertise itself. Yet even as they railed against institutional power, these researchers were careful not to disavow their own status as spokespersons. Rather than simply emboldening their neighbors in the northwest to take action as "citizen scientists," environmental researchers positioned themselves as shrewd yet compassionate mediators. It would be local scientists who would help the region manage its ecological futures, they suggested, if only the power that was promised to them returned.

In subtle ways, many of the researchers I came to know in Smithers implicitly framed their own professional mobility as a latent threat to the region itself. Some described their loss of formal institutional attachments as proof of their commitment to the Bulkley Valley. In private conversations and in public events like the November summit, these researchers also compared the instability of their and their spouses' professional positions to the looming ecological crises facing the region—crises that they were continually reorganizing their work to address. These comparisons were not confined to spoken narratives, however. Much like the speeches in which local politicians hailed them as historical actors, the stories these researchers told about the pasts and futures of the rural north were invariably enmeshed with documents. Pauline and others routinely cited biodiversity indicators, ecological succession models, and other technical artifacts as both illustrations of their own research as well as material proof of their work as activists. Frequently underlining how specific, intimate obligations had come to motivate their ongoing research, many of the scientists I came to know in the region presented themselves as both producers of original research as well as caretakers of documents abandoned by the state. Their relationships to these documents, they suggested, and the knowledge required to update and mobilize them in the future would be key to securing the future health of the region's forests. By highlighting the intentional movements and professional relationships that enabled these critical documents to persist, however, their assertions invited a difficult question: Whom, or what, would the labor of caring for documents be most likely to save in the end?

Arrival Stories

The sheer number of scientists living in Smithers might, at first glance, seem paradoxical: as the presence of provincial government institutions in the town steadily shrank through the first two decades of the twenty-first century, the number of scientists living there has, if anything, increased.

Anchored around the BVRC, this self-consciously peripheral cluster of experts and their expanding rosters of independent projects have continued to draw more and more researchers to live and work in the northwest, despite the fact that the government ministries that continue to fund and organize much of their work have drastically downsized and restructured. I often heard working-class Smithereens derisively refer to these newcomers as "amenity migrants": young professionals who began moving to Smithers during the War in the Woods intent on building technical careers while enjoying the spectacular mountains, parks, and wilderness areas surrounding the Bulkley Valley.[9] For many of these migrants, though, achieving professional mobility meant more than gaining access to far-flung professional networks: upon arriving in Smithers—often with partners who were themselves researchers—and deciding to call the place home, most learned to use their mobility as a means of remaining in place.

Over the course of the twentieth century, the ways that different researchers "arrived" in Smithers and cultivated senses of belonging there gradually shifted in concert with changes in the administrative structures of extractivism. Established to support a new railway depot in 1913, Smithers eventually became the commercial relay for resource extraction in the northwest quarter of the province. By the time large-scale clear-cut logging began expanding throughout the region in the early 1970s, the town's Forest Service office had also become a planning hub for the provincial government's sustained yield forest harvesting system. Even as later researchers began moving to the region to focus on wildlife habitat and watershed restoration research, though, a sense of connection to earlier central planning regimes persisted in the ways that they articulated their senses of place. Many people I met in Smithers narrated the town's histories to me through numbers. Projected ore tonnages. Timber harvest volumes. Dam-generated kilowatt hours. Over time, I found myself describing Smithers's administrative catchment areas through these imposing statistics as well. West of the Rocky Mountains and north of Highway 16 (the northernmost route to Canada's Pacific coast), only a few of towns interrupt the nearly 300,000 square kilometers of forests before the Yukon border—an area nearly as large as Germany. Rather than reflecting on their distance from Victoria as a form of isolation, though, Smithers-based researchers presented themselves as sentinels overseeing the province's vast northern hinterlands.[10]

As the War in the Woods began to unfold in the 1990s, Smithers became renowned throughout the province for its rising population of young professionals who brought university degrees, government connections, and urbane politics and tastes to a region otherwise dominated by timber mills and mining camps. I first heard the nickname "Nelson North" applied to Smithers while sitting in on a meeting of biologists at the University of Northern British Columbia in the city of Prince George, four hours east of Smithers. The joke paired the highly educated and oft-outspoken activist community of Smithers with the more famous town of Nelson, a haven for American draft dodgers and leftist expatriates who migrated to Canada during the Vietnam War to live amid the ski resorts of British Columbia's southern Rocky Mountains. Many of the people I met around Smithers championed the town's geographic isolation as providing a similar sense of distance. Separated from southern British Columbia by a fifteen-hour drive or a notoriously expensive two-hour plane ride, Smithereens rarely missed an opportunity to deride runaway housing prices in the sprawling suburbs of Vancouver, or to trade stories of urban rudeness encountered on recent trips south.

Particularly for the full-time government employees who were able to remain in Smithers after the town's offices began closing, the distance between Smithers and Victoria was something to be relished. For most of the year, they admitted, their superiors in Victoria effectively left them alone, allowing them to divide their time between organizing research projects and administering to the mines, timber supply areas, and provincial parks scattered throughout the northwest corner of the province. For the many scientists who had left government jobs for the private sector, their reliance on contract work kept them close with their few former colleagues who remained with the state. In spite of their precariousness, they assured me, they remained in the northwest by choice. Compared to the tense atmosphere at the main dirt ministry offices that many of them had left behind in Victoria, the egalitarian attitudes that they encountered in and around Smithers came as a relief. Eventually, I came to know many of these people over Friday evening happy hours and Saturday mornings at the downtown farmers market. Many of the most prominent scientists in Smithers were women. Among these, several were former government scientists turned consultants, nearly all of whom complained about the "toxic cynicism" of the larger government offices in Victoria from which they had "escaped" before moving to Smithers. As I grew closer with them and their families, some of these researchers shared stories with me about delayed promotions, lost maternity leaves, and other encounters with gender discrimination that precipitated their own journeys away from the provincial capital.

During my first months in town, I encountered dozens of researchers who were ostensibly in Smithers only for temporary stays. Biologists from eastern Canada stopped by for a few weeks to observe familiar bird species in unfamiliar habitats. Tree disease specialists from Vancouver drove north between semesters to see how a pest dispersed throughout the province interacted with the kinds of trees that grew in the region's forests. Others had first come under similar circumstances before deciding to attempt to live in the region full-time. Some returned years later for multiyear post-doctoral appointments or, like me, for prolonged bouts of research for PhD degrees supervised by advisers at distant institutions. Dividing my time in town between the ramshackle meeting rooms at the main office of the BVRC and my borrowed cubicle in the Northwest Community College's glistening new LEED-certified building two blocks away, I spent a few days each week meeting with BVRC researchers and affiliates for coffee and talking with them about their lives and their work. Many shared stories about their experiences in other kinds of private and government-driven forestry research, and their anxieties about the provincial government's seemingly endless restructuring. We gossiped about the developing projects and daily dramas at the BVRC, and the broader ambitions of its enthusiastic directors.

As I came to know dozens of different researchers through the BVRC and in other informal spaces of interaction, our conversations about "rootedness" typically bifurcated into two distinct temporalities. For a small handful of researchers, their stories focused on parents who had moved north during the expansion of industrial logging, or earlier relatives who had established homesteads in the early twentieth century. For many others, however, their sense of commitment to the region had begun with their own decision to remain in the area beyond the end of a specific research project. The prevalence of this latter frame of experience made my own arrival in the Bulkley Valley immediately legible to my interlocutors as a potential prelude to a permanent move. To both the environmental researchers and resource workers I met during my time in the northwest, I was simply another researcher who had arrived in the region thinking of himself as a temporary visitor, little different from the steady stream of visiting scientists whose expressions of interest in local politics betrayed an emerging desire to make the destination a home.

For some of the people I befriended in Smithers, particularly ranchers and resource workers whose families had lived in the region for multiple generations, the idea of a recent arrival trying to claim the town as their own was frustrating, but familiar. "You're not a local until you've buried someone here," one of these friends half-jokingly informed me, including once while scolding me for citing as a "local" a resident who had, in the words of my critic, "only just moved up north in 1978." Most of the environmental scientists I met in the region, though, deployed altogether different criteria when judging their neighbors' connections to the region. Many of the people whom these scientists celebrated as "locals" were other researchers who had simply turned down repeated opportunities to move away. For researchers who emplaced themselves in the region through their vocal disdain for "fly-in consultants" and other seasonal researchers, the end of summer brought relief. One Smithers-born, government-employed sociologist summarized for me the feelings of many of his colleagues as we chatted at Pints and Politics, a monthly event that brought many researchers and other government employees to a local pub to chat informally with the town mayor about local gossip and concerns. "November is everyone's favorite month," he admitted. "That's when you find out who's really here."

Position and Place

"Who's really here," I understood, included those who seemed likely to remain: through the winter doldrums between summer field seasons, and through persistent uncertainty between contracts and grants. Nearly all of the scientists I came to know in the region had migrated as adults north from Vancouver or west from urban centers in Ontario and Quebec. Even the few who could claim northwestern roots by birth narrated their lives in the region as moments of conscious decision. Growing up in Kitimat, a small town located a three-hour drive west of Smithers, Pauline had been a young girl when her father had broken with the American-led Steelworkers Union to lead the formation of the Canadian Association of Smelters and Allied Workers in 1967.[11] Coinciding with the spectacular media attention generated by Expo 67, the world's fair held in Montreal, the sudden formation of a Canadian-led worker's union at what was then one of the largest aluminum smelters in the world quickly turned Pauline's father into a regional celebrity as well as a favored target of conservative political attacks. "That kinda influences your attitude about taking charge of your own destiny," she wryly acknowledged. Her career decisions, she admitted, had begun to feel like a coherent narrative only when she considered them in the light of her father's professional life.

Compelling autobiographies were not the only resource that researchers drew on to lend their careers a sense of coherence, of course. Months before the November summit, I joined Pauline for a firsthand look at some of the maps she had helped to construct during her first years as a forestry scientist. One of the few women to enter the prestigious University of British Columbia forestry program in the 1970s, Pauline spent a formative summer conducting field research in the northwest as she transitioned into graduate study, assisting a Smithers-based botanist to adapt a landscape classification system developed in southern British Columbia for the forests of the northern coast.[12] For several hours, we flipped slowly through stacks of old biodiversity reports in her office, an unassuming room above the garage at the home she shared with her husband, Dennis. As we talked through the morning, Pauline occasionally gestured over her shoulder to a set of enormous paper maps adorning the walls of her office: biogeoclimatic classification system–based maps (similar to the one pictured in figure 1.2) and cross sections, several of which she had helped to produce as an intern more than thirty years earlier.

Visiting other home offices around Smithers, I often saw aging ecosystem maps displayed as wall art. Particularly for researchers who had conducted fieldwork in the service of defining the maps' boundaries, polygons denoting statistical distributions of groups of tree species held a subtler sense of meaning than the features on a conventional political map. Many such maps were simply beautiful objects in their own right, Pauline offered. Full of cascades of fading colors, each map conveyed the unfathomable immensity of the northwest: magenta for the grand cedars along the coast, for instance; teal for the narrow swaths of aspen following the trunks of the region's largest rivers; indigo as the Douglas fir of the coastal mountains gave way to the cyan of the interior plateau's vast monotony of industrially planted lodgepole pine; chartreuse for the alpine tundra that slid lower and lower, off ridges and peaks and eventually into the valleys of the Spatsizi Plateau as the map ranged northward past the Yukon border.

By the time I began visiting Pauline in her home office, I had grown accustomed to seeing researchers deploy maps as storytelling devices. Time and again, my interlocutors would begin searching through filing cabinets or point to documents pinned to their walls as they explained to me how they had arrived in the region, and how their projects and positions had shifted in the years since. Gesturing at the many maps decorating the walls and ceiling of her office throughout my first visit to her home, Pauline shared stories about the work of building relationships and getting to know herself in the field. The fieldwork involved in constructing the maps, she remembered, had been grueling and mundane. "It was basically walking fifty meters, putting down a stake, counting trees; walk another fifty

FIGURE 1.2 Biogeoclimatic map of Canada, displayed on the wall of a geographic information systems consultancy in Smithers (not Pauline's office). Photo by Johanna Pfalz.

meters . . ." she laughed. "Most of the maps here are way, way out of date by now, of course, but they still have sentimental value for me." The work, she reflected, had also proven to be politicizing in ways that she did not understand at the time. She and several of the other young botanists contracted to help extend the new classification system across the province bonded over the shared sense of frustration they experienced in working across the provincial government's administrative boundaries, few of which mapped well onto the ecological zones then emerging from their taxonomical studies. As they continued to produce and collect these discordant documents, Pauline's stories suggested, the sense of estrangement she and her fellow researchers felt toward the provincial government steadily deepened.

In addition to comparing the lines on their maps in their musings about the region's futures, a few of my interlocutors reflected on looming institutional change by comparing their own experiences of transition with the experiences of other researchers. Unlike many younger researchers in Smithers, Pauline reflected, her own experiences with earlier government layoffs allowed her to view the 2002 closing of the local Forest Service office in a comparative light. After completing a master's degree in Oregon in 1979, Pauline had moved to Smithers with her husband, Dennis, a forest ecologist who had migrated to British Columbia from eastern Canada, and they both began working for the provincial government full-time. The timing of the move gave Pauline her first taste of government abandonment. Two years after arriving in Smithers, both Pauline and Dennis were left unemployed as both the BC Forest Service and the BC Ministry of Environment (Dennis's employer at the time) were reorganized by the government of the Social Credit Party, populist conservatives who diminished the role of both organizations' research divisions after a brief period of rapid expansion (Wilson 1998, 149–82).[13] After the provincial government's reliance on sustained yield forest management practices was challenged by a short-lived NDP government in the early 1970s, the Social Credit government sought to blame the emergence of new conservation-oriented protests throughout the province on the expanded role that the NDP-led Forest Service had accorded to ecological restoration research. "Everyone with minimal seniority got thrown into the street, kinda overnight," Pauline admitted. Not yet committed to building institutions of their own, she and Dennis decided to follow the example of many of their newly unemployed colleagues and simply moved away.

The relative ease with which the two researchers first left the northwest was not lost on Pauline as she reflected on how her sense of place in Smithers had changed in the decades since. Their credentials had given them options, she remembered, a luxury many of their earliest friends in Smithers had yet to experience. At the same time, their time away had made them both wary of living in fear of future government cutbacks. Determined to confront this fear, they decided to return to the northwest and find work only after they arrived—just as the War in the Woods was beginning to develop in earnest. Their optimism, not yet fatigued, turned out to be well placed, even if their efforts to distance themselves from the provincial government proved to be short-lived. Within weeks, Dennis was recruited to begin work as a research scientist for the Forest Service. Soon thereafter, Pauline began receiving offers of consulting work from contacts and friends she had accumulated during her earlier years as a Forest Service employee. By the late 1980s, she had begun soliciting contracts for her new owner-operated consultancy, cataloging habitat sensitivity information throughout the area for environmental impact assessments and government-funded reports.

Shifting her professional position did not immediately transform Pauline's sense of place. Her primary research on postdisturbance plant succession and autecology (the study of the relationship between individual species or organisms and broader environments), for instance, "barely changed," she remembered, when she left the Forest Service and began working as a consultant. Even as she established herself as an independent contractor, the BC Forest Service and other government institutions in Smithers continued to shape her social and professional worlds. "Wherever there's a regional office, there's this clump, this cluster of consultants partly because you're in tune to what's going on, you get these contracts," Pauline explained to me. "But also a lot of spouses are involved, right? A lot of people, one part of the family works in government and . . . the other partner's a consultant; they've got the pension and all the health benefits. . . . Doesn't matter which partner it is, who's making more money, it's just a nice arrangement for stability. And that's a stay-at-home kind of job, usually." Over the next two decades, Pauline continued to build relationships with researchers still moving to the region as she settled into the rhythms of working from home. As her understanding of continuity took shape against her ability to keep working in place, though, she felt a growing compulsion to help secure continuity for others.

Pauline's reflections on her transition from full-time government researcher to independent contractor underline the many subtle divergences between the lived experience of government downsizing and broader structural explanations of the process. In her narrations, each new institutional attachment further enabled her to rearticulate her position in both cumulative and retrospective terms. Contracts and grants came and went; working documents piled up and eventually began to gather dust. As she began to consolidate a sense of her voice as a researcher, though, Pauline felt increasingly compelled to bring this voice to bear in new domains of activism as a committed *resident* of the region, rather than as an expert per se. Her cleverly balanced consulting schedule provided more time and energy to devote to advocacy work, a "hobby" she feared would disappear completely were she and Dennis to take up new jobs in Victoria. "When the land use planning started," she chuckled, "I had babies, and I really needed to do something other than just be a mom." By the early 1990s, tensions surrounding the War in the Woods had helped the NDP to win its first provincial elections in two decades. Promising to act as the stewards of an environmentally and economically "sustainable" approach to forestry, the new government began inviting rural residents to form local committees that would oversee an entirely new land use planning process.[14] In late 1991, the Bulkley Community Resources Board, or CRB, was elected to construct what would become the Bulkley LRMP—British Columbia's first community-authored land management document.[15] Relishing her new role as a scientist turned citizen, Pauline joined the process as one of the CRB's founding members.

A Founding Document

Since the Bulkley LRMP was formally adopted into provincial policy in 1998, the document itself has led multiple lives. As an administrative document, the practical legacy of the LRMP has been relatively modest. Based on the recommendations of the CRB, the provincial government set aside 5 percent of the 7,600 square kilometers comprising the Bulkley LRMP area as protected parks.[16] Within several years of the plan's adoption, though, the sophisticated data-gathering strategies and development analysis protocols that the board outlined for the areas outside these parks had been almost entirely written out of government law. This is not to say that the original plan simply died when its stipulations were voided, however. As a document that could be read, cited, copied, and saved, the 148-page final report has been continually resurrected: not as a bitter chapter in the history of the northwest, but as a vision of ecological stewardship and coherence to which the region might one day return.

The Bulkley LRMP, like the town of Smithers itself, residents often tried to impress upon me, was different. Compared with other LRMP documents begun throughout the province during the 1990s, the detail and specificity of the Bulkley LRMP starkly reflected its drafters' technocratic ambitions. Perhaps more subtly, though, the framing of the plan also belied a sense of faith that the provincial government would recognize these ambitions, and reward them with concrete authority. As the final plan was sent to the provincial government for approval, the technical meanings and spatial extent of each of the board's five different use designations had been pulled into focus and mapped out with considerable precision (see figure 1.3). Within the "integrated resource management" areas that took up 64 percent of the district, a cascade of subdivisions outlined a complex list of subtly different management regimes. Other designations not introduced in the original terms of reference proposed entirely new systems for arranging different forms of use within constrained areas. Descriptions of new "ecosystem network" polygons sketched out intricately organized arrays of habitat migration corridors, intensive forestry development areas, and protected "visual quality" areas, including highly visible mountain slopes in proximity to provincial parks.

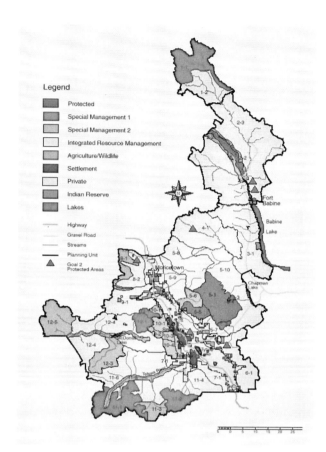

FIGURE 1.3 Bulkley LRMP area coded by land use designation. Note the preponderance of land classified for "integrated resource management." Scale bar is in kilometers. Modified from Bulkley Valley Community Resources Board 1998, 38.

Not all parts of the plan area were subject to such baroque specifications. Areas where the board had been unable to reach consensus were marked as "special management zones," listing general provisos constraining how and where certain kinds of development could occur. A permanent CRB, refreshed through regular elections, would parse new proposals, and would be consulted by government officials wherever disagreements over implementation arose. Pauline and several members of the original CRB admitted to me with weary embarrassment that they had all believed that the government officials in charge of implementing the plan would appreciate their attention to detail. With plans for continuous monitoring approved as part of the plan itself, the board expected to be allowed to make regular revisions to their outlines as relevant ecological maps and data sets were updated and as new contingencies emerged.[17]

To those who participated in the planning process and the many others who signaled their affinity for it in later years, the document was both an impressively polished product and a symbol of things left undone. Describing for me the genesis of the LRMP over cups of tea in her home office, Pauline's narratives swayed between individual modesty and collective pride. When I arrived in Smithers early in 2013, the Bulkley LRMP was still cited around the province as a triumph of participatory planning. Of more than a dozen LRMPs produced in the province prior to the implementation of the far more government-directed, developer-centric Strategic Land and Resource Plan (SLRP) model by the BC Liberal Party–led government in 2006, only the Bulkley LRMP had won widespread support, and only the Bulkley CRB continued to meet after its plan was approved by the province (Forest Practices Board 2008). For the dozens of conservation activists already living in the region by the early 1990s, the initiation of the LRMP process had been a watershed moment in its own right. Hundreds of people attended the first CRB planning meeting in the gymnasium at St. Joseph's Catholic School in Smithers. At the urging of Irving Fox, a retired professor of planning and longtime conservation activist in the northwest, dozens of attendees gave short speeches and volunteered for board membership, choosing from a brief list of "community values" they would represent if elected to the committee (forestry, fishing, hunting, conservation, or mining, to name a few).[18] After hours of debate, a dentist, a timber mill manager, a wildlife biologist, a hunting guide, a logging technician, a self-described housewife, an exploration geologist, and several others were nominated to convene as the original CRB.

The references I heard to the LRMP as a technical document were frequently couched in reflections on the document's construction. For many of the researchers who came to celebrate the document in the years after it was drafted, adopting the LRMP as an artifact of personal history allowed them to treat the confrontations that preceded the planning process into moments of convergence for the Bulkley Valley as a whole. Smithers, researchers acknowledged, had long been divided by differences in profession, class, and birthplace. As clear-cut logging rapidly expanded throughout the northwest in the 1980s, though, Pauline and others insisted, a pervasive sense of anxiety had begun to transcend these apparent divisions. In Pauline's recollections of the meetings that led to the formation of the CRB, the original board members had primarily been concerned with the rate of timber removal throughout the region. "There's always the redneck versus the enviro-people stuff, and the local people versus the urban people, but they were pretty united about the fact that, when the wood ran out, we'd be kinda up the creek." Rather than explicitly enrolling nonscientists throughout Smithers into an established conservation project, she suggested, Irving Fox and the other organizers of the Bulkley CRB had merely provided residents with tools for expressing their fears about the possible futures of local landscapes.

All of the original board members who spoke with me about their experiences on the CRB explicitly presented their senses of connection to the Bulkley Valley as compulsions that had driven them to participate in the LRMP process, rather than as products of their time on the board. Some, though, admitted that they had actively considered how their ties to the region would evolve in response to the shape of the final document. Wary of another transition in government like the one that had prompted her first move out of the region, Pauline had been surprised when none of her fellow board members began negotiations by advocating for the creation of new provincial parks—the only form of provincial protection that carried a promise of permanence. Even those who explicitly aligned themselves with anti-clear-cutting activists were uneasy about dismissing outright the livelihoods of the other members of the board.[19] "They all had a reason why they didn't want parks," Pauline explained, "and each one was different." One participant, for instance, a vocal member of other Smithers-based conservation groups, "made his living building log houses," Pauline admitted, "so he had a lot of respect for people who cut down trees."

Whenever the researchers I met around Smithers referenced the LRMP by describing early stages of the drafting process, they invariably mentioned the affective ties between the original board members as a reason for the continuing persistence of the document in Smithereens' collective imagination. In subtler ways, though, some researchers also pointed to the influence of these same friendships when explaining how the plan had begun to erode as an effective instrument of policy. Pauline dwelled on the personal anxieties each member had shared with her during the committee's first years, particularly as the group weighed the prospect of banning developmental activities across broad regions, far into an unknowable environmental future. "I was a little bit concerned that we were all just a little too mild-mannered," she laughed. "We were all good Canadians." Her own experience building ecosystem classification systems as an employee with the BC Ministry of Environment had allowed her to see firsthand the ease with which government policymakers could reorganize elaborate resource use protocols. Rather than attempting to persuade the group to commit to an inflexible set of demands, though, Pauline recalled, she eventually al-lowed herself to believe that their calls for continual monitoring and updates would be taken in good faith.

Over time, Pauline remembered, she and the other board members gradu-ally grew less preoccupied with the formal administrative limits governing the process. Meeting roughly once per month for four years, they worked through different planning scenarios. Pauline's technical background enabled her to ask critical questions of the rotating cast of government researchers who vis-ited the board for consultations. Hydrologists, botanists, grizzly and caribou biologists, and other specialists joined their meetings for a few hours at a time, each one sharing their research and answering questions about specific parts of the district. Together, the board members projected the effects of each proposal on the future populations of particular animal and plant species, the available area of agricultural land, and the rise and fall of predicted timber harvests, typically decades into the future. As the plan progressed, they held public feedback sessions to explain the different management scenarios they had experimented with during the previous months. For several years, Pau-line recalled, the board struggled to convince the residents of Smithers and neighboring towns that the project was not simply another government-run endeavor. Pauline herself had worked to keep the group's government col-laborators sidelined during the board's periodic public meetings, she admit-ted, even as she and others frequently called on these collaborators to help them answer technical questions. "They would help us with maps and stuff," Pauline joked, "but we would be up there pinning stuff to the wall."

Numerous researchers that I met in Smithers described the years spent drafting the LRMP as a process of affective and intellectual convergence. In the process of recounting debates and conversations from individual CRB meetings, though, Pauline consistently emphasized her fellow participants' shifting senses of self. Only a few years removed from the original War in the Woods, the independent researchers who had helped to convene the committee constantly emphasized their distance from their government peers. "We didn't want to have any government people on the committee," Pauline laughed. Over time, though, she admitted, some of these distinc-tions became more difficult to sustain. As board members grew more en-gaged with the physical maps of the district, their initial suspicion toward the government planners gradually thawed, and they eventually overcame their resistance to the physical space of the BC Forest Service district office in Smithers. "We didn't meet there for the longest time because we didn't want to be tainted," Pauline admitted, half-jokingly. "So we met in all these places, but eventually we kinda gave that up and met there because all the maps were there. I remember we were at the library and various things. So that was just a couple years of getting comfortable that the Forest Service wasn't trying to run the process—but of course, they gradually did."

In her retelling, Pauline referenced the gradual expansion of her own technical aspirations in subtle and indirect ways. As the process wore on and the publicity surrounding the initial board elections slowly dissipated, she recalled, the scope of the government's interests in the process "became more apparent" to the remaining members of the board. The rate of timber harvest in the region, or annual allowable cut, that the government set anew each decade was off limits, and would continue to be calculated by a small cadre of Forest Service programmers based in the provincial capital (see Özden-Schilling forthcoming). These officials continued to circulate public discussion documents detailing basic aspects of their rationale for the annual harvest limit set for the region overall (usually on the order of 800,000 cubic meters per year), but even as the LRMP process began to take shape, the quotas outlined in Forest Service planning documents did not change. Her sense of disenchantment, she admitted, extended to the highest levels of the provincial government. Despite sponsoring a raft of new projects to research the effects of large-scale, sustained yield harvesting, the NDP was proving to be just as loyal as other parties had been in ensuring that the province's timber companies received the allocations they desired. For board members and supporters brought to the process by a desire to play active roles in timber management, the revelation was a heavy blow.

In our private conversations about her role in the process and the institution-building work she had undertaken in the years since, Pauline remained circumspect. Not everyone had had the same ambitions for the final document, she reminded me, and not everyone had experienced the same frustration. Even as she modestly disclaimed the representativeness of her own experience on the board, though, she nevertheless invoked the interests of a silent community. Describing for me the confusion she had come to feel during the final year of the LRMP drafting process and in the years following its ratification, Pauline's narratives shifted between private moments of disenchantment and imagined trajectories of regional change. "There was always this sense that they'd just keep grabbing more and more timber, and everything would become merchantable and then they'd just take it," Pauline explained. "We had so much wild country, you could see this happening. . . . When [the LRMP process] actually happened, people said, 'Oh, we're not going to be able to address the rate of cut . . . that's not part of the mandate.' But certainly, that was a huge driver for everybody, the rate of cut. But you know, government. You get to do this, you get to do that. People had this vision that they'd be able to address the rate of cut, but they didn't." Such a vision of intervention, Pauline suggested, would eventually have to be secured through other means.

Saving a Place

In its original incarnation, the Bulkley LRMP was championed throughout British Columbia as the work of devoted nonspecialists. The document had given form to popular anxieties that the forests of the northwest were disappearing, and that social life throughout the region would likely change as a result. It was primarily local researchers and politicians, however, who eventually leveraged the document to assert that these popular anxieties had been ignored. When I asked environmental scientists in Smithers if the plan had become more influential as memory than it might have been as law, few rejected the idea outright. Unlike dozens of other, less ambitious planning documents authored throughout the region in the years after the War in the Woods, the LRMP was still cited in celebratory speeches like those given at the November summit described at the beginning of this chapter. Like the yellowing ecosystem maps pinned up on the walls of home offices around the town, the document came to carry multiple kinds of weight in the years since provincial government officials had begun to overwrite its prescriptions and recommendations. In meetings organized to discuss new policy initiatives, for instance, I occasionally saw scientists revisit the text of the LRMP to extract planning unit descriptions and other technical details. At other times, I observed researchers invoke the document in broad, wistful speculations about how the character of the region might have developed differently if the plan had retained the force of law. Whenever scientists reflected on the drafting and dismantling of the document, though, they invariably referred to the precariousness of their positions in the northwest as well. For the nonspecialists who had devoted years of their lives to drafting its recommendations, their musings suggested, the LRMP might well live on solely as memory, but for researchers struggling to stay in the northwest, it had also become a platform for social renewal.

As I began visiting Smithers in 2013, nearly a decade after the LRMP had been effectively dismantled, I found the document mediating relationships between researchers in both intimate and programmatic ways. On more than one occasion, a new contact asked me if I had read the plan in its entirety before consenting to sit for an interview, or pressed me to explain how my own ethnographic research would contribute to the document's original aims. To my interlocutors, these questions were not meant to be taken as mere symbolic gestures: time and again, I was asked to refer to the PDF of the plan available for download on the website of the Bulkley CRB, and invited to frame my ongoing work through the document's terms of reference. Surprisingly, several of the people who quizzed me about my knowledge of the document had themselves moved to the region after the original LRMP process had already been completed. A few of them had participated in similar planning initiatives elsewhere in the province. Nearly all of them, though, presented the ecological monitoring work on which these and other initiatives had been based as an obligation that transcended boundaries between institutions and policy regimes. Rather than invoking the document solely to index a particular moment in time, then, these recent arrivals hailed the Bulkley LRMP as part of an emergent moral economy of independent research.

Since the beginning of the twenty-first century, the moral economy of conservation research in British Columbia has been powerfully shaped by nostalgia. Calling attention to the dispiriting fates of land use plans and other ambitious technical artifacts has done more than offer attachments to scientists whose lives have been defined by transitions: it has also allowed them to mourn the passing of a regime that never fully came to pass. In subtle ways, these acts of mourning have also had productive effects. Environmental scientists seeking to contest industrial development, Tim Choy (2011) suggests, frequently leverage nostalgia as a kind of promissory logic to legitimate their own expertise. Choy's concept of "endangerment" offers key insight into how the temporality of nostalgia shapes the way retrospective articulations operate in the world. "Like nostalgia, endangerment moves along an imagined timeline, retrieving something from earlier, recasting it as later. But within the conceptual coordinates of this temporal ecology, endangerment positions its subjects in the future, looking backward, watching with dismay at the ruining of our present. And because it proffers this clairvoyant view, it can engender politics—because with foresight, the future can be changed" (49).[20]

The nostalgia of experts makes particular claims on the pasts and futures of others, as well. A similar contradiction, Boym (2001) suggests, underlies all attempts to translate nostalgic feelings into new social bonds and rearticulated senses of self. "Nostalgia is paradoxical in the sense that longing can make us more empathetic toward fellow humans, yet the moment we try to repair longing with belonging, the apprehension of loss with a rediscovery of identity, we often part ways and put an end to mutual understanding" (xv). By equating the government's dismantling of the LRMP with the abandonment of the rural north, in other words, the researchers who continued to celebrate the document tacitly characterized sociality writ large as a product of expert intervention. In narrativizing their struggles to justify the value of their research in the face of continual downsizing, Smithers-based environmental scientists routinely contextualized their own institution-building efforts as convergent with other historical processes. Proponents of the Bulkley LRMP often invoked the document to talk about how one could come to feel themselves to be part of the Bulkley Valley by emplacing their work in the region. The innovative governance initiatives that might one day coalesce in the northwest already had their own histories, they suggested. Any new researcher could write themselves into these futures and pasts, provided they recognized the authority of science.

In many ways, researchers' stories about arriving in the Bulkley Valley and developing affinities with the Bulkley LRMP frame history as a series of choices, rather than compulsions. The nostalgia that so frequently animated researchers' reflections, however, revealed senses of intentionality constrained by resignation. In her reflections on the LRMP process and its aftermath, Pauline presented the document's unraveling as a muted inevitability. As she described the kinds of research projects that she had helped to organize in the years since, her musings about her shifting professional ambitions frequently drifted into the past tense. In these retellings, even the geographical scope of the original document transformed into forebodings of eventual detachment. "My interests were always much more regional than district," Pauline admitted while recounting her initial years on the CRB, gesturing as she spoke toward an enormous ecosystem map of the Pacific coast that she had helped create as a research assistant in the early 1970s. "It was a whole new thing for me, the 'Bulkley District,' this piddly little thing—and I did coastal forests." She reminded me that this orientation was reflected in her consulting work as well. "To get that focus on the Bulkley District—we went over every little speck of land, so I did have a pretty good appreciation for it, but my interests were broader." Standing in as artifacts of her earlier selves, Pauline's aging maps betrayed grand ambitions, deferred.

For some people who moved to the Bulkley Valley after the LRMP was already formalized, organization-spanning life histories like Pauline's offered models of continuity as well as portents of approaching gaps. Pauline's eagerness to mobilize the expertise she had acquired through consulting, she admitted, was in part a strategy of preemption. By looking ahead to new collaborative initiatives like the BVRC, she could devote herself to urgent concerns even as she actively prepared for each new program's potential unraveling. Beth and Paul, two ecologists who moved to the region in the late 1990s and had immersed themselves in BVRC-directed research and governance initiatives ever since, gave a more ambivalent assessment. Vacillating between their enthusiasm for flexible consulting work and their bitter memories of other failed planning initiatives elsewhere in the province, Beth and Paul expressed the frustrations felt by many midcareer scientists struggling to reconcile their ambitions to the limits of a downsizing state. For them, the independent research programs and other initiatives that had helped to make Smithers a destination for younger scientists were not panaceas, but reminders of precarity's duration.

As I came to know Beth and Paul over the course of several years, I often found them describing their careers and their reliance on one another in ironic and self-effacing terms. Fixtures at technical workshops around Smithers and frequent collaborators with other scientists throughout the region, they were the first Smithereens to introduce me to the term *amenity migrants*, and often used the phrase to refer half-jokingly to themselves. At times, though, their humor shaded into litanies of prior disappointments. Although they had not settled permanently in Smithers until several years after the provincial government had already begun to dismantle the Bulkley LRMP, they had both worked as consultants on other land use plans throughout British Columbia before and after their arrival in the northwest. Prior to moving to Smithers, Paul had been hired to develop biodiversity indicators for other LRMP documents throughout the province. Like the Bulkley LRMP, though, these other plans had also been dismantled following the 2001 change in government, and had left little behind other than the borders of new provincial parks. Recounting the ways his own models and monitoring plans had been excised from these other documents, Paul remained bitter about what he saw as the relentless undermining of the original LRMP process. "The model was set up so that it could have worked," he complained to me. "If they hadn't disemboweled the LRMPs and tried to sweep them to the side because they saw them as interfering with their decision-making, then they could've worked."

Meeting me for coffee the day after the November summit, Beth and Paul were in a reflective mood. We had originally intended to use our visit together to expand on pieces of stories they had already shared with me about their first years living in northwest British Columbia. In earlier meetings throughout the year, they had described how they initially came to feel at home there, and how their views of the Bulkley Valley had shaped their thoughts on other places in turn. Like other researcher couples I spent time with in Smithers, they often talked in tandem, interrupting one another and completing each other's sentences when they came to a point that they were particularly adamant that I understood. They shared the exhausting joy they had experienced while roofing their new off-grid cabin over a decade earlier, beginning the process mere hours after Beth defended her doctoral dissertation in behavioral ecology. As we became closer, we talked together about the trepidation they felt watching their son prepare to leave Smithers for college in southern British Columbia.

As the weak autumn sun drifted down toward the western horizon, we quickly descended into jokes and gossip. After a few minutes of breathless anecdotes and fits of laughter, though, the conversation slowed down. The speeches we had heard the previous morning, they admitted, had left them both feeling deflated. Beth was preparing to run in the next round of CRB elections scheduled to take place in a few weeks. The board still looked to the original LRMP as its founding document, but after government support for twice-a-decade revisions to the plan were delayed indefinitely in the early 2000s, the group had eventually redirected its attention to other, smaller conservation initiatives. The SLRP model that had replaced the LRMP process in 2006 had recognized the CRB as an official "stakeholder" group, and allowed the board to submit input during smaller-scale planning process (Government of British Columbia 2006). The allowable purview of CRB-authored suggestions remained much more modest than the proposals that Pauline and others had put forward while drafting the original LRMP, but the submission and feedback process still enabled CRB members to provide contract-based researchers in Smithers with opportunities for paid work. In addition to helping another computer modeling specialist organize a series of technical workshops on salmon health for researchers based throughout the region (see chapter 5), Paul had spent part of the summer working for the CRB as a private contractor, programming landscape simulators that would be used to construct a proposal for a new recreation access management plan for the Bulkley District. Reflecting on the long hours he had spent refining his code and the occasionally tense meetings through which members of the CRB had debated the implications of his findings, though, he admitted that he was eager to move on to new projects as well.

We laughed aloud as we recounted together some of the more melodramatic lines from the previous day's event. "They're all nice guys," Beth offered with a smile, trailing off as she struggled to explain what purpose the meeting had served. Beth's weary appraisal of the meeting found fault not with the speakers, but with her peers in the crowd. "We never really got an answer to Nathan [Cullen]'s question," she sighed. "'How do we change?'" For Beth, Paul, and other researchers who had come to rely on the funding and imprimatur of the BVRC after government grants radically dwindled, "change" had come to signify more than another transition between states of policy. Other land use plans they had worked on since the collapse of the LRMP "up here and along the coast," Beth insisted, "have kept government out of the picture, and have moved further along by going it alone." In recent years, she and Paul had advocated for the value of "going it alone" in building their own careers as well, and rejected recruitment entreaties from powerful environmental consultancies that would have provided more dependable paychecks and research resources in exchange for regular hours. "'Beth and Paul's friendly little consulting company' means that we work part-time," Beth acknowledged, "and that works fine for us."

For many people who had moved to Smithers after beginning their careers elsewhere, consciously articulating the terms of professional uncertainty was often a first step toward living within it. Committed to continuing their lives and careers in Smithers amid regular erosions in government support, Beth and Paul presented the futures of their distended networks as projects of continual narration. "The two things you need to make a good story is someone who knows all the literature, and someone who knows the local terrain," Paul offered. "And the one advantage that we've got here is that we still have research scientists in the district. I think the only way you converge on the truth is by putting your story out there explicitly." They embraced the diversity of institutional forms available in the region for funding their work and bringing it to larger audiences. A shrinking state wouldn't keep them from leading the lives they wanted to live, their weary smiles conveyed, even if it sometimes gave their stories an elegiac cast.

History as Choice

As I observe throughout this book, more and more policy-oriented research in rural spaces like northwest British Columbia is being performed by experts with only fleeting attachments to conventional planning institutions.

In the coming years, examining how these kinds of untethered scientists are writing their own lives into and through their research will become increasingly important to understanding the implications of these shifts for the futures of northern forests. The vision of history undergirding individual experts' arrival stories in the Bulkley Valley and the affinities they formed with the Bulkley LRMP typically frames participation as choice, rather than compulsion. Understandably, ethnographers and others have been rankled in the past by the suggestion that such comparatively powerful identities could be assumed at will. For Arun Agrawal, the resentment he encountered among forest users in northern India toward multiple generations of state foresters obviated any sympathy these forest users might have felt for their neighbors struggling to inhabit their officialdom. One of Agrawal's informants put the matter bluntly: "Government employees don't really have any interest in forests. It is a job for them. For us, it is life" (Agrawal 2005, 2).

In northwest British Columbia, the lines dividing lives and careers are not drawn by everyone in the same way. The obligations expected to accompany certain forms of research, for instance, almost certainly correlate with the capacity to see one's credentials, like one's race, as an inalienable form of property (Reardon and TallBear 2012). The ecologists I met in Smithers were also not the first knowledge workers in the region to complain about their identities and expertise being constantly put "on trial." Despite comprising over 35 percent of the population of the Stikine electoral district in which Smithers is represented in the Legislative Assembly of British Columbia, Gitxsan and other First Nations people have been unevenly involved in many of the "community-oriented" research projects supported by the BVRC and other institutions based in the region.[21] These omissions reflect more than the persistence of disconnects between the region's White and First Nations residents, however. Many BVRC affiliates have collaborated closely with First Nations individuals on research projects and land use plans. Others, including Pauline herself, have even provided expert testimony supporting land claims lawsuits filed by these groups against the provincial and federal governments (Monet and Skanu'u 1992, 105–41). As I will argue in the following chapter, however, the fading of these earlier collaborations reveals dramatic differences in the ways that White and First Nations environmental scientists have been able to translate institutional uncertainties into political influence, professional mobility, and new forms of community coherence. The shrinking of the regulatory state, in other words, has not provided all experts with the same means for working in place.

The improvisational approach Smithers-based experts have taken toward the narration of regional histories suggests a configurable sense of obligation. The hope that has allowed so many non-Indigenous researchers to move to the northwest, however, also betrays a lingering sense of expectation. Early GIS mapping experts from the nearby Gitxsan First Nation championed adaptive management in their work and drew on the same government funding initiatives for watershed restoration research that supported forest succession experiments (see chapter 3) and participatory planning processes like the Bulkley LRMP in the 1990s. Yet unlike the many amenity migrants who have managed to remain in the northwest amid the loss of these programs, the constrained professional mobility gained by Gitxsan experts has effectively forced many of them to move out of the region to find work. For some of these individuals, mapping became less a job than a calling that they felt compelled to embrace for its more-than-material rewards. In the following chapter, I will examine a darker side of rural research, and attempt to answer how a similar campaign to grow expertise in situ left some experts living in exile.

FIGURE 2.1 Stegyawden (Hagwilget Peak, Rocher Déboulé Range),
from Hagwilget Canyon Bridge, Gitxsan territory. Photo by author.

2

Calling

The Returns of Gitxsan Research

Lori couldn't wait to tease us as we came down the attic stairs from her husband's office. "He used to wear this T-shirt that said, 'If my lips are moving, you'd better be taking notes.'" She had been waiting for more than an hour, she reminded us, to prepare dinner and get the kids ready for bed. Yet again, what was supposed to be a brief chat had turned into a four-hour saga, as her husband, Russell Collier, a Gitxsan man, proudly scrolled through folders upon folders of digital maps and shared the stories behind their construction.[1] After dinner, his stories continued. Stepping out into the brisk October air to relieve our eyes, Collier explained the construction of his family's sleek, angular cabin as he took me on an ambling tour of his solar heating installations, chicken pens, and trio of aging pickup trucks, each a part or two short of working order. He occasionally had to assure himself that the projects were all coming together, he admitted, even if he felt convinced that he was always running out of time.

Whether we talked about mapping, politics, farming, or fatherhood, my conversations with Collier often dwelled on the uncertainty of returns. Since first learning digital mapping techniques in a two-week-long training program in the early 1990s, he had transitioned from his professional beginnings as a tech-savvy employee of the Gitxsan Treaty Society (GTS) to one of the most widely known Indigenous land use planning experts in North America. As a cofounder of the Gitxsan Strategic Watershed Analysis Team, or SWAT, Collier helped initiate the digital countermapping movement that had transformed Indigenous land disputes worldwide.[2] His perpetual search for steady employment brought him into conversation with policymakers and First Nations activists across Canada. By the time we met in 2013, however, it had also drawn him far away from his wife and two young children.

Whenever we exchanged emails or talked on the phone, Collier grumbled about the interminable thousand-mile bus ride between his farm and Fort McMurray, the boomtown of the Alberta tar sands and the closest city to the Mikisew Cree First Nation reserve where he had recently taken a job as a development consultation coordinator. ("It's a $1,400 plane ride away," his wife had despaired when I met her at a farmers market earlier in the summer and carelessly asked if she had visited him recently.) Despite the exhausting trip that awaited him the next day as we slowly toured his yard, Collier exuded pride in each of his unfinished projects. His trucks, chickens, farm, and family: each added to the narrative Collier offered of his life as a self-made expert and "cultural entrepreneur." He assured me that situating his cabin near Telkwa, a predominately White, middle-class town over an hour's drive from the nearest Gitxsan reserve, simply helped him better accommodate his growing roster of contacts at First Nations resource management offices and environmental NGOs across North America. The ambivalence that colored his narratives, though, cast this distance in less neutral terms.

Like his musings on the projects scattered around his farm, Russell Collier's elliptical retellings of the story of SWAT lingered over grand plans and unfinished business. Ushered in by the *Delgamuukw and Gisday'wa* trials, the War in the Woods, and other legal battles over Aboriginal rights and title, the team's efforts to digitize territorial boundaries established through trial research had catalyzed the creation of new infrastructures of Gitxsan self-governance throughout the 1990s. With nearly six thousand people claiming Gitxsan ancestry in a recent Canadian census, including hundreds living outside British Columbia, SWAT-produced maps had also helped to shape other, more idiosyncratic articulations of Gitxsan belonging.[3] In many places—homes in Vancouver, gas stations in Kispiox and other reserve villages—territory maps were prominently displayed on walls. Vinyl stickers juxtaposing Gitxsan slogans with the same iconic borders decorated truck bumpers throughout the region. By the late 1990s, a few of the team's maps even appeared in comic books written to explain Gitxsan histories to children across Canada. In the same way that many White scientists I had come to know in Smithers narrativized their professional trajectories, Collier often emphasized how the diverse products of his work had been shaped by intentional decisions. Even if the most visible artifacts of SWAT's work did not bear his actual signature, Collier joked, seeing evidence of his labor throughout western Canada helped to assuage his doubts about the arc of his professional path.

Other former members of SWAT offered humbler interpretations of the team's rise and dissolution. Meeting with me for the first time more than a decade after the collapse of SWAT, Darlene Vegh, a Gitxsan and Gitanyow woman, still lived on the Gitxsan territories, and occasionally conducted new mapping projects throughout the region (see chapter 4). As she reminisced with me over cups of tea in her kitchen, Vegh's assessment of the team's impact was bittersweet. "I always thought that if I could heal the land, I could heal the people," she offered as we thumbed through her old field notebooks. Rather unlike Collier's habit of pivoting between celebratory narratives of the early days of SWAT and the subsequent global proliferation of Indigenous-authored countermapping techniques, Vegh persistently tempered her reminisces with frank assessments of what she had come to see as the team's relatively meager impacts on provincial policy-making. When I asked her once if other Gitxsan shared her assessment, she offered a weary laugh. "You know what? I think people have kinda forgotten about Gitxsan GIS." Gitxsan institutions—whether house groups, civil society organizations, or emergent resource management and mapping divisions—had been locked in litigation with the provincial and federal governments and with each other for years. By 2013, some of these divisions were burning hot and bright, spilling out over the pages of the *Three Rivers Report* and other local newspapers covering events on the five Gitxsan reserves along the Skeena River between Kispiox and Kitwanga. Other conflicts had largely faded from memory, or lay dormant as frustrated litigants regrouped for injunctions and appeals. Unlike Collier, though, Vegh had managed to move on from these conflicts without having to move away.

Russell Collier and Darlene Vegh came of age during a period of profound transition, a period now strongly associated with an epochal series of land claims trials in which few young Gitxsan at the time had directly participated. To some residents of northwest British Columbia, SWAT had been little more than a footnote in the still-unfolding story of *Delgamuukw and Gisday'wa v. The Queen*, a decades-spanning Aboriginal land title lawsuit lodged in 1984 by forty-seven Gitxsan and Wet'suwet'en hereditary chiefs to regain ownership of their vast traditional territories in northwest British Columbia.[4] Other Canadians came to know the *Delgamuukw and Gisday'wa* decision as one of the defining moments of the modern land claims era. At the time the longest and most expensive series of legal trials in Canadian history, the Supreme Court of Canada's decision on the *Delgamuukw and Gisday'wa* claimants' federal appeal in 1997 secured standing for hereditary First Nations leaders and oral histories in Canadian courts for the first time. Particularly among White researchers eager to filiate their own work with regional narratives of struggles toward equity and justice, the trials signified globally significant legal precedent and progressive potential.[5]

As a framework for a new era of First Nations institution building, however, some Gitxsan who were alive while the trials were taking place have come to regard them with a sense of ambivalence (Napoleon 2010, 2019). More than two decades since the federal appeal ended with a call for a new trial, the governments of British Columbia and Canada have yet to recognize Gitxsan title. While fragments of jurisdiction were parceled out among an array of new Gitxsan institutions—including a development corporation, a fisheries monitoring office, and a forestry consultation group—during the years before and immediately after the 1997 Supreme Court decision, most activists engaged in day-to-day work on the territories have long ago come to see ownership and the meaningful realization of ownership and rights as part of far more laborious struggle (see Manuel and Derrickson 2015; Pasternak 2017). Even after the *Sparrow* decision explicitly reaffirmed Aboriginal hunting and fishing rights in 1990, Vegh and Collier each reminded me, Gitxsan and Wet'suwet'en fishers continued to be harassed and arrested. For several years after the decision in the *Delgamuukw and Gisday'wa* federal appeal formally recognized provincial governments' duty to negotiate with First Nations about developments on their traditional territories, numerous forestry companies operating throughout the Skeena watershed still managed to avoid consulting with the house groups with claims to the territories in question.[6] Persistent disconnects between the letter of British Columbian and Canadian law and the provincial government's mechanisms of enforcement, in other words, spread tensions within nascent Gitxsan institutions, even as the public aura of the *Delgamuukw and Gisday'wa* trials continued to grow.

In many contemporary conversations over the potential futures of Gitxsan political action, the story of SWAT remains a footnote as well. Founded during a lull between the provincial and federal appeals to the initial *Delgamuukw and Gisday'wa* decision, the team's original mandate had been to facilitate "consultation" between Gitxsan house groups and the BC Forest Service (Burda et al. 1999). What exactly "consultation" would entail, however, had initially been difficult to define. After Gitxsan-led blockades reached a crescendo in the summer of 1993 (see Blomley 1996), the Forest Service had agreed in 1994 to provide information about, if not necessarily seek approval for, proposed tree harvests on Gitxsan-claimed territories while the *Delgamuukw and Gisday'wa* claimants continued to pursue their claim in court. Shortly after the consultation process officially began, however, SWAT's role on the territories rapidly expanded. Young team members demonstrated digital mapping techniques for clusters of students gathered around their computers at the office of the GTS. They helped to organize strategic discussions over printed maps arrayed atop folding tables at Gitanmaax Hall and other reserve community centers. By the end of the 1990s, traditional leaders throughout the territories were hailing their work as a new phase of the Gitxsan political project (Holyk 1999).

Outside the region, the same maps that mediated conversations between young Gitxsan activists and their elders were positioning mapmakers as new kinds of expert authorities. The ambitious vision of SWAT for a "Gitxsan model" of forest management brought SWAT-produced maps into circulation through magazine articles and conservationist and GIS industry newsletters (see, e.g., Convis 2000; Kuin 1998; Lewis 2000; Natcher 2001). As SWAT's media exposure increased, both Vegh and Collier became celebrities in the growing world of Indigenous countermapping. They shared stories and strategies in GIS training sessions at other First Nations reserves around British Columbia and Canada. They were invited to lecture government officials, university departments, and conservation groups. As their databases grew, they offered broad reflections on First Nations treaty negotiations in meetings of the provincial parliament and provided expert testimony in legal hearings against consultation-averse logging companies. Over time, though, each new juncture in their professional paths found them answering new questions about how their work would contribute to Gitxsan sovereignty writ large.

Almost as quickly as it had arisen, the organizational support behind SWAT collapsed, leaving Vegh and Collier without the funding they required to keep up with their growing roster of projects. By 2002, the same year that the election of a new provincial government led to the closing of the regional Forest Service office in Smithers, the original members of the team had already begun to disperse. When my own fieldwork began in earnest in 2013, few of the team's original founders and collaborators lived near the Gitxsan territories, and several who did had distanced themselves from the political leaders with whom they had originally worked. As I learned shortly after I arrived in Smithers, many of the cartographers and anthropologists enlisted as researchers for the original *Delgamuukw and Gisday'wa* trial had also long been ostracized from the central leadership of the Gitxsan First Nation, now externally represented by the GTS (Napoleon 2010, 2019; Penikett 2006). Some had chosen to move away from the territories and perform consulting work elsewhere in Canada, where the "aura of Gitxsan GIS," as Collier put it, remained uncomplicated. As I sat down for conversations with some of these people in their homes throughout the province, though, most of them ruminated over the same questions: What, after so many years, had their labor meant to other Gitxsan? And how would each of them be welcomed them if they tried to return?

Promising Returns

This chapter examines Vegh and Collier's reflections on what drew them into Gitxsan governance and what eventually pushed them out. During key transitions in the institutional and technical architecture of the Gitxsan sovereignty project, the founders of SWAT were treated alternately as the leaders of a new political movement and as the beneficiaries of unevenly distributed investments. Some, like Vegh, wove the skills they accrued during the period into rich and idiosyncratic relationships with traditional leaders and other activists. One hundred kilometers south of the Gitxsan territories and a decade removed from its politics, however, Collier's reflections on his work with other First Nations and his lonely self-labeling as a "cultural entrepreneur" cast the team's legacy in a different light. Together, Vegh and Collier's stories exemplify how the forms of authority that took shape in the wake of the War in the Woods have hinged on the promise of *returns*— that Indigenous experts would devote their specialized labor to a collective cause; that their patrons would see material benefits; and that, eventually, the experts themselves would come "home," and merge their new professional networks into their nation's social worlds. For many First Nations researchers, these expectations operate as critical sources of inspiration and fulfillment (see, e.g., Goeman 2013; McCreary 2018b; L. M. Johnson, Vegh, and Morgan 2019).[7] Others, though, have also come to understand the returns attending their participation in institution-building and governance work primarily in terms of deferral: lawsuits stalled for want of government support; paychecks and project budgets delayed; sophisticated environmental monitoring projects planned, but never carried out. On some reserves, these deferrals have strained working relationships between technical staff, traditional leaders, and their various patrons. Throughout North America, these deferrals have also provoked uneasy questions about what experts owe to collective sovereignty projects, and what rewards are owed to individual experts in return.

The paradoxical demands that Indigenous researchers face in their everyday work underscore the challenge inherent in examining lives affected by bureaucratization. As the following pages aim to make clear, individual researchers have found complex forms of meaning and belonging in the process of devoting their lives to research. In order to take seriously their processes of meaning-making without separating them from other currents of Indigenous collective life, though, the interplay between individual labor and shared aspirations requires a broader analytical frame. For Max Weber, the growing tendency of institutional actors to characterize their jobs as vocations during the twentieth century embedded new forms of meaning in technical work, yet these meanings were mainly cloaks for control (see also Rabinow 1996). "The modern entrepreneur," Weber argues, "gave to his employees, as the wages of their ascetic devotion to the calling and of cooperation in his ruthless exploitation of them through capitalism, the prospect of eternal salvation" (1961, 269–70). As I argue throughout this chapter, Weber's distinction between devotional and contractual labor can be powerfully useful for tracking the social shaping of Indigenous research. Yet unlike the broad institutional transformations that Weber theorized over the course of his career, the Gitxsan sovereignty project is not and never has been premised on either a progressivist teleology or an abstract portrait of deindividuated labor. In order to theorize the lives of Indigenous researchers as mobilized by a sense of calling, in other words, we must first recognize the irreducible specificity of the meanings that different researchers attribute to this labor—particularly when these meanings appear to diverge.

As I will argue below, excavating Western theories of bureaucratized life to account for the worlds of Indigenous researchers requires sustained dialogue with Indigenous modes of theorizing. Such an approach demands attention to more prosaic forms of meaning as well, including the meanings attributable to the very language of Western social theory. For many First Nations people who grew up in the twentieth century, the word *vocation* itself offers an unwelcome reminder of their encounters with Indian residential schools, some of which had *vocational* in their official names.[8] Indeed, British Columbia's government-run residential schools—the last of which was closed only in the late 1980s—played oblique yet persistent roles in many of my interlocutors' accounts about the experiences that drew them into lives of research.[9] During SWAT's laborious training sessions for Gitxsan youth, for instance, many trainees whose parents had been forcibly sent to residential schools visited their family's *wilp* territories for the first time when Vegh and Collier conducted mapping exercises on them. In other conversations, some SWAT team members briefly mentioned events from their own parents' time in residential schools. They explained how certain experiences had transformed their parents' relationships with their territories, or had kept their parents from teaching them the Gitxsanimx and Gitsenimx languages or undertaking outdoor activities with them when they were children.

The narratives that former SWAT affiliates shared with me were never simply stories, however. Their acts of sharing these narratives were also critical moments of theory-making—moments that my interlocutors' lives as researchers had made them uniquely adept at navigating (Million 2011). Even when we spoke in detail about how Gitxsan encounters with residential schools had transformed kinship ties throughout the region, my interlocutors presented their intergenerational relationships as sources of empowerment and resolve. It had been through these concrete relationships, they reminded me, that they had first learned about the violence endured by their ancestors and their ancestral territories. But it had also been through these relationships that they had come to see themselves as capable experts, whose work could potentially redress historical wrongs (see Z. Todd 2016).

The accounts I relay in the following pages share resonances with what Dian Million (2008, 2009) describes as "felt theory." The term, Million explains, foregrounds the productive effects of Indigenous people sharing personal narratives in specific settings, particularly narratives about intimate events. Through these acts of sharing, Indigenous people—and Indigenous women especially—"honed and developed a profound literature of experience" (Million 2008, 272) on violence, marginalization, and estrangement. But they also became adept at mobilizing this literature of experience to reframe critical discussions about how the particularities of individual perspectives ought to matter to the political futures of their collectives. Like the accounts addressed in Million's work, the gendering effects of colonialism emerged with quiet consistency in my interlocutors' accounts of the work opportunities that were made available to them, and in the sense of narrative control each researcher projected over stories about their own lives. By highlighting, however subtly and implicitly, the gendered discrepancies between different researchers' post-SWAT trajectories, these accounts persistently unsettled my efforts to track how researchers' sense of themselves as individuals changed as new Gitxsan governance projects emerged. Yet, as if they were echoing Eve Tuck's (2009) call for scholars to stop reproducing portraits of Indigenous communities as irreversibly "damaged" by colonial traumas, Vegh, Collier, and their former colleagues were also consistently adamant that I not lose sight of the many ways that they had drawn new senses of empowerment from difficult periods in their lives. The fact that several of them had come to feel underappreciated by former patrons did not mean that they saw their associated worlds in despairing terms. As they reflected on the persistent sense of estrangement that colored many of their narratives, though, my interlocutors remained wearily aware that their efforts to make sense of these relationships would echo into the lives of other Gitxsan as well.

Taken up as a tool for distinguishing how collectivized hopes and anxieties become routed through individuals and their labor, the concept of *the calling* offers a path for exploring the tensions that have come to structure the worlds of Indigenous experts. During and after the War in the Woods, individual Gitxsan researchers became prominent members of promising, if short-lived, institutions. They produced documents around which, as I show throughout this chapter, new professional communities were constituted. Throughout this period, their work continually reshaped conversations about the scope of a sovereignty project in whose realization they each hoped to take part. By the time I met Vegh and Collier in 2013, though, more than two decades had passed since Indigenous-led digital mapping groups and initiatives had begun to proliferate around North America.[10] The young men and women initially recruited to manage these projects were no longer young.[11] Like other aging non-Indigenous scientists I came to know throughout northwest British Columbia, the handful of former SWAT members still working as GIS experts who spoke to me about their approaching retirements each expressed doubts about how their work would be remembered. Few expected that their own deaths would occasion the same ceremonies and news coverage that often accompanied the deaths of the chiefs who participated in the *Delgamuukw and Gisday'wa* trials.[12] Their experiences had occasionally offered them privileged positions at the center of Gitxsan political activity. At other times, though, these same experiences had positioned them on the outside looking in. While some of them discussed their experiences in feast ceremonies and other house-level processes of traditional governance with me, most held only limited power in their respective house groups. Several had grown up off reserve with comparatively wealthy families. A few already had high school diplomas and college degrees before beginning their work on the territories, qualifications that had strongly encouraged Gitxsan elders and GTS executives to recruit them for technical positions in the first place. Some had spent the majority of their adult lives away from the Gitxsan reserves and territories, yet still promoted their work through references to the competencies they had acquired there. For some former members of SWAT, though, the experiences they had accrued while living away from the territories had complicated their paths of return.

In recent decades, anthropologists and Indigenous studies scholars have increasingly called attention to the ways that travel undertaken by Indigenous individuals can carry consequences for the trajectories of collectives. Through her work with urban Indian communities and activists in California, Renya Ramirez shows how "Indians' movement into the cities has increased the possibility for gathering and politically organizing" (2007, 2). Secured through the work of enterprising activists, many of them women, each of the many "Native hubs" organized through urban networking have come to function simultaneously as a "vision of urban and rural mobility" and as a "mechanism of cultural and identity transmission" (24). Notwithstanding the wrenching circumstances under which many of these migrations occurred, Ramirez argues, the geographical dispersion of Indigenous people has generated political resources and social ties that are now central features of Indigenous life (see also D'Arcus 2010; Dorries et al. 2019; Goeman 2009; Weiss 2018). As more Indigenous researchers have developed careers that require them to spend much of the year on the road, access to these resources and modes of relationship building have also enabled them to navigate potentially exploitative relationships with White conservationists, developers, and other settler groups even while communicating with their colleagues and kin across great distances (Callison 2014; Hirsch 2017; Hirtz 2003; McCreary 2013a; Neale and Vincent 2017).

Particularly for geographically isolated First Nations communities, both the outgoing travels of individuals and their anticipated returns can be treated as shared and generative processes. Haida Gwaii, for instance, an archipelago located roughly one hundred kilometers off the coast of northwest British Columbia, is home to hundreds of members of the Haida Nation, including several globally renowned Haida artists who played starring roles in earlier anthropological discussions of Indigenous mobilities (Clifford 2004). Rather than discouraging young Haida from leaving the islands to continue their education or establish their careers, many elders actively devise ways to support these people in their travels. Describing the endless stream of feasts and community raffles that he participated in while living and working in the Haida reserve village of Old Massett, Joseph Weiss (2018) underscores the powerful, deliberate symbolism underlying travel fundraisers as a constitutive force that simultaneously dispels anxieties about population dispersal and reassures departing individuals that they will be warmly welcomed when they decide to return. "Young Haida leaving home are never 'alone' if they have been the subjects of a fundraiser; rather their mobility has been authorized through collected social value" (75). Weiss describes the affective interplay set into motion through these experiences as a process of "homing," a term he borrows from Haida artist David Armstrong, who describes Haida Gwaii as a "homing beacon" that inexorably draws people back to the islands later in life. Yet the term itself, both Weiss and Armstrong acknowledge in different ways, helps to enact the sense of optimism and inevitability it purports to describe. The insistent sense of a "future perfect" underlying everyday assertions among Old Massett residents "that 'everyone comes home,'" Weiss argues, "has the significance it does precisely *because* it is not currently clear whether or not Haida who leave will always necessarily return" (66).

As Ramirez, Weiss, and other scholars make clear, of course, not all Indigenous individuals travel for the same reasons. While the forms of communally supported travel that Weiss describes were relatively ubiquitous among his interlocutors because of the lack of postsecondary education institutions on Haida Gwaii, the activists, artisans, and other cultural brokers who often play central roles in scholarly accounts of Indigenous mobilities are frequently members of elite families (see, e.g., Blackman 1982; P. J. Deloria 2019; Fienup-Riordan 2000; Sterritt 2016). They often enjoy economic resources and forms of political agency, whether in traditional or bureaucratic systems, that extend far beyond the means of their neighbors (Clifford 2004; De la Cadena 2015; Dombrowski 2001; Mason 2002). With these privileges come different pressures. As James Clifford (2007, 2013) argues throughout much of his work, the power and prestige enjoyed by the individuals who become prolific travelers are often judged by others in anticipation of specific kinds of future returns, the mere possibility of which can serve to reaffirm and expand particular senses of collective identity: wayfarers and politicians returning from far-flung travels, bringing new goods and relationships to incorporate into local cultural repertoires; artifacts dislodged from museums by new repatriation laws, sometimes bearing new stewardship agreements to tether Indigenous communities to centers of academe.[13] If the questions that first drew anthropologists to study Indigenous mobilities implicitly mirrored the prerogatives of cultural elites, in other words, the consequences of these travels must be weighed with a broader range of relationships in mind.

The movements of Gitxsan digital mapping experts—both through space and between institutions—have been shaped by diverse pressures and privileges. As representatives of the Gitxsan political project, Gitxsan mapmakers traveled frequently, and navigated a wide range of jurisdictional scales as they went. Their standing shifted continually as Gitxsan leaders focused their attention on different political battles, from fishing rights, to land title, to resource royalties, to development partnerships. As managers of the documents and digital databases through which each of these projects was pursued, however, these researchers were often forced to negotiate rapid redistributions of technical labor, as well as redistributions of credit and blame. Given the high stakes attending the construction and circulation of maps of traditional territories, it is perhaps unsurprising that the individuals responsible for this work have been judged—and occasionally judged harshly—by the family members, political leaders, and other people whose collective political aspirations have been invested in their labor.[14]

If the concept of *the calling* is to be a useful aid in examining the lives that Indigenous experts invest in research, these heterogeneous investments must be kept in clear view. The aspirations enframing Gitxsan sovereignty cannot be treated as forms of enchantment, even—perhaps especially— when sovereignty's elusiveness brings individuals into conflict. Sovereignty projects, like all social institutions, Audra Simpson (2014) argues, pose paradoxes that their adherents must negotiate in the everyday. The allure of land title and its unsteady promise as a panacea for political and economic control has already shaped the lives of generations of First Nations people in British Columbia, where nearly three decades of formal treaty negotiations involving dozens of First Nations have as of yet generated only four final agreements.[15] Indigenous and Euro-Canadian leaders alike have deployed promises of deferred returns to harmonize responses both for and against timber harvests, pipelines, and other contentious developments. Throughout North America, the sense of the collectives at stake in these processes has shifted in numerous directions. In some places, traditional and other leaders have reevaluated their commitments to government-run negotiation processes and pursued their own interests through practices of refusal or through new regional affiliations (Kulchyski 2005; Coulthard 2014; Simpson 2014; Pasternak 2017). In other communities, however, particularly those straining under debt accumulated through treaty negotiations, criticisms of specific collective projects are occasionally branded as excesses of individualism. Some researchers have spent years struggling to situate their work in "the unacknowledged space between two legal orders" (Napoleon 2010, 10) that the *Delgamuukw and Gisday'wa* trials and the original War in the Woods both helped to deepen. In the following pages, I recount the paths of professionalism into which these researchers were first recruited as teenagers. Through their own ruminative accounts, I then examine the interplay of expectations that has structured these paths and caused others to evaluate their lives and sacrifices in divergent terms.

The Loneliness of Networks

As the remainder of this chapter aims to make clear, the divergent meanings attributed to Indigenous expertise by Indigenous leaders, by community members, and by experts themselves index experiences that take years to unfold. Attempting to track these unfoldings ethnographically presents a range of practical challenges. The individuals whose stories occupy the following pages were once linked through personal and institutional bonds, but now live in various states of professional exile. Of the six former SWAT members and collaborators with whom I spoke over the course of my fieldwork, two had not been involved in any countermapping projects or GIS work for many years. They all nevertheless shared meals with me as they answered my questions and connected me with other lapsed mapmakers who had been affiliated with the program. Some reflected at length on how their early facility with computer programming had shaped their later careers. One had become a technician for environmental assessment consultancies. Another had recently been promoted to operations manager at a major timber mill. A few of those who still lived on or near the Gitxsan reserves invited me to join them for regular visits or to meet with them during their occasional trips into Smithers, the site of the only major grocery stores and shopping centers within an hour's drive of the eastern reserves. Among the others who had left the reserves and were now scattered across the small towns of British Columbia's vast northern interior, my visits were limited to brief stopovers at their homes and offices during my monthly trips to Prince George, or on my semiannual journeys between Smithers and Vancouver.

None of those living away from the territories had severed their ties entirely. Even those who had become alienated from Gitxsan political figures following the collapse of SWAT periodically return to visit family members and attend certain house group feasts. Most of them have Gitxsan feast names through lineages, like nearly all traditional governance relations among Canada's First Nations, that are affirmed through maternal connections. Almost all of them also hold band membership through one of the Gitxsan or Gitanyow reserves—bonds that, like the federally administered band system in general, were originally accorded through patrilineal descent. Regardless of their relationships to the people currently in positions of power, though, my questions picked at awkward memories. Nearly all of my interlocutors were critical of the overwhelmingly expensive centralized treaty process, which they readily complained had reorganized allegiances and deepened linguistic and other historic divisions among the *huwilp*.[16] As we discussed specific aspects of the Gitxsan traditional governance system, I was routinely reminded that the *wilp* has been and continues to be the primary seat of power among the Gitxsan, and that any attempt to represent the interests of an individual *wilp* by another group without the permission of the *wilp* violates significant aspects of Gitxsan legal protocol (Daly 2005; P. D. Mills 2008; Napoleon 2010).[17] Several former members of SWAT complained that most of their original maps and field notes remained inaccessible to them, locked away in the office of the GTS.[18] In the course of our interactions, some took the opportunity to extensively criticize personnel changes and what they saw as institutional corruption across different Gitxsan governing bodies. Most, however, carefully avoided particular subjects and refused to discuss certain individuals by name.

By the summer of 2013, tensions between Gitxsan house groups and bureaucratic leaders had become regular topics in provincial news, particularly as protests against the proposed Enbridge Northern Gateway pipeline brought specific industry contracts and collaborative agreements under increased scrutiny (see, e.g., Canadian Press 2012; Gitxsan Unity Movement 2012a; Posadzki 2014; Jang 2017). A months-long blockade of the GTS office led by critics of the province-run treaty negotiations had been dissolved the previous year, but the office remained closed to the public—and to former GTS employees as well. As they had been doing for years, GTS executives and their allies continued to trade accusations with dissident chiefs in local newspaper articles. Echoes of these long-standing tensions often seeped into other conversations I shared throughout the region. Non-Indigenous environmental scientists living in Smithers, roughly an hour's drive south of the nearest Gitxsan reserve, often glibly switched between tones of respect and suspicion when describing to me their engagements with Gitxsan groups and individuals. They sometimes sarcastically dismissed the prospect of engaging with significant Gitxsan institutions, even while citing specific individuals within these same institutions as cherished collaborators. However cynical, these narrow interpellations nevertheless recognized—and reproduced—a key legacy of the post–*Delgamuukw and Gisday'wa* era: namely, that the work of seeking sovereignty had become, for some First Nations researchers, an increasingly isolating endeavor.

The accounts of the former members of SWAT are not meant to serve as typologies of the vast range of experiences accrued by Indigenous researchers working throughout North America, or even in northwest British Columbia. Commonalities, though, did emerge. While none of my interlocutors explicitly mentioned gender while describing their formative experiences or more recent careers, our conversations nevertheless carried subtle echoes of the gendered tensions, silences, and divisions of labor that Dian Million locates in the foundations of felt theory. With Darlene Vegh and her SWAT-trained daughter and sister, I learned how consultation procedures initially took form, and how the team learned to systematize its methods in the field to keep itself agile and responsive to shifting demands. My conversations with Russell Collier followed unpredictable paths. Often responding to simple questions via email with long and complex narratives, his reminiscences of SWAT's place within the broader Gitxsan political landscape could quickly become guarded and vague. In some ways, the textures of our conversations mirrored the rhythms of their recent professional lives. While Vegh retreated from activism for several years following the demise of SWAT before eventually reorienting her work around the needs of individual Gitxsan house groups and other First Nations governing bodies, Collier's professional networks steadily expanded, linking him with audiences, clients, and collaborators throughout North America. A major theme in our conversations, then, became his fluencies with the digital mapping technologies and data standards that allowed him to traverse these networks.

Russell's ruminations on these skills cast him as an active, and, to follow Million, decisively male protagonist in a story of adversity and technological change. By continually seeking out more stable venues from which to pursue his work, though, Collier resigned himself to professional networks that drew him farther away from the place he once called home.

Collier and Vegh's stories exemplify the divergent trajectories that Indigenous researchers and the artifacts of their work can take following periods of intensive litigation and institution building. This divergence also underscores the uncertain place of the individual's burden within narratives of Indigenous sovereignty. The experiences SWAT members accrued during their training, their uptake of digital mapping technologies, their enrollment in nascent Gitxsan governance institutions, and their subsequent dispersal have been deeply personal and idiosyncratic. By considering First Nations–led mapmaking work as a calling, I wish to call attention to these burdens, and to weigh their effects on an artifact-laden politics of affiliation that has alternately positioned these experts as translators, saviors, and self-interested entrepreneurs. Examining professionalization as a process of responding to a calling also reveals other legacies of the capacity-building projects launched in the midst of the *Delgamuukw and Gisday'wa* trials and the War in the Woods. As new relationships and subject positions that took shape during this period have begun to outlive the expert institutions that originally produced them, how have individual Indigenous researchers sought to carry on the burdens and aspirations associated with these institutions into other spheres of their professional lives?

In the years since the Gitxsan mapmakers who participated in SWAT first attempted to move into consulting and other lines of work, each leveraged their Gitxsan identities with different degrees of critical distance. Some, like Vegh, eventually decided to eschew both the allure of far-flung professional networks and the tumult of work as a full-time administrator to focus on modest projects with people living nearby. For Collier, though, the critical distance with which he could articulate his sense of his Gitxsan identity played a constitutive role in shaping his career. Following the collapse of SWAT, Collier took on a wide range of temporary positions and quickly established himself as an international authority on Indigenous mapping, as it began to be known, writ large. His sense of Gitxsan identity, Collier often insisted to me, was not contingent on where he lived, but was rather something that he inhabited through work and travel. Even as this work won him professional prestige away from the Gitxsan territories, however, he brooded over the recognition that seemed to elude him at home. In the conclusion of this chapter, I will examine how some of Collier's erstwhile colleagues addressed this quest for recognition in the context of a more somber form of return.

"Pretty Little Maps": Darlene Vegh's Story

Darlene Vegh and I first met in her home, a large, two-story house high on a bluff overlooking the Skeena River and the Kispiox Valley. Thanks to articles that other friends throughout the region had been sharing with me for months prior to my visit, I had already come to know about Vegh's collaborative work on linguistic surveys, archaeological digs, botanical succession experiments, and innumerable animal habitat and trail mapping projects.[19] Few of her academic visitors, she admitted with a laugh, sought her out primarily to hear personal stories. Fewer still seemed to be interested in learning about SWAT, by then already a decade since the group's demise. Like other scientists I had come to know in Smithers who were struggling to find new trainees to whom they could pass on old projects (see chapter 3), Vegh was also contemplating the end of her career as an active field mapper. "I had this vision of myself retiring until Gitanyow called me again," she sighed. The Gitanyow Office of Hereditary Chiefs (GHC), the administrative center of the neighboring Gitanyow First Nation, had provided much of Vegh's contracting work since her departure from SWAT. Never quite filling the role of a permanent professional home, the GHC had nevertheless enabled her to contribute to projects in the region without preventing her from leading a full life.

Vegh had not grown up on reserve, although she did not experience Collier's middle-class upbringing. She had learned to speak Gitxsanimx, the Gitxsan dialect of the eastern village reserves, later in life, slowly formalizing the inchoate sounds of childhood visits to relatives' houses through deliberate conversations and tutorials with her elders as she grew older.[20] Vegh's political and familial associations throughout the region were layered and complex. "My lineage emerges out of Gitanyow. But my Indian status comes out of Gitanmaax [a federally organized Gitxsan reserve]. . . . I've got family in Gitanyow and in Gitxsan." As it had for hundreds of thousands of other First Nations people throughout Canada, the original federal process of awarding band membership based on patrilineal descent, rather than on the matrilineal relationships that structured most First Nations house groups, clans, and other hereditary governing bodies, lived on as an awkward tension between Vegh's overlapping social worlds (see Blackburn 2009). Sitting across from each other at her kitchen table, we paged through her old field notebooks and laminated checklists. Every few minutes, she would get up and walk to her filing cabinets in the living room to retrieve a specific map, unfolding it and flattening it out on the broad table to orient old stories and point out the locations of particular dramas. Some confrontations she remembered with a mirthful chuckle: last-ditch efforts to catalog fishing rocks and campsites on the other side of a tense road blockade; surreptitious trips through patches of old growth to remove ribbons from intricately carved and other culturally modified trees that roving timber cruisers had promised to leave out of their harvest plans, yet had tagged with ribbons to mark them for removal anyway. Other battles had been so draining that she visibly tired even as she began trying to recall them.

Her memories slowly returning as we flipped together through piles of old maps, Vegh reflected on the profound sense of excitement she had felt upon returning to the region during the War in the Woods after several years of living in Vancouver. After briefly moving away from the territories after finishing high school, like many other Gitxsan youth, she had eventually grown eager to build on her experiences with the traditional government system she had participated in as a child. As she prepared to move back to the territories, she remembered, she also became increasingly determined to solidify the political commitments she had begun developing with other activists in southern British Columbia. She recalled how this excitement quickly merged with a sense of personal obligation as she joined the first cohort of the Gitxsan Territorial Management program in 1991, a two-year course on environmental mapping, wildlife habitat assessment, and provincial law. Even if national newspapers remained fixated on the blockades that were still proliferating on the Gitxsan territories, Vegh and many other young Gitxsan were equally thrilled by the explosion of institution-building and organizing work that was already unfolding in parallel.

Much of the work that Vegh and others encountered and contributed to upon returning to the territories was supported by middle-aged Gitxsan who themselves had participated in an earlier phase of Gitxsan returns. In 1973, Neil J. Sterritt (Mediig'm Gyamk)—the man who would eventually become the director of research for the *Delgamuukw and Gisday'wa* land claim and the leader of the joint Gitksan-Wet'suwet'en Tribal Council—was recruited by Gitxsan elders to return to the territories to manage 'Ksan, a reconstructed village, museum, and cultural center established in the late 1960s that was already becoming a hub for First Nations artists throughout the northwest coast. Like Walter Harris (Geel), another Gitxsan artist who helped to establish 'Ksan and subsequently found considerable fame for his masks, jewelry, totem poles, and other wood carvings, Sterritt had originally pursued technical training and work in the resource industries (see epilogue). Harris had begun carving through an apprenticeship program at a timber mill, and had subsequently drawn on the professional networks he had established as an artist (including his appointment to Canada's federal Fine Arts Committee in the late 1970s) to introduce other Gitxsan to new spaces of political dialogue (Sheenan and Gallant 2019). Harris's sister, Doreen Jensen, also helped to establish 'Ksan and introduce the artists and chiefs affiliated with the center to national audiences. Jensen had curated a major exhibition on coastal First Nations ceremonial robes for the University of British Columbia's Museum of Anthropology in Vancouver (L. Todd 1994) in 1983, the year before Sterritt, Alfred Joseph (Gisday'wa), and Earl Muldoe (the first of three chiefs to hold the name Delgamuukw over the course of the trials)—the latter men both master carvers and art instructors themselves (Hoffman 2019)—formally presented their land claim at the provincial court house in Smithers. When Muldoe, Joseph, and other chiefs began asking Sterritt to help them record stories and construct maps of their house territories shortly after the epochal *Calder* decision was announced in 1973, the institutions that they and others were building to support Gitxsan education and cultural outreach provided the beginnings of an infrastructure for research.

Two decades after Neil J. Sterritt's initial return to the Gitxsan territories, the region's institutional landscape had grown considerably more complex. By 1993, the consolidation of the BC Treaty Commission (BCTC) had led to the formation of the GTS, a small bureaucratic group that organized itself as an intermediary between the nation's hereditary chiefs and the provincial government's ministries.[21] Within a few months, GTS leaders had reorganized and expanded the Gitxsan Education Society, which ran Vegh's certificate program, and were actively recruiting graduates to develop and lead an entire series of new Gitxsan institutions. Once the idea of a Gitxsan-led environmental mapping and forestry consultation group began circulating among GTS officials, Vegh remembered, the genesis of SWAT was dizzyingly abrupt. Only days after graduating, she met Don Ryan (Mas Gaak), a leading figure in the blockades of the late 1980s and early 1990s and the new leader of the GTS, in the halls of the GTS building, whereupon he summarily invited her to lead the society's newly created forestry department.[22] The scale of the job was immense: Vegh was to oversee forestry consultations for the entirety of the Gitxsan traditional territories, even as the BC Forest Service was still developing its own protocols for engagement.

While Vegh modestly downplayed her role in shaping the consultation process, she acknowledged that, for many Gitxsan, the new procedures had cued a generational shift. Within months of the founding of the team, SWAT had already attracted as trainees and assistants dozens of Gitxsan men and women who had been too young to participate in preparations for the *Delgamuukw and Gisday'wa* trials. They recruited teenagers who had grown up on the reserves, some of whom had played central roles in logging blockades during the War in the Woods, as well as others who had been reluctant to join direct actions. Others, like Collier and Vegh themselves, had only recently returned to the region after spending several years living away. Even before the team had produced its first map, SWAT was already eliciting returns.

Regardless of the aspirations that had led dozens of younger Gitxsan to join SWAT or participate in team-led activities, however, Vegh remembered, the technical organization of the Forest Service–run consultation process led to frustration almost immediately. Tasked with assessing new logging proposals even as they were rushing to generate their own maps of existing clear-cuts, government-mandated deadlines for response simply did not provide the team with enough time to attend to all of the sites that came up for review (see Devlin 2009). "It was just taking up way too much time, and it was going nowhere and it meant nothing," Vegh complained. "It was just dotting the i's and crossing the t's for the province, to go through consultation that led nowhere." Creating maps of their own, then, rather than simply summoning new testimony each time loggers proposed to begin work in a new area, quickly became the team's primary goal. By the mid-1990s, the team had begun to systematize their own databases from the reference points and observations they gathered through trail mapping sessions and the hundreds of binders full of *Delgamuukw and Gisday'wa* territorial affidavits and other research materials stored in the GTS office. In addition to streamlining their work in the field, the databases also shifted their tone of engagement. "In the early '90s, when we first started," Vegh told me, "before we were involved in GIS, we used to get 1:20K topos [topographic maps] or forest cover maps and hand color the polygons. And forestry officials used to kinda snicker at us and say, 'Oh, you've got pretty little maps there.' But they were pretty powerful, actually. They started changing the way forestry officials dealt with us."

In much the same way that shifts in forestry policy became seismic events in the lives of other activists living nearby (see chapter 1), members of SWAT experienced the ongoing digitization of environmental management protocols as a constantly shifting terrain of engagement. Throughout the 1990s, provincial officials were busily transposing into digital databases the paper records of boundaries, infrastructures, and measurements of environmental change accumulated by government scientists and planners throughout the twentieth century.[23] In 1994, though, shortly after SWAT began its first consultations with government foresters, the introduction of a new watershed management policy framework complimented by a generously funded ecological research initiative known as Forest Renewal BC (FRBC) greatly accelerated this transition. In addition to forcing the provincial government to begin reformatting its voluminous archives, new digital data standards swiftly transformed how Forest Service personnel and other government-employed researchers conducted everyday work in the field. Data standards initiated in tandem with FRBC policy changes included laborious instructions for taking measurements, making lists, performing calculations, and defining the attributes of new entries to be programmed into GIS databases. The new standards also redefined how georeferenced units could be compiled and analyzed, and provided a legal language for identifying new protected entities.

The sense of familiarity that Vegh and others quickly developed with the new standards transformed the social experience of research by shifting who SWAT affiliates associated with in the offices they visited, as well as how they worked together in the field. Standards for cataloging field observations proved crucial in helping Vegh to coordinate the work of SWAT's everchanging roster of field mapping assistants (see chapter 4). New cooperative management projects begun with FRBC funding also provided some of their first opportunities to collaborate meaningfully with non-Indigenous scientists.[24] During the initial years of these collaborations, a few SWAT analysts were already more skilled than their government counterparts at writing in the DOS coding language required for early GIS interfaces. Working side by side, however briefly, with government scientists also helped SWAT to become more adept at securing specific sites within more robust conservation classification systems. "If you can overlay data for berry areas on forest ecosystem network or hydroriparian zones," Vegh explained, "then it's already protected and logged, so we don't have to say 'this is our berry area,' that's already established in provincial law."

As digital data standards swiftly reorganized the management practices of Gitxsan governance institutions during the 1990s, their associated bureaucratic terms offered SWAT team members new resources for challenging their government counterparts as well as new frameworks for assessing their own successes. Reading from a collection of journals that she kept during the late 1990s, Vegh occasionally laughed out loud as she recounted the pointed barbs and sarcasm she and her SWAT collaborators had lobbed toward Forest Service officials during meetings at government offices, industry conferences, and elite academic venues like the University of British Columbia (UBC) Department of Forestry. Rarely did they miss opportunities to aggressively tease registered professional foresters (RPFs) for their naivete about traditional government systems and their reluctance to participate in consultation. "We were pretty bold and audacious back then, eh?" she laughed, remembering a specific lecture series meant to introduce incoming foresters to new procedures of First Nations consultation. "We titled our module for UBC foresters, 'Boldly to Go Where No RPF Has Gone Before.'" As she dwelled on these confrontations nearly two decades later, she continually referenced annual allowable cuts (AAC) and other Forest Service terms and metrics that framed the nostalgia of other, non-Indigenous researchers that I had come to know throughout the region (see chapter 1). "When I first got into this . . . I thought, 'OK, five years, I'm gonna have downward pressure on the AAC,'" she offered with a weary smile. "But I didn't."

As she quietly recounted the pressures that had shaped her day-to-day work with SWAT, Vegh rarely betrayed any lingering ambitions to build new institutions. "I'm a field person," she insisted. "You're always involved in politics and stuff like that, but mostly I spent a lot of my time in the field." While both she and Collier shared duties in leading mapping exercises, the rapid computerization of their work led to a de facto division of labor that often kept Collier in the office while Vegh led expeditions on the territories, often with other women like her daughter and sister. Building on the mandate of the Gitxsan Education Society, through which both of them had received their initial training, Vegh and Collier routinely organized with other SWAT collaborators to host GIS analysis and trail mapping training sessions for local Gitxsan youth. For Collier, who referred frequently to these early students during our conversations, teaching GIS lessons often meant contending with two dozen students crowded around a single computer, and explaining complicated coding practices to teenagers and young adults with little or no prior experience with computers. For some of the children and grandchildren of residential school survivors who joined Vegh for trail mapping sessions, working with SWAT sometimes also meant visiting their families' *wilp* territories for the first time.

Like the ad hoc training sessions through which Vegh and Collier began their careers, the temporalities of SWAT's projects were also frequently punctuated by the unpredictable demands from government offices or unexpected events in the lives of the team's family members and neighbors. Time and again, Vegh remembered, the death of an elder disrupted a project schedule, as house group members and other relatives temporarily redirected their energies to organizing a commemorative death feast, collecting donations, and handling the transfer of feast names and other matters of hereditary succession.[25] The already unpredictable tempos of Forest Service demands and funding allotments made these interruptions even more destabilizing. Vegh invoked these layered uncertainties while defending the decisions of several of her family members to leave behind countermapping work and seek out corporate careers. "The projects are always stop and start, stop and start, and my daughter, my sister, they have families, and they just need steady employment." Many participants, she admitted, were simply ready to move on.

The search for steady employment, many SWAT members soon learned, brought with it a wide range of new tests and strains. As I will show below, Collier's professional networks soon grew to include a broad range of conservation NGOs, government committees, and First Nations management offices. Most of the early SWAT collaborators who followed him away from the reserves, however, eventually took on roles within the logging industry. Speaking to me from her office at a forestry planning and mapping consultancy based in a town several hours east of the Gitxsan territories, Mabel, an early SWAT trainee, reflected that the computer training she received from Collier and Vegh had helped her to move away from the territories, but had also effectively removed the temptation to return. Her initial sense of moral conflict over working within the forestry industry, she admitted, had long since faded. "The only milestones that shaped where I work and why is opportunities. There weren't a lot of them for someone with my skills. There still aren't a lot," she explained. "I have chosen to stay [away] . . . working for a forest consulting organization because I'm paid well, and have had a full-time job here for the past ten years." Few of her former SWAT colleagues, she admitted, had been nearly as lucky.

"A Fighting Force": Russell Collier's Story

Building a career as an Indigenous mapper, a few former members of SWAT lamented to me, meant getting used to living far from home. Not long after my arrival in the north, Collier had begun a job as the consultation coordinator for the Mikisew Cree First Nation in northern Alberta. His brief visits back to his small farm half an hour southeast of Smithers were his only chance to spend time with his wife and their two young children. As I busied myself with visits to the homes and offices of other Gitxsan mappers still living in the region, Collier and I connected in other ways. Throughout the summer, I occasionally bought chicken from his family's stand at the weekly farmers market in Smithers, and I listened to his wife's laments about the strains of living and working long-distance. The boredom and isolation he experienced during his months in Alberta, though, Collier admitted, also gave him the time and freedom to do other things, including writing long and thoughtful accounts of his life in response to the questions I sent him by email.

Like other former members of SWAT that I came to know throughout the region, Collier initially claimed to be reluctant to place himself at the center of a collective story. Continually looping his reminiscences back through the physical devices of his early work, Collier characterized SWAT's early discussions with hereditary chiefs less as scenes of expert translation than as his enrollment into a decades-long conversation between Gitxsan houses and the provincial government. Basing their consultation work around house group territories, as opposed to the exterior borders of the overall Gitxsan First Nation, Collier reminded me, meant interfacing between hereditary *wilp* chiefs, clan matriarchs, and other house members, as opposed to the elected bodies of the band councils that ran reserves or the self-appointed board of the GTS. Rather than having a disaggregating effect on the team's overall work, however, this mode of interaction immediately put Collier and others into consequential mediating roles.

Initially, the structure of the consultation process offered SWAT multiple potential sources of legitimacy. Despite being recruited by new bureaucratic leaders whose roles would eventually become clouded in acrimony, Collier and Vegh's work was routinely validated by leaders within the traditional system. As Collier put it:

> The hereditary chiefs and clan matriarchs supported this kind of work
> and this kind of training. Indeed, they felt proud at seeing us all doing

this kind of work. In those earlier days, there was a lot of activity from within the communities that my work and my students' work fit into. We were part of a larger dream and it felt pretty good to be of service. The really active community members were the most curious about our work. . . . Without having the jargon, or the respect of the government-industry folks, they nevertheless [knew] pretty well what they wanted to see achieved. They voted to create us and our work, and they patiently asked questions of us at community meetings. The [Gitxsan-Wet'suwet'en] Education Society work, and the GIS map department work, was driven by a combination of response to whatever current battle was occurring, and the longer-range vision we were all trying to achieve.

The move to digital mapping, Collier insisted, was merely pragmatic. "Anybody in the [Gitxsan] leadership or among the tech people could see really fast that this was a useful way of handling more information than one person alone could handle." Computerized tools, though, redistributed technical labor in the office even as they generated new modes of earning prestige. Collier rarely downplayed the novelty of SWAT's computer technology while explaining the growth of his personal ambitions. In an email describing his initial work in the GTS's Technical Department, the organization that preceded the creation of SWAT, Collier emphasized the relative novelty of the computer resources made available to him at the outset of his career:

That shop ran an early Unix-based version of ESRI's ArcInfo [a major proprietary GIS program], on Sun OS SparcStations. The shop also had copies of the PC ArcInfo, and I learned them both, picking up Unix systems administration along the way. . . . Those were the early days of GIS in the community, you have to remember. Very few First Nations at that time had GIS capability; we were one of the early adopters of the technology. It was horribly expensive. I think my office spent $27,000 apiece on 2 SparcStations with ArcInfo installed to each . . . it was a huge commitment for all of us to make.

Constantly describing the group's technological tools as proof of a broader strategy of collective investment, Collier's reflections on his privileged role in authorizing access to these tools conveyed his awareness that he was an object of investment as well. "The cool factor at being able to work at something that expensive and that advanced was very high, because only government and some industry had the funding to get not just one but two licenses [for the ArcInfo software]," he excitedly recalled. "It signaled to all that we were going to be a force to be contended with." Collier qualified his fascination with the computer technology he worked with by referring to himself as a "ponytail geek," a class of tinkerers, he explained, "who tend to get into the graphic design end of things, who are forced into or maybe gravitate toward social situations where they interact with a lot of other people." Collier's accounts of the genesis of the team echoed Vegh's insistence on their roles as bureaucratic "translators," but emphasized the thrill of being thrust into unexpected managerial roles. "The new job was challenging, because not only were we required to do mapping, we also had to understand what was important to different kinds of map users: lawyers, biologists, hereditary chiefs, and a wide variety of other professional folks. And so I picked up a smattering of all the users' lingo and training."

In Collier's retelling, digital data standards quickly became handles for subversion, tools that agile field-workers could use to transpose their observations into multifaceted legal and scientific arguments against provincial authority. "One of the questions we got asked a lot was if the technology drove our results, or were we able to resist having our ideas packaged by technology," Collier reminisced while describing the early years of SWAT's rise to prominence and their subversive efforts to leverage government-authored technical work to expand their own limited jurisdiction. "I actually found that to be a hilarious question. We were taking tools the province provided grudgingly, such as forest cover digital data, with databases attached, and then subverting them for our own ends." Much of the team's advantage, Collier explained, came not only from their facility with the new standards, but from their willingness to physically visit the areas depicted on Forest Service maps. Before high-resolution satellite photos became widely available, simply checking the basic accuracy of the ministry's depictions of road locations and old-growth blocks with backpack-carried and handheld GPS devices proved to be a rewarding, if time-consuming, confrontational strategy. "It used to really piss them off to find that by ground truthing the forest cover, we could correct polygon contents and make better decisions with better data," Collier bragged. "We also could find holes in their regional and landscape planning, because we could find holes in their data." That the tools and data standards of the provincial government's new environmental modeling programs were initially shared with such hesitation meant that SWAT could frame their work as both a compromise with government epistemes and as a unifying gesture of defiance. "I don't think the province or industry realized that if they'd only taken a conciliatory approach," Collier reflected, "and given us an inch here or there, instead of fighting us to the bitter end every step of the way, we'd not have become such a good fighting force."

Collier's self-presentation as an assertive political actor enframed both his reflections on his time on the Gitxsan territories as well as his narratives of his movement away. After consolidating his sense of himself as a technical expert, his stories suggested, he was able to approach the dissolution of SWAT as a moment of personal choice, much like how White scientists in Smithers presented their own arrivals in the region as the realization of intentional acts. As the *Delgamuukw and Gisday'wa* appeals wore on, lingering ambiguities over the separation of powers between hereditary clans and house groups and the self-appointed GTS had devolved into public disagreements over consultation procedures and development proposals. Influential Gitxsan leaders left the region for bureaucratic jobs and consultancies in Ottawa and southern British Columbia. By the time the BC Ministry of Forests suspended its financial support for First Nations consultation work in 2002, many of SWAT's original trainees and collaborators had already left the region to look for work. "People just got burnt out," Collier admitted. Perhaps even more so than his colleagues, Collier was ready to see how his own professional persona would transform as he traveled. "With some trepidation," he offered, "I hung out my shingle."

In Search of Recognition

Following the collapse of SWAT, Vegh's and Collier's careers took markedly different paths. Vegh temporarily retreated from countermapping projects altogether before returning in the mid-2000s to oversee occasional mapping projects for the GHC (see chapter 4) and other local groups. Collier began a peripatetic journey across western Canada, selling his services as a GIS technician and traditional ecological knowledge (TEK) consultant for First Nations groups and environmental NGOs, many of which were engaged in forestry-related conflicts of their own. Living away from the Gitxsan reserves and territories, Collier divided his time between a wide range of groups, and often supported himself one project at a time. Each First Nations group with whom Collier worked also faced their own uncertain timelines and sudden gaps in project funding, not unlike the situation at the GTS that he had earlier sought to escape. Few of his "permanent" positions kept him in one location for longer than a year. While working for one First Nation band office in central British Columbia, for instance, he assembled a computer interface to model risks around a proposed mine. When the prospective developer sold the claim to another mineral exploration company, Collier's salary disappeared. Other engagements were even more limited in scope. With numerous coastal First Nations groups already embedded in long-standing relationships with international conservation NGOs like Greenpeace and the Sierra Club, Collier's GIS and GPS training sessions typically lasted only a few days at a time.

While the financial uncertainty characteristic of his time working with Gitxsan organizations remained relatively unchanged, Collier's expanding networks provided him with something he claimed that his Gitxsan employers had long refused to provide: acknowledgment of his expertise. "I'd say that developing a professional identity has been instrumental in kicking me out of the nest, so to speak," Collier offered once, as a conversation outlining one particularly disjointed period began to darken his mood. "To more than a few influential leaders in my home communities," he lamented, "I'll never be more than the junior GIS mapper I started out to be." His original patrons, he bitterly suggested, had hoped to exploit his devotion to the Gitxsan First Nation's cause even as their practical aims transformed over time. Away from the GTS, though, the terms of professional recognition were cynical, but more straightforward. "I wasn't charging very much and learned that to be considered professional, I had to charge the going rate for this kind of work. I hiked my day rate from $200/day to $350/day and right away found that people's estimation of me went up."

Within months of increasing his rates, Collier secured a multiyear appointment with Ecotrust Canada, one of the largest conservation NGOs in British Columbia. Despite often being forced to occupy an awkward intermediary position between the organization and the small First Nations communities where they conducted much of their work, his association with the organization quickly thrust Collier into prominent roles. He helped to assemble a comparative report on forestry certification programs on Indigenous resource rights and political mobilizations, a task he later reprised as the National Aboriginal Advisor to the Canadian Boreal Forest Agreement (R. Collier and Hobby 2010). He also helped to establish the Aboriginal Mapping Network (AMN), an online discussion board that aggregated job postings for GIS technicians, map construction methodologies, information on ongoing countermapping projects, and links to new online atlases assembled by First Nations groups and other Indigenous offices.[26] Like most other traditional land use mappers working at the time, his work consisted primarily of assembling map biographies: interviewing elders, fixing lines and icons to correspond with elders' stories of their experiences on their territories, and collating the results to produce visual plots of Indigenous groups' collective presence within particular regions.[27] By helping to standardize these techniques and publicizing this work through the website, Collier's name soon reached an even more dispersed array of Indigenous groups and potential patrons, just as the proliferation of free and open source GIS software was pushing hundreds of new groups to pursue countermapping work for the first time.

Reflecting on the celebrity he enjoyed from his association with the *Delgamuukw and Gisday'wa* appeals and with SWAT, Collier occasionally referred to his Gitxsan identity in explicitly instrumental terms. "There has been some magic in the 'made in Gitxsan' label," he explained during one of our early email exchanges. "My part in mapping for the fabled Gitxsan-Wet'suwet'en land claims court cases . . . in the second stage and the appeal . . . lends a certain shine to [other projects], because they have a real, live Gitxsan mapper, one of the best in the country, at their service for a contracted chunk of time." That it had become easier for Collier to feel recognized as Gitxsan by *non*-Gitxsan groups said much about the burdens and disappointments that had freighted his earlier work. The pride of recognition Collier expressed as we scrolled through folders of new maps he had created during his most recent consulting work often came interspersed with subtle criticisms of his former patrons. "Other, non-Gitxsan, communities . . . welcomed me with an enthusiasm that astonishes me. They are more ready to accept me and my growth than my home communities ever have." His present success was provisional, his reflections suggested, and would likely remain tied to the gains of his clients for the remainder of his career. The still-unfolding Gitxsan sovereignty project, though, he had long since transformed into a prologue of his account of himself.

Collier was far from the only former member of SWAT to express an attenuated sense of allegiance. Mabel, a SWAT trainee turned forestry technician now working in central British Columbia, responded bluntly to my questions about the recognition she had enjoyed since leaving SWAT. "I have not heard from anyone and have never been called upon by any Gitxsan group to lend my expertise," she explained to me during an email exchange. Like Collier, the fading of her connections to the GTS and the other management offices on the reserves had pushed her toward other kinds of groups and networks to assuage her sense of estrangement. Still, her early experiences had made her wary. "I have never worked for any first nation organization as a GIS analyst (directly)," Mabel told me over email. "However, I have taken on contracts with [another First Nation office in central British Columbia]. I believe that because I myself am also first nation (although from a different nation) [I] am more trusted." The roots of this trust among other First Nations personnel, Mabel suggested, emerged from their similar experiences dealing with marginalization. Yet in emphasizing her embrace of more distanced gestures of recognition, she acknowledged that her early experiences of professionalization had left a lingering psychic toll.

The way that Mabel vacillated between expressions of solidarity and alienation mirrored the ambivalence that other Gitxsan researchers expressed while reflecting on their experiences honing their craft. All of the former SWAT members with whom I spoke expressed considerable pride about the meagerness of their initial credentials. Unlike many other Gitxsan who assisted him with mapping projects, though, Collier had spent time at university before returning home to work on the territories in the 1980s, and he had continued to pursue postsecondary credentials after leaving the region again in the early 2000s. Early into our first email exchanges, he directed me to the master's thesis he had recently written as part of an environmental education and communication degree (R. Collier 2012).[28] Built around a series of interviews and linguistic explorations with Gitxsan friends and family members, the thesis highlighted Collier's acute reflexivity about the mapping methods he had helped to develop throughout his career. The language of the thesis also repeatedly emphasized Collier's conviction in his own uniqueness as a "cultural translator," a man who had been "trained in two worlds" and could pass effortlessly through the liminal spaces between traditional governance and provincial technocracy. And yet, even amid his obvious enthusiasm for the work of translation, the conversations with elders he recounts in the dissertation reveal a man resigned to navigating these liminal spaces alone.

Departing from Collier's house one evening, only hours before he was set to board a Greyhound bus back to northern Alberta, I felt weary under the weight of his stories. Even after talking for more than four hours, though, Collier had apparently found his second wind. As I gathered my things, he outlined plans for us to reconvene as soon as he returned home for his holiday vacation in December. He again offered long lists of names of people working throughout the province—NGO affiliates, environmental scientists, government officials, other First Nations mapmakers—who had joined him at various stops in his professional travels, and who could add texture and perspective to his narratives. "I know how the research process works," Collier assured me. Fact-checking. Story triangulation. Multiple return visits and endless follow-up questions. As he walked me down his porch steps and back to my truck, Collier promised to be prepared. "These kinds of things only begin to make sense over time. I'm still learning that myself."

Obligation and Expertise

Finding fulfillment in the pursuit of a calling, like the realization of a collective political goal, can only occur with the passage of time. Gitxsan experts took up digital mapping tools at almost precisely the same time that the government of British Columbia ceased to govern through paper maps.[29] Both transitions were managed by individuals—individuals whose aspirations were shaped by the affordances of their changing tools. In the three decades since these transitions began, these associations have come to carry a symbolic weight for some Gitxsan, particularly those who have become frustrated with the apparent returns of the post–*Delgamuukw and Gisday'wa* era. As I have argued throughout this chapter, anthropologists working in Indigenous communities have said little about these forms of estrangement. Many ethnographic analyses of Indigenous-led mapmaking remain tethered to the beginning of the modern land claims era, years before the chiefs, researchers, and expert witnesses who became famous during this era began to die. For better or worse, this emphasis reflects a time before land claims research institutions became entrenched, and before the tools that these institutions developed to pursue their original aims began to generate their own forms of life (but see Thom 2009; Neale and Vincent 2017). For Gitxsan mapmakers who began their careers at the dawn of the digital countermapping movement, traversing boundaries has been neither automatic nor cost-free. In order to enjoy the mobility and influence promised by professional networks, many Indigenous experts first had to distance themselves from the groups who first recruited them into technical careers (see Nadasdy 2005b). As the stories recounted in this chapter make plain, though, these acts of renunciation are rarely explicit, and the breaks they engender are never clean or complete.

Narrative accounts of lives spent on research must be appreciated as consequential acts of theory-making. In order for this to happen, however, the estranging dimensions of professionalization must be carefully distinguished from the disenchantment and anonymization that social theorists often ascribe to bureaucratization writ large (see, e.g., Hoag 2011; Babül 2017). As Max Weber himself insists, the pervasive urge to position experts as bellwethers of collective trajectories, a defining feature of European pro-gressivism, is one that can only be countered through attention to the par-ticularities of experts' experience. Lecturing at Munich University in 1917, Weber warned that students' insistence on seeing their instructors and other scientists as heroes of progressivism and misrecognizing the ephemeral, undecidable character of scientific work had unsettled the balance between the ethic of responsibility and the ethic of conviction that he believed ought to underlie a career in research. Unlike prophets and other religious figures, he chided his audience, scientists cannot offer meaningful answers to the question, "Which warring gods should we serve?" (Max Weber 1958, 131). Mutually fulfilling relationships between researchers, institutions, and their broader social worlds, he suggests, would be grounded not in relentlessly striving toward idealized social forms, but in the reflexivity of the many people with investments in these processes. "We can force the individual," Weber offers, "to give himself an account of the ultimate meaning of his own conduct" (130). It is only in these individual accounts, he suggests, that the true obligations attending research can begin to take tangible form.

Of course, as Indigenous scholars, and Native feminist scholars in partic-ular, have argued for years, narratives about concrete experiences of settler colonialism are never reducible to "individual accounts" (J. Barker 2017; see also Talaga 2017, 2018). Dian Million explicitly connects the political affordances of experiential accounts to the limitations of conventional pro-gressivism. "Native women in Canada often distanced themselves from white feminism, instead choosing strategies and language that located them within the heart of their own experiences," Million writes. "They walked a tightrope between their need to organize on intimate issues and the neces-sity to argue for self-determination for their communities" (2008, 269). Former members of SWAT often described their professional paths as pro-ceeding along similar tightropes. The accounts that they shared with me about their sense of the callings that led them onto their territories and into lives of research painted dense webs of social relations structured by compet-ing obligations at every node. These accounts foregrounded how each indi-vidual's sense of themselves as a researcher was shaped by the expectations of specific individuals. The researchers also dwelled on the expectations that these other individuals bore from still more people and institutions as well. By emphasizing how the everyday encounters they negotiated through their work steadily shaped these long-term relationships, their accounts troubled the many categorical distinctions—traditional and bureaucratic; expert and novice—that have often made First Nations experiences of technical research subject to compartmentalizing analyses.

The ways that experiential accounts of settler colonialism can help to unsettle analytic categories has for many First Nations people become indispensable to the remaking of worlds. During the decades leading up to Canada's Truth and Reconciliation Commission on Indian residential schools, Dian Million (2009) shows, stories played critical roles in rendering "private" issues "public"—including gendered experiences of violence that Canadian policy-making had first helped to render "private" through its overwriting of Indigenous women's roles in family planning, property relations, and governance. Experiential accounts authored by Indigenous elites can also enact important theoretical insights, even if the increased visibility of some of these accounts can pose distinct challenges of interpretation. Careful attention to the autobiographies of Indigenous activists, for instance, has helped to illuminate pressures that may have caused politically prominent individuals to articulate the meaning of their professional labor in particular ways. Renya Ramirez's (2018) life history of her grandfather, a prominent Winnebago leader named Henry Cloud, addresses this tension directly by showing how Cloud's idiosyncratic pursuit of multiple kinds of callings came to matter to Native American–led institution building and policy-making writ large. "Some could consider Henry Roe Cloud as 'assimilated,' a 'sell-out,' and 'inauthentic,'" Ramirez writes, "because he was a 'progressive' Indian who encouraged Native Americans to become modern and Christian. . . . These categories are stuck in creating binaries between 'progressive' and 'traditional' Indians in which 'progressives' are defined as wanting to assimilate into American society and 'traditionals' are described as maintaining a strong connection to their tribal communities and traditions" (2009, 79). Weaving a close reading of Cloud's autobiography with reflections on policy reports, personal letters, and other archived documents connected to the man's life, Ramirez shows how her grandfather consistently obviated these categories through both his aspirations and his intentional acts. She also carefully highlights the tensions that might have caused Cloud to frame his experiences in ennobling terms—not wanting to upset his many White Christian readers, for instance, with stories about himself and his classmates suffering physical punishment for speaking their native language. As Ramirez makes clear, the fact that such conflicting expectations persisted throughout Cloud's lifetime did not prevent the man from leading a meaningful and fulfilling life. Yet the lack of a clear resolution to these conflicts nevertheless affects contemporary scholars and kin, who must continually work out how their elders' experiences of toil and meaning-making might reverberate into the future.

Darlene Vegh and Russell Collier's stories lay bare the exhausting pressures of translating knowledge between different legal orders and bureaucratic spaces. Perhaps surprisingly, they and their former SWAT colleagues often acknowledged these tensions directly. They acknowledged that the meaning of their research would remain ambiguous as long as the space between these legal orders persisted, and as long as enacting sovereignty through research remained an everyday practice. Their reflections on their efforts to make peace with this ambiguity offer new ways of reading Max Weber's portrait of science as a calling: "Why does one engage," Weber asks, "in doing something that in reality never comes, and never can come to an end? . . . Each of us knows that what he has accomplished will be antiquated in ten, twenty, fifty years" (1958, 115–16). For Weber, the answer was a pedagogical one—an answer that he effectively modeled through the form of his public address. Finding peace with one's future disappearance and impressing it upon those patrons who demand prophecy in scientific work, to those students seeking leaders rather than teachers, Weber insists, is not merely crucial to a successful research career: it is foundational to any search for fulfillment in the practice of collective life.

Throughout his writings on different conceptualizations of the calling, Weber's emphasis on the disenchanting effects of progressivism caused him to treat the promises framing organized research as illusions to be eschewed. For Indigenous experts, however, such detachment is a dangerous luxury. The many conversations I shared with former members of SWAT about sovereignty as a continual practice conveyed a clear sense that none saw their political futures in teleological terms. Yet they also consistently conveyed the sense that these futures would remain elusive, and that amid this elusiveness, the expectations that other Gitxsan invested in their work would continue to generate periodic disappointments. As I show in chapter 4, the dramatic decline in government support for First Nations–led mapping projects over the past two decades has forced researchers to develop relationships with other kinds of patrons in order to continue contributing to long-term collective projects. This includes the very corporations whose activities First Nations researchers actively leverage their work to contest. For the researchers attempting to negotiate these new relationships and draw out their affordances for the pursuit of sovereignty, however, sharing personal accounts of these processes with the many people invested in their work may yet offer some measure of peace. At the least, these accounts will serve as reminders: that the proper returns of research, like the homeward returns of many researchers themselves, still have yet to arrive.

Given to a Name

Two weeks after the November summit described in the previous chapter and three days before Russell Collier's scheduled bus ride back home from Alberta, a friend in Smithers forwarded me a link: a Facebook page had been set up to collect donations for Lori, Collier's wife. The previous night, midway through the annual Christmas party on the Mikisew Cree reserve, Russell had collapsed and died on the dance floor. By the following afternoon, his family's initial call for a small, informal memorial service later in the spring had given way to preparations for a large, formal funeral and death feast to be hosted jointly between multiple Gitxsan houses, the likes of which had become rare in the years since Collier's departure. For a single night, the posthumous culmination of Collier's perpetually deferred return collapsed his disparate networks into a single room. Executives of the GTS, members of the provincial and federal parliament, dissident chiefs, and many of SWAT's scattered original members crowded into the feast hall for hours upon hours of meals, performances, speeches, and exchanges of gifts.

As attendees returned to their dispersed homes and institutions in the following days, some offered eulogies for additional audiences. People who had not spoken to Collier for years penned thoughtful editorials for blogs and local newspapers. Months later, Nathan Cullen, the Smithers resident, federal parliamentarian, and leader of the opposition in the House of Commons of Canada whom we met in in the previous chapter, offered his tribute during a session of parliament.[30] Referring to Collier as "one of British Columbia's foremost Aboriginal land use planners, a cultural translator between his ancient Gitxsan heritage and his knowledge of modern science," Cullen acknowledged Collier's ties on reserve even as he interpellated him within the professional networks that had drawn him away from home. Former collaborators around Smithers offered similar thoughts in research meetings and chance encounters with each other throughout the winter, citing the persistence of Collier's memory throughout the region as proof that his influence had never left. Recognized as Collier's recent interlocutor, I was pulled into some of these conversations as well. People in Smithers and around the reserves who had been vaguely aware of my research expressed sudden interest in the histories I was struggling to reconstruct. They asked after the tenor of the many stories Collier had shared with me during his final year, and wondered aloud what might have happened if he had ever decided to move back to the region and work with the Gitxsan full-time.

With Collier gone, my already precarious fieldwork methodology took different turns. I brooded over the uncomfortable fact that I had crowded into the final meal Collier had shared with his family, a nosy anthropologist eager to unsettle painful memories yet largely oblivious to the quiet, difficult work he had been doing for years to repair these broken bonds. Reading again and again through our voluminous email exchanges in the following months and reflecting on Collier's personality and legacy in long and occasionally tearful conversations with people on and off the reserves, I gradually discovered a more patient man than the one I had first captured in my daily annotations. One story in particular stood out: Responding to a cluster of questions I had asked about the unraveling of SWAT's GIS training exercises as the funding for the team collapsed, Collier offered a long and personal story, the relevance of which I only began to grasp in the months after his death. My fixation on the dynamics of technical training that I saw at the root of SWAT's capacity-building project, Collier had suggested gently, had caused me to miss key aspects of the longer-term processes in which these exchanges were meant to be understood. Reflecting on his own Gitxsan name, Collier drew analogies to the long-term training process through which *wilp* chiefs and clan matriarchs prepared their young successors for the leadership roles they would eventually assume within their house groups and clans.

"My name is Hli Gyet Hl Spagayt Sagat," he told me. "It means 'The Man Who Comes Down From The Sharp-Pointed Mountain.' It's a local landmark in the Gitsegukla Valley." Having grown up off the reserves, Collier had neither a feast name nor a baby name when he was given to the name Spaiyt Sagat in his midthirties. The name itself was a new invention. He was to be its first holder.[31] In Gitsenimx, the name was a triple pun. The first two meanings of the name, he explained dryly, were fairly straightforward: among his family and house group, he was already known as the "mountain man," the mapmaker who led different groups into the hills to mark trails and gather data. As with other Gitxsan men his age, he was also known for retreating to the mountains while mulling over life transitions and important decisions ("to seek visions or whatever," Collier joked).

The third part of the name referred to the end of the journey: the return. "Coming back down," Collier chuckled, shaking his head. "'You will spend most of your life trying to grow into it,'" the chief of his *wilp* had told him during the naming feast, Collier remembered to me over two and a half decades later. "'And it's only later, when it's towards the end of your life, that you'll finally understand what we meant when we gave you to that name, what we intended for you.'" Collier paused, as if allowing me time to feel the weight of these painfully ambiguous expectations. Was his ongoing story of professional exile part of his time in the mountains? A prelude to his necessarily deferred return? The words of his chief offered nothing, simply the promise of time to work and wonder: "'What you'll do in the meantime is up to you.'"

FIGURE 3.1 Dennis cuts through a treatment unit on a recently renovated boardwalk trail. Photo by author.

3

Inheritance

Replacement and Leave-Taking in a Research Forest

"OK, Tom—let's see how well you've been paying attention. Why do you suppose these trees are growing so close together?" Dennis waved his hand toward the dense wall of young spruce that he, two young assistants, and I had just finished fighting our way through. Outside the stand, peering back from the airy openness of an old-growth grove of hemlock trees, the fast-growing second-growth spruce looked even more chaotic than it had seemed when we had been lost inside it moments earlier, rarely able to see more than a few inches in front of ourselves. Kristen and Sanjit, appreciating the chance to catch their breath, waited for my answer. My eyes traveled upward, toward a narrow band of sunlight streaming in through a slit in the canopy ninety feet above us. Dennis followed my glance and corrected me before I began to answer. "That's part of it." With his right hand, he traced

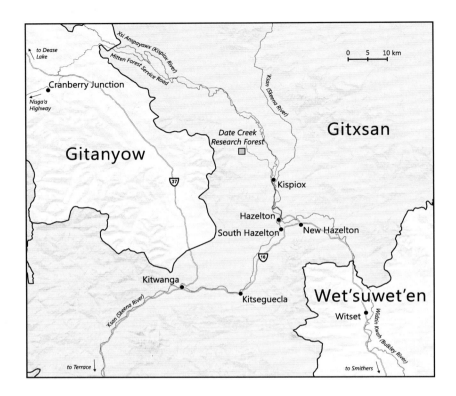

MAP 3.1 Map of Date Creek Research Forest, Cranberry Junction, Gitxsan villages, and environs.

the wall of spruce from east to west, back toward the road where we had parked earlier that morning.

"An old skid trail, right?" I ventured.

Kristen smiled and nodded. "Good to know, right?" she said. "In case you get lost and want to find your way back to the road. They're all over the place in this section." Sanjit and Dennis had already picked up their clipboards and begun walking again, Sanjit scanning ahead for the yellow metal tag denoting our next measurement point (see figure 3.6 at the end of the chapter). My eyes lingered along the base of the winding wall of spruce for a few more moments. I imagined the path cut by the skidders—tractors that, a little over two decades earlier, had dragged out the trees felled when Dennis and two other researchers with the BC Forest Service had won a government grant to create the Date Creek Research Forest. Throughout the summer, Dennis had led Sanjit and me through dozens of similar conversations, usually with an eye toward improving the accuracy of the notes we took as we worked. Sanjit, a computer modeling specialist, had just moved to Smithers to begin a short-term position as a researcher at the Bulkley Valley Research Centre (BVRC; see chapter 1). Although he could already assemble elaborate ecological simulations to project how different parts of Date Creek might evolve over the coming decades, he and I both had only begun learning the rudiments of forestry fieldwork. Kristen, an ecologist who was also based at the BVRC in Smithers, had conducted soil surveys and other kinds of field studies all over northwest British Columbia, but was only visiting Date Creek for the first time that summer as well. As Dennis patiently offered instructive explanations and challenged us with occasional quizzes, she usually stood by quietly, sometimes offering additional details or questions of her own.

At first, I glibly referred to these guided conversations as "reading lessons"—my own indoctrination, I assumed, into the narratives, heuristics, and formal descriptions Dennis had developed for turning novice observations into coherent data.[1] Only a few weeks into what promised to be a hectic summer field season, it was clear that Dennis depended heavily on these kinds of contributions. Even if he took substantial time away from his office duties in Smithers and neglected the other field sites that he managed throughout the region, his goal of completing a total remeasurement of Date Creek before the coming winter still felt impossibly ambitious. Hundreds of representative plots distributed throughout the research forest would have to be located. A dozen or more trees at each site would have to be measured and described. If the research forest was simply waiting to be read, it seemed, it would have to be parsed through our mundane agendas, and committed to memory as we moved at high speed.

Our hurried work was freighted with other kinds of anxieties as well. Within a few years, Dennis was planning to retire. With luck, he hoped to persuade the Forest Service to replace him with Kristen. As the summer progressed, though, his hope was growing dim. Along with the other silviculturist who had helped Dennis to establish Date Creek in the early 1990s and who was himself on the verge of retirement, Dennis was one of only a handful of Forest Service researchers based in the northwest to have survived the provincial government's extensive personnel cuts in the early 2000s. "There's little doubt that they're not going to replace both of us," he had told me during one of our final trips to the research forest later that summer. "They might replace one of us. And even right now I'd say that's unlikely. So if we're both gone, there isn't going to be anyone to go out there and keep things going. It's as simple as that." As I immersed myself in the quiet drama surrounding Dennis's uncertain succession, I began to hear his stories in somber tones. The reading lessons Dennis offered me weren't simply indexed to the unfinished business of our summerlong survey, I worried. As my own field notes filled up with Dennis's reflections on the decades of experience he had accumulated at Date Creek, I found myself sensing a fear that the very language of his lessons was about to be lost.

The quiet resignation Dennis seemed to convey while reflecting on his legacy found its twin in the unassuming presentation of the research forest itself. Cloistered along a series of unmarked dirt roads in the Kispiox Valley, over half an hour's drive away from the nearest town, I initially assumed that Date Creek was designed to be obscure. It hadn't always been that way. Launched alongside half a dozen other alternative silvicultural research stations around British Columbia in the early 1990s, the long-term experiment Dennis and his collaborators proposed for Date Creek had formed a tacit part of the Forest Service's response to the dozens of anti-clear-cutting blockades and other protests that had taken place in the region during the War in the Woods. "When Date Creek first went in, we had a mind-boggling number of tours," he reminisced to me shortly after we first met. Politicians from Europe. Groups of children from nearby schools. At the height of the so-called war, executives from Greenpeace and the Sierra Club took time away from a scheduled meeting with a group of blockade leaders at a nearby Gitxsan reserve to join Dennis for a personal tour. The main experiment they encountered there was deceptively simple: after selectively logging groups of trees to create a patchwork of differently sized holes in the canopy, Dennis measured the rates of growth for each remaining tree in the forest as a function of its distance from the nearest opening to direct sunlight (figures 3.2 and 3.3).[2] The design of the experiment had helped Dennis and his collaborators call attention to growth dynamics within the forest's so-called secondary structure, the smaller trees and minor tree species growing underneath the forest's upper canopy (figure 3.7). In the first years after Date Creek's inception, the prospect of using ecological research to inform forestry planning had made Dennis a pariah within the BC Forest Service. Twenty years later, his published work had helped to encourage internationally dispersed researchers and policymakers to treat secondary structure as both a bellwether of climate change and a valuable future resource in its own right. Outside in the forest, secondary structure was often all one could see.

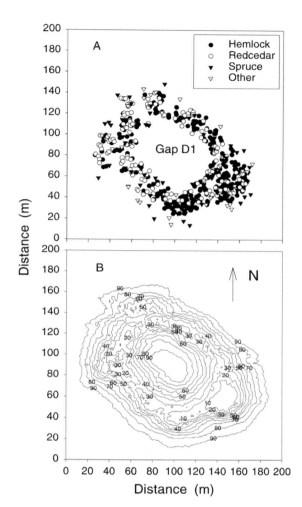

FIGURE 3.2 Schematic diagram of tree stem location (A) and light distribution (B) relative to a 0.33-hectare gap, as modeled in SORTIE-ND. Numbers in B denote extent of shading; area outside polygon devoid of trees. Figure modified from Canham et al. 1999, 1782.

Dennis's lighthearted interactions with Kristen belied the sense of duty and expectation that I often found myself imagining in their work. By midsummer, I decided to ask them both outright how they planned to cope with the possibility that so much institutional memory might suddenly disappear if Dennis retired without a formal successor in place. "Forest ecology folks are relativists," Dennis insisted, half-jokingly. "We don't usually like to talk about 'losing' things." Even if other researchers' access to Date Creek disappeared when he retired, he mused, his work there would live on in other ways. Collaborative work, much like professional life in the rural northwest

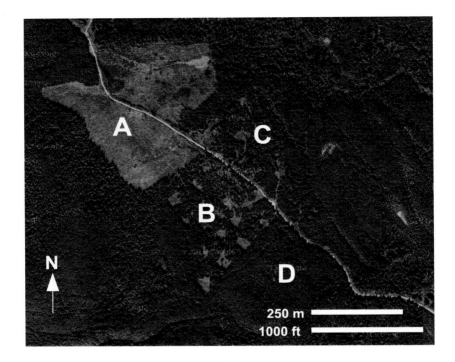

FIGURE 3.3 Satellite photograph of Date Creek Research Forest ca. 2016 (twenty-five years after initial creation of treatment units). The different removal areas are labeled by letters: A, clear-cut; B, 60% removal; C, 30% removal; D, 0% removal (control unit). The pale line winding through the center of the image is the Kispiox Forest Service Road. Satellite imagery © Province of British Columbia.

corner of the province, was inherently precarious. "People kinda just accept that. When something happens, they move on with their lives," he offered. As I pursued the subject throughout the summer, Dennis's insouciance periodically gave way to wistful complaints. "We're a five-and-a-half-hour drive from Prince George. We're a really long way away from Vancouver. There's a lot of places that university professors can send their students that are a lot closer than here. We've had students come up over the years. But it'd be pretty hard to have somebody come up, to be here." Whoever took over the research forest and extended its life as a space of science, Dennis suggested, would have to see it as more than an interchangeable laboratory in an arbitrary space. Most of the reading lessons I had been offered that summer had cast the value of the objects I was taught to recognize primarily in terms of their duration: whoever inherited the task of managing Date Creek's futures, it seemed, would have to do so while managing its pasts.

The kinds of research questions Dennis had eventually come to pursue at Date Creek had expanded dramatically in recent years. His continuing devotion to the initial selective harvesting experiment, however, had left him tacitly responsible for an expansive and unruly infrastructure of research. Following his design for the initial experiment, the patterns of light and shade produced by each canopy opening had slowly produced yet another grid of potential "fields" for smaller-scale experiments. Over time, other researchers established their own plots within the forest to study the decay rates of rotting logs or the habitat preferences of birds, bats, and rodents. Others came to track the intricate competitions that developed between the many species of lichen growing close to the forest floor. Under monumental cedars, mycologists marked out single-meter plots to track minute changes to fungi populations crowding against the cedars' massive trunks. Every few years, Dennis and his collaborators tried to assemble a new list of publications generated by each project, and to map their locations within the forest.[3] As their databases expanded, they struggled to keep pace with the frequent turnover. Some research groups returned every year, and slowly established relationships with Dennis, Kristen, and other ecologists living throughout the region. As we worked our way through the research forest in 2013, though, most of the experimental plots we encountered had been abandoned for years, the still-growing plants within them forgotten as papers were published, degrees were earned, or travel grants were used up (see figure 3.8).

Many of Dennis's interpretive lessons were bracketed with similar forebodings of erasure: any confident "reading," he suggested, could unravel over time, especially if no one remained to receive it. On the same early summer afternoon, a few minutes after quizzing me on the spruce-covered skid trail, Dennis stopped again and pointed to the ground. "Those big guys back there aren't the only things that grew up here after the skidders came through," he offered with a grin. Crouching on the ground, he peered closely at a dense carpet of tiny green trees, toy-sized miniatures of the fast-growing spruce we had just passed through. "These little guys are spruce too. They might be just as old as the ones growing in the middle of the trail." Dennis peered up at the canopy again. "Or maybe they're only five years old. Hard to tell." Stepping to the side and peeling away a small clump of moss with his boot, Dennis assured Kristen that if she returned to the same spot a few years from that time, the new divot would be full of inch-tall saplings, just like those growing in great clusters on either side of the skid trail. "All of these long-term experiments are tricky, though," Dennis admitted. "Some students came up here to study these tiny saplings a few years ago, but they didn't stick around long enough to see them get swallowed up when the moss came back in." In order for the new trees to have any hope of remaining, they needed to grow fast enough, or in great enough numbers, to keep the disturbed moss from reclaiming its old domain. Replacement, he hinted, rarely proceeded as one might expect.

Restoration and Replacement (or Deciding What to Keep)

Collaborative ecological research is suffused with scenes of inheritance—encounters where knowledge, ambitions, and objects of research are conveyed between senior scientists and their younger colleagues, often with the tacit hope that particular senses of place and purpose will live on after the former retire and die. Rather than simply reproducing institutions and hierarchies, such exchanges can enable successors to reconceptualize their institutional attachments. Conceptualizing the sharing of work as an inheritance can also reveal epistemic instabilities—the kinds of instabilities through which scientific disciplines are alternately destroyed and rebuilt. In referring to these transmissions as a form of inheritance, though, I also mean to underline a certain irony. As we saw in the previous chapter, Gitxsan representatives have struggled for decades to earn recognition for hereditary structures of governance and land ownership, watching as younger generations' understandings of both land and inheritance have changed in the process. Meanwhile, scientific projects begun long after these title claims were initiated have already existed long enough to generate succession dilemmas of their own.

Frequently, it seemed, Dennis talked about the ways another scientist might inherit the projects he had begun at Date Creek less to reflect on the substance of his legacy there than to dwell on the ways that it all might unravel. As anthropologists and historians alike have noted, conversations about inheritance arise most forcefully when a transfer is threatened, or a medium of exchange undergoes an unalterable shift. Many analyses have continued to focus on land and property as conventional guarantors of social reproduction (see, e.g., Hann 2008), often by treating landscapes as privileged mediators in intergenerational transfers of wisdom (see, e.g.,

Basso 1996; T. F. Thornton 2008). In western Canada and many other places, however, development, dislocation, and the overwriting of hereditary chieftainships and other systems of traditional governance by settler colonial institutions have left many people dispossessed of the things and territory their progenitors once worked to secure (Simpson 2014). As Hispano families living in northern New Mexico were forced to sell off farmlands they would have bequeathed to their children, for instance, Angela Garcia (2014) writes, heroin use and addiction took up the place of territory in conversations about what family members might share and pass on. Treating instructions on drug use as moments of care within relationships defined by shared suffering, Garcia's ethnography refocuses attention away from the object inherited to the shared social worlds its transmission secures. As Clara Han and Andrew Brandel (2020) argue, though, Garcia's consistent if implicit framing of inheritance as genealogical transmission has the effect of naturalizing her subjects into predetermined positions: the mother as teacher; the daughter as learner; and only later the latter as teacher herself.

As Kristen and Dennis walked the forest together with the prospect of succession at once looming and remote, little of what Kristen stood to inherit was being shared through explicit instructions. Early into the summer, I had begun to recognize some of the gestures and forms of attention that Dennis had learned in his years with the Forest Service. While he rarely had time to reflect on how his own awareness of the history of the region had influenced the techniques he had developed for working there, none of the rest of us then learning to watch, listen, think, and move in the forest were doing so by ourselves. Like the fragmentary conceptual knowledge that Sanjit and I picked up through our own sidelong encounters, though, the sense that our developing skills nevertheless felt so self-taught—the sense that these techniques were taking root within us as embodied, inarticulate knowledge—rendered our own debts to Dennis ambiguous. The continuing contraction of British Columbia's resource ministries made future episodes of replacement less likely and examples of successful succession harder to find. It was probably becoming easier for some young researchers to imagine themselves as sui generis scientists, we mused together, unbeholden to older researchers whose old field sites they sought to reanimate through their work.

The transformations engendered by government downsizing have changed the meaning of inheritance for many kinds of colleagues and kin living in British Columbia. Much as they have for Garcia's interlocutors in New Mexico, these dramas have largely played out through bodily activities and contingent relationships to land. When I first began working alongside

Dennis, Kristen, and Sanjit in 2013, the uncertain future of the forest itself rendered all of the roles that we worked to inhabit there subject to retrospective change. These ambiguities also manifest themselves in the ways Dennis and others negotiated conceptual aporias within the discipline of forest ecology. Even for a domain of research that takes radical uncertainty as an organizing premise, the prospect of not having a future collaborator in place to gather the results of a decades-long experiment underlined the intergenerational tensions that permeated our work. Long-term collaborations, in other words, carried their own kinds of urgency as well.

For several years after my first summer working in Date Creek, it seemed as though what I had witnessed there had been a failure of succession, rather than a process of intentional replacement.[4] Dennis had already spent several years building relationships with nongovernment researchers in the furtive hope of keeping parts of particular experiments running after he and his colleague retired. He had successfully enlisted the BVRC, where Sanjit and Kristen both worked, to provide funding and personnel for Date Creek's first grand remeasurement in 2005. After Kristen joined the BVRC in 2007 and began collaborating with Dennis shortly thereafter, she gradually picked up some of his ambitions for the projects he had started throughout the region, even as she was initiating studies of her own. When I met her in 2013, she was steadily building her own career as a soil ecologist. The prospect of inheriting a new infrastructure for research meant a chance to design new experiments and articulate them with her mentor's impressive legacy in secondary structure research. As Kristen told me shortly after we began traveling to the field together, the data collected in 2005 was already invaluable for showing the long-term viability of selective harvesting, and the data that we gathered together in 2013 would be more valuable still. We agreed that reproducing the same measurements another twenty or thirty years in the future would be an impressive accomplishment. It was less clear, though, what other kinds of continuity a successful transfer would help to secure.

The call finally came in 2016, three years after our first trip together to Date Creek: the BC Forest Service would hire Kristen as Dennis's formal replacement. Remarkably, the other aging cofounder of the research forest would also be replaced by another researcher based in a neighboring city. The relief that Kristen felt was almost immediately replaced by an altogether different set of anxieties. As she began to take over the day-to-day operation of the research forest the following summer, she was suddenly tasked with assembling ad hoc fieldwork teams, applying for internal grants, and increasing her publication output to reflect her broad new roster of active projects. As the primary manager of the Date Creek Research Forest, she also felt compelled to build relationships with some of the dozens of other groups and individual scientists who periodically visited the space to conduct research projects of their own. Forest Service officials had largely left it to Kristen to decide which of Dennis's projects in the northwest to continue. As she admitted to me several times in the years after starting the position, simply deciding which of Dennis's ongoing projects to "keep," and which to conclude or "hand off" to other Forest Service researchers elsewhere in British Columbia wound up keeping her busy for months.

The continuing usefulness of the grand experiment that Dennis initiated at Date Creek in 1992, she acknowledged when we spoke in early 2018, still had to be demonstrated for Forest Service officials and other government personnel. A research forest could always lose funding, she lamented. Some installations elsewhere in the province had recently been opened up to logging with little to no warning for the scientists working within them. Kristen was keenly aware that she could also be reassigned to another research station, or, more likely, to another office, somewhere else in the province. Dennis and the other founders of Date Creek all had PhDs, she reminded me, while she had yet to progress past a master's degree herself; working anywhere else in British Columbia would mean losing the autonomy she had cultivated through years of local work. Maintaining a viable future in the region for herself and her two children, then, suddenly demanded that she learn to articulate questions through Date Creek that distant observers would find compelling. If the forest I thought I was learning with Dennis was a landscape whose histories could be passively read, encountering it with Kristen as an inherited obligation found the same historicity bound by fragile and seemingly arbitrary threads.

For Jacques Derrida, the deliberate, fragmentary labor of sorting through a predecessor's possessions, assigning new meanings to them, and allowing the overall process to compel oneself toward new goals does not degrade the spirit of a transfer. "An inheritance is never gathered together, it is never one with itself," he writes. "Its presumed unity, if there is one, can consist only in the injunction to reaffirm by choosing. 'One must' means one must filter, sift, criticize, one must sort out several different [possibilities] that inhabit the same injunction. And inhabit it in a contradictory fashion around a secret. If the readability of a legacy were given, natural, transparent, univocal, if it did not call for and at the same time defy interpretation, we would never have anything to inherit from it" (Derrida 1994, 18). The self-effacing relativism that Dennis expressed throughout our summer together, in other words, was misleading: much like the long-term experiment for which the research forest was initially created, Kristen's work of replacement would not be measured in the stories she remembered or the experiments she saved, but through the act of continuance itself.

Researchers affiliated with spaces like Date Creek consistently position their connections to the forests of northwest British Columbia as relationships under threat. And yet these are not property relations in any conventional sense. What Dennis talked about potentially losing there, what he hoped Kristen would be able to gain, was a form of life on the land: learned modes of bodily labor; shared and evolving clusters of scientific concepts; and companionable relationships with other researchers. Like the other scientists whose stories I explored in chapter 1, the ways that researchers articulated these relationships to me were at once genealogical and speculative. While Dennis and others often reflected in detail about the experiments they had completed at Date Creek, they consistently presented the main value of their work as setting the stage for others. "The worst kind [of research forest] is the one that's been in the ground for twenty years," Dennis complained to me, "and people have gone out and measured [the trees], and all the data's in a filing cabinet, right? So, we've published a lot." The object of Kristen's inheritance, then, was not reducible to knowledge, per se, even though the knowledge generated through her research there was already valuable to the discipline of forest ecology. If anything, the experimental system for which she was formally assigned responsibility in 2017 presented itself less as a roster of stories and technical accomplishments than as a battery of emergent choices. Faced with the task of deciding which long-running experiments to keep, which to abandon, and which of her own project ideas to install as she went, what would it mean for her to call herself Dennis's successor, with so much still subject to change?

Reproducing Experiments

In asking by what measure the Date Creek Research Forest might remain "itself" amid the personnel shifts, institutional transformations, and other persistent uncertainties caused by a downsizing government, I mean to examine how researchers confront the impossibility of imagining a world beyond specific configurations of concepts and practices. In some sense, the labor of confronting epistemic limits is a defining feature of scientific work. Within long-established environmental research sites like Date Creek, much of this labor plays out through shifts in the spatial and temporal scope of an evolving project. Since the establishment of the Date Creek Research Forest in 1992, the focus of Dennis's work there has expanded beyond his initial questions about post-clear-cutting succession dynamics to more open-ended explorations of the assumptions undergirding conventional silviculture. Tree diseases, pest outbreaks, and other climate change–related effects would play increasingly important roles in determining the shape of forests to come, he and his collaborators argued, even if provincial officials continued to ignore this broader inheritance. Reckoning the vectors of transition between these later projects as a form of inheritance in its own right, Kristen could only resecure the substance and legacy of Dennis's work by articulating its limitations, and eventually replacing it altogether.

Philosopher, historian, and biologist Hans-Jörg Rheinberger finds in the inexorable movement of epistemic limits a description of scientific activity as a whole. "The sciences are characterized by a permanent process of reorientation and reshuffling of the boundary between what is thought to be known," he writes, "and what is beyond imagination" (1997, 11). Responding primarily to other philosophers of science who treat the temporary closure of debate around scientific problems through the inertia supplied by the norms of experimental practice and the convergence of persuasive rhetoric (Kuhn 1962; Lakatos 1976; Galison 1987), Rheinberger shows instead how specific arrangements of terminology and representational schema collapse earlier descriptions into inaccessible traces. In *Toward a History of Epistemic Things*, he charts a series of such arrangements, or "experimental systems," through the post–World War II transformation of a set of laboratory practices that eventually came to be known as in vitro protein synthesis. By addressing each set of formalized experimental conditions, or "technical objects," with the particular material entities or processes ("epistemic things," in Rheinberger's parlance) that these conditions make visible, Rheinberger uses the analytic of experimental systems to underline both the institutional shaping of scientific knowledge and the radical contingency of any act of interpretation:

> It is through these technical conditions that the institutional context passes down to the bench work in terms of local measuring facilities, supply of materials, laboratory animals, research traditions, and accumulated skills carried on by long-term technical personnel. In contrast to epistemic objects, these experimental conditions tend to be characteristically determined within the given standards of purity and precision. The

experimental conditions "contain" the scientific objects in the double
sense of this expression: they embed them, and through that very em-
bracement, they restrict and constrain them. . . . Within a particular
experimental system both types of elements are engaged in a nontrivial
interplay. (Rheinberger 1997, 29)

Undecidability, Rheinberger argues, underlies all acts of scientific description. Even in this groundbreaking articulation, though, key vectors
of continuity are taken for granted. Within Rheinberger's model of gen-
erativity, "institutional context" merely "passes down"; "skills" are "accumulated," and even then by personnel signified by their "long-term"
commitment to the work at hand. Expanding on this process of mutual
embedding in a later essay, Rheinberger again contrasts the procedural
surprises that bring new knowledge into being with the predictable unfolding of a bounded and idiosyncratic "culture." "Scientific objects come into
existence as a result of unprecedented events," he argues, "that time and
again subvert the finite capacities of imagination of a scientist who remains
always embedded in a particular thinking frame and a local experimental
culture" (2000, 273).

By focusing his analysis on the networked spaces of successful research
laboratories, Rheinberger tacitly establishes a critical set of spatial and
temporal boundary conditions around his historiography. Chief among
these assumptions is his faith in the inevitable reproduction of the research
community itself. Like his interlocutors, Rheinberger is still ultimately concerned with how communities dedicated to the production of new knowledge eventually come to be sure of their concepts, their instruments, and
themselves, in spite of the ultimate instability of any experimental appara-
tuses.[5] For Peter Galison, this self-assurance is achieved through the steady
removal of specific conditions of possibility. "Each individual move [in the
development of an experiment] imposed a further constraint," Galison
writes in *How Experiments End*. "Together they established the reality of
the phenomenon by articulating the boundary between effect and artifact"
(1987, 263). Scientists move readily between disparate tools, concepts,
and rhetorical resources, he argues, guided by a faith that their technical
arguments—and the reality of their objects of study—will eventually be
resolved in satisfying, demonstrable ways.

Like many historians of science, Rheinberger's preoccupation with formal
classifications and institutional boundaries often distracts him from other
lived experiences of limits. "In following the development of epistemic things

rather than that of concepts, topics, problems, disciplines, of institutions," he asserts, "boundaries have to be crossed, boundaries of representational techniques, of experimental systems, of established academic disciplines, and of institutionalized programs and projects. In following the path of epistemic things, classifications have to be abandoned" (Rheinberger 1997, 34). Yet as Lyle Fearnley (2020) shows, for instance, in his ethnographic work with virologists studying potential human-animal transmission routes among poultry breeders in southern China, tracing the history of an epistemic thing beyond the walls of a well-funded laboratory quickly leads to places where novelty and prestige are no longer the only goals of research. In some spaces, research also offers its practitioners a means of negotiating everyday marginalization. Rather than simply enabling scientists to produce new marvels for an active and attentive audience, some research practices are rather designed to hold open a space where new questions might be asked in the event that a dwindling audience eventually returns.

Over the past two decades, many Canadian environmental scientists have been tasked with shepherding complex experimental systems through processes of institutional succession. For government researchers still reeling from decades of budget cuts and personnel losses, the looming prospect of future contractions has become embedded within these experimental systems themselves. In Dennis's later published work, the growing agencies of nonhuman actors increasingly betrayed his own shrinking sense of control. By the time I began visiting Date Creek with him in 2013, Dennis and his collaborators were devoting far more attention to the long-term effects of pest outbreaks, tree diseases, and other agents of forest change further removed from human intervention than they had been when the research forest was first established. Whenever we talked about the earliest years of the research forest, including the original partial cutting experiment for which Dennis and a colleague had established the space, Dennis consistently downplayed the notion that the founding of Date Creek had been part of an explicitly political project. Regardless of how he contextualized the beginning of experimental work in Date Creek, though, the mere fact of its persistence had allowed it to help some researchers to make political points through their work. At minimum, it had allowed a handful of people to keep living in northwest British Columbia, and had given dozens of others a reason to visit for extended stays. More subtly, the relative stability of the research forest had also allowed many of these researchers to present their own well-tended experiments there as evidence of the broader value of long-term research. By leveraging their own ongoing forest succession experiments in Date Creek to call attention to *Dothistroma* needle blight and other emergent agents of change, Dennis and Kristen pointedly underlined the fact that the embodied knowledge and collaborative relationships that they relied on to generate new questions were themselves subject to uncertain futures.[6]

In chapter 1, I explored how environmental scientists in northwest British Columbia have negotiated the ambiguities facing their professional futures by framing aging research and planning documents as pieces of a shared history. As the dilemmas of inheritance surrounding Date Creek make clear, though, the strategies rural researchers have developed for coping with a shrinking state encompass far more than public citations of old documents. Outside in the forest, this aspirational labor continually overwrites what one might interpret from a conventional instruction in technique. In the decade and a half since the BC Forest Service closed its local office in Smithers and began to contract across the province, new questions of belonging have come to inhere in research forests like Date Creek and other spaces of experimental forestry. How could anyone hope to "pass on" land that they did not own? If not the land itself, then what exactly was being transferred through the intergenerational engagements that I witnessed there? Perhaps most urgently, how could anyone allow themselves to treat a research forest as an object of emotional investment, particularly when government agencies have continually subjected them to abrupt funding cuts and closures whenever a new administration has seen fit?

Science in a Heritable Space

For most of the twentieth century, the BC Forest Service treated its experimental stations as proving grounds for nascent industrial planting, periodically establishing new sites throughout the province as industrial forestry expanded northward (Franklin 1989; Hansen et al. 1995; McClellan et al. 2000).[7] Most, like Date Creek, encompassed little infrastructure beyond a few metal signs, and were situated close enough to active logging sites to allow researchers to access them via existing roads. ("That's *hard* silviculture—plantation, even-aged management, which trees are best. It's an experiment by geneticists," Dennis once volunteered as we passed by one such sign near the southern entrance to Date Creek.) Several of these older sites were still visible throughout the Kispiox Valley. In the years after my first visits to Date Creek, I eventually discovered a small handful of historic research forests that had been equipped with their own office buildings, sleeping quarters, and training facilities. As I came to know other forestry scientists who had worked at these sites, however, I soon learned that all of them, no matter how elaborate or seemingly established they became, had been subject to sudden funding cuts and personnel reassignments.

The Aleza Lake Forest Experiment Station (later known as Aleza Lake Research Forest), roughly four hundred kilometers east of Date Creek, was initially established in 1924 as the first long-term forest research installation in northern British Columbia (figures 3.9 and 3.10). Log cabins built for work camps during the Great Depression housed dozens of technicians and researchers who organized planting and growing experiments at the site until its first closure in 1939. The same buildings housed yet another generation of researchers from 1957 until 1964 (figure 3.11). While most of the early research sites established by the Forest Service in southern British Columbia were situated to allow for easy commutes from the metropolitan centers where most government personnel lived, Aleza Lake was among the first long-term government research facilities in western Canada to effectively force its employees to relocate for their work. At the time, the remote location of the research station proved to be a galvanizing force (figure 3.12). With few other options for entertainment and socialization, Aleza Lake's staff and visitors had little choice but to spend their nonworking hours hiking, hunting, and fishing in the surrounding forests (Revel 2007). Many developed close friendships that would endure far longer than the station itself. When the provincial government summarily abandoned the Aleza Lake station a second time and began dismantling its buildings in 1964, a technician who had worked at the site purchased the main cabin for himself, hauled it by tractor to a nearby town, and lived in it with his family until he died over three decades later.

The handful of informal memoirs from retired foresters that the BC Forest Service has published to document the "histories" of Aleza Lake and other northern research outposts are almost all written as cheerful frontier stories, full of unexpected encounters and obstacles to be overcome. Some of the researchers who worked at these places, however, eventually came to reflect on their attachments to them through stories of abandonment and loss. As Kristen was beginning to take over Dennis's work in 2017, I met a technician who began his research career at Aleza Lake after moving to northern British Columbia from England in 1957. By himself, he had continued to collect data there for several decades after the second closure of the experimental station in 1964 (figure 3.13). It was not until nearly three decades later that he was able to lobby the then newly constructed University of

Northern British Columbia to reopen the research forest altogether in 1993. When I met with him at his home near Prince George nearly two decades after his retirement, he wistfully credited his brief period of formal work at Aleza Lake rather than his more than thirty subsequent years of employment with the BC Forest Service for establishing his sense of connection to the landscapes of the northern interior. After all, he reminded me, he had had to seek out university funding to reopen the site. Perhaps his lifelong employer simply could not see either his research or himself as objects of long-term investment.

By the time the Date Creek Research Forest was opened in 1992, the rapid expansion of industrial logging throughout northern British Columbia and the growing presence of provincial government ministries in the region had rendered much of the region substantially less "remote" for the scientists who sought to work there. While nearly all of the researchers and support staff who worked at the Aleza Lake Research Forest from the early to mid-twentieth century were new arrivals to the northern interior, several decades of Euro-Canadian migration into places like Smithers and Prince George meant that what counted as a "convenient" field site by the 1990s had steadily shifted as well. For Dennis and his collaborators, the sudden availability of Forest Service funding for a research forest in the Upper Skeena offered an opportunity to secure a space for research close to where they already lived. If Aleza Lake's scientists initially treated their time at the research station as temporary encounters with an unruly frontier, the scientists who began moving to Smithers at the end of the twentieth century set their sights on more distant horizons.[8]

The duration of an experiment alone, generations of BC Forest Service personnel learned throughout the twentieth century, was rarely reason enough for the provincial government to keep a site open. By the end of the 1960s, the broad transition toward clear-cut logging in provincial forestry policy meant that most of the long-term experiments running at sites like Aleza Lake were no longer relevant to industrial forestry. In order to keep Date Creek open long enough for intergenerational inheritance to become conceivable, Dennis and his initial collaborators reasoned, the site would have to be tethered to more elusive goals. For dozens of researchers working throughout the province, the international attention generated by the War in the Woods and an accompanying chorus of academic criticism provided a critical opening. Funds dispersed through the Forest Service's new Watershed Restoration Research program were used to establish dozens of new experimental sites throughout the northwest corner of the province. Other scientific initiatives explicitly charged new sites with pursuing political goals. By the middle of the decade, both the provincial and federal Forest Services had incorporated alternative harvesting and habitat research programs into cooperative land management projects organized with First Nations governments all over British Columbia.

Initially, many of the scientists involved in these projects worked to cultivate long-term attachments by explicitly presenting their experimental sites as spaces of reconciliation.[9] The Long Beach Model Forest, established as a partnership between Forestry Canada and the Nuu-Chah-Nulth First Nation, promised "to 'model' scientifically the best practices of a more sustainable forestry" (Davis 2009, 36) in Clayoquot Sound on Vancouver Island—one of the original epicenters of War in the Woods. By framing their research as performances of exemplary management practices, however, the silviculturists, botanists, and other scientists who organized experiments there found themselves repeatedly criticized by some Nuu-Chah-Nulth and other area residents for presenting their experimental work as justifying jurisdictional claims for policy-making for the broader region. In the eyes of loggers whose livelihoods were threatened by severe harvesting restrictions imposed in the model forest in response to scientists' recommendations, the researchers were not long-term residents building meaningful attachments to the area, but were simply "some people play[ing] around in the woods on the federal payroll" ("Model Forest No Help to Alberni-Clayoquot," *Alberni Valley Times*, November 4, 1996, quoted in Davis 2009, 47).

As the War in the Woods entered new venues over the course of the 1990s, most of the provincial government's attempts at direct engagement were foundering over questions of commercial access and long-term jurisdiction. Experimental spaces framed by more abstract goals, however, were flourishing. Following examples set by the US Forest Service amid other anti-clear-cutting protests then raging throughout the American Pacific Northwest (Prudham 2005), the BC Forest Service began funding large-scale studies of selective harvesting in turbulent regions throughout the province in the 1990s as part of the Alternative Silvicultural Systems program. Unlike with the Model Forest program, however, Date Creek and the other sites established under the Alternative Silvicultural Systems program would stand as tacit endorsements of emergent policy initiatives without explicitly committing their users to a particular political project. By articulating their critiques of provincial land use policies through scientific models of tree growth and succession, Dennis and his collaborators reinforced the government's claim to the physical space of Date Creek even as they undermined other government researchers' analyses that had been used to justify large-scale clear-cutting in the first place.

During the final years of the twentieth century, a sea change in the tenor of conservationist politics appeared to be taking place across northwest British Columbia. By the time the New Democratic Party lost its leadership of the provincial parliament in 2001, the BC Liberal Party had actively courted racial animus by publicly decrying the newly centralized treaty process and accusing conservation activists of destroying the provincial economy (Rossiter and Wood 2005). For Dennis and dozens of other scientists who had only just begun building their careers in the region, the infrastructures they had established for their experimental work swiftly retreated from public attention. Only loosely coupled in the collective memory of the northwest to the blockades that had helped bring them into being, Date Creek and a small handful of other research sites like it have nevertheless fostered new kinds of attachments as their users continued to age. As Dennis and Kristen's careful, repetitive work in the forest shows, the sites eventually came to offer the researchers who tended to them a place from which to ponder their own roles in possible conflicts to come.

Walking Lessons

Reflecting on her first few months as the head of the research forest, Kristen admitted to me that she sometimes struggled to distinguish her inheritance of Dennis's position with the Forest Service from her inheritance of Date Creek itself. At times, she addressed her attachment to the space as both a weight and a point of pride. "Now I'm the head of Date Creek," she offered resolutely, "so it's my life." Other times, she quietly acknowledged the research forest's potential for future abandonment by framing her inheritance from Dennis in terms of "his data and ideas." The future of Date Creek would be as a multimodal transfer; she was not the only one, she suggested, to have inherited something of Dennis's work there. Some of the smaller experiments that Dennis's colleagues had begun under the Alternative Silvicultural Systems program had already been reproduced and modified elsewhere. Other researchers who began their careers in Smithers had adopted some of the tenets of Dennis's work as they struck out on their own. Some had returned to Date Creek periodically to coauthor new studies with Dennis, or had invited him to their own university departments or government centers for extended stays. Nearly all of them, however, shared their data with Dennis to show how their efforts to adopt his theories were playing out in other research forests around the world. The more I learned about these entangled conceptual worlds, the more it felt as though the experimental system encompassing secondary structure research had long since transcended the forest itself.

In myriad ways, my interlocutors' interactions with the forest itself forced me to consider their labor against more distant horizons. Initially, I had received Dennis's reading lessons as a nostalgic form of what Charles Goodwin (1994) refers to as "professional vision": a careful training of discernment and gesture, accompanied in this case, perhaps, by a fear that the structures that gave meaning to the techniques were themselves about to disappear. As I became preoccupied with the drama surrounding Kristen's potential succession, it grew increasingly difficult to imagine the future of the research forest without dwelling on the knowledge that would be lost, the histories that would be occluded, and the many experiments that in all likelihood would be abandoned there. Time and again, though, Dennis, Kristen, and Sanjit patiently reframed these anxieties. Much of what Dennis hoped to pass on as he took his leave from Date Creek was diffuse: gestures and ways of moving that Kristen and others would learn, then refashion; modes of historicizing objects within the forest that added texture to the labor of taking measurements and notes. Together, the shared gestural and narratological experience of fieldwork was as much a part of Kristen's inheritance as the grand partial cutting experiment that created the forest, or any of the experiments that had been established there since. And yet the long-term experiment was anterior to all of these things. In order to keep these inheritances alive, the experiment would have to be maintained, and remeasured every decade or so, inevitably with informal assistants who would require their own reading lessons in turn. Like any proper inheritance, Kristen's would largely lie in the mundane labor of repetition.

Taken together, Dennis's reading and walking lessons revealed an experimental grid shot through with traces of meaning. "It's very hard to make sure that everyone who comes in here to take measurements receives the same level of training," Dennis complained as he patiently guided us through each step. With each poorly tied ribbon and misplaced tag, he reminded us, the likelihood diminished that another researcher would be able to return for follow-up measurements years later. His commitment to repeatability, though, was not quite the same as insisting that everyone work the same way. Over time, it became apparent that Dennis saw our exercises against a broad and deeply personal continuum of techniques. As a young man in the 1970s, working summers as a consultant for corporate logging firms, he had learned to maximize his efficiency even as he taught himself visual cues for recognizing tree species at a distance. During his first years with the Forest Service, he had spent months coordinating painstaking sample plot measurements as part of his informal initiation into full-time government work. The concepts he had learned through establishing plots and returning to measure them were impossible to separate from these bodily skills.[10] Take long strides, Dennis insisted, and count every other step. After taking a compass bearing, pick a tree roughly twenty meters away (assuming one could see that far) and walk straight for it. Climb over deadfall, wade through bogs, but unless the path becomes completely impassable, never leave your imaginary line.

By each afternoon that first summer, Sanjit, Kristen, and I would settle into a routine. We guessed which trees our survey would require us to measure as we approached a still-to-be-marked grid point. We then swiftly moved in a clockwise circle, calling out measurements and species names (see figure 3.4). Between grid points, we counted our steps, challenging each other to maintain an even stride. Over time, we began noticing grid point marking plates from farther and farther away, and intuiting where missing plates might have been torn away by downed branches. Planning our routes in expanding loops around the truck, we pushed toward goals of greater efficiency. We fell into a relentless rhythm: moving, counting, and moving again. Seven grid points before lunch time. Eight more before calling it a day.

Wary of the numbing allure of speed and efficiency on new recruits to the measurement crew, Dennis encouraged us to slow down and learn as we worked. Time and again, he pointed out the small whorls of bark on a lodgepole pine and the narrow blisters bulging under the skin of a subalpine fir. Moving between grid points, he repeated Latin names for moss, trunk-clinging lichens, and shrubs. The common names, he occasionally forgot. Seeing me stumble and grasp the spine-covered stem of a devil's club, Dennis called out with a wily grin: "*Oplopanax horridus!*" My hand still red and swollen a week later, the name echoed in my head.

As the summer went on, Kristen offered new reading lessons, too. Confronting a cluster of juvenile trees in a small patch of sunlight one morning, she showed me how to estimate their ages by counting the branches jutting out at regular intervals along their trunks. "It's usually just one major branch per year," she assured me. It was Dennis, though, who projected his stories deepest into the past. Earlier in the summer, he pointed out a

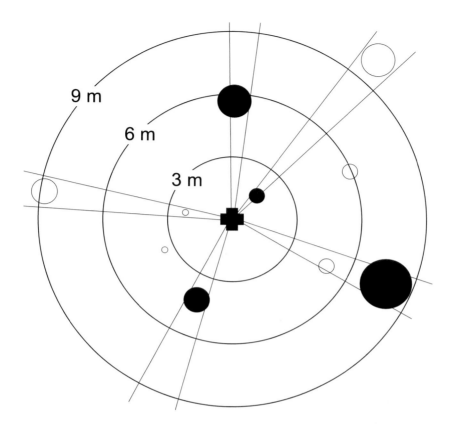

FIGURE 3.4 A schematic depiction of a prism plot. The cross denotes the center of the survey, and the concentric circles denote three-meter-distance intervals from the plot center. Based on the prism used for this particular survey, each tree stem depicted by a darkened circle would be counted as "in" (and thus its diameter would be measured and recorded), and each stem depicted by an empty circle would be counted as "out" (and would thus be ignored).

streak of blackened wood poking out from a scar on an enormous cotton-wood.[11] "This one was big enough to survive the fire that created this forest," he intoned, referring to the sprawling forest fire that had leveled the Kispiox Valley in 1855 (see Parminter 1983; Sterritt et al. 1998, 194–242).[12] According to ecologists, the fire had opened space for the enormous hemlock and western red cedar that dominated the landscape in the twentieth century—the same trees that eventually lured industrial loggers deep into the Kispiox Valley in the 1980s. Even as Dennis encouraged us to imagine fire scars and skid trails as constituting the history of a singular space, he framed his lessons around fungible skills.

As Dennis frequently reminded us, the speed and precision of our movements would affect more than just the accuracy of the original selective harvesting experiment and the ability of other field-workers to update it in the future. Every hour or two, another experimental plot would appear beneath us as we stood to rest between grid points. Once we noticed the first ribbon, we scanned around our feet to find the corners of the plot. Succession experiments focused on shrubs and saplings might occupy four square meters of forest floor; moss and lichens, a single square meter. Larger "woody debris" plots could span up to twenty-five square meters of rotting trunks and branches, all marked with a profusion of blue ribbons denoting to returning researchers which pieces to measure and which to ignore. The first time I encountered a lichen competition plot along the corner of a separate plot for woody debris, I remarked on the puzzle in my notes: "grids within grids within grids!" Since their plots were calibrated to the gradients of shade crafted by Dennis's original experiment, dozens of experimentalists would come to depend on Kristen's repetitive labor whether she knew what they were up to or not. Over time, perhaps, they would come to conceptualize the continuance of their work through succession and inheritance as well.

Inheriting Experiments

Jacques Derrida spent much of the last decade of his life thinking through the ambiguous and often contradictory compulsions attending the inheritance of grievances and goals. Driven in part by the collapse of Soviet communism as well as by his own advancing age, he repeatedly turned his attention to unfolding scenes that seemed to defy resolution, treating each new failure of governance or outburst of violence as a legacy that would be transferred between generations with no explicit instructions attached.[13] In *Specters of Marx*, Derrida collapses the progenitors of these problems into the figure of the ghost—a paradoxical absent presence who cannot be directly addressed, but whose injunctions nevertheless carry an irresistible, if ambiguous, force.[14] By continually returning his attention to the lingering voices of departed figures, Derrida underlines the exhausting labor of crafting a sense of self after a critical companion has taken their leave.

While the forms of life that link scientists together around shared projects are typically described through idioms of collaboration, experimental research relies on diverse forms of companionship. This is particularly true for long-term experiments in rural areas and other settings where personnel are few and processes of replacement are never guaranteed. Less transactional than the commitments that define the formal limits of collaboration, companionship also entails meeting expectations that have been left unsaid. By urging his readers to think of the inheritance of knowledge not as a positive accumulation but as a practice of anxious projection, Derrida frequently treats intellectual legacies—including the legacies he inherited from Nietzsche, Heidegger, and others, as well as the legacy he himself has already passed on to others—primarily as injunctions to recognize and negotiate the seemingly contradictory dependencies that arise from attempting to think with others (see also Das 2007; Brandel 2016).[15] At times, these injunctions may manifest as an urge to articulate a vision of a collective future in the language of an imagined, coherent past. At other times, the injunctions that comprise an inheritance are taken up in the quieter labor of learning how to live one's own life. Like the shifting texture of companionship itself, the directness of the "address" relaying the injunction "hesitates," too, Derrida writes, "between address as experience (is not learning to live experience itself?), address as education, and address as taming or training" (1994, xvi–xvii).

Treating intergenerational transfers of long-term field experiments as processes of intellectual inheritance underlines a critical facet of Derrida's work on legacy: the everyday experience of inheriting involves few opportunities for grandiloquent statements, but rather demands countless hours of mundane, repetitive labor. "There would be no future without repetition," Derrida (1998, 80) bluntly insists in *Archive Fever*. It is in these repetitions that the lasting entailments of companionship are finally affirmed, he suggests, and where the past ambitions of others are made into the substance required for working on democracy "to come" (Derrida 2005b). Throughout his later work, Derrida finds in companionship not an escape from or disavowal of the political, but a foundation for politics itself. "To whom, finally, would an obligation of justice ever entail a commitment, one will say, and even be it beyond law and beyond the norm," Derrida writes in *Specters of Marx*, "to whom and to what if not to the life of a living being?" (1994, xx). In *The Politics of Friendship*, Derrida elaborates the intimate obligations that impel political action by routing them through the language of kinship. "The concept of politics rarely announces itself without some sort of adherence of the State to the family," he writes, "without what we will call a schematic of filiation" (2005a, viii).

For Samir Haddad, each of these forms of intimacy composes a part of the project of making the self, a project that underlies the work of both intellectual criticism and everyday political activity. "Through his emphasis on the role of self-critique in democratic practice," Haddad argues, "Derrida can be read as asserting that participants in democracy must inherit if they are to pursue its promise. Democracy is thus not only inherited; it also contains the injunction to inherit, and democratic action requires an active response to this injunction" (2013, 4). A similar point could be made about the intergenerational demands of collaborative research. As Kristen learned to attune herself to the impositions and affordances that Date Creek offered to the scientists who worked within it, Dennis's decades-long efforts to keep Date Creek open through broad shifts in the provincial government's funding prerogatives and political sensitivities offered her a useful model of self-critique. Not unlike the inheritors of explicitly political projects, in other words, the scientists assigned to manage long-term research projects also faced ambiguous injunctions that would have to be worked through if they wished for their experiments to remain workable in the present.

In some sense, all scientists eventually learn to treat their own epistemic inheritances as incitements not only to repeat, but also to defer and forget.[16] In his early philosophical work, Hans-Jörg Rheinberger borrows from Derrida the term "historiality" to present his own approach as a hermeneutics of scientific narration. Part of asking what "history" means to a scientist, he insists, means first asking what "history" is. "Are they looking at a past that is the transformation of another, foregoing past;" he asks, "or are they looking at a past that is the product of a past deferred, if not of a presence?" (1994, 65). In much the same way that anthropologists like Angela Garcia (2014) and Clara Han (2020) have shown how dispossession reveals the shape and limits of inheritance, Rheinberger demonstrates how epistemic objects destabilize as relationships between experimental practice and formal representation are forced to change. "The retrospective view of the scientist as a spontaneous historian is not only concealing but in many respects also revealing," he argues. "It reminds us that an experimental system is full of stories, of which the experimenter at any given moment is trying to tell only one" (1997, 185). And yet for forest ecologists coping with the uncertainties of replacement, telling even a single story requires confidence in its eventual unfolding. The reading lessons that Dennis offered as we worked in the forest underlined this challenge: How was a researcher meant to narrate the history of epistemic thing while its futures remained mired in doubt?

Returning to *Specters of Marx* a quarter century after the book was first published helps to underscore Derrida's elegiac tone. Many of the democratic projects that had only just been abandoned at the time Derrida was writing have long since given way to the numbing uncertainties of structural adjustment. As chapters 2 and 4 of this book show in detail, Gitxsan and Gitanyow people have endured far more destabilizing uncertainties than most of the White residents of northwest British Columbia. For post-Soviet citizens and First Nations activists alike, scholars have argued in different ways, neoliberal reforms have slowly replaced much of the frustration attending these earlier failures with a resigned sense of diminished possibility (see Bell 2023; S. J. Collier 2011). At times, though, by explaining these changing attitudes through recourse to collective narratives of decline and abandonment, some critical work has inadvertently obscured the forms of companionship that can emerge around the projects of past regimes. Reexamined as the slow unfolding of an intellectual inheritance, an aging scientist's acquiescence might yet become their inheritor's call to arms.

A new spokesperson, Dennis might have gently added, can also push their inheritance into the future by experimenting with what later audiences may be willing to hear. If the Date Creek Research Forest was originally meant to make the "sovereignty of science" (Helmreich 2009, 141) visible in the contested Kispiox Valley, its continuing existence after nearly three decades owes much to its apparent detachment from the new narratives of conflict that had come into circulation in the years since it was founded. As Kristen, Dennis, Sanjit, and I worked our way through Date Creek together in 2013 and reflected on its possible futures, the Gitxsan-led blockades that had helped to bring the research forest into being entered our conversations only through tangents. Talking as we worked or on the long drives to and from the site, Dennis patiently answered my questions about the blockades—what he remembered of particular confrontations, or how he had been received while presenting his initial experimental plan to the Gitxsan chiefs whose territories encompassed the research forest. As I corresponded with Kristen shortly after she took up Dennis's post, however, she reflected on these earlier exchanges with an altogether different sense of urgency.

In 2016, the Forest Service had directed Kristen to begin her own consultations following the precedent-setting decision in *Tsilhqot'in Nation v. British Columbia*, the first modern legal action in British Columbia to result in an award of Aboriginal title (see Borrows 2015). Not only had the decision reaffirmed the Supreme Court of Canada's ruling in its *Haida* decision nine years earlier—namely, that the provincial government had a duty to consult parties with outstanding Aboriginal title claims to lands subject to forestry developments (Olynyk 2005)—but the award also provided forestry companies active throughout the province with a strong reminder that lands where Aboriginal title had been successfully claimed would no longer be subject to the provincial government's Forest Act. The *Tsilhqot'in* decision also established a much stricter interpretation of the provincial government's duty to consult than the interpretation put forth in *Delgamuukw and Gisday'wa*, which took the normal functioning of the forestry industry and the general application of provincial forestry laws as sufficient grounds for eschewing consultation (Mancell, Waatainen, and Hunter 2014). With dozens of land claims and treaty cases still pending throughout British Columbia, the decision reminded Forest Service personnel that practically any forested area in the province might eventually be removed from provincial control. Persuading the hereditary chiefs, band governments, and other groups and individuals who would then finally have decision-making power over these landscapes to stay in dialogue with the White researchers who had come to feel invested in these spaces, Kristen knew, would require an altogether different approach to listening and learning—one that even the most well-intentioned senior Forest Service researchers had never been forced to develop.

The walks and conversations that she had begun having with Gitxsan custodians, Kristen admitted as we caught up in 2018, were still tentative. "I'd like to think that people [in the Forest Service] are realizing it's the right thing to do," she reflected to me doubtfully. Her initial meetings with the Gitxsan custodians about the future of Date Creek, she told me, had probably been far more interesting for her than for any of her new interlocutors. Still only dimly aware of Dennis's own attempts at engagement during the initial establishment of the research forest decades earlier, Kristen saw refashioning the process as central to her new role. Her inheritance contained no instructions for moving forward; only the injunction that she somehow proceed.

Going Home

Already more than half a decade into her job as the head of Date Creek as I write this chapter in 2022, Kristen's inheritance has indeed become an all-consuming project of professional self-creation. The research forest has secured her place in the northwest, for a time at least, and offered her a place from which she can speak as both a full-time government researcher and citizen activist. Even as the formal transfer of control over the space in 2017 indelibly underlined her professional filiation with its former manager, the everyday work of actually becoming Dennis's replacement has called forth new vectors of differentiation. Despite working alongside Dennis as his collaborator for nearly a decade and, after 2016, another year as his replacement-in-training, Kristen evinced little of the nostalgia that Dennis often expressed for the way that the Forest Service had been run in the past. When Kristen began her career in Smithers, the wide-scale restructuring that had unmoored so many researchers in the region was already several years underway. Learning to navigate the hierarchies and conventions of government work after spending nearly a decade at a small, independent research center had been challenging, she admitted, but her basis of comparison was different. She was pleasantly surprised, for instance, that the Forest Service consented to let her begin the job several months before Dennis formally left. "Overlap hardly ever happens in government anymore," she cheerfully noted.

When I spoke to Kristen in early 2018, five years after we first met, it had been almost a year since Dennis's retirement. Perhaps because the prospect of replacement had remained doubtful for so long, she had gotten used to Dennis outlining his hopes and plans for the projects at Date Creek in resigned and speculative tones. More likely, though, she suspected, the indirect nature of Dennis's instructions reflected a permanent sense of restraint. As was often the case while she had been working as Dennis's collaborator at the BVRC, the advice she received from Dennis upon becoming his nominal replacement was offered modestly and without expectation. "Lots of times, Dennis just seemed happy that someone was taking things over. He wasn't trying to control things." Rather than telling her which of his projects he hoped she would continue, he often simply waited to be asked. "When I needed input," she reflected, "then he could fill in that more senior scientist role." At a time when so many researchers had left or were leaving their government jobs, she admitted that she felt compelled to fulfill as many of his beleaguered ambitions as she could. One of Kristen's friends in Smithers summed it up for me with a sigh: "Survivor's guilt."

Even during my own modest work alongside Dennis in Date Creek, I frequently found myself awaiting explicit instructions that never arrived. Perhaps like some of the dozens of other part-time collaborators who had spent time with Dennis there over the years, though, I eventually came to understand that these forms of waiting and thinking played a small part in keeping the site's long-term experiments alive. By the end of September 2013, five months after our grand remeasurement of Date Creek had begun, snow had already crept down from the peaks around the Kispiox Valley and had left its first dusting on the roofs and roads of Smithers. The aspen trees around the Bulkley Valley slipped from green to yellow to leafless within three short weeks; from one week to the next, the days were growing shorter by more than half an hour. Not yet appointed to be Dennis's official successor, Kristen had her own commitments to attend to before winter set in. With predictions of heavy snow looming in the extended forecast, she energetically solicited volunteers to help her collect the final soil samples of the season before the changing weather rendered inaccessible another field site she visited for her work, a second-growth forest 200 kilometers southeast of Date Creek. In a small upstairs office at the BVRC, Sanjit had already been busy for weeks, too, tabulating the hundreds of pages of handwritten notes and figures recorded on our trips. By the time the valley began to fill with snow in early October, he would be ready to begin the first full-scale calculations with the data we had collected throughout the summer.[17]

Hemmed in by days of freezing rain, Dennis and I made our final field trip of the year together in early October, aiming to pick up the last few plots that had been missed in other sections and begin a survey of wind damage that he and Kristen would conclude the following year—yet another experiment that Kristen would continue into the coming decades. "Too bad we didn't bring along a bottle of scotch to toast the end of the field season, huh?" Dennis smiled. As we finished the final plot and returned to the truck to exchange clipboards, Dennis coached me through the methods that would guide our next count. "First things first, you gotta determine whether a downed tree is actually windthrow or whether it just fell down on its own. Wind isn't the only thing that kills trees out here, you know." We took a few steps into the treatment unit closest to the truck. Rotting hemlock trunks were strewn everywhere (figure 3.5). "Anything with moss on it was probably knocked down in the big windstorm a few years ago," Dennis assures me. "We don't need to worry about those—we're just looking for the new stuff." Previous years' measurements were spray-painted and tagged. Flipping to a printout in his clipboard, he located our unit. "At this heading, this big guy should be already marked. There it is: number 115. Let's keep moving." Eyes fixed on our compass, we wound north and then south through our treatment unit in fifty-meter increments, measuring only the trees that fell across our narrow line. Without any fanfare or much sense of closure, one experimental reading of the forest ended, and another abruptly began.

FIGURE 3.5 A particularly daunting series of obstacles within the windthrow study area. Photo by author.

Despite his insistence that ecology was a discipline for relativists, Dennis was not immune to feelings of loss. As we hoisted each other up and over downed trunks and waded through the bogs and thickets separating each clearing, Dennis's reminiscences morphed into wistful speculation. We wondered together about succession patterns within the Kispiox Valley, and the future shape of clear-cutting along the Skeena. We guessed about the likelihood of future layoffs in research offices in Smithers and Victoria, and thought out loud about how other forest ecologists in Canada and elsewhere might eventually adapt, replace, or simply forget about Dennis's own published work on the relationship between shade levels and growth dynamics in temperate forests. Dennis mused at length about the changing fortunes of other senior researchers who, like him, were nearing retirement, and about the impending loss of their accumulated knowledge and skills as the provincial government continually refused to hire new researchers to replace them. We both worried after the fate of his experiments in Date Creek, and about the new generations of forestry researchers who might or might not choose to devote time, money, and energy to maintain its intricate plots. "It could be tremendously useful for some graduate students in the future if some university professors know it exists. There's a lot of old experiments . . . that are well taken care of for ten or fifteen or twenty or twenty-five years, and then they kinda fade away." Over time, Dennis reminded me, shifting to an unsentimental, matter-of-fact tone, the boundaries of research forests often simply fade from provincial management maps, leaving carefully tended stands open to roving industrial logging crews. If these spaces were not known through continual labor and refashioning, his remarks suggested, they would soon enough not be remembered at all.

Driving toward the bridge to Kispiox on our way back toward Smithers that night, we encounter no other drivers. As we cross onto asphalt and begin winding our way south toward Hazelton and Highway 16, Dennis reaches for the transmitter of our CB radio to let the Forest Service dispatcher in Smithers know that we are in for the evening. Along the banks of the Skeena, Gitxsan men in tall gaiters cast lines into the river while others with long-handled nets and gaff hooks wait downstream. The autumn run of coho salmon has just begun. In Moricetown Canyon, half an hour north of Smithers, all eyes are on the river. Wet'suwet'en and other fishers line gangplanks along the walls of the canyon, gaffing fifteen-pound coho as they struggle to leap their way up and over the cascading falls. Smithereens and Witset residents mingle along the sides of the highway, leaning out the windows of parked cars to watch the action in the river below. No one looks up as our truck rushes past.

FIGURE 3.6 A typical grid point label. Photo by author.

FIGURE 3.7 Fog rolls into a treatment unit gap. Photo by author.

FIGURE 3.8 Unidentified experimental plot markers. Photo by author.

FIGURE 3.9 Landscape near Aleza Lake (Aleza Lake Research Forest 1976).

FIGURE 3.10 Experimental plot close-up (Aleza Lake Research Forest 1935).

FIGURE 3.11 Aleza Lake Forest Experiment Station (Aleza Lake Research Forest 1936a).

FIGURE 3.12 Young Men's Forestry Training Program crew digging plumbing trench for research station (Aleza Lake Research Forest 1936b).

FIGURE 3.13 Harry Coates (Aleza Lake Research Forest 1969).

4

Consignment

Trails, Transects, and Territory without Guarantees

It was half past six in the morning, but Darlene Vegh, Alan, and I had already been up for two hours.[1] The fire we had built to stave off the early-autumn chill was dying down; the generator whined, charging our lanterns, satellite phones and GPS devices. Cheerfully, anxiously, we plotted the day's route on an enormous paper map spread out atop Vegh's firewood box. Moving back and forth between the map and a scattered stack of high-resolution satellite photos, we compared the shapes and locations of the logging roads depicted on the map to the pixelated brown lines winding through the photos, noting each inaccuracy spread out along our intended path. Every few minutes, Vegh glanced at her watch. "He was supposed to be here at 5 a.m.," she muttered. Catching my worried glance, Vegh smiled and shrugged. Alan, a White biologist who often performed contract-based mapping work alongside Vegh and other First Nations researchers, read through kilometer

FIGURE 4.1 Darlene Vegh annotates a topographic map in preparation for a transect walk.
Photo by author.

markers along our day's route as Vegh wrote them down and keyed them into her GPS device. Alan finished, paused, then slowly read through the list of points a second time. Gerry, the assistant who the Gitanyow Office of Hereditary Chiefs (GHC) had promised to send along for the day, still hadn't shown up.

At a quarter past seven, an old GMC Suburban lumbered into camp. From the passenger seat, a tall, gray-haired Gitanyow man stepped out, hastily stuffing canteens, a sweater, and bags of food into a small backpack before bidding his driver goodbye and turning to greet us. Smiling apologetically, Gerry admitted that he had misplaced the directions he had written down explaining the way to our meeting site near Cranberry Junction, a remote intersection of a highway and Forest Service road near the Nass and Cranberry Rivers. After finding the directions and already on his way to our camp, he had had to return to Kitwanga, a village over seventy kilometers south, when his driver reminded him that he had left the house without packing any protective clothing. Reaching into his backpack with another sheepish grin, he pulled out a heavy pair of bright white and neon yellow reflective overalls. "Couldn't find my hunting pants either, so I had to bring these. Worked as a flagger for a highway crew this summer. Better than nothing I guess."

After a fresh round of coffee and a few jokes, we returned to the stack of maps arrayed atop the firewood box and explained to Gerry the purpose of the project as we sketched out the day's route. As Alan pointed out each kilometer marker, road crossing, and incline, Gerry nodded along, occasionally asking after the names of particular roads or rivers. One challenge of working with such complicated maps, Alan admitted, was that many of the roads they depicted had long since been decommissioned. Several recently constructed logging roads, too, had yet to be incorporated into the government-authored shapefiles that the GHC used to compile their maps. Gerry's experience hunting bear and moose and picking mushrooms nearby had taught him how to move through the region, but like Alan, his awareness of the state of the area's roads and bridges was embedded in old memories and anecdotes. His eyes roving along the thick red line marking the route that we would follow for the next several weeks, Gerry gently chimed in with Gitxsan and English place-names as Alan described the landscape along the path. "I knew lots of moose used to be in there, eh? Quite a bit," Gerry offered. "Used to see them all in there." Poring over the map together, the two men cross-referenced each other's mental inventories with stories (figure 4.4 at the end of the chapter).

As the four of us shuffled around the dwindling campfire, Vegh patiently explained the broader project to Gerry. The TransCanada Pipelines (TCP) Corporation was planning to build a natural gas pipeline from northeast British Columbia to Prince Rupert, the main Pacific port city for the northern half of the province. A seventy-kilometer section of the proposed pipeline was planned to bisect the traditional territory of the Gitanyow—a Gitxsan people with separate band governments, hereditary chiefs, and traditional territories from the neighboring Gitxsan First Nation. As the company had done with more than twenty other First Nations band governments with active claims to territories along the proposed path, TCP officials had reached out to the GHC for their endorsement of the project. It was not clear what effect, if any, critical feedback from the GHC would have on the TCP project, Vegh admitted to Gerry, but the office had nevertheless accepted financial support from the company to perform their own research on the proposal as well.

As part of their evaluation, GHC staff had hired Vegh's team to map out an alternative path for the pipeline. "I just wanted to talk about the elephant in the room before we got started, you know," Vegh joked. Some younger assistants balked at the idea of accepting pipeline company money for their work, she admitted. Gerry simply nodded and smiled. As Alan and I began to pack the car with our supplies for the day, Vegh continued to explain the Gitanyow chiefs' "strategic" aims. The GHC'S initial proposal for an alternative pipeline route, she explained, was a kinked path, oriented primarily through clear-cuts and other previously developed areas, and curving away, as much as possible, from old-growth forests, rivers, and lakes. A tentative digital map of the path had been created by two full-time technicians employed by the GHC in Gitanyow reserve village. It was up to Vegh and her assistants, though, to "ground truth" this path in the field. It was also up to us to make the most out of our chance to gather new field data, Alan offered, now that support for major mapping projects had become so sporadic.

Ground truthing, Vegh explained to Gerry, was a laborious and physical process. For the next several weeks, we would be traveling along the entire length of the potential alternate path, describing the terrain, and noting any inconsistencies between the locations of objects and the categories of land cover depicted on our printed maps and the qualities of the land that we actually encountered. Unlike the exhilarating first wave of GPS-assisted trail mapping expeditions that had introduced Vegh and many other First Nations men and women to technical work in the 1980s and '90s, though, our group was to spend the next several weeks walking transects. By surveying the GHC-proposed route in transects—straight line segments along which we would fan out to find and count traces of animal activity, and, if we were extremely lucky, archaeological artifacts—we would avail ourselves to random encounters, and generate a statistical picture of the landscape in all of its heterogeneity.

Particularly for new assistants, the labor of ground truthing through transect mapping also meant becoming acquainted with documents and their attending institutional ecologies. As Gerry pointed to differently shaded lines and colored areas along the route, Vegh set down her device and carefully explained the GHC's system. "That's Gitanyow's land use plan, and that's an old-growth management area," she offered, following Gerry's roving finger with her eyes. The Gitanyow Strategic Land and Resource Plan (SLRP), an environmental management program generated collaboratively between the GHC and planners affiliated with the BC government, had been formalized only a few months prior to our trip. The plan, Alan acknowledged, was similar in structure to the Bulkley Land and Resource Management Plan (LRMP) and other land use plans produced throughout the province in the late 1990s. Unlike Smithers residents who invoked the Bulkley LRMP in "hallowed tones," though, Alan joked, the Gitanyow researchers who had helped to assemble the SLRP maintained no illusions about its long-term authority. Provincial government officials would almost certainly find ways to undermine the new plan as soon as it began to interfere with the ambitions of resource developers; it was important to take advantage of the document before these conflicts inevitably arose.

Our project, Vegh had explained the previous evening, was to be one of the first on the Gitanyow territories to utilize the new plan as its organizing framework. The finely detailed habitat sensitivity information, archaeological data, and environmental management goals outlined in the plan had been crucial to the efforts of GHC staff to chart out a potential alternative route for the pipeline. As a structure for continuing environmental monitoring efforts, the plan would also help to secure a place for the different data sets that Vegh and future researchers would accumulate while working in the field. Out in the field at that moment, though, the plan was equally vital. The many maps that had been generated during the preparation of the new plan provided substrates for conversation with new trainees—including trainees like Gerry, who readily admitted that he hadn't heard of the SLRP prior to arriving in camp that morning. Perhaps ruminating over the fact that the project we were about to begin together would likely be her last with the Gitanyow before she retired, Vegh politely ignored Alan's pleas for everyone to rush to the morning's first waypoint in order to make up for lost time. It was important, she told Gerry, that he feel comfortable asking questions. It was important for him to absorb each detail.

As Vegh returned to the land cover designations on the map, Gerry responded to her technical explanations with stories. "Oh yeah, there's some pretty old growth in there," Gerry offered, remembering a mushroom gathering excursion there years earlier as Vegh pointed to a nearby polygon. He talked about what he had found on that trip, and struggled to recall the name of the outlet creek that had led him to a particular grove. Vegh remembered the landscape around the grove, too, but in more immediate terms. "The only trouble is, we can't get in here without a helicopter," she laughed. Together, Gerry and Alan pieced together recent histories of infrastructure development across the territories. The destruction of a bridge along a branch of a primary Forest Service road had kept most hunters out of one particular region for over a decade. Moose scared away by the development of the original power line next to Highway 37 several decades earlier had moved back in, and were now so numerous that they had displaced the herds of caribou that had once lived there as well. Now that the old line was being decommissioned, the corridor along its path was "greening up" with dense, second-growth spruce forests. A new transmission line with a much wider right-of-way was being cleared along a new path; many moose were once again on the move. Her experiences with different projects had given Vegh a rich, if fragmentary, knowledge of changes across the Gitanyow territories. Like the chiefs whose office funded her mapwork, though, she insisted, her sense of the integrity of the territories as a whole was always in the back of her mind.

Rejecting Selection

The precise ways that fragmentary knowledge about traditional territories informs researchers' relationships to territorial wholes can be difficult to disentangle from how skirmishes over the meanings of territories have played out in Canadian courts. Whenever we discussed the legal contexts enframing a particular mapping project, the researchers I met in northwest British Columbia invariably had specific details from several of these skirmishes ready to hand. Only a few kilometers west of the temporary campsite that Vegh, Alan, Gerry, and I shared on the Gitanyow traditional territories, the traditional territories of the neighboring Nisga'a First Nation were perhaps the most visible of all First Nations–claimed landscapes in the province. For more than two decades after a case initiated by Nisga'a chief and politician Frank Calder had caused the Supreme Court of Canada to first recognize the prior existence of Aboriginal title throughout British Columbia, Nisga'a negotiators had made national headlines by forging a new path toward a comprehensive treaty agreement with the BC government (Blackburn 2005). The resulting final agreement—the first new treaty to emerge in the province since the mid-nineteenth century—recognized Nisga'a ownership over 1930 square kilometers of land. While the Nisga'a were granted territorial control over less than 10 percent of their original claim area, the fact that provincial government officials had also acknowledged a far broader "traditional territory" stretching 24,000 square kilometers had enabled diverse parties to celebrate the treaty as a symbol of territorial coherence (Sterritt 1998).[2] During the lead-up to the signing of the agreement, these celebratory citations eventually helped to draw dozens of other First Nations throughout the province into a newly centralized treaty-making process.

For a time, the Gitanyow chiefs invested hope for territorial coherence in the promise of a treaty as well. Aided by a young Gitanyow chief-in-training who had spent the prior decade assisting researchers for the original *Delgamuukw and Gisday'wa* trial with mapping work on the neighboring Gitxsan territories, the GHC had filed a transparency agreement, a negotiation framework, and a mapped statement of intent for their claim with the BC Treaty Commission (BCTC) within two years of the establishment of the commission in 1993. Like it had for nearly all of these groups, however, their process had quickly devolved. The fundamental flaw in the treaty negotiation process, Gitanyow negotiators argued, was the "land selection model," the province's preferred method for separating claims into small subregions in order to translate broad questions of ownership and jurisdiction into more localized issues of rights and title (Devlin 2009). While some province-wide First Nations governing bodies like the First Nations Summit and the Assembly of First Nations generally supported the centralized process, other groups that had been more supportive of direct action protests during the War in the Woods, particularly the Union of British Columbia Indian Chiefs, excoriated BCTC officials for forcing claimants to agree to the federal government's extinguishment of their broader claims in order to have a chance of receiving title for any lands whatsoever (Wood and Rossiter 2011).[3]

The very premise of the land selection model and its underlying principle of extinguishment, its critics argued, was rooted in a racist and logically flawed legal philosophy (Culhane 1998). Even as the Supreme Court of Canada had repeatedly affirmed the prior existence of Aboriginal title in the *Calder, Sparrow, Delgamuukw and Gisday'wa, Haida, Taku River Tlingit*, and *Tsilhqot'in* decisions, the government of British Columbia continued to assert that none of the lands in the province had been subject to sufficiently organized use to constitute prior ownership when British sovereignty had first been proclaimed over the region. Not only did First Nations claimants bear the burden of proof for establishing their underlying claims, provincial negotiators insisted, their opportunities to do so in court would remain predicated on the federal government's authority to extinguish these claims through its own legal and legislative processes—an insistence that British parliamentarians and legal experts had repeatedly warned the Canadian government was already damaging the moral legitimacy of the nation as a whole (Manuel and Derrickson 2015). Practically speaking, the land selection model had forced negotiating First Nations throughout western Canada to translate diverse concepts of land use, access, and stewardship into the discretely bounded, autochthonous model of territory preferred by government negotiators (Harris 2002; McCreary and Milligan 2014). In some places, these processes had already radically intensified disagreements between neighboring groups over the positions of boundaries and long-standing shared use agreements (Nadasdy 2017). The power that government officials wielded over competing claims, Vegh and other Gitxsan researchers lamented, had only increased as these arguments had grown more intense.

During the months leading up to our project, Vegh and her former colleagues occasionally shared stories with me about how the scope of their work had shifted after the BCTC grew entrenched. At times, their reflections suggested that the elusive possibility of outright control over territory had made it more difficult for First Nations leaders to recruit researchers to small mapping projects and other modestly framed endeavors. Perhaps paradoxically, though, a few acknowledged, the abrupt closure of this possibility had helped to reenergize Gitanyow land defense by forcing the chiefs to develop new modes of engagement. When Nisga'a leaders and the government of British Columbia signed their Final Agreement in 1998, nearly all of the territory outlined in the Gitanyow claim was recognized as Nisga'a traditional territory (Sterritt 1998). After complaints to the province about the Nisga'a agreement went unanswered, Gitanyow representatives suspended their own treaty negotiations and sued the BCTC for failing to negotiate in good faith (Gitanyow Hereditary Chiefs 2009; Krehbiel 2004; Peeling 2004).

Thanks to her confrontational work with the Gitxsan Strategic Watershed Analysis Team (SWAT) during the 1990s, Vegh had long been skeptical of government-led treaty-making processes. Like many researchers and activists who had joined land defense projects as *Delgamuukw and Gisday'wa* made its way through the provincial and federal courts, Vegh had seen her own day-to-day work perpetually reconfigured as government officials had responded to First Nations' demands for ownership and jurisdiction over their lands by promising new mechanisms for government-led consultation—mechanisms that prior to the *Haida* and *Taku River Tlingit* decisions in 2004, Vegh reminded me, had been only sporadically enforced (Olynyk 2005). By the late 2000s, most of the First Nations that had begun negotiating treaties with the BCTC had effectively come to reject the land selection model too, but had remained nominally enrolled in negotiations to prevent the provincial government from demanding the legal fees that they had accrued during the process—enormous sums that, for many negotiating groups, would have rendered their governments insolvent (Wood and Rossiter 2011).[4]

Like the GHC, though, Vegh had also developed new tools and techniques for engaging with territories in the absence of treaty-based promises—tools and techniques that had become increasingly crucial to her ability to treat mapping as a collective practice.[5] As we prepared to enter the forests near Cranberry Junction together in the autumn of 2013, her GPS devices, her field notebooks, and the data-coding system she first developed while leading field mapping exercises with SWAT helped to structure the territories as a space of temporary sanctuary. In different ways, each tool enabled Vegh to consign competing pressures to her peripheral vision and to focus on the demands of the day. Throughout the morning, she had gently urged Gerry to find a modest sense of focus for his own experience in the field as well. If Gerry had signed on to the project hoping for exciting discoveries, she warned with a laugh as we piled into Alan's minivan to head toward the day's first grid point, he was likely to be disappointed. But if he thought of the other mapmakers who had worked on the territories before us and the many who would come along after, it seemed to me, he might yet find his own reasons to keep working there as well.

Territory without Guarantees

The rise of developer-funded, contract-based mapping in northwest British Columbia has complicated First Nations researchers' efforts to invest their labor in collective projects. Among the many people living in the region who are critics of these new arrangements, the proliferation of contracts has brought into sharp relief the radically discordant timelines separating development project deadlines, ecological cycles, traditional governance processes, and the time required to train individual technicians. For Indigenous mapping experts who have come to depend on developer support to carry out new projects, though, the technological shifts required to engage in contract work have generated new political affordances. The digital mapping tools and techniques that make contract work possible have come to anchor a process of deferral that I call *consignment*.[6] Consignment combines the intentionality of a gesture embedded in a technological form—an audio recording of a story, a digital map of a grown-over hunting trail, a photograph of a soon-to-be-defaced site—with the ambiguous promise of deferred returns. Consignment is a way to safeguard possessions, borrow time, and generate small, temporary gains. While consignment does offer individual researchers a means of deferring their emotional investments in specific development consultations, it also entails considerable risk, since aspirations stored away may be lost or change form over time.

The sense of quiet patience that Vegh displayed during our time in the field together belied her acute awareness of the precariousness of her situation. Her individual capacity to halt the pipeline on technical terms was constrained from the outset by the brevity of her contract and by the narrowness of TransCanada's solicitation for input. Neither Vegh nor Alan expected the syncopated project timelines that were driving this dispersal to shift within their lifetimes. For First Nations offices throughout British Columbia, they admitted, relying on corporate support for countermapping had long ago become a fact of life. The rhythms of contract work kept my own ethnographic ambitions circumspect as well. When I first joined Vegh's mapping group several days after their project had begun, I feared that I would be lost playing catch-up, and that my engagement with the field of their work would be trapped in medias res. As I quickly learned, however, the project, like many others, had no clear beginning or end, but was rather defined by the limits of what the group could accomplish in a given day. Once the team located a section of their intended path, they chopped up the work into segments. In practical terms, working through transects made my own participation expendable, since any new assistant could simply take over wherever I left off. Gerry undertook the mundane labor and tacit activism inherent in the job without questioning directly the broader rationale of the project. Yet by entering the territory with experts long practiced at building maps and databases from the contributions of temporary assistants, Gerry's labor added new marks to a field long defined and sustained by these partial connections. Equal parts workplace and imperfect laboratory, the linked chain of forest transects we walked together kept the politics of pipelines in our peripheral vision even as Vegh trained her sights farther and farther ahead.

As I came to know numerous First Nations researchers who had begun their careers during the War in the Woods, I often heard the temporalities of fieldwork described in jarringly discordant terms. Building up viable land claims and functioning resource management offices, researchers liked to remind me, required many years of devoted labor. Yet the demands, and occasionally the financial support, of prospective developers emerged suddenly and at unpredictable intervals. Responding simultaneously to such pushes and pulls, they lamented, often felt like an insurmountable challenge. As trainers of field personnel, translators between chiefs and government officials, and authors of bureaucratic documents, however, researchers like Vegh were nevertheless responsible for ensuring a sense of continuity across many different spaces of political engagement. The fact that Vegh and many others now pursued this labor through contracts rather than as full-time employees of specific First Nations offices did not in itself lessen their sense of investment. It did, however, offer a persistent reminder of their mounting dependency on support from other researchers, even as it caused them to keep their broader designs on decision-making power firmly in check.

By the time I began working with Vegh, Alan, and Gerry on the Gitanyow territories, more than three decades had passed since the United Nations Rio Declaration on Environment and Development had helped to formalize the use of Indigenous knowledge in globally dispersed courts and policy-making venues (Agrawal 1995; Dove 2006; Sillitoe 1998). Since then, anthropologists have debated over how Indigenous researchers' experiences navigating these spaces have reshaped their individual subjectivities and collective aspirations. Inspired in part by their own professional experiences working with Indigenous groups on land claims research, treaty negotiations, oral history projects, and other collaborative endeavors, many anthropologists have focused on how these experiences have been mediated by specific technoscientific tools. At times, scholars have struggled to reconcile the tension between positivist, instrumental understandings of so-called traditional ecological knowledge and analyses emphasizing social damage and disenchantment. Many ethnographic accounts of Indigenous-led research have remained fixated on the apparently irreducible tension between Indigenous ways of knowing and engaging landscapes and the "abstracting" (Agrawal 2002) efforts of settler governments and other bureaucratic organizations to translate the products of this research into technical documents. Whether by following oral histories and experiential knowledge into planning documents and government databases (Houde 2007) or by cataloging the historical ruptures caused by the errant placement of lines on government maps (Bryan 2011; Chapin, Lamb, and Threlkeld 2005), though, scholars have typically given greater credence to the form of the documents and representational techniques at issue rather than to the social obligations and practical demands borne by the researchers involved.

Over the past three decades, the rapid professionalization of Indigenous-led environmental research has added increased urgency to Claudio Aporta and Eric Higgs's (2005) insistence on the "need for a new account of technology" in the shaping of these settings and encounters. Indeed, a steadily growing range of scholars and activists have begun to grapple with the elusive emancipatory potential promised by Indigenous-led mapping projects and their attending professional and political networks (Callison 2020; Cruikshank 2005; Whyte 2013; Thom 2009). Yet, despite growing scholarly sensitivity to the complex roles that technoscientific navigation and mapping tools have come to play within Indigenous forms of life, some anthropologists remain primarily concerned with the apparent threats these tools pose to the epistemologies they see undergirding these worlds. Throughout his ethnographic work and theoretical writings, Tim Ingold pointedly refuses to "translate" Indigenous concepts of territory into what he refers to as Western languages of space and power (see also Hirtz 2003; Rundstrom 1995). In their rush to produce synoptic portraits of landscapes and their inhabitants, Ingold argues, anthropologists and other social scientists have long favored discretely organized lines of inquiry, and thus eschewed the idiosyncratic forms of navigation, wayfaring, and storytelling through which individuals and groups have come to know their environments. "The more one reads into the land," he cautions, "the more difficult it becomes to ascertain with any certainty where substances end and the medium begins" (Ingold 2008, 8). For the people who live in "the field" of anthropological work, he surmises, "quotidian life is experimental through and through" (Ingold 2011, 15), and its study thus demands attention to embodied knowledge unique to particular people and locales.

In his recent work, Ingold's long-standing emphasis on embodiment and experience has transitioned into a nostalgia for the holism of trails, navigation, and other continuous forms of human-environment interaction. Rather than explicate how the shape of these interactions has been influenced by specific confrontations and material histories, however, Ingold locates these transformations in the postmodern rupture of a particular spatiotemporal form: the line. "Once the trace of a continuous gesture," he writes, "the line has been fragmented—under the sway of modernity—into a succession of points or dots" (Ingold 2007, 75). For Ingold, the "fragmentation" of the line introduced by mapping clashes with the boundlessness of "life" and its "meshwork of habitation" (103). In his earlier work, Ingold recognizes the inevitability of rupture in the practices and social relationships linking people with particular landscapes. "Skills are not transmitted from generation to generation," he argues, "but are regrown in each" (2000, 5). Yet by contrasting the ambiguities and fissures of "postmodern" representation with the immediacy and apparent continuousness of embodiment, Ingold tacitly endorses a troubling assertion: namely, that it is merely technologies of representation, and not actual forms of Indigenous life, that have been subject to rupture in the contemporary era.

By highlighting the exhaustive deliberateness, even awkwardness, of contract-based transect mapping and the contingent relationships that these projects call into being, I mean to offer a counterpoint to both the nostalgic and celebratory accounts of mapping and wayfinding that constitute much of the ethnographic literature. Mapping is *not* a "quotidian practice." As Darlene Vegh, Alan, Gerry, and I moved and mapped together on the Gitanyow territories, our work drew continuously on our individual skills and experiences, but always in highly selective ways. The outputs of mapping, whether material or semiotic, require similarly deliberate acts of curation. Depending on their audiences, Gitanyow mappers like Vegh might represent their territories as bounded, autochthonous spaces of Indigenous belonging, as the homes of their ancestors, or as "working environments" of scientific knowledge production (Kohler 2011; see also Fearnley 2020). Regardless of the vision of landscape at stake in each of these discussions, Vegh's reflections on mapwork invariably accounted, however tacitly, for an array of interests and perspectives. The multiple patrons who supported her work, she acknowledged, had complex, and sometimes conflicting goals. The assistants who accompanied her into the field varied from project to project, as well. Each one brought different technical skills, experiences on the land, and intensities of political interest and involvement to bear on the way they approached their tasks.

For mappers and ethnographers alike, the word *transect* carries different meanings. In First Nations resource management offices and treaty research centers, where field data are compiled into diverse maps and arguments, the transect is merely an environmental mapping technique. It is a mode of navigating space along straight lines; enumerating particular kinds of objects, including plant species, animal activity, and isolated remnants of human use and occupancy; and measuring each object's distance from an axis of travel (figure 4.2). Designed for rapid, quantitative cataloging and easy extrapolation, the uptake of transects and other surveying techniques during the last decades of the twentieth century by First Nations mappers mirrors other "statistical revolutions" that transformed ecological and archaeological field practice during the same period (see, e.g., Klassen, Budhwa, and Reimer/Yumḵs 2009; Lynch 1985; Webmoor 2005).

Perhaps just as significantly as their political and legal affordances, transect mapping techniques also offer practitioners alternative ways of attributing new meanings to territory in the wake of dramatic environmental change. Throughout northwest British Columbia, the rapid expansion of clear-cut forestry during the 1970s and '80s destroyed many of the original trails and culturally modified trees that were to serve as legal and symbolic anchors for emerging land claims and comanagement projects (Nicholas 2006). As numerous First Nations groups formed strategic (and often contentious) alliances with environmental advocacy groups in the decades to follow in an effort to push land claims into other legal domains, their reliance on data from biological and ecological field mapping projects steadily grew (Braun 2002; Wilson 1998; Dove 2006). Taken up within the scaffolding of ecological classification systems, transects became a way for First Nations resource management offices to generate "knowledge" about their territories even as the trails and historic sites that had previously grounded their claims were destroyed by the expansion of industrial logging. As the sense of momentum generated by the direct action protests of the War in the Woods has shifted in tone and form, the maps and data sets generated from transects have continued to offer purchase for Indigenous experts struggling to exert influence within evolving land management institutions.

The many contingencies that shape the meanings of research can be difficult to acknowledge—let alone negotiate—in spaces shaped by intractable conflicts. In many of these settings, arguments between would-be allies often hinge on temporal concerns, including disagreements over which terms of engagement should be considered first (or last). Writing amid the rise of Thatcherism in the United Kingdom, Stuart Hall famously chides adherents of structural Marxism for impoverishing their analyses of ideology by insisting on the determining influence of the economic "in the last instance," rather than exploring "the setting of limits" or "the defining of the space of operations" (1986, 43). Challenging his colleagues in the field

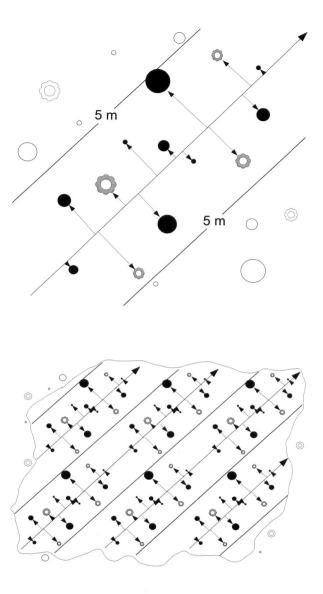

FIGURE 4.2 Schematic diagrams of a single transect line and a broader research area subdivided by multiple parallel transects. The large arrow denotes the direction of travel, and the darkened circles and flower icons denote objects counted within the transect study area (defined in part by their distance—small arrows—from the transect line). In both cases, nonshaded objects outside either the single 10-meter-wide study area or the broader research area would not be counted.

of cultural studies to consider a more contingent image of ideology and to theorize a vision of "marxism [*sic*] without guarantees," Hall insists that "we have to acknowledge the real indeterminacy of the political—the level which condenses all the other levels of practice and secures their functioning in a particular system of power" (43). By extrapolating Hall's warning to the forms of the political engaged and produced through contemporary Gitanyow mapwork, then, I seek in this chapter to invite similar indeterminacies to center stage.

The indeterminacy that Stuart Hall invokes while reimagining Marxian theory for a neoliberalizing United Kingdom bears much in common with Gerald Vizenor's conceptualization of survivance. Telling stories about possible futures, Vizenor suggests, and threading these stories through creative accounts of shared pasts was and remains fundamental to the ways his characters and interlocutors engage with otherwise unbearable uncertainties. "Survivance stories," Vizenor offers, "create a sense of presence and situational sentiments of chance" (2008, 11). Such stories also provide Indigenous peoples with crucial resources for situating themselves in social and environmental dramas that promise to keep playing out for centuries. In recent years, Indigenous science and technology studies scholars and their allies have hailed Vizenor's work while examining how the labor and imaginative horizons of activists come to be reoriented around interminable crises like environmental toxicity. "Ethics, rather than an anticipated result, is at the core" of the practices that Max Liboiron, Manuel Tironi, and Nerea Calvillo, for instance, describe as "slow activism" (2018, 342). In much the same way that relationships between isolated mapwork and broad territorial projects come to be mediated through processes of consignment, the gestures, modes of accounting, and forms of reason that these scholars highlight are often indirect in their affect and effects. Yet by eschewing the specific goals and quantitative thresholds around which conservation campaigns are typically organized, this practiced indirectness enacts a form of survivance by enabling practitioners to share indeterminacy itself.

Like survivance, consignment has become for researchers like Darlene a method for maintaining collaborative life. By focusing on the interrelations between the embodied and temporally unfolding labor of contract-based mapping and the mediative work required to weave map data into broader political goals, this chapter explores how Gitanyow mappers negotiate the contingencies of fieldwork in the wake of government downsizing. In particular, I examine how the day-to-day conduct of technical research sustains precarious relationships and knowledge-making practices by embedding them into easily reconfigurable media. In much the same way that scholars have expressed grave concerns over the increasing adoption of private land purchases as a strategic defense against appropriation elsewhere in Canada and the world (Kohlbry 2018; Pasternak 2015), First Nations mappers' increasing reliance on corporate support has provoked concerned discussions both on and off reserves over the potential complicities inherent in these partnerships (Veltmeyer and Bowles 2014). Nevertheless, the forms of transect mapping supported by these grants have enabled Vegh and other marginalized experts to compile substantial databases and manage more easily the partial contributions of a dispersed cast of assistants and activists. For project managers like Vegh, the logic of consignment enables her to help other leaders gather individual assistants' discrete enactments of agency into articulations of collective will by facilitating the construction of larger maps and temporally dynamic models as well as by enabling leaders to revisit these data at later dates. Such affordances made contract-based mapping a worthy enterprise, Vegh insisted, even if they temporarily required her to withhold more forceful critiques. This form of work also provided a simple structure that would enable other researchers to take over after she eventually takes her leave—whoever these other researchers might be.

From Territory to Transects and Back Again

In the three decades since the standardization of BCTC treaty negotiation protocols, the scope and structure of mapping and environmental fieldwork on traditional territories has undergone continuous change. As I show in chapter 2, numerous First Nations researchers who participated in countermapping and resource comanagement projects set into motion by the War in the Woods and by land claims litigation throughout western Canada during the 1980s and '90s have since built careers as GIS experts and traditional land use consultants. After the government of British Columbia drastically reduced funding for First Nations–led mapping and environmental monitoring work in the early 2000s and devolved regulatory powers and data-gathering responsibilities to developers in the subsequent decade, many of these people were forced to seek out new modes of engagement and new sources of financial support.

Since the mid-2000s, First Nations defensive fieldwork strategies have entered a new phase. Weary of divisive and overwhelmingly expensive treaty negotiation protocols that have as yet generated only a small handful of comprehensive agreements, nearly two dozen First Nations groups across British Columbia have begun constructing new incremental treaty agreements (Aboriginal Affairs and Northern Development Canada 2008). Typically comprising a combination of short-term revenue sharing agreements and collaborative roles (alongside government planners) in the production of new resource management and access plans, interim agreements have generated mixed feelings among First Nations communities (Alcantara 2013; A. Barker 2009). Some community leaders have welcomed the increase in timber and mineral production royalties and the simplification of consultation procedures (Blackburn 2005). Others have complained that the agreements serve only the interests of capital, securing for developers certainty over land access in the short term even as the environmental consequences of new developments and more substantive matters of First Nations rights and recognition are perpetually deferred (Pasternak 2017). Yet as both sides acknowledge, the work of tracking and projecting the effects of new projects must proceed.

In 2012, the GHC established its own interim Recognition and Reconciliation Agreement with the province (Clogg 2012). In keeping with the skepticism surrounding other interim treaty agreements throughout British Columbia, Gitanyow men and women have expressed mixed feelings about the new agreement (Meissner 2012). According to its supporters, the goals outlined in the agreement were modest and pragmatic. This circumspection, some Gitanyow suggested, reflected the GHC's awareness of the negative consequences of other, more ambitious treaties and legal agreements established throughout Canada in recent decades. The Yukon Umbrella Final Agreement, for instance, set out a territory-spanning framework for granting land title and establishing self-government agreements with all fourteen of the federally recognized Indian bands in Yukon. The relatively swift conclusion of negotiations and the subsequent dispersal of titled lands among eleven of the fourteen bands was initially hailed as a coup by advocates and lawmakers alike. In recent years, however, new borders imposed by the agreement have fostered new expectations of exclusive use and access, provoking tensions between members of neighboring First Nations who had freely granted hunting access to each other's lands in the recent past (Nadasdy 2017; see also Daly and Napoleon 2003; Egan 2013; Overstall 2008). Blaming these shifts primarily on tools and discourses spread by Euro-Canadian bureaucratic institutions, some, like Dene theorist Glen Coulthard, have lamented such tensions as part and parcel of a general "reorientation of the meaning of self-determination . . . [and] Indigenous struggle from one that was deeply *informed* by the land as a system of reciprocal relations and obligations . . . to a struggle that is now increasingly *for* land, understood now as a material resource to be exploited" (2014, 78).

For some First Nations leaders, practicing a coherent politics amid ongoing shifts in conceptualizations of territory has meant articulating specific legal agreements against other modes of performing intent. By framing each new mapmaking project as a challenge to the land selection treaty model, the Gitanyow have sought to highlight the persistence of their claims amid so many transient plans and technical agreements. In the wake of their 2012 Recognition and Reconciliation Agreement, the GHC produced a set of finely detailed maps of old-growth forest management areas, animal habitats, and other conservation zones in collaboration with the provincial Forest Service. A year later, the GHC put their new maps and digital shapefiles online, supplementing them with court transcripts and other historical documents outlining their struggles with the province over the weight and structure of its consultation procedures (Gitanyow Hereditary Chiefs, n.d.). Technicians working for the office added GHC logos to each map and replaced many of the colonial names for mountains, rivers, and other features with Gitanyow markers and Gitsenimx language place-names. Perhaps more importantly, however, the GHC also added their own polygons to the maps too, derisively depicting the pitiful extent of the regions that the province offered the Gitanyow during earlier stages of land selection–style treaty negotiations that they had been engaged in for nearly twenty years. Rather than treating the new maps simply as emblems of locally produced knowledge, however, the GHC emphasized their omissions and dated details—features that Gitanyow demanded to fill in themselves.

Maps, I was often reminded, were far from the only means for the Gitanyow to document their continuing engagement with their lands. On the GHC website, accounts of earlier lawsuits against timber companies and other developers operating without permission on the Gitanyow territories were followed by links to documents generated by the Gitanyow SLRP, which was formalized in 2013 (Gitanyow Hereditary Chiefs, n.d.). Explicitly organized as a timeline of Gitanyow opposition, both kinds of documents position iterative, long-term fieldwork as evidence of the GHC's rejection of the colonial ideology of the land selection model. Reframing their narrative of opposition around these other forms of work, the question of "complicity" begins to blur. Whether each related mapping project was conducted in defiance of, or in collaboration with, state and corporate interests and support, the timeline suggests, the documents certify the GHC's belief in their right to engage, in whatever terms available, with the totality of the territories outlined in the initial Gitanyow land claim.

For researchers, chiefs, and other Gitanyow alike, the overbearing influence of the land selection model has not fundamentally altered the meaning of Gitanyow territory in everyday life. The kinds of bureaucratic processes that First Nations throughout northwest British Columbia initially developed to respond to land selection–based treaty procedures, however, have affected how the Gitanyow and their neighbors have experienced new conflicts. As I drove west from the town of Smithers to meet Vegh and Alan at their campsite, I crossed through the territories of three different First Nations, each potentially about to be bisected by proposed pipelines. In keeping with their divergent bureaucratic histories, representatives of each group had encountered these proposals in different ways. Members of the Office of the Wet'suwet'en (OW)—like the GHC, the OW houses the council of hereditary chiefs for participating Wet'suwet'en house groups— had spent the past several years leading province- and nationwide protests against a contemporaneous proposal by the Enbridge corporation to build a bitumen pipeline across their territories to the south.[7] Their approach to the TCP Coastal GasLink project—a separate proposed pipeline that was not planned to cross the Gitanyow territories—had been similarly direct. After the company submitted their initial environmental assessment report with the province in 2014, the OW immediately followed suit with a submission to the same office, insisting that the TCP report had failed to account for outstanding Wet'suwet'en claims to Aboriginal rights and title (Office of the Wet'suwet'en 2014). When Canadian police eventually arrested six Wet'suwet'en land guardians and dismantled several blockades against the Coastal GasLink project in February 2020, the steadfast opposition of Wet'suwet'en leaders helped to inspire hundreds of sympathetic blockades and protests across Canada (Bellrichard and Brand 2020; see epilogue).

As we prepared to enter the field in late 2013, the stance of the Gitxsan First Nation, the Gitanyow Nation's neighbors to the east, remained difficult to predict. During early negotiations with the Enbridge corporation, members of the Gitxsan Treaty Society (GTS) had signed a unilateral agreement with the company, inspiring a series of lawsuits and a six-month-long blockade of their headquarters by Gitxsan chiefs who opposed the pipeline (Canadian Press 2012).[8] In the summer of 2014, however, GTS executives spontaneously evicted Enbridge and TCP surveyors from their territories for "violating Gitxsan territorial sovereignty" (Posadzki 2014). As with other confrontations between the Gitxsan, the provincial government, and prospective developers over the past two decades, residents of the Gitan-yow reserves read their neighbors' responses in multiple registers. The night before I joined Alan and Vegh at the campsite, residents of Kispiox, a nearby Gitxsan reserve village, had held a meeting to denounce the unex-pected discovery of TCP surveyors on Gitxsan territory, a clear violation of the provincial government's already weak consultation protocol. The over-crowded meeting, which drew numerous White activists from the nearby town of Smithers, inspired another round of angry denunciations of the leaders of the GTS, whom many in attendance assumed were complicit in the surveyors' work.[9]

With a far smaller population, landbase, and operating budget than either their Gitxsan or Wet'suwet'en neighbors, the Gitanyow Nation's initial response to the TCP proposal was circumspect. Working within the spatial structure of the recently adopted Gitanyow SLRP, technicians working for the GHC began negotiations by proposing an alternative path for the pipe-line. On the maps we brought with us into the field, the simplicity of the projected route belied the diversity of materials that had been assembled to construct the new SLRP maps (figure 4.3). In the weeks before we entered the field, GHC technical staff had sifted through discarded treaty charts, land management data sets, and GIS shapefiles assembled by provincial for-esters and other government analysts active throughout the area. Pointing out the different data sources competing for space on our maps as we pored over them at camp each morning, Vegh occasionally tried to reassure us by pointing out an inescapable fact: any kind of map we produced for the area, she chuckled, would remain a work in progress as well.

The diversity of managerial styles among the different First Nations of-fices in the region mirrored the shifting attitudes with which Vegh had ap-proached her work during different stages of her life in research. Nearing the end of her career when I met her in 2013, Vegh had long since retreated from the confrontational tactics that characterized her years working with SWAT, the GIS mapping group she had helped to create in the early 1990s to over-see Gitxsan consultations with the BC Forest Service (see chapter 2). (She remained an ardent supporter of the people who ran new blockades near her house in the Kispiox Valley and other sites on the Gitxsan territories, how-ever, and often visited the people there to bring them food and supplies.) The financial support for her work with the GHC, once drawn primarily from government grants, came increasingly from corporate budgets for environ-mental assessment work around proposed mines, energy infrastructure projects, and tree harvests. Another recent mapping project that Vegh had

FIGURE 4.3 Satellite photos and Forest Service tree cover charts arrayed atop the GHC's 1:50,000-scale route map. Photo by author.

begun with Alan had been supported by a public utility company preparing to clear new rights-of-way for power transmission lines (figure 4.5). The transect-based maps that Vegh and Alan had created as a result spanned the length of the Gitanyow territories, from north to south. The fact that hunters on four-wheelers would inevitably begin traversing the new rights-of-way, she admitted, had weighed heavily on their minds as they worked.

Whenever we speculated over the likely impact of her work on the project, Vegh consigned her feelings about the pipeline proposal to a longer-term commitment to tracking changes on the land. Even if the goal for the project was apparently, as Vegh joked, to "find nothing" that the GHC would feel strongly compelled to protect, neither she nor Alan saw themselves as capitulating to the whims of their funder. Set against a backdrop of maps and data sets that Gitanyow officials had compiled with BC Forest Service officials in preparation for the interim treaty agreement, the alternate pipeline route proposed by the GHC challenged TCP's definition of "path of least resistance." The nearly seventy-kilometer route proposed by the company would represent a small yet crucial section of the Prince Rupert Gas Transmission Project, a planned 900 kilometer extension of the company's nation-spanning network of pipelines.[10] Overlaid atop the imposing topography of the Coast Mountains range, the TCP-proposed route offered a straighter path with minimal elevation gain, hewing closer to the rivers and lakes feeding into the Skeena, Nass, and Cranberry Rivers that drained the Gitanyow territories. At the very least, the data we collected as we walked would offer the GHC a technical base for confronting the TCP proposal. If construction impacts were deemed too severe for even the least vulnerable swaths of the territory to sustain, Gitanyow advocates would stand a far greater chance of halting the project entirely. Once added to the GHC's database, however, our data would also serve other ends. Vegh speculated about the negotiations behind the project while consigning her most fervent hopes to later confrontations. "Who knows what will happen?" she admitted. "If something happens, it'll be better to have our path on the books too."

Training in Transit

Disengaged from day-to-day Gitanyow politics but a longtime ally and frequent contractor for the GHC, Darlene Vegh's skill and her measured approach often made her the GHC's first choice to lead mapping projects on the territories in cases where the consequences of mismanagement would be severe. After the office received the TCP grant earlier in the summer, though, even Vegh had struggled to coordinate the resources she needed to produce a map quickly enough to challenge the company's initial proposal. She had hoped to spend my first day with the team flying the length of the proposed route and scouting for potential landing sites. A chain of level clearings on mountain tops, sandbars in rivers, and other surfaces would, ideally, allow her to maximize the team's logistic efficiency by dividing the route into walkable segments and reducing our exposure to steep inclines. The long-promised helicopter service, however, a common feature of remote field mapping campaigns throughout the province and a basic necessity along several of the most rugged patches of the GHC's proposed path, kept being pushed back as TCP introduced new bureaucratic hurdles.

The GHC's need to leverage TCP funds to support local employment initiatives brought other practical challenges as well. Throughout more than two decades of work with the Gitanyow, Vegh had overseen dozens of mapping projects with an ever-changing roster of field assistants, untrained helpers recruited by the GHC through online ads, Facebook posts, bulletin board announcements, and word-of-mouth calls around the reserve villages of Kitwanga and Gitanyow. Many of the people who responded to these ads were older men, motivated to engage in physical, outdoor work, yet still looking for part-time employment. Training Gerry, our new arrival, would occupy Vegh's main assistant for our first two days in the field together. Alan, her assistant, often worked for the GHC, assembling wildlife population projections and leading a range of other mapping exercises. As a registered professional biologist, Alan could also lend his signature to technical documents requiring the certification of a provincial government-registered scientist. In addition to training Gerry, Alan would also serve as our navigator, calling out waypoints as we walked, and leaving Vegh free to keep her eyes on the ground.

The constant communication and subtle collaborative labor required to sustain transect mapping exercises mirrored another facet of Vegh's career that she had come to dwell on as she approached her retirement. With each new assistant, she reflected, she had to be prepared to start over, even if her fundamental goal was to keep decades-long knowledge-making projects in motion. With federally recognized "Indian status" through a nearby Gitxsan reserve, maternal lineage in Gitanyow, and a host of family members and previous mapping projects spread across both territories, Vegh's two decades of experience as a GIS expert in the region had made her a familiar face among developers and activists alike. This was true even among younger researchers and new arrivals in the region who had never heard of her work with SWAT (see chapter 2). Over the course of her career, Vegh's collaborative relationships on the Gitxsan and Gitanyow territories had undergone continual change. After the provincial government scaled back its support for First Nations–led field mapping and GIS training programs in the early 2000s, she had met a revolving cast of temporary assistants, training them on the fly to navigate, take notes, and log GPS waypoints. Only a handful of these trainees had returned for a second project, although a few had found technical positions with consulting companies operating nearby. Many of these assistants she never again encountered after their first project together drew to a close. Others, though, like Alan, became her close and lasting friends.

Alan and Vegh's patient efforts to train Gerry in the field reminded us all of Alan's impending departure. On this project, like many others, the GHC could afford to hire him for only the first few days of fieldwork before transferring his responsibilities to a Gitanyow assistant. Some of the assistants hired through this route, Vegh admitted, simply were not up to the grueling demands and social isolation of protracted fieldwork. A few became regular contributors and took advantage of their time in the field to ask her questions about the databasing and analysis work she undertook back at camp at the end of each day. With opportunities dwindling for formal training on the territories, these interactions had become her best means for getting other Gitanyow excited about working on the territories. Yet like the transects they haltingly walked together, establishing continuity meant working patiently through chance encounters, and entering the field time and again with the hope of eventually turning such partial connections into a more comprehensive whole.

The overwhelming need for flexibility was made clear to me during my first morning in the field with Vegh's team. At eight o'clock, after we had been waiting anxiously for nearly four hours, the GHC finally relayed the news from TransCanada: no helicopter for the day. Clustering around a giant paper map, Alan and Vegh swiftly assembled a new set of waypoints covering a relatively flat section of the route that Vegh had hoped to save for the end of the project. A broad swath of twenty-five- and fifty-year-old second-growth timber set within a five-kilometer gap between active logging roads, the route promised few interesting finds. Alan offered more hopeful angles: with few clear landmarks and a profusion of dense undergrowth disrupting lines of sight, he suggested, the terrain would force Gerry to hone his navigation skills quickly.

"Won't we just be using the GPS the whole time?" Gerry asked cautiously.

"As soon as you jump in the bush, you're using your compass," Alan explained. The thick, second-growth forests in the region often made GPS devices unreliable (figure 4.6). Our devices were meant solely for marking finds and waypoints along each transect, he reminded us, and for periodically ground truthing the locations of our finds on the paper maps we carried in our packs.

The risks inherent in consignment, including the possibility that goals deferred would change shape or be lost, weighed on us as we worked. The random encounters generated by our transect-oriented survey meant that while our measurements were likely to be recombined with other mappings in subsequent years, our observations would never be repeated in exactly the same way. Such warnings kept us focused on our work, even as we struggled simply to maintain our footing. At first, the only markers we encountered as we walked were the neon-pink ribbons left behind by TCP surveyors who had been cutting new trails through the area the previous week. With little rise or fall in the land to help orient us after the initial climb up from our parking site, Alan tacked constantly between compass, navigation target, and folded map. Anything an approaching pipeline construction crew encountered after we left would either be destroyed or displaced, he pointed out. However unimpressive our finds proved to be, the sense of the field that we captured in our notes would offer a critical historical perspective on the region if the pipeline were eventually to be built.

As we groped our way forward, most of the few points of orientation we encountered were long-abandoned roads or right-of-way paths cleared for other recent infrastructure projects. At each encounter, Alan pointed out the discrepancy between the location of the intersection depicted on the map and the position he measured with his GPS device (figure 4.6). If the province recommissioned these roads during the lead-up to pipeline construction, Vegh lamented, inaccuracies would invariably cause disagreements. "We might as well start noting them now." Even upgraded and expanded roads might once again fall into disuse (figure 4.7), she suggested, but it would remain important for other mappers to know where they all were.

Gerry and I stayed close to Vegh as she walked, relaying her detours and pauses ahead to Alan. Moving swiftly, Vegh offered patient tutorials over piles of animal droppings, clean-stripped patches of berry bushes, and dozens of claw-torn tree stumps (figures 4.8 and 4.9). Gerry shared anecdotes from his fur trapping experiences in the mountains farther south, helping me to spot holes in rotting logs that had likely been dug out by weasels. As we called Vegh over to investigate each find, she explained, for instance, what kind of weasel had likely made a particular hole, and when. When Gerry asked how she accounted for signs she couldn't quite place, Vegh was straightforward in her modesty. "If I think it's really important," she offered, "then I take pains to describe it." Less than an hour into our walk, she showed Gerry her field notebook, already filling up with rows of check marks next to coded category headings, each corresponding to one of several dozen different kinds of frequent finds. Separate categories for identifying traces of ungulates, carnivores, rodents, and birds. Shorthand codes for classifying whether encounters had taken place through seeing, hearing, or smelling live animals. Another set of codes for classifying evidence of their trails, homes, scat, and remains. Flipping forward within the notebook, Vegh showed Gerry more than four pages of tightly packed columns bearing shorthand descriptive notes and codes next to a corresponding list of spatial coordinates. "I wouldn't be able to work this fast," she assured us, "if the three of you weren't here to help me."

I quickly learned to consign my own tacit hope for exciting "discoveries," as well. Throughout the first morning, Vegh continually apologized that she had invited me to accompany her on such a "boring" project. Gerry admitted that when he had signed on to help, he had expected to find more "cultural stuff," too. Most of the marked trees, trails, and dwelling sites that had once existed in the area, Vegh lamented, had been destroyed during the first years of logging on the territory, shortly before such artifacts were protected by provincial law. The few known objects that remained were marked and coded as small orange polygons on the maps we carried, but, by design, few of these polygons sat anywhere near the land we would be crossing as we worked. This did not mean that the tangled thickets of second-growth trees growing in the wake of these removals were devoid of value. New forests provided food and shelter for moose and other animals evading humans through the autumn hunting season. Coding the notes that she accumulated during the day while sitting at her laptop back at camp each evening, Vegh projected more ambitious futures for our mundane finds. Once numbered, generalized and extrapolated along our route, each point would help GHC staff scientists to question and improve upon the animal habitat polygons and other conservation data that the office periodically shared with the provincial government.

After breaking for lunch (figure 4.10), Alan invited Gerry to take up his compass and begin leading the way. Gerry moved slowly at first, constantly referring to Alan's GPS readings to determine how far he was straying from the route as we walked before gradually picking his bearings based on targets farther and farther ahead. As Vegh and I set to work a dozen meters behind, I probed for her thoughts on Gerry. "He seems to be learning fast, which is great," she offered. With Alan's contract set to expire in two days, Gerry's competence could determine the success or failure of the trip as a whole. After almost twenty-five years bringing novice field mappers into forests to work, Vegh could decipher immediately whether a new recruit would take to the technical tasks each project required. Assessing how new assistants would manage the exhaustion, vulnerability, and other emotional stresses of fieldwork, however, was less automatic. As we returned to camp late in the afternoon, Vegh's easy rapport with Gerry reflected her long experience assuaging the anxieties of new mappers, still uncertain of their place in the field. At fifty-three years old, Gerry was only a few years younger than Vegh. Both had grandchildren already in their late teens and family members scattered across the Gitxsan and Gitanyow reserves. Gerry inquired several times about Vegh's knowledge of the Gitsenimx language, and listened intently as she explained the family dramas that had kept her away from her grandparents and forced her into English-language-only schools.

By condensing their work in the field into a medium that could be easily shared and expanded on by others, the form of the transect allowed Vegh to translate Gerry's labor into both the work at hand and the broader Gitanyow political project without belaboring their apparent differences in professional status and expertise. When I met them both, Vegh was already an internationally recognized mapping expert. Gerry was still learning to read, after leaving school as a child and spending much of his adult life in temporary jobs at a string of timber mills along the Skeena River. As a teenager, Vegh had worked for local logging outfits too, hewing freshly fallen trees into the rough logs that tractor drivers pulled out of the forest. Even after transitioning to full-time mapping work in her twenties, though, she keenly remembered the allures and hazards of industrial labor. Vegh was pleased to hear Gerry reflecting on the day's mapping work as an engaging contrast to the drudgery of life at the mill. Physical endurance acquired through logging work translated well into the demands of transect mapping, and many of the young men and women she had taught to map and navigate during her time with SWAT moved between the two domains as work opportunities emerged and disappeared. The revolving door between industry and activism on the territories heightened tensions around development controversies, she admitted, since new proposals so often found members of the same families and house groups entangled on opposing sides.

Approaching her projects one transect at a time, the iterative nature of her work matched the circumspect tone she adopted while musing about her maps' possible consequences. "For me, it's just little pieces," she insisted as we drove back to camp one evening. "I'm not part of these house groups, so I'm not involved in the decision-making with what happens to the data. I can give my suggestions . . . and I do give my recommendations all the time when I'm putting this data together." Freed of the day-to-day burdens of governance, working in the field allowed Vegh the flexibility to impart her experience and expertise on potential novitiates while adding new layers—however partial—to the GHC's working image of their landbase. The defiant gestures of her earlier work with SWAT had transformed into a subtler politics of collecting, refining, and repurposing data drawn from decades' worth of chance encounters in the field: depoliticized in the instant, perhaps, but latent in their power, and consigned for confrontations to come.

Digital Maps and Energy Dreams

The shape of future confrontations in British Columbia, of course, will likely owe much to the patterns of development and land defense established through earlier conflicts. In 1978, anthropologist Hugh Brody moved to a Beaver Indian (Dane-zaa) reserve near the town of Fort St. John, BC, to assist residents in documenting their use and occupancy of land in the region prior to the planned construction of the Alaska gas pipeline.[11] Hired by the Union of British Columbia Indian Chiefs to assemble maps depicting the group's subsistence activities throughout the region, Brody drew on his own experience as a government consultant in the High Arctic, adopting the novel mapping methods that he had helped to pioneer there while helping to assemble the first comprehensive maps of Inuit territory in Canada (Brody 1976).[12] The maps that Brody produced for the consultation process were not depictions of territorial boundaries, but rather charts of movement, work, and adaptation (see also Aporta and Higgs 2005). Many of the Beaver men and women Brody encountered on the reserves had been relocated there less than two decades earlier. They still drew heavily on the income they earned from fur trapping on their families' registered traplines, and on the hunting rights formalized with the signing of the Canadian government's Treaty 8 in 1899.[13] While certain elders played central roles in Brody's study, the younger men who led many of the hunts in which Brody participated eventually became some of his most vital interlocutors. At times, these young men directly criticized Brody's initial assumptions that the methods and motivations behind their own hunts were somehow less legitimate than their fathers' were.

Brody recognized a troubling paradox in identifying Indigenous groups by their adaptive skills rather than on the attributes of their cultural ephemera. "There is a difficult tension," he writes, "between insisting, on the one hand, that Indians are surprisingly flexible, and saying, on the other hand, that they are now economically and socially threatened as they have never been before" (1981, 248). Brody's image of the frontier, a liminal zone enmeshed with aspiration and latent conflict, had first proven instrumental in the Mackenzie Valley Pipeline Inquiry, which had concluded with Justice Thomas Berger's startling assertion that pipeline construction in northwest Canada should not proceed until Aboriginal treaties had been established throughout the entire region (Berger 1978). Long after the conclusion of the Berger commission introduced Brody's arguments to a national audience, the image of the frontier he established there continued to influence his research and advocacy work for the rest of his career. During the mid- to late 1980s, this work included a full-time position as an anthropological research consultant for the Gitxsan and Wet'suwet'en claimants in the original *Delgamuukw and Gisday'wa* trial. Despite his connection to the trial, however, it was Brody's reflections on the intimate and intergenerational tensions surrounding pipeline politics that has kept his image of northern British Columbia's energy frontier salient in the minds of many Canadians more than four decades after his research in the region began. *Maps and Dreams*, the monograph that Brody wrote about his engagements with Beaver Indian hunters and trappers, forebodes of a future in which rising oil prices and expanded transport infrastructure would bring far more prospectors and developers to the region and introduce changes far more expansive than those that the Beaver were already struggling to contest (see also Mason 2013).[14]

By the time I set out with Darlene Vegh and her colleagues onto the Gitanyow territories in late 2013, natural gas produced in northeast British Columbia had become one of the province's most valuable export commodities, a source of fees and royalties that by the early 2010s was providing an average of over $1 billion in annual provincial revenues.[15] With the aid of a new, 48-inch-diameter pipeline to connect these growing gas fields to the port city of Prince Rupert, provincial government officials argued, producers would enjoy direct access to the rapidly expanding energy markets of East Asia. Accommodations for First Nations groups with territories along the proposed path, company officials announced, would be handled as a matter of course. In some ways, the popular success of *Maps and Dreams* was directly responsible for increasing precisely the kinds of research support that were then being promised by TCP officials. Advocates for the Beaver's claims against the Alaska gas pipeline proposal pioneered the consultation process in the late 1970s, generating a new class of regulatory forms in the process. Among the Gitanyow and the other First Nations groups whose territories would be bisected by the new pipeline, however, reinhabiting these forms four decades later has meant articulating connections to landscapes within an altogether different professional world.

For some anthropologists and First Nations advocates, the transition from trail mapping to transects as a primary modality of land defense still provokes a frustrated sense of nostalgia (Joly et al. 2018). For the resource managers and other Indigenous experts struggling to find methods of contesting development that are likely to remain viable through uncertain futures, though, this shift reflects similar changes in the organization of many Indigenous individuals' social worlds. Transect mapping techniques have enabled GHC-hired contract mappers to observe long sections of land in quick bursts, and to record agile data sets that can be recompiled as new needs and challenges arise. However productive, of course, such an iterative system highlights the challenges the GHC faces in attempting to invent new forms of institutional memory to replace earlier First Nations experts' mastery of continuous trails and their ability to undertake frequent sessions of fieldwork.

As she explained to me while compiling her field notes every evening, Vegh perpetually compared trends that emerged in her notes with observations from nearby transects and trails that she had walked in previous years. Her accumulated experience helped her to predict general shifts in forest health and animal distribution with impressive accuracy, but her projections did not always find their way into her employers' recommendations, let alone into the policies of the provincial government. Officially, she could only watch, write, compile reports, and add to an interlacing archive of transects stored at GHC headquarters. As Vegh prepared to retire, though, she knew that it would take far longer for other, less experienced mappers to translate the results of new transect-based surveys into nuanced pictures of territory change. Unlike the scientists at Date Creek awaiting specific successors to carry on their work from the security of full-time positions (see chapter 3), any mapmakers who wished to replace Vegh would have to build on her legacy one contract at a time.

In April 2015, a year and a half after Vegh concluded what she assumed would be her final stint of paid fieldwork on the territories, the GHC voted to endorse the TransCanada project (Fee 2015). A little more than a year later, though, the project as a whole was indefinitely postponed, temporarily undone by an abrupt decline in global prices for oil and natural gas. The subsequent response on the territories was at once celebratory and circumspect. Many Gitanyow residents celebrated the project's failure in road signs, T-shirts, and Facebook posts throughout the autumn of 2016. Yet few of the people I met in the region during visits in the following years had critical words for the GHC's original endorsement. Had the project been approved and completed, TCP had promised to provide the GHC with annual payments, job training programs, and continuing support for environmental mapping work. The GHC's emphasis on support for technical work was consistent with the Gitanyow constitution, some reminded me. The recently implemented Gitanyow SLRP would further the aims of the constitution by integrating the results of Gitanyow-run fieldwork projects with data drawn from government research. Even the most hopeful discussions of these new collaborative initiatives, though, underlined an uncomfortable fact: in order to pursue these constitutional aims, Gitanyow researchers would continue to rely on developer support.

In some ways, the exhausting labor of fieldwork itself made these paradoxes easier to bear. In much the same way that hunting offered Brody's interlocutors respite from the tensions surrounding development even as hunting-related travels generated politically meaningful data, mapwork offered Vegh and her collaborators a similarly powerful space of retreat. Rising public debate over the broader pipeline project hovered overhead as we worked our way across the territories. And yet, our manner of speaking kept its forebodings at arm's length. The transect-focused technical terms we employed as we worked offered a means of temporarily depoliticizing our observations. Every evening at camp, Vegh steadily repackaged these observations into discrete descriptions and quantitative arguments. Regardless of what happened with the pipeline, she insisted, the GHC would still need these data when contending with other development proposals in the years to come. Immersed in the intricacies of her work, the field became for Vegh both laboratory and sanctuary, a place where changes could be pondered and conflicts deferred.

Not all activists feel this way, of course. Through more than two decades of work throughout the Gitxsan and Gitanyow territories, Vegh has seen the ambitions of many former colleagues collapse under the contradictions of contract-based mapwork. Yet she has also learned that questions of continuity often simply cannot be taken head-on. As she patiently listened to my restless worries over the likely "impact" of our work on the overall pipeline proposal, her modesty belied a broader conception of the place of territory in Gitanyow lived experience. The chiefs and the house groups knew where their territories were, and they understood their obligations to care for them, she reminded me. The provincial government's continuing insistence on the land selection model would not change these ideas and commitments. The data she compiled at her laptop each evening conveyed only slices of the whole, Vegh insisted. Nearing the end of a long career spent assembling arguments from hastily compiled maps and imperfect data sets, she was well aware that one could hardly predict how her work might be read in the future. The challenge in the meantime was simply to keep walking, and to find others to keep walking when she could no longer carry on.

The Road to Cranberry Junction

By the end of Gerry's second day in the field, the topography of our path had tilted sharply. A succession of steep ridges broke up the featureless monotony of the previous day, but the new terrain brought additional hazards. Scrambling to the top of an outcropping for a view of the path ahead, Alan had punctured his thumb on a splintered branch, leaving Gerry to manage the compass alone for much of the afternoon. Vegh began the morning by stumbling over a grounded hornets' nest, awaking a small swarm that stung her on her hands and face. Toward the end of the day, I had tripped over a wayward root while picking my way down a short slope, aggravating an ankle I had sprained at the nearby Date Creek Research Forest (see chapter 3) two weeks earlier. Only Gerry had managed to survive unscathed, although the day's constant climbing had left him exhausted. Piling into Alan's minivan at the end of the walk to begin the long and winding drive back to camp, Vegh jokingly offered macabre predictions about the injuries we were likely to sustain as the weeks wore on. Her frustrated calls to the GHC had yet to earn a clear answer about our long-awaited helicopter, she reminded us. We had better start getting used to all of this climbing, since the remaining flat sections of our path were becoming fewer and farther between.

As we rounded a sharp curve hemmed in on both sides by tall, yellowing aspens, our helicopter finally arrived. There it sat: parked in the middle of a dip in the logging road, set between a gravel pit and a small clearing (figure 4.11). Its rotor blades lay still, with no pilot or passengers in sight. As Alan slowed to a stop, Vegh laughed. "That's probably the one we were supposed to rent today," she mused. Strange as it was to see a helicopter parked in the middle of a road, none of us was particularly surprised. A pair of helicopters had been hovering over the Cranberry Junction region for the past two days. One carried a team of TCP surveyors; the other, "some nature photographers," Vegh informed us. (With few pilot contractors available in the region, she explained, the GHC had gotten a fairly good grasp of each pilot's upcoming schedule as they argued with TCP representatives over the terms of their own rental.) After a few minutes of waiting, Vegh reached over from the passenger seat and tapped on Alan's horn. Three people, one man and two women, all White and middle-aged, emerged from the clearing. With large cameras dangling from their necks, the women waved cheerfully and jogged back to the helicopter, settling into their seats as the pilot set the rotors into motion. Leaning out of the windows of the van to take pictures of the spectacle, we waved back, then looked at each other and shrugged.

Dust and leaves buffeted Alan's windshield as the helicopter slowly lifted into the air. "Wonder what they're thinking up there, hey?" Gerry chuckled. "A couple of Indians and a couple of White guys in a busted-up minivan out here in the middle of nowhere. Hiding drugs or poaching moose or something, I'll bet. Up to no good." As we rolled up our windows and watched the helicopter rise and turn south, our laughter filled the car. Gerry grinned. "Yeah, probably wondering about that one really good."

FIGURE 4.4 Early-morning map discussion at camp. Photo by author.

FIGURE 4.5 A 100-meter-wide right-of-way through Gitanyow territory cleared for the Northwest Transmission Line. The preponderance of post-clear-cut second-growth forest (the shorter tree
stands in various different shades, versus the darker areas along
the far ridge) throughout the region becomes visible immediately
when seen from above. Photo by author.

FIGURE 4.6 Alan and Gerry confirm our position on a georeferenced map of the study area, uploaded onto a GPS-enabled iPad that we carried into the field during the early stages of the project. Photo by author.

FIGURE 4.7 A de-
commissioned
logging road, over-
grown with saplings.
Photo by author.

FIGURE 4.8 Bear
diggings. Photo by
author.

FIGURE 4.9 A wayward moose antler, with GPS device nearby for scale. Photo by author.

FIGURE 4.10 Alan stops for lunch. Photo by author.

FIGURE 4.11 The
elusive helicopter,
with Alan's minivan
in the foreground.
Photo by author.

5

Resilience

Systems and Survival after Forestry's Ends

"What the hell are we even doing here, man?" Charlie had been pacing along the side of the classroom for most of the morning, confronting speakers with abrupt questions and sarcasm. After pretending not to hear the previous half dozen interruptions, Oliver finally stopped writing notes on the whiteboard. Turning toward Charlie, he managed a strained and narrow smile.

For two hours, the workshop organizers had been saying the same thing: It wouldn't all make sense right away. We needed to trust the process. Building a cumulative effects model, they assured us, was supposed to be messy. Aesthetically at least, it was difficult to disagree. The whiteboard at the front of our large classroom in Northwest Community College (now Coast Mountain College) had long ago filled up with scribbled words and arrows. Large sheets of paper covered with additional keywords and diagrams were quickly filling up the wall behind the organizers' stage as well. Our task was to enumerate risks faced by salmon attempting to spawn in British Columbia's Morice River watershed. Simply trying to agree on appropriate scales for discussing each issue raised, though, provoked argument after argument. Paul, a computer modeling specialist who served as one of the workshop's organizers, sketched examples that telescoped in size from specific bends in the Morice's minutest tributaries to the entire Coast Mountains range. In the coming six months, I would eventually befriend Paul and routinely join him and his wife, Beth, for coffee and conversation, including in the days after a series of speeches by local elected officials cast the region's researchers as indefatigable heroes (see chapter 1). That morning in June, though, I was simply another workshop attendee who was struggling to decipher how all of Paul's sketches and comparisons would add up. By ten o'clock, Paul's efforts to cajole the audience into identifying the "main" factor influencing water flow across the region had devolved into a hostile exchange. Biologists detailing fluctuating rainfall were interrupted by other people describing depleting glaciers. Other scientists demanded to know why the meeting was happening at all.

In the three and a half decades since the conflicts over industrial logging in northwest British Columbia first began making international headlines, arguments over the terms and stakes of collaborative research in the region have remained a common feature of everyday life. As we have seen in previous chapters, however, the institutional landscape linking researchers throughout northwest British Columbia has steadily grown more complex, and processes of succession and replacement within individual organizations have grown more uncertain. Some Smithers-based researchers, I had quickly learned upon moving to the town, responded to these uncertainties by articulating their sense of place in the region through celebrated land use planning documents and other artifacts of conservation-based activism (see chapter 1). Others effected quiet detachment (see chapter 3). At workshops designed to foment new data-sharing initiatives between disparately positioned researchers and organizations, though, arguments over the possible shape of collaborative life betrayed altogether different hopes and anxieties. Many research programs initiated after the War in the Woods had offered ambitious horizons, often predicated on assumptions of continuing government support. What, some Smithereens wondered, had the researchers who wished to remain in the region learned from these failed expectations? How might they reenvision their ties with their work and collaborators, so that future episodes of abandonment would be easier to bear?

The goal of our workshop was to condense scientists' knowledge about the Morice and its salmon into a series of "risk thresholds": simplified quantitative indicators designed to specify the limits beyond which diverse environmental variables like stream temperature, road density, and the timing of spring runoffs could irrevocably harm salmon health. Analyzed together as parts of a region-spanning cumulative effects model, Paul explained during his opening remarks, these thresholds might allow researchers to convey the vulnerability of the watershed as a whole. Few in the audience required any convincing that the region's salmon required serious attention. The previous year, the federally organized Cohen Commission had concluded a three-year-long barrage of scientific studies and policy reports to address crashing salmon populations throughout the Fraser River watershed, an enormous network of salmon spawning beds and First Nations harvesting areas covering nearly all of southern and central British Columbia. Some critics had already charged the Cohen Commission report with deferring to industry interests by downplaying the role of coastal fish farms in spreading diseases (Sutherland 2021). Other conservation-oriented researchers, however, particularly those working in watersheds farther north, cited the Cohen Commissions' findings as evidence that other funders—and other sources of legitimacy—would have to help organize future initiatives to keep industrial interests in check. Each threshold authored by our workshop group, Paul explained during his introduction, would inform the nascent BC Cumulative Effects Framework (CEF), a policy initiative that, like a growing range of conservation projects across the region, was funded jointly by the provincial government and an enormous philanthropic group called the Gordon and Betty Moore Foundation (the Moore Foundation for short). Designed by a team of government and independent scientists, the framework would transform the beleaguered environmental impact assessment (EIA) process governing new proposals for roads, mines, and forestry operations throughout the province.

If the policy goals of the CEF were formidable, the scientific principles driving its organizers signaled broad and expansive ambitions. Both of the men who served as the meeting's organizers were ardent supporters of resilience theory, a branch of ecology initially developed to describe how food chains, watersheds, and other complex systems might adapt in response to sudden shocks (Holling 1973). As I began visiting Smithers in 2013, the concept of *resilience* had become a common feature in conservation and resource planning initiatives throughout Canada (Berkes, Folke, and Colding 2000). Working from university laboratories, government offices, and private consulting firms, biologists and other scientists promoted cumulative effects analysis and other modeling techniques to show how interactions between biological processes and management practices—fish breeding rates and species-specific catch restrictions, for instance—could produce unexpected and far-ranging effects. In recent years, however, tools and concepts associated with resilience theory had also spread to a sprawling array of other institutions charged with managing future risks (J. Walker and Cooper 2011). As Oliver, a mathematician who served as Paul's co-organizer for the workshop, explained the premise of our meeting, he excitedly described how resilience-based modeling techniques had been taken up by other expert bodies around the world, including disaster response agencies, climate change adaptation aid organizations, and urban design firms (see Barrios 2014; Cons 2018; Grove 2018). Across each space, Oliver offered, experts were reframing risks by treating their objects of intervention as "complex adaptive systems." By helping to construct the BC CEF, he implied, researchers in Smithers would be doing more than adding yet another conservation initiative to the town's long history of research-based activism; they would also be adapting themselves to the demands of a global transformation in expertise.

On paper—or rather, in the detailed flow charts and methodologies that the organizers of the workshop had distributed before the meeting— the design of the CEF was at once elegant and imposing. If implemented as scheduled in 2021, the framework would coordinate data-sharing and decision-making processes between multiple government ministries tasked with facilitating environmental assessments (Government of British Columbia 2016). Organized according to the sophisticated mathematical precepts of resilience theory, the framework would bring to fruition the sense of promise that ecologists had invested in cumulative effects analysis since the early 1980s, when scientists first began using the term to criticize EIA processes for failing to consider the combined effects of ongoing developments in evaluations of new proposals (see Duinker and Greig 2006).[1] Unlike many earlier attempts to revise EIA procedures in the province, the designers of the framework also explicitly sought input from First Nations resource managers at multiple stages of planning and implementation. Stewart, a full-time researcher employed by the Office of the Wet'suwet'en (OW), had opened the workshop by welcoming the attendees to the territory of the Gidimt'en Clan. During his opening remarks, he had called attention to the fact that he was the sole First Nations person in attendance. His Wet'suwet'en colleagues had been working on their own cumulative effects plans for several years, he offered, and he hoped that there would be time during the meeting to move beyond mere solicitations for input so that the organizers might better understand the Wet'suwet'en plans and their attending objectives. As he wound down his brief introduction, Stewart quietly admitted that he was skeptical of the fantastic promises surrounding the new framework, but he remained eager to hear what everyone else had to say.

Other researchers in the audience were more vocal in their skepticism. Charlie, a regular guest at both planning workshops in Smithers and direct action protests throughout northwest British Columbia, was an independent biologist and mapmaker who had conducted fieldwork in the Morice for four decades. With varying degrees of scorn and sarcasm, he had loudly criticized the premise of the meeting throughout the morning. After yet another reminder from Oliver that the question about water flow had been on the table for nearly an hour, though, he finally relented. "You want a simple answer?" Paul nodded impatiently. Charlie responded in a measured tone. "The timing has changed."

"From forestry?"

"Oh yeah."

The audience murmured in agreement. The second-growth timber that dominated northwest British Columbia after industrial clear-cutting expanded there in the 1970s drew far more groundwater than old-growth forests, a hydrologist explained, readily depleting small streams. As Paul scribbled notes, scientists who had remained silent throughout the morning began to vent. "All of these processes are super stochastic," complained another hydrologist. "You need a field component. You can't calibrate your indicators using only models."

Sensing he was losing the room again, Oliver immediately tried to broaden the scope of Charlie's remark into a series of questions about the watershed's likely futures.

"When our glaciers start to leave . . ."

Before Oliver could finish the sentence, Charlie's voice shot through a cascade of groans from the audience "Go fly it tomorrow, man. The change is already here. The Morice is kicked."

As a gloomy silence settled over the room, Paul offered a half-hearted joke. "Normally we have our first indicator figured out before lunch."

A government biologist sitting next to me, bemused that the organizers' entreaties were inspiring such passionate resistance, leaned over to whisper his agreement. "It's true," he smiled. "Moose are way simpler to model."

Adaptation and Expertise

Like many scientists recruited to participate in resilience-based initiatives, researchers in Smithers often disagreed over whether the transitions they were helping to initiate were productive or depoliticizing. In different ways, their debates have paralleled arguments among social scientists about "what kind of thing" resilience has become in the decades since its inception (B. Anderson 2015; see also Joseph 2013; Nadasdy 2007). To some critics, the language of resilience enables developers and government institutions to leverage beguiling metaphors of survival to present radical disruptions in optimistic terms (Brown 2014; Reid 2012). To proponents in rural areas like northwest British Columbia, though, the same terms and technical tools have come to offer researchers practical means for reorganizing the data collection, analysis, and advocacy work that now occupy their everyday lives. Resilience-based cumulative effects analysis, Oliver argued at the workshop, would be critical for understanding the interlinked impacts of climate change and resource extraction on the region's landscapes and wildlife, and for helping researchers to explain "systemic" risks "in terms that decision makers understand." Perhaps just as importantly, Oliver intimated, the process would enable the overstretched scientists still living in the region to maintain a measure of resilience of their own.

In the decades since the War in the Woods helped to turn northwest British Columbia into a destination for environmental scientists, researchers have increasingly emphasized the contingency of professional life in the region as inextricable from their sense of place and their relationships with other researchers. These contingent lives—at once models and metaphors for theorizing resilience and sets of empirical problems for resilience theory to address—pose a unique challenge for ethnographic inquiry. What might it mean for Smithers-based researchers and their expertise to continue to "survive" in a rapidly changing institutional environment? If one follows Gregory Bateson in defining "the unit of survival" as "a flexible organism-in-its-environment" (1972, 457), how are anthropologists to make sense of the epistemic boundaries that resilience theory's experts are learning to draw around themselves, their data, and their professional attachments, particularly in the wake of government downsizing? Despite the recent proliferation of resilience theory across a wide range of expert institutions and an eruption of critical debates about the consequences of these transitions (see, e.g., Simon and Randalls 2016; Brown 2014), few scholars have examined how new collaborative practices and discourses of adaptability have transformed the lives of experts, particularly experts living in and administering rural areas. These transitions have become especially acute for conservation researchers in northwest British Columbia, who for years have deployed normative concepts of extinction and survival to justify their research even as they confront the fragility of these concepts in daily practice (see also Parreñas 2018).

Three decades ago, a series of demographic shifts, governance initiatives, and new experimental techniques converged around the War in the Woods and helped to turn long-term research into new forms of life (see Fischer 2003). As the subsequent contraction of government support has forced researchers to devise new kinds of social arrangements to sustain their projects, new questions have emerged about how individual researchers and their aspirations come to matter to the continuance of these forms of life. Rather than asserting that resilience discourse directly enacts or excuses processes of downsizing and decentralization, this chapter examines how resilience-based initiatives pressure rural researchers to translate their idiosyncratic goals and practices into forms that specific audiences—particularly government policymakers and private funders—have come to recognize as sufficiently "collaborative" to address "complex" problems. Resilience proponents present this work of translation primarily as a shared process of narration, whereby the products of field-based research are made legible and usable to broader communities of experts. Some of the skeptics that I came to know in Smithers, however, have come to regard the "collaborative" assembly of cumulative effects models as a prelude to the permanent simplification of their research and the eventual replacement of themselves as researchers. For Charlie and a handful of other White researchers in the region who actually participated in blockades during the War in the Woods and other conflicts in the following decades, the concomitant retreat away from direct confrontation has introduced new strains into already precarious relationships with other researchers. Particularly for senior field-based researchers approaching the ends of their careers, the increasingly abstract portraits of collaborative life promoted by some Smithers-based researchers have made the vagaries of aging more challenging to bear.

Many arguments that I observed between scientists in Smithers, both at the Morice salmon workshop and at other events that I attended there in the following years, implicitly revolved around a key paradox in the way resilience theorists attribute agency to individual experts. According to

Kevin Grove and David Chandler, two political theorists who present resilience as a source of conceptual tools uniquely suited to contemporary problems, "Resilience and neoliberal thought converge around a shared critique of centralised planning that emphasises the limits complexity poses to human cognition and any attempt to manage complex ecological or economic phenomena, respectively" (2017, 81). Rather than treating these limits as reason to retreat from such tasks, Grove argues instead that contemporary "intervention requires constant monitoring and reflection that will allow humans to adjust (or more precisely, adapt) their interventions to the unpredictable effects that result" (2018, 5). The scientists recruited to design or participate in resilience-based initiatives, in other words, might very well usher in a new era of dynamic, research-based governance. To do so, however, they must continually reorganize their professional lives even as they recognize new limits to their expertise.

For the past two decades, the spread of the "gospel of resilience" (Nadasdy 2007) throughout rural North America has closely paralleled the decentralization of resource governance processes and the expansion of contract-based research (Lave 2015). Particularly in northwest British Columbia, the rise of resilience has also been accompanied by transitioning anxieties around ecological crises. While I was preparing to begin ethnographic fieldwork in the region in 2013, government-employed forestry modelers had recently begun predicting an impending collapse in timber supply for the entire province, a casualty of nearly a century of overly permissive harvesting quotas. Even as institutionally diverse as Smithers had become since the onset of the War in the Woods, some of my interlocutors acknowledged, taxes from timber sales remained the primary source of funding for conservation research throughout the province (W. Anderson 2017; see also Innes 2003). As traditional sources of revenue withered even more quickly than they had during the initial years of government downsizing in the early 2000s, numerous researchers I met throughout the region admitted that they struggled to imagine how their own careers might unfold over the decades it would take the region's emerging second-growth timber to mature.

Scientists in Smithers routinely recognized the possibility that their careers might not end on their own terms. Rather than treating this possibility as a topic for solitary reflection, though, the organizers of the Morice salmon workshop found ways to encourage their fellow researchers to correlate their own futures with the region writ large. Throughout the morning, Paul and Oliver repeatedly described the researchers living near Smithers as a community whose existence was under threat, even as they presented the entirety of northwest British Columbia as a single emergent system, one that these same researchers were obliged to secure. They warned that all researchers were equally threatened by further downsizing, regardless of their institutional or disciplinary affiliation, and encouraged attendees to recognize the kinds of narratives and quantitative proof expected by the new financiers of conservation science.

As both organizers repeatedly acknowledged, everyone in the audience was well aware of these pressures. During the months I had spent living in Smithers, I had already come to know dozens of researchers who had refashioned their research around the prerogatives of philanthropic groups like the Moore Foundation. Many also earned income by taking part-time contracts assembling EIA reports for developers and government ministries, or by refashioning their research into "adaptation services" (see Keele 2019) for resource developers seeking to redesign their infrastructure and work processes in the region in anticipation of the effects of climate change. While sharing stories with me about the kinds of lives they had attempted to build in Smithers, many of my White interlocutors emphasized that the relative independence, institutional flexibility, and other affordances of these forms of employment had become indispensable to their work as activists. Others, however, framed their own transitions toward contract-based work primarily as practical strategies for making ends meet.

Smithers-based researchers often expressed solidarity with other scientists living outside the region, particularly those who had previously worked for the provincial government. The ways that they linked the practical challenges associated with institutional restructuring to their sense of commitment to one another, though, proceeded along divergent lines. Of the two dozen attendees at the workshop—government-employed biologists, NGO representatives, computer modeling specialists, and others—half had flown to Smithers from urban offices in southern British Columbia. Many had already met at other CEF-related events the previous year. Nearly everyone complained about the challenge of obtaining useful data as government ministries devolved analytical tasks to developers (Luckert and Boxall 2009). Each group, though, articulated the sense of loss they associated with these transitions in strikingly different ways. To some, field measurement programs that had been canceled or privatized registered simply as "gaps" or "data quality issues" that could be "calibrated" through additional computer simulations (Marian Weber, Krogman, and Antoniuk 2012). Rather than complaining about dwindling numbers of field researchers, modeling specialists like Paul and Oliver consistently translated their colleagues' concerns about precarious data collection practices into problems of sharing and analysis. They argued that cumulative effects analysis could empower their fellow researchers to cope with declining resources, and pleaded with them to use simulators to help prioritize their conservation objectives and research plans. In the process, however, these simulation specialists also implicitly framed the broader "survival" of environmental research in the region as an abstract, systemic process—one that depended more on the persistence of universally accessible data than on the persistence of particular personnel. For some First Nations researchers and other aging scientists who were already wary of ambitious promises, these entreaties simply reaffirmed their sense that they had already been left behind.

The following section, "Systems and Survival," charts the development of the concepts of ecological resilience and complex adaptive systems theory, and follows debates initiated by their proliferation into other disciplines and bureaucratic domains. I show how some of the most revolutionary promises undergirding resilience-based initiatives—including, in the case of regulatory programs designed around cumulative effects models, the promise of continuous monitoring—build on creative reimaginings of the limits and capacities of individual experts (see Chandler 2018; Grove 2018). While these portraits of experts and expertise identify subtle interdependencies between individual circumspection and collective action, they frequently rely on ideal-typic renderings of collaborative life that obscure the everyday pressures that drive experts into tense partnerships and precarious working arrangements. Rather than joining other critics in equating resilience with "embedded neoliberalism" (Joseph 2013), however, I argue that this paradox echoes the radical challenge that researchers themselves face in attempting to imagine their futures with other scientists amid widespread institutional restructuring.

The second half of the chapter examines the kinds of relationships that Smithers-based researchers have come to develop with data from long-term research projects amid the regional transition toward contract-based research. I also track how these transitions have affected researchers' sense of the value of their contributions to shared projects, as well as their sense of dependency on other researchers. As I show through an account of an extended argument at the Morice salmon workshop, the scientists who organized the meeting presented cumulative effects modeling as an egalitarian process open to contributors across the region. Ultimately, however, Paul and Oliver successfully generated new indicators only while working with a select group of researchers after most workshop attendees had gone home. Their insistence on securing future research resources by tethering them to ambitious policy goals drove them to align with entrepreneurial scientists, and to valorize streamlined, corporate-produced data visualizations that obviated First Nations jurisdictional claims and emphasized risks in simplified terms. This strategy underlines a long-standing frustration among aging environmental researchers throughout northwest British Columbia: namely, that the most vocal critics of government inaction are often influential supporters of the same private consulting firms that have helped to entrench a services-based model for environmental research. As one Wet'suwet'en researcher's succinct criticisms at the workshop suggest, the rise of privatized research will not necessarily help to bring White- and First Nations–led stewardship projects into closer alignment, particularly if new initiatives are continually routed through the imagined capacities of abstractly defined experts. I conclude the chapter by returning to the paradoxical promise of resilience. With each new plea for pragmatic adaptation, proponents of resilience initiatives are generating new tools to help their fellow researchers continue their work amid continual disruptions. Meanwhile, they are deepening an epistemic divide between their present precarities and an ideal-typic community of future collaborators—collaborators who may never arrive.

Systems and Survival

Wherever they have worked—well-funded laboratories at elite universities, corporate positions in densely packed cities, or independent research centers in rural resource peripheries—ecologists' efforts to theorize survival have long been entangled with debates over the organization of expertise. Writing in the *Annual Review of Ecology and Systematics*, a British Columbia–based ecologist named Crawford S. "Buzz" Holling (1973) coined the term "resilience" to describe how the complex interlinking of actors within an ecosystem could generate both surprising vulnerabilities as well as unexpected capacities for persistence. Explaining his analysis through examples of coevolving predator and prey populations under varying environmental conditions, Holling provocatively opposed the term to "stability," the lodestar that had long guided ecology as a scientific and managerial discipline. The near disappearance of sturgeon from the North American Great Lakes in the 1920s and their subsequent failure to return to precrash numbers offered Holling a foreboding exemplar. The emphasis that conventional resource managers had placed on predictable succession patterns, he argued, obscured subtler processes like temperature shifts, pH changes, and siltation in adjoining rivers, combinations of which had led to an unexpected and spectacular collapse. To keep track of the risks posed by these flexible processes, Holling explained, technical experts, policymakers, and their respective institutions would all have to be equally adaptive.

By introducing sophisticated modeling techniques into ecological analysis and emphasizing new parameters for articulating complexity, Holling empowered new kinds of experts even as he placed limits on their individual authority. The sudden collapse of a fish population and its continuing failure to "rebound" offered both a conceptual system for defining a problem in holistic terms and a practical framework for reorganizing research—one that would shift decision-making authority away from experts beholden to specific disciplines and institutions and toward scientists collaborating in flexible, multidisciplinary arrays. In the ensuing decades, Holling and a growing number of acolytes developed sophisticated analyses of wetlands rehabilitation, wildfire mitigation, agricultural transitions, and urban development by drawing on the tools of systems theory, an interdisciplinary approach for conceptualizing and quantifying relationships between seemingly disparate phenomena (Berkes, Folke, and Colding 2000). By articulating new models for translating ecological crises into problems of interdependence, though, these scientists challenged not only the content of prevailing ecological theory, but also long-standing conventions for federating expertise. Individual government agencies and even entire academic disciplines, they argued, were too "compartmentalized" to effectively conceptualize complex systems.

Throughout the 1980s and '90s, "adaptive management," Holling's program of recursively interconnected ecological science and administration was taken up by government-run fisheries conservation programs and other community-based resource management initiatives throughout western Canada, as well as in Australia, Scandinavia, and elsewhere (Armitage 2005; Holling 1978). While each initiative materialized the principles of resilience in different ways (K. Lee 1999), the rapid spread of terminology and the assistance of Holling's network of collaborators reinforced a sense among many experts involved in these programs that they were contributing to a coherent political project (Parker and Crona 2012). In Smithers, early proponents of adaptive management helped to embed its principles into the Bulkley Land and Resource Management Plan (LRMP) during the 1990s, the first community-authored land use plan adopted by the BC government (see chapter 1). Numerous researchers who moved to Smithers in the years after the LRMP was adopted and then disassembled cited with pride these aspects of the plan. A few explicitly framed the initial success of the Bulkley LRMP as playing a significant role in the global expansion of Holling's methods and ideals. They also knew that, as government research opportunities had been rapidly shrinking in British Columbia, the professional networks of resilience-focused researchers had been growing by leaps and bounds. By the early 2000s, Holling's collaborators had formed the Resilience Alliance research network and were quickly expanding their influence into still more domains of planning and policy-making. In many new institutional contexts, Resilience Alliance researchers had already shifted from treating resilience solely as a framework for modeling systemic risks to articulating it through empirical qualities that could be engineered into existence, whether through the selective control of animal populations or the deliberate modification of landscapes (B. Walker et al. 2004).

Half a century since Holling first defined the term, resilience-based concepts and management practices have proliferated across myriad domains of research and policy-making, from urban design and architecture to military security and disaster response. In their attempts to explain the sheer ubiquity of the term and its seemingly relentless diffusion, though, social scientists have offered equally diverse explanations about "what kind of thing" (B. Anderson 2015) resilience actually is. Scholars have alternately defined the word as both a descriptive and normative concept (Brand and Jax 2007); a form of rationality (Lakoff 2007); a policy buzzword (Chandler 2014); an ethos for design (Grove 2018); a "post-political term of art" (Simon and Randalls 2016, 4); and an "idiom of global governance" (J. Walker and Cooper 2011, 144). Many explicitly link the profusion of the term to contemporaneous processes of regulatory devolution and structural adjustment, particularly within institutions responsible for conservation and resource management (Brown 2014; Reid 2012). The alternately subtle and overt ways that justifications for neoliberal reform come to be embedded in everyday life, Jonathan Joseph (2013) argues, mirror the diverse ways that proponents of resilience reshape managerial interventions, often without making explicit political claims. "There is a commonality across this distribution" of definitions, Stephanie Simon and Samuel Randalls suggest, "which is the generality and flexibility of resilience that names a positive future, or desirable conditions of possibility, yet makes no promises" (2016, 5).

At stake in many critiques of resilience are divergent ways of understanding how processes of neoliberalization legitimize specific configurations of expertise (S. J. Collier 2017). Some proponents have celebrated transitions toward resilience-based management as opportunities to examine "how governance is seen to operate without the handrails of modernist ideas of rationality and progress" (Chandler 2018, xv). Others contrast emergent programs with the "false faith" invested in "command and control" (Grove 2018, 98) technocratic decision-making. Critics, meanwhile, decry proponents' claims of circumspection as convenient covers for technocratic ambition. Biologists who designed adaptive comanagement programs meant to conserve wild sheep populations in Yukon, for instance, Paul Nadasdy writes, criticized hunting restrictions proposed by other program participants by impugning "the concept of 'management'" itself as "deeply problematic" (2007, 209). The explanations that program organizers shared while discussing their work, Nadasdy observes, often contrasted "a constructivist account of equilibrium-based ecology . . . and a positivist account of non-equilibrium ecology" (2010, 42). In addition to downplaying the political entanglements of resilience, he suggests, such narrations also discredited other theoretical frameworks and modes of organizing research.[2]

Other scholars have argued that the rhetoric of resilience seems to signal tacit acceptance of structural changes already underway. Michael Watts (2011) and Julian Reid (2012) each note parallels between government-run adaptive management programs and discursive shifts toward sustainable development, accusing champions of resilience theory of leveraging "vitalist metaphors" and other forms of "ecological reason" to aid the agendas of resource developers by creating a false sense of empowerment among communities affected by extraction (see also Brown 2014). The same metaphors, others have argued, also give resilience theory purchase as an "operational strategy of risk management" (J. Walker and Cooper 2011, 143) in military planning and humanitarian aid (see also Barrios 2014; Duffield 2012). "Living systems are said by ecologists to develop not on account of their ability to secure themselves prophylactically from threats," writes Reid, "but through their adaptation to them" (2012, 71). Across each domain, Reid and others argue, articulations of resilience theory naturalize neoliberal frameworks of governance by encouraging individuals to develop personalized strategies for mitigating risk, and by presenting existing institutions as unequipped to deal with future threats (Lakoff 2007).[3]

In Smithers, many researchers revealed their assumptions about the likely futures of governance institutions in private conversations as well as at public events. I was startled, for instance, by pat defenses of free market policies that I encountered in climate change workshops held for local residents throughout the year. At one "scenario planning" exercise organized earlier in the year to generate timber harvesting policy recommendations for the nearby Nadina River watershed, Oliver distributed pamphlets juxtaposing four speculative narratives depicting different possible effects of climate change in the region. Without explanation, "severe average global temperature increase" was directly correlated to "increased barriers to international trade" in both of the more catastrophic scenarios, while "free trade" and "minor to moderate average global temperature increase" were linked in the less disruptive scenarios. When I noted this to Oliver shortly after the workshop, he laughingly explained that he had devised subtly different scenarios for each exercise in the hopes that attendees would find them engaging and provocative. The purpose of the thought exercises was not to convince Smithereens that certain scenarios were inevitable, he assured me, but to force them to consider how many aspects of their lives could be subject to spectacular changes. Discussing these possibilities in groups also helped residents to consider the many roles that scientists could play in preventing these disruptions. Perhaps, though, I found myself wondering, these discussions could also provoke new fears about what these futures might look like if scientists were no longer around.

In workshops and many other spaces of discussion, Oliver frequently invoked abstract participants—both researchers and nonspecialist rural residents alike—in order to explain how the implementation of resilience-based governance programs would affect the lives and landscapes of northwest British Columbia. Whenever he did so, however, he spoke with acute awareness about his own concrete place in a historically evolving system of expertise—a sense of reflexivity he rarely accorded to the subjects of his stories. Academic critics of resilience theory are often guilty of similar discrepancies. By emphasizing discursive similarities between resilience and neoliberal theory rather than the practical consequences of specific reorganizations of expertise, some critiques have obscured how adaptive management and other resilience-based governance programs come to be shaped by the experiences and aspirations of individuals, including the experts who design and operate these programs. This lacuna points to a common tension in the way both critics and practitioners articulate resilience: to the extent that they are referenced in concrete terms, the experts who act within complex systems are often imagined to be at once more powerful and more vulnerable than conventional technocrats. Examining the specific demands and opportunities that resilience-based programs generate for their intended participants, Ben Anderson finds a multiplicity of potential subjects. "The 'resilient subject,'" Anderson writes, "is more than a liberal 'self-securing' subject. The 'resilient subject' is, among other things: a subject who is encouraged to make preparations; a subject who is to be protected by the state (specifically emergency services); a subject who is a member, or may become a member, of different kinds of community; and a subject who accepts state help in order to return to a pre-emergency normality" (2015, 61).

The elusiveness of the "resilient subject" mirrors the ambiguous place of environmental researchers in emergent research-based governance initiatives. As the arguments that transpired during the Morice salmon workshop made clear, researchers' relationships with one another are also subject to radical disruptions, and their continuing professional survival—whether together or separately—is far from assured. Rather than explicitly identifying what facets of these relationships researchers ought to work hardest to protect, however, resilience theory's advocates in Smithers often echoed Holling himself by asserting that their fellow researchers ought to prioritize flexibility above all else. Defining as resilient not discrete species, but rather relationships that persist through dramatic changes, Holling's original definitions of extinction and survival pointedly eschew concrete coordinates for assessing individual relationships. "If we are dealing with a system profoundly affected by changes external to it, and continually confronted by the unexpected," he observes, "the constancy of its behavior becomes less important than the persistence of the relationships. Attention shifts, therefore, to the qualitative and to questions of existence or not" (Holling 1973, 1).

In their efforts to establish new modes of collaboration throughout places like northwest British Columbia, contemporary resilience theorists have effectively transposed Holling's conceptualization of survival and extinction onto the very institutional structures of research that his own work helped bring into being. Resilience theory, Paul and Oliver argued, could help displaced researchers adapt to changing circumstances by offering them new terms for articulating the aggregate value of their work. By grounding the legitimacy of the CEF in locally authored reports, CEF organizers implicitly promised that researchers living in rural areas would be guaranteed future funding and would thus be better protected from (professional) extinction— much like the province's salmon. They encouraged their colleagues to treat the milieu of conservation research and advocacy as a complex adaptive system, and to develop new research skills and communication practices that would facilitate their survival within the evolving system. And yet: their promises also provided a telos against which both White and First Nations researchers were encouraged to reimagine their relationships with other rural researchers in contingent and configurable terms.

In British Columbia and elsewhere, the sophisticated forms of reflexivity employed by systems ecologists and other resilience theorists have become crucial to their jurisdiction as experts in an ever-expanding array of governance processes (B. Anderson 2015). Yet the flexible definitions of survival undergirding this jurisdiction belie an incongruity between theoretical articulations of resilience and lived experiences of research, one that manifests as a persistent tension among collaborating experts. In addition to using the terms of resilience theory to reconceptualize their own sociality, both proponents of resilience and the many other researchers who contribute to resilience-based initiatives must also plan for the futures and afterlives of their own research. The arguments that transpired at the Morice salmon workshop suggest that some of these researchers are still struggling to reconcile the divergent meanings of survival that give form to these different processes. These struggles are rarely apparent from the scientific papers and policy documents generated through initiatives like the BC CEF. Arguments over the design and implementation of technical practices like cumulative effects models, though, can nevertheless serve as "points of articulation" (Simon and Randalls 2016, 4) through which concepts of resilience come to act on the world.

In the second half of the chapter, I examine how Oliver and Paul's efforts to promote abstract conceptualizations of survival elicited several different forms of critique. One argument was precipitated by the organizers' enthusiastic endorsement of visualization tools produced by a private consultant—tools that critics accused of presenting a dangerously relativizing portrait of the crises facing different sections of the Morice watershed while also obscuring key gaps in field-based data about these same areas. In the second argument, Stewart, the sole First Nations participant at the meeting, succinctly accused the organizers of taking for granted the participation of the Wet'suwet'en First Nation, whose territories encompass the Morice. The fact that the organizers and many other participants seemed to be wholly unaware of the salmon conservation planning work that he and other Wet'suwet'en researchers had already undertaken, Stewart suggested in his remarks, betrayed a dim view of how contributors' actual experience and perspectives would be accounted for in the overall CEF. While the organizers eventually developed their indicators and the workshop ended on relatively cordial terms, both arguments laid bare tensions that have existed among the region's researchers since the beginning of the War in the Woods. If the personal commitments and jurisdiction underlying First Nations researchers' work failed to register in new initiatives, and if the accumulated labors of other senior scientists were so easily effaced in new bids for influence, to what extent could one say that rural research—as a form of life—had survived government downsizing after all?

Trust the Process

A mathematician by training and a senior researcher with the BC Ministry of Environment, Oliver was regarded as something of an evangelist among scientists living in Smithers. Like Dennis (see chapter 3), Oliver had been one of the few senior government researchers in Smithers to successfully retain his position while also resisting pressures to relocate to the provincial capital during the first wave of government downsizing in the early 2000s. He collaborated frequently with consultants, academic researchers, and other government employees throughout the province, and copublished journal articles on the kinds of risk indicators and modeling techniques around which he and others had sought to organize the Morice salmon workshop. Like Pauline (see chapter 1), Oliver had also taken an active role in managing the Bulkley Valley Research Centre as the provincial shift away from prescriptive forestry management policies strained the livelihoods of many of his collaborators.

Despite the myriad ways that he had sought to support his fellow researchers in Smithers and improve their access to resources for long-term work, Oliver's efforts to promote resilience as a totalizing framework for research in the region had nevertheless made him a polarizing figure. At meetings with local politicians and scenario planning workshops designed to solicit public engagement with climate change policies, Oliver routinely described the region and its researchers in parallel and complementary terms. By using Moore Foundation and provincial government funds to organize a voluntary workshop around the cumulative risks affecting salmon, he highlighted the interdependence of the research prerogatives of scientists from highly diverse fields and backgrounds, many of whom would not have been able to travel to Smithers without the travel support and accommodations that the workshop sponsors provided. More provocatively, though, Oliver also put forth the fish as a metaphor for the struggling professionals. Resilience and adaptability were not only properties to be found among animals and ecological systems, he insisted: they were also qualities that the researchers who studied these systems should be able to cultivate in themselves.

Oliver's comparison between the fates of the region's salmon and scientists was not the first time I heard rural researchers described as a species on the verge of extinction. Numerous Smithereens I met deployed the word *resilience* while describing the professional changes they expected to endure as shrinking glaciers and migrating animals transformed their landscapes and economies. Others invoked the term to describe their admiration for colleagues who continued to live in the northwest through decades of inconsistent employment (see chapter 1). Oliver, though, was perhaps the most prolific in weaving metaphors of resilience into everyday conversations. Perhaps as a consequence, he was also the most vocally self-conscious of my interlocutors in Smithers about being "studied" by an anthropologist. Earlier in the year, I had seen Oliver promote data-sharing initiatives among contractors and other former government researchers by promising them a sense of coherence and legitimacy that had been eroded by a decade of downsizing. Cumulative effects analysis was a common "mission," he assured them, albeit one in which modeling experts must take leading roles.

The "mission" underlying cumulative effects analysis took much of its inspiration from the sense of investment that researchers had developed with northwest British Columbia in the wake of the War in the Woods. As I observed Oliver interact with a broad range of scientists over the course of my time in Smithers, however, it gradually became clear that his sense of this new mission occasionally required other researchers to downplay the particularities of their research as well. In 2002, the government of British Columbia had radically scaled back support for environmental fieldwork and data collection after the newly elected BC Liberal Party initiated a period of dramatic deregulation and restructuring across all of the province's resource-focused ministries. In the years that followed, researchers' complaints about the transition largely diverged into two registers. In newspaper editorials and public speeches in Smithers and other towns throughout the northwest, many scientists clamored for the BC Forest Service and other ministries simply to rehire field-workers lost to downsizing (Luckert and Boxall 2009). Other researchers, however, argued that both current and future contractions should be countered by steering existing resources through elaborate systems for prioritizing conservation objectives, research questions, and physical locations for research (K. Price and Daust 2009). Redesigning rural research according to such models would ameliorate the effects of downsizing, these advocates insisted, by steering field-workers still in the region toward critical locations. In the meantime, data-driven prioritization would also enable simulation specialists to make more efficient use of the data they already had.

To researchers who equated their expertise with long-term, situated fieldwork, the broadening influence of modeling in conservation initiatives provoked a deeper sense of estrangement. At another cumulative effects workshop earlier that year, several researchers had criticized the modelers who had organized the meeting for assuming that further downsizing was inevitable, and that vacated full-time government field-worker positions were unlikely to be replaced by new personnel. In practical terms, these critics understood that establishing a new collective "voice" from dispersed data sets would eventually diminish their opportunities to refine old analyses and provide critical feedback. Modelers who were already resigned to the disappearance of field-based researchers, they complained, were more likely to devote their time to working with data that were already available, regardless of their source or quality, than to cultivating relationships with aging personnel. Indeed, much of the data to receive attention during the Morice salmon workshop came not from researchers living near Smithers, but from consulting companies based in Vancouver. Long accustomed to selling data sets and interpretive analyses to developers, conservation NGOs, and government ministries alike, these companies had already adopted precisely the kinds of indicators for communicating their work that CEF organizers wished to develop for the framework as a whole.

After decades of initiatives focused on restricting industrial logging, the rising resonance of salmon among conservation scientists in the northwest further reflected the ways that the constraints of contract-based research were becoming embedded in everyday life. In conversations throughout the spring, numerous Smithers-based scientists admitted to me that they had grown weary of politicians insisting that conservationism was responsible for recent mill closures and layoffs. By reframing their research around risks faced by migrating salmon, they could emphasize the productive aspects of resource governance, rather than the regulatory prescriptions that developers readily equated to lost jobs. Salmon researchers had also experienced downsizing's effects in particularly acute ways. No matter how elaborate the sampling methods involved, studying salmon in the Morice required people, both to count the fish as they swam through artificial channels scattered throughout the region's rivers and to tag a subset of arrivals near each river's mouth before recapturing them farther upstream. Some tasks had been taken over by volunteers and minimally trained contractors. Myriad other factors influencing water volume and quality, though, were increasingly left unmonitored.

In 2001, the year before the BC government began radically reducing its ministries' staff and research budgets, the Moore Foundation began their Wild Salmon Ecosystems Initiative. Over the next fifteen years, the initiative dispersed nearly $300 million to groups spread out from California to Alaska, supporting projects ranging from habitat biology and ecotourism businesses to Indigenous governance and data-sharing trusts (Gordon and Betty Moore Foundation 2017). When I began visiting Smithers in 2013, though, many researchers there who had received Moore Foundation grants were already preparing for the scheduled sunset of the Wild Salmon Ecosystems Initiative in 2017. When I asked scientists how they felt about being abandoned yet again after already surviving a decade of government downsizing, most insisted that the Moore Foundation's departure did not carry the same sense of betrayal. Its limited duration, they had been told, was expressly designed to "incubate" new institutional connections. The month Oliver and Paul convened their workshop, the foundation awarded a $1 million grant to the North Pacific Wild Salmon Organizational Resilience Project, a grant that would "support a fund aimed at enhancing the impact and financial resilience of North Pacific wild salmon conservation organizations through use of new tools to diversify their supporter base" (Gordon and Betty Moore Foundation 2013). It was incumbent on the region's experts to devise strategies for weathering uncertainties, the announcement suggested, particularly since salmon were already doing the same (see also Hébert 2015).

The range and complexity of factors affecting the salmon spawning process made it an ideal problem for cumulative effects analysis. The Morice watershed's sinewy, glacier-fed streams could easily turn muddy and barren if a badly placed road sent soil tumbling into them at an inopportune time of year. Declining annual snowfall and the shrinking of dozens of glaciers feeding the watershed had dramatically shifted the timing and volume of spring runoffs. Thousands of salmon died every year struggling to navigate these unpredictable flows, unable to begin building their spawning nests before reaching the precise location where they had grown up from eggs into tiny smolts and begun their journey to the ocean half a decade earlier. Such a fraught migration process also offered compelling metaphors for researchers eager to distinguish their personal interests from those of their employers. An anadromous fish that lives in the ocean between being born and dying in freshwater streams, salmon regularly traverse provincial and federal boundaries. Part of the CEF's task, Oliver joked, was to help policy-oriented researchers gain similar professional mobility.

Some of these metaphors impinged on explicit policy concerns. Throughout the workshop, participants complained that some of the most grievous issues facing Pacific salmon—commercial overfishing and diseases spread from fish farms—happened in the ocean, which fell primarily under the jurisdiction of Fisheries and Oceans Canada, a federal agency. Rather than critiquing directly these jurisdictional boundaries, though, CEF proponents defined the emergent framework in terms of "valued ecosystem components" that transcended any specific institution (Auditor General of British Columbia 2015). The anodyne language of "values," an overtly apolitical term designed to solicit engagement without hailing participants by political party or profession, was already common throughout Canadian conservation initiatives (Mackenzie and Dalby 2003). Values that could not be articulated through quantitative indicators, though, Paul insisted, rarely received attention from regulators (see, e.g., Adams 2016). If an indicator could be explicitly tied to conservation benchmarks already outlined in provincial law, he suggested encouragingly, it would be harder for policymakers to ignore related research.

As Oliver and others acknowledged, organizing regulatory initiatives around collectively defined "values" was hardly a new idea in the region, whether for Euro-Canadian governance initiatives or for technical programs run by First Nations. Even as their representatives expressed ambivalence about the programmatic aims of the CEF and sometimes bristled at the presumptuousness of the framework's spokespersons, the OW and several other First Nations–run resource management groups throughout the province had already incorporated cumulative effects analysis into their own consultation procedures and resource management policies. Indeed, even as early as the mid-2000s, several provincial-scale bureaucratic assemblies, including the First Nations Fisheries Council of British Columbia, had already drafted their own cumulative effects implementation plans in an effort to structure their own negotiations with provincial and federal ministries. Similar documents had also been produced by the Yunesit'in, Tl'esqox, and Xeni Gwet'in First Nations, members of the Tsilhqot'in National Government. When the Tsilhqot'in were awarded 1,750 square kilometers of a land claim in 2014, these implementation plans were repeatedly cited in the Supreme Court of Canada's final decision (Borrows 2015).

In the years immediately after the *Tsilhqot'in* decision was announced, forestry companies and other developers began looking at First Nations–produced land use plans much more carefully as a means of anticipating eventual legal action, in the event that an underlying claim was successful (Mancell, Waatainen, and Hunter 2014). As we gathered together for the Morice salmon workshop in 2013, though, Paul and Oliver primarily referenced First Nations–produced plans less as existing frameworks that would have to be engaged than as evidence that cumulative effects analysis was already proliferating across the province. The sheer number and heterogeneity of these and other plans, furthermore, they interpreted as yet another reason for individual researchers to simplify their claims. Referring to a CEF-produced comparative study of cumulative effects–based land use plans that had been developed throughout northwest British Columbia over the previous decade, the organizers mentioned that just three of these plans together listed eighteen different values—far too many, CEF representatives insisted, for the overcommitted researchers in the region to address in any detail. Worse still, the reviewers continued, only a handful of the values listed in these earlier reports were defined in quantitative terms against which "acceptable conditions" could be discerned (Auditor General of British Columbia 2015). The possibility that the researchers who helped to articulate these values might be appealing to other jurisdictions and decision-making bodies, though, was never addressed in the comparative study.

By 2013, the CEF working group had published an initial list of five values, including old-growth forests, aquatic ecosystems, grizzly bear, forest biodiversity, and moose.[4] Aquatic ecosystems, for instance, was further divided into eleven indicators, including thresholds for riparian disturbance and the maximum flow of individual streams. If a project was judged likely to push an indicator—the number of roads crossing streams within a given area, for instance—past a specific threshold, CEF team members argued, the assessment should trigger additional review or even an automatic regulatory prohibition. By presenting each risk indicator as a thoroughly considered consensus articulated by experts from across the province, though, the framework's designers also aimed to generate direct confrontations. In an article outlining the risk estimation methodology that had already been used to guide multiple CEF workshops throughout the province, two Smithers-based independent researchers made explicit the moral compulsion they hoped to expose. Once each indicator had been adopted into government policy, "all objectives [accounted for by the resulting model would] have been agreed to by multi-stakeholder committees and signed by government. Hence," the authors coolly state, "we assume that failure to achieve any agreed-upon objective is a consequence that requires evaluation and potential management response" (K. Price and Daust 2009, 1882). The reports produced through CEF-led expert workshops, the authors suggested, would provide a technocratic paper trail, one that could secure rural researchers' collective voice, even in the absence of conventional regulatory authority.

Precisely what kind of collective voice might be enacted from expert reports was more challenging to explain. The goal of cumulative effects modeling, Paul reminded us throughout the workshop, was to "estimate the risks associated with making a decision, so that the decision maker doesn't have to." Yet as their critics countered, the model of political legitimacy imagined in these gestures remained resolutely—and perhaps resignedly—centralized. By treating the evaluative process as one of disinterested, if hurried, contemplation, the organizers tacitly assigned the many precariously employed researchers living in the northwest to uncertain, peripheral roles. The title of the article outlining the process the organizers used, "Making Monitoring Manageable," begged critical questions: manageable for whom, and to what ends?

A More Coherent Story

Like other workshop organizers I had come to know in Smithers, Oliver and Paul took pains to define their fellow researchers as a coherent community with singular goals. At the Morice salmon workshop, they saluted local field-workers in the room and humbly disclaimed their own modest knowledge about salmon while reminding visitors from Victoria that multiple researchers in their midst had been working in the Morice for decades. Several attendees had not only accumulated critical data sets on stream flow velocity and water temperature throughout the watershed, but had also spent weeks at a time navigating the region on foot. One of the first speakers of the morning had worked in the Morice since the early 1970s. In addition to gathering data and attending to his own long-term studies, the man had also assembled multiple synthetic documents meant to join together his own research with other government, academic, and developer reports that he had accumulated during his work in the region. Some of his own reports were also explicitly framed around "prioritizing" certain questions and areas for immediate study. In one coauthored report published in 2002, he admitted that even the selection of the Morice itself as a space of study had been an outcome of a process of prioritization (Bustard and Shell 2002, i). In the report, the authors listed and described "information gaps" for each of the nine species of fish covered in the report and outlined tentative plans for follow-up fieldwork in later years. Rather than proposing to fill these gaps with simulated measurements, however, they presented them as questions and physical sites to which individual researchers would eventually return.

Throughout his presentation and published reports, the speaker alluded to the specificity and presence of rural researchers in other ways, as well. In the coauthored report, he explicitly warned his readers to approach the document with skepticism, particularly the arguments he and his coauthor had communicated through their crude if colorful maps. As they primly wrote in their introduction, "relying on these maps to tell 'the whole story' is not advised" (Bustard and Shell 2002, 2). At the workshop, his presentation slides contained few maps, but many images of rivers throughout the Morice where he had taken specific measurements. He described beaver dams that flooded meadows and diverted small tributaries for seasons at a time. He relayed to rapt attention stories from his experiences counting salmon nesting sites in swift-moving water as grizzlies lingered nearby. The surprises one encountered through conventional fieldwork, he suggested, were innumerable. As other biologists in the audience asked how his practice had changed to cope with declines in funding, he admitted that his sampling methods had grown less laborious. "I don't have as many people out there with me as I used to," he admitted. "It's really important to trust the folks you get." After a few more slides, the speaker concluded by encouraging his audience to consider their own relationships in similarly dependent terms.

As the morning wore on and Smithers-based biologists' presentations were followed by talks from modeling experts, an altogether different sense of place and codependency was attributed to the research labor under discussion. Peter, the final presenter of the morning, echoed the organizers' and audience's praise for the region's senior biologists. Without their "tireless work," Peter effused, the work of "fly-in consultants" like himself "just wouldn't be possible." As he deftly pivoted from signaling solidarity with northern researchers to showcasing the elaborate data visualizations that were the signature of his company's work, however, it became clear that the organizers had given Peter the morning's final slot for a reason. The company Peter worked for was one of the largest ecological consulting groups in the province. Founded in the 1980s by graduate students of C. S. Holling himself, it had been among the earliest research groups anywhere in the world to adopt resilience theory as a foundation for private consulting. Peter's presentation covered sections of the Skeena watershed, a much larger river system that wholly encompassed the Morice. As the organizers' laudatory introduction made clear, though, Peter's style and methods were meant to be seen as exemplary.

The boundary conditions guiding Peter's study were far more explicit than in any other presentation. He promised to break down his discussion into sub-basins of the Skeena, and to describe the risks identified by the project through the specific conservation units (fish populations defined by their spawning locations) believed to be most affected by them.[5] Moving briskly through his opening slides, Peter extolled the virtues of methodical prioritization. Unlike most of the audience, he had spent years immersed in resilience theory. His felicity with its acronyms occasionally forced others in the room to ask him to stop and explain. "The whole point of cumulative effects modeling is safeguarding VECs," he insisted, before catching himself and explaining that VECs were the "valued ecosystem components" or "values" undergirding the CEF as a whole. By setting out a handful of guiding terms and assumptions, he went on, risks could be compared in ways that "invited more people" to "understand the overall process."

After racing through his introductory remarks, Peter then set about explaining the complex visual grammar through which his company communicated its work. "It's important for all of our clients to be able to tell at a glance where the problems are," he insisted, "whether it's a mining company or an NGO." The region's dramatic topography, he went on, made such visualization methods both convenient and necessary. Aided by satellite-produced maps, his company had separated the Skeena into sharply defined "zones of influence," each of which was broken down into minute sub-basins, including sections of lake shores and individual river valleys. The effect was a kaleidoscope of tiny red, yellow, and green polygons, each one broadcasting a relativized category of risk. If the value of a particular indicator—acid drainage from local mines, for instance—in one sub-basin landed in the "better half" compared to the average value of the indicator measured throughout the watershed as a whole, the polygon for the sub-basin was colored green. Each slide displayed half a dozen variations on the same spatialized "zone of influence," with the sub-basins recolored for each new risk factor.

Before Peter could begin explaining his first set of maps, a hydrologist interrupted him. Gesturing toward a mapped zone of influence comprising a pair of large, heavily logged tributary valleys, the man expressed concern that the "rolling averages" displayed on the map had cloaked grave problems in fields of green.

"Shouldn't that entire map be red?"

Peter flashed a smile; he had clearly been anticipating the question. "We're still waiting for the experts up here to tell us what the thresholds for these areas should be," he offered. "That's part of the reason I flew up here today—to talk about these kinds of numbers." In the meantime, Peter went on, working with relativized values allowed the company to bring risk indicators to wider audiences. "Images like these aren't really meant for specialists," he demurred. "We call them 'report cards.'" The NGO that had paid for the project had already posted much of these data online, and were in the process of designing simple geographic information systems (GIS) mapping tools so that nonspecialist users could explore data sets and design simple maps of their own.

The hydrologist was unconvinced. "But aren't you worried about misleading people? Nobody has good data on some of the places you're showing here, but from the way these maps look, you'd have no idea."

"Yes," Peter nodded, "these are all just spatial snapshots right now." As he elaborated, his tone became more accusatory. Like other researchers in the region, his company had yet to perform the detailed follow-up studies required to make their models statistically meaningful. As means of procuring "community buy-in" from several rural villages in their study area, though, the company had recruited "local assistants" to count and measure fish. Anticipating another follow-up critique, he then added that his company had also developed "correction algorithms" to account for the variances they expected to encounter when compiling measurements recorded by minimally trained field-workers.

Returning to his slides, Peter attempted to press on with his talk through a flurry of scatter plots and bar graphs depicting other relativized issues with water flow, air temperature, and sedimentation. Within moments, Charlie stood up and interrupted, and asked Peter to return to the report cards. "This is the problem with environmental assessments," Charlie complained. "They'll use any available piece of data they find, and then if they can't find anything, they'll say there's no problem."

Before Peter could answer, Oliver and Paul had already stepped back onto the stage. "Guys, the government is flying blind right now!" Oliver pleaded. Peter's company wasn't trying to water down the other research and monitoring work being conducted in the north, and they weren't trying to replace anyone, he tried to assure the audience.

"I know this sounds cynical, but we need a more coherent *story*," Paul acknowledged. "We're still trying to make the entire process more transparent for the public. But we've got to do it. This gives us a stronger voice." Shouting to cut through the rising tumult, Oliver promised to field more questions after everyone broke for lunch. The indicators, he sighed, would have to wait.

Selling Out

As the workshop reconvened after lunch and the speakers who had presented throughout the morning took their chairs among the rest of the audience, Oliver and Paul made it clear that the indicators could wait no longer. Well over a dozen people were due to fly back to Vancouver and Victoria the following evening, they pleaded with the audience, and their supervisors would likely want to see proof that traveling to Smithers had been worth their time. Revealing a simple chart that they had drawn up during the lunch break to replace the whiteboard scribblings and taped-up sheets of paper containing the accumulated notes from the morning's discussion, the two men announced that they would begin the afternoon by focusing on backcountry road density, and that they would use the process of developing this indicator to more fully explain how their risk curve modeling methodology was meant to connect experimental research to policy. They then proceeded to ask audience members to begin listing quantifiable effects of road construction from which they could estimate simple thresholds beyond which further development should cease. The time for dwelling on detailed historical studies and layering each point with qualifications had passed during the morning's presentations, the organizers insisted. The point now was to offer simple numbers and keep moving.

Upon seeing the simplified diagram drawn up on the whiteboard behind the stage, Charlie was up on his feet. "Don't you understand? This shit doesn't work! All of the changes you're talking about are already here!" Reminding the audience that the meeting was ignoring work that First Nations researchers had already completed, he pleaded with Paul and Oliver to stop the meeting to consider what could happen if their simplified models and management protocols were actually adopted as government policy. "Every time you talk about 'decision makers,' you're just selling out the Wet'suwet'en. Why would they want any of this? These models are just going to enable more development."

At first, Charlie's impassioned speech was met with awkward silence. Oliver turned to Stewart, the natural resources manager for the OW. Like several of the government employees sitting near the front of the room, Stewart had remained silent for most of the day. After offering a brief opening prayer and welcoming the group to Gidimt'en Clan territory, he had sat impassively next to Charlie throughout the morning's arguments, occasionally whispering with Charlie during other speakers' presentations or nodding after uncontroversial points. With Oliver asking for a direct rejoinder, however, he quietly got up from his seat.

"I think Charlie's right," he calmly offered. "Shouldn't we be talking about the political basis of these objectives first? I appreciate the work that everyone is trying to do here, but I don't understand how this is supposed to account for the Wet'suwet'en land use plan, or for the data-sharing plans we've already set up. If this is just another data-sharing initiative, couldn't we have started with a clearer explanation of what's expected of us than all of these calls to 'trust the process'?" With the attention of the audience firmly on him, Stewart continued. For most of the previous decade, Wet'suwet'en people had caught so few salmon on their territories that the OW had had to import fish from the Nisga'a and other coastal First Nations simply in order to have sufficient amounts for ceremonial purposes, let alone provide a sustaining food source for their members. Turning to face the organizers, Stewart apologized for not emphasizing this fact during his welcome statement earlier that morning. The OW saw the situation in dire terms, he went on, and it was frustrating that many people in the provincial government seemed to hold different priorities. "The entire Forest Service should have salmon protection as its chief focus, not just as one more species on their list of animals warranting attention." The group had spent the entire day hearing about the critical importance of salmon to the Wet'suwet'en and other people living in the region, he intoned, but the researchers in the room were still hiding behind "risk thresholds" and other inoffensive terms instead of conveying a real sense of alarm. After speaking for less than two minutes, Stewart thanked Oliver for inviting his input, then quietly sat back down.

Stewart's succinct criticism sent the meeting into disarray. After spending the entire day treating Charlie's attacks as embarrassing distractions, the organizers were immediately chastened by Stewart's suggestion that Wet'suwet'en participation had been taken for granted. Paul promised to sit with Stewart and Charlie during dinner, and to ask detailed questions about the salmon recovery plan that the OW had developed several years earlier. Oliver offered to email all of the workshop participants with articles detailing the risk curve methodology, and to spend the following morning fielding more questions about the overall CEF. Other participants in the audience, though, continued to reiterate Charlie's accusations. Independent research groups and NGOs had already developed sophisticated risk assessments for salmon throughout the Skeena watershed, they insisted, and most of their warnings about the effects of more development activities were far more dramatic than the precautionary measures outlined by the CEF. What did the organizers hope to accomplish by ignoring this work? The government of British Columbia had been ceding analytical responsibilities to these groups for more than a decade; why should researchers help to reconsolidate the authority that the government had lost in the process?

Within minutes of Stewart's brief remarks, Paul and Oliver abruptly decided to end the meeting for the evening and reconvene the next day. "Today's been . . . ambitious," Paul sheepishly acknowledged, earning a few scattered laughs. He admitted that he had been hoping to generate as many as four risk curves during the day, but he welcomed one attendee's suggestion that a small subset of the group build tentative curves on their own that could be sent around for critique and revisions. As Paul clustered together with a handful of attendees around the whiteboard at the front of the room, four of the scientists who had flown up from Victoria followed Charlie out to the balcony at the back of the classroom. Together, they quietly chatted with Charlie as he smoked a cigarette, and gently cajoled him to think of Paul and Oliver's methodology as a meager life raft for beleaguered government employees. Passing beside me as he left the balcony and walked back into the classroom, Charlie clapped me on the back; the meeting that he and I had tentatively scheduled for later that afternoon would have to wait. In the meantime, he would go find Paul and Oliver and attempt to conclude their conversation with a truce. "I gotta go make sure the fence isn't too torn," he sighed.

I eventually made my way back into the classroom, where my companion from the morning was rolling up the half dozen maps she had printed for the meeting. "Fights like these kinda come and go," she offered with a weary laugh. "Everybody will see each other again at the next big meeting. By then, they will have forgotten 90 percent of what happened the last time." Waving a hand at the clusters of people still standing around the room and half shouting to be heard above their loud and lively conversations, she reminded me that the apparent divide between "locals" and "fly-in guys and gals" was a subtle and complicated one. "Oliver probably works more closely with people in Victoria than he does with most people up here, but the same thing is true in reverse, too, sometimes." A few of these people spent so much time in Smithers and the surrounding area that they would bristle if they were told they weren't "locals," she laughed, even if they had never lived in the region themselves. "We're all pretty spread out. So it's nice to come together like this sometimes. But it's hard too." Like several other researchers who had already begun to leave for the day, she had worked with the OW on multiple projects in the past, and she wasn't surprised by Stewart's criticisms. "He probably just feels like he's been wasting his time, but I'm sure he'll be here for the next meeting." The fact that Stewart still had to explain Wet'suwet'en research and land management projects to White scientists in Smithers despite attending similar workshops for more than a decade, though, she suggested, made her wonder why he bothered with government-led initiatives at all.

By five in the afternoon, most of the workshop attendees had begun to make their way to the Aspen, a hotel bar along the highway that was popular with Smithers-based scientists. As we walked to the bar in small groups, I expected the tension and bitterness that had dominated the workshop to devolve into complaints about wasted time. The two visitors from Victoria who walked alongside me, however, were jovial. Sounding surprisingly genuine, they insisted that it was exciting for them to see researchers who had yet to "completely give up hope." As my companions soon made clear, a subtly different form of nostalgia inflected the ways some scientists from metropolitan British Columbia viewed their counterparts up north. As we walked by modest suburban-style houses and soccer fields, both men echoed an idea that I had often heard proudly proclaimed by Smithereens. Significant shifts in government practice, they insisted, often began in rural peripheries before ministry headquarters amended their ways. Neither scientist referenced the Wet'suwet'en plans. Both of them, though, hailed Stewart as a shrewd and valuable contributor, and insisted that they were eager to see their hosts in Smithers invite him to future meetings.

As I gradually caught up with other workshop attendees in the months to follow, a few scientists from southern British Columbia were more ambivalent about the pathos of their northern counterparts. In the early autumn, I met with Peter outside his company's office in Vancouver. When I cautiously brought up the criticisms he had faced during his presentation in Smithers, he let out a long and gentle laugh. "I understand why people up there get so angry," he admitted. "As far as they're concerned, there really isn't any substitute for just having more people in the field. And in a lot of cases, they're totally right too." Like the government employees who observed Smithereens from afar, Peter continually spoke of his company's relationship with northern researchers as one of collaboration, rather than replacement. His reflections on the likely futures of the region, though, presented these assurances in less patient terms. "We're going to keep going up there. And hopefully, eventually, people like Charlie will decide to work with us. I think he knows we're both on the same side." Numerous First Nations governing councils had already hired his company to generate risk assessment models, he reminded me. A few groups had also been in conversation with the company about designing training modules for their member nations, so that they would eventually have risk modeling specialists closer to home. As our conversation slowly drew to a close, Peter's vision of northwest British Columbia grew at once darker and more hopeful. If field researchers who wished to remain in the region decided to eschew new collaborative tools, their work and careers would eventually be forgotten, he offered matter-of-factly. "A lot of scientists down here in Vancouver would love to be able to move up to Smithers," he admitted. If the people who already lived there would not do what was required to make their research resilient, he hinted, more adaptable researchers would be happy to take their place.

Promising Resilience

In cumulative effects workshops and other spaces where new forms of collaborative life are being worked out, resilience theory's advocates present their fellow researchers with a discordant set of demands: accept unconditionally the conditions of the present, even as you plan for a radically open future. This discordance underlines a key intersection between the new economics of decentralized science and the promise of resilience-based reform. Researchers are increasingly being told that by making concrete, individual sacrifices in organizing and carrying out their work, they will increase their chances of achieving collective, if ambiguous, returns. Rather than enacting these changes solely through the imposition of new laws or institutional mandates, though, the scientists recruited to participate in resilience-based initiatives are encouraged to perform self-conscious forms of accounting at every step of research, and to suppress the sophistication of their analyses by being selective about what they choose to "contribute" in collaborative settings.

Despite the aura of novelty surrounding recent invocations of resilience in northwest British Columbia, the compulsion to prioritize individual research activities is hardly new for the many researchers still living throughout the region. As I have argued in each of the previous chapters, these researchers' winding professional paths exemplify their contingent places within networks of power—places that have always depended on translating their work into formats acceptable to government ministries, funding bodies, and other powerful institutions. As the rush of public funding and institution building that followed the War in the Woods has given way to corporate- and philanthropic-sponsored research, individuals have still found ways to position their work so that it might be meaningful to future collaborators to come. Both White and First Nations senior researchers described some of their own strategies for prioritization as forms of deferral and detachment. Throughout my fieldwork, I observed how these researchers deferred the sense of urgency around particular field sites and questions, even as they affirmed commitments that they or their future successors should eventually return and pick up where they left off.

Proponents of resilience theory articulate different connections between the labor of prioritization and the horizons of collaborative life. A resilient collective voice, the organizers of the Morice salmon workshop suggested, would have to be continuously legible within networks of power. Whether by finding new sources of funding, new experimental techniques, or new terminology and visual tools for communicating findings to nonspecialists, whoever wished to remain part of this voice would have to adapt to keep a foothold in these networks. Rearticulating one's research through the language of cumulative effects analysis has for many rural researchers become a promising route for both achieving this flexibility and lending a sense of coherence to an otherwise scattered collective voice. By consistently reorienting their efforts around already-articulated policy goals rather than saving questions for later, proponents of resilience insist, disparately positioned scientists can ensure the survival of rural expertise even as individual researchers depart and surrounding landscapes continue to change.

For many White and First Nations researchers in northwest British Columbia, the promise of resilience continues to be elusive. Among those who remain skeptical of ambitious projects like the CEF—or, to be more precise, who continue to participate in resilience-based initiatives despite their ambivalence and periodic frustration—the model of rural research envisioned through resilience forebodes of estranging and dispiriting futures. If one assumes in advance that resources for research will remain meager and does not allow themselves to come to peace with their disappointments through their own practices of deferral and detachment, what will become of their personal investments in their work or the experiences they have accrued with other scientists? What will become of rural research as a form of life? Such questions underscore the paradoxical promise of resilience: even if scientists continually reframe their work around transcendent collective problems, their livelihoods will likely remain precarious, and their sense of investment in their research will depend ever more heavily on meanings attributed by others. But the system, at least, will survive.

Epilogue

In the early hours of February 6, 2020, Sleydo' (Molly Wickham), a Wet'suwet'en woman and spokesperson for the Gidimt'en Clan, posted two brief videos to Facebook. A tactical team of Royal Canadian Mounted Police (RCMP), she informed those watching, had just arrived at their checkpoint and were aggressively "clearing out the camp." For months, Sleydo' and other Wet'suwet'en activists and allies had maintained a road blockade to prevent surveyors and other construction workers from entering the Gidimt'en territories to continue building the Coastal GasLink pipeline. Intent on carrying out an injunction against the checkpoint awarded to the TransCanada Pipeline Corporation (TCP) by the BC courts, the RCMP team had finally arrived to arrest the organizers of the blockade. Over the next five days, RCMP officers made arrests at four additional checkpoint camps that other Wet'suwet'en activists had established along the proposed pipeline path. As I followed the events from my home in Baltimore through cascading text message exchanges with friends in Smithers and the surrounding area, Darlene Vegh's words from our visit the previous spring kept ringing in my ears: "It's pretty obvious to the folks who live up here that the conflicts never really stopped." Nobody won the War in the Woods. The War in the Woods never went away.

Within hours of Sleydo's posts, dozens of First Nations–led blockades and other protests initiated in solidarity with the Wet'suwet'en had sprung up throughout British Columbia and the rest of Canada. In Vancouver, protesters blocked access to four major seaports (Little 2020). In eastern Canada, protests at bridges, highway interchanges, and railway stations disrupted traffic for days, and generated tense confrontations between law enforcement officers, government officials, activists, and other residents (Bracken and Cecco 2020). A sympathetic blockade established on the Tyendinaga Mohawk reserve in Quebec blocked the main rail connection between Toronto and Montreal, severing passenger and freight connections between the two largest cities in the country (Bains 2020). By the end of the week, the arrests and the mushrooming local and national response had become front-page news around the world (Austen 2020; *BBC News* 2020; Kestler-D'Amours 2020).

In the month that followed the Wet'suwet'en checkpoint arrests, debates over First Nations' territorial claims and their jurisdiction over resource and infrastructure development became the singular focus of Canadian politics and public discussion. Rather than immediately offering new proposals for still more bureaucratic interventions into the conflicts, though, many commentators emphasized pervasive mistrust among affected communities and looming possibilities for retaliatory violence. Compared to most of the confrontations over clear-cut logging that unfolded during the 1980s and '90s, some observers argued, the militarized police teams that conducted the new raids seemed intent on instilling a sense of fear among the activists they encountered. Journalists active near the camps were forcibly removed and threatened with arrest if they photographed the RCMP officers conducting the sweeps—a tactic that RCMP officers had adopted from the tactical police teams that had conducted mass arrests at the Standing Rock Sioux protests against the Dakota Access Pipeline three years earlier (McIntosh 2020; Estes 2019).[1] Such overwhelming displays of force, government spokespersons argued shortly after the initial arrests, were necessary to protect Canada's precarious pathways for shipping resources to the outside world (see Cowen 2014). Leaving unbuilt the country's future extraction infrastructures or surrendering current systems to disruption, officials' comments suggested, would not simply cost developers access to lucrative global markets: such actions would induce an interminable national crisis. Even as commentators purported to feel sympathy for the interests of First Nations activists, many nevertheless bemoaned the "billions of dollars at stake" (Bains 2020) each day that the Tyendinaga Mohawk blockade prevented railway traffic from moving through eastern Canada. Canada's appetite for reconciliation, it seemed, could only extend so far.

Almost as abruptly as the protests had first arisen, an altogether different phenomenon emerged the following month to sever transport links within Canada and across the globe. In late January, a British Columbia resident returning from a trip to China became the province's first official case of COVID-19 (Canadian Press 2020). By the second week of March, an exponentially rising number of cases throughout Canada prompted near-universal shutdowns of schools, workplaces, and informal social activities. While some activists in rural areas were able to remain at—or return to—the camps and checkpoints where they had been maintaining their protests, most of the sympathetic blockades still running throughout the country dissolved as activists moved indoors to safeguard the health of their communities (Noakes 2020). In the months to follow, negotiations and legal disputes continued to unfold between Wet'suwet'en leaders, TCP executives, and provincial government officials (Cecco 2020). The sudden suspension of everyday life, though, effected for many activists and researchers in northwest British Columbia a prolonged period of reflection and doubt. What, after so many years of uncertain engagement, had their labor meant to the actual stewardship of the region's landscapes? What new kinds of stewardship claims and what new would-be stewards might emerge in the coming years, if the possibility of violent reprisals continued to linger?

For some researchers who had built careers in northwest British Columbia in the wake of the earlier War in the Woods, the February 2020 raids offered damning evidence that the bureaucratic systems established to mollify Indigenous resistance against resource extraction were not functioning as their initial proponents had promised. The fact that an international conflagration had begun on Wet'suwet'en land underscored this failure in particularly dramatic terms. The Office of the Wet'suwet'en (OW), a bureaucratic office chaired by the hereditary chiefs of each of the twelve Wet'suwet'en house groups, maintained a carefully integrated system for evaluating development proposals and consultation requests on their territories. They employed multiple full-time resource management specialists, and frequently organized or participated in collaborative research projects with government ministries, conservation NGOs, and individual scientists who worked on their territories. Like a growing number of other First Nations resource management offices throughout British Columbia, OW personnel and their contract-based researchers had even developed their own modeling tools for performing cumulative effects analysis, and actively solicited new data sets from developers working on their traditional territories.

Yet despite the OW's long-standing investments in these research and consultation processes, much of the popular media coverage of the arrests and subsequent protests nevertheless emphasized the apparent intransigence of the Wet'suwet'en hereditary leaders by contrasting them with the federally organized Wet'suwet'en band councils who had already expressed support for the Coastal GasLink pipeline (see, e.g., K. Coates 2020).[2] Only a handful of reports on the "historical origins" of Wet'suwet'en resistance acknowledged that OW staff had proposed an alternative route for the Coastal GasLink pipeline—a path that had secured the endorsement of almost all of the Wet'suwet'en hereditary chiefs—only to see TCP officials reject their proposal on the grounds that the new path would increase the project's construction costs (Kurjata 2020). To my Gitxsan and Gitanyow interlocutors who followed the progress of the Wet'suwet'en's consultation process from close quarters, the stalemate was as frustrating as it was predictable. More than twenty years after Gitxsan Strategic Watershed Analysis Team (SWAT) researchers were received with bemusement for insisting that provincial government officials appreciate the coherency of Gitxsan-produced maps and data sets, their Wet'suwet'en neighbors who had spent their entire lives as professional researchers remained stuck in a similar and still "unacknowledged space between two legal orders" (Napoleon 2010, 10), looking for ways to keep moving.

To say that individual researchers have persisted with their work while encountering similar misunderstandings is not the same as saying that nothing has changed. It does mean, however, that the individuals whose careers have come to span different phases of prolonged contests over stewardship and sovereignty often find themselves responsible for interpreting what forms of continuity are worth keeping. The final Wet'suwet'en camp invaded during the sweep of arrests in early February had been the Unist'ot'en Camp, a site that had been running continuously for nearly a decade. Originally established to monitor mineral exploration activity on the Unist'ot'en Clan territories and subsequently expanded to prevent surveyors and other technicians from continuing work on the now-canceled

Enbridge Northern Gateway pipeline project (see chapter 1), the Unist'ot'en Camp had since become the host of a healing center and other permanent buildings, where Freda Huson and other Unist'ot'en Clan representatives engaged with a growing roster of institutional supporters and held meetings with journalists, academics, and activists (McCreary and Turner 2018). Smogelgem (Warner Naziel), a hereditary chief with the Likhts'amisyu Clan and one of the primary spokespersons of the Unist'ot'en Camp during its initial years, had been one of Darlene Vegh's classmates in the Gitxsan Territorial Management course in the early 1990s—the same course where Vegh had first begun to learn geographic information systems (GIS) mapping techniques, and where she had first adopted the phrase "Heal the Land, Heal the People."[3] For several years, Smogelgem had produced traditional use study maps as a consultant for the OW before his frustrations with OW leadership inspired him to begin pursuing direct action protests instead (Khalfan 2015). The fact that their career paths as technical workers and activists had developed along such different registers, though, was less compelling for Vegh than the fact that she and Smogelgem were still working toward similar goals. After all, she observed, Smogelgem and others at the Unist'ot'en Camp had long ago adopted the slogan from the territorial management course for their public announcements and promotional materials too (Spice 2019).

My conversations with Vegh and other researchers about the February 2020 raids requires a significant qualification. Perhaps because I had first come to know staff at the OW and other Wet'suwet'en chiefs with whom Unist'ot'en leaders were sometimes at odds, I did not visit the Unist'ot'en Camp during my fieldwork in the region. While I shared a few informal conversations with some of Smogelgem's family members, I never met Smogelgem, Freda Huson, or any other leaders of the five Wet'suwet'en checkpoints that were temporarily dismantled by RCMP officers during the 2020 raids. As I have tried to illustrate throughout the text, the Gitxsan and other First Nations activists I came to know since beginning my research in 2013 each have contending positions and motivations, much like my White interlocutors. In hindsight, I wish I had sought out more land defenders like Smogelgem to complicate the stories of my other aging interlocutors, and to learn directly from them about their own experiences in bureaucratic research processes as well as the motivations behind their direct action work. Even as the War in the Woods was still playing out around me, I had to remind myself, my efforts to make sense of earlier episodes sometimes obscured my attention to the ways that the relationships engendered through these episodes were still taking shape in the present.

When I admitted these misgivings to my Gitxsan and Gitanyow interlocutors, several of them reminded me that the full breadth of their own experiences and attachments were never accessible to them all at once. Making sense of their lives as researchers—and of their roles in the lives of other researchers—their responses suggested, were narratological processes that could only unfold over time. The salience of certain connections were only triggered belatedly. Despite the fact that Vegh and I had talked about her initial training in mapmaking, and about her time with the Gitxsan Territorial Management course in particular, on and off for almost seven years, it had not occurred to Vegh to mention Smogelgem's presence in the course until the raids on the Wet'suwet'en camps and checkpoints had become international news. The ways that she and other Gitxsan researchers reflected on Smogelgem's consulting work and activism in our conversations about the raids and their possible aftermaths, then, made it clear that they expected their sense of connection with one another to continually evolve as new circumstances emerged, experiences were accrued, and generational transitions unfolded. That two lives spent on research and activism had converged for a while before apparently proceeding along different paths did not preclude the possibility of shared futures. In the meantime, conversations about such convergences could still provide prompts for engaging with other colleagues and kin, and for finding peace in the tumult of collaborative life.

Coming Home, Again

Precisely what future shape First Nations land defense and other claims to stewardship may take in the coming decades remains impossible to predict. For the men and women leading contemporary efforts at Wet'suwet'en checkpoints and elsewhere, though, the life stories of other activist researchers in the region underscore the incredible range of investments that can obtain within a single life spent on research. Sadly, one of the best-known of these life stories began to circulate in everyday conversation again recently after the researcher in question passed away.

On April 9, 2020, two months after the RCMP sweeps of the Wet'suwet'en camps began making international headlines and only four weeks after the spread of COVID-19 across North America had completely upended everyday life, Neil J. Sterritt (Mediig'm Gyamk), a Gitxsan researcher and political leader, died of cancer on his seventy-ninth birthday (*CBC News* 2020). Even as the coronavirus spread throughout Canada, Sterritt's death occasioned detailed obituaries in both provincial and national news outlets. For decades, Sterritt's work had made him a prominent figure in Indigenous politics throughout Canada. In the 1970s and '80s, he had served as both the original leader of the Gitxsan-Wet'suwet'en Alliance and the director of research for the original *Delgamuukw and Gisday'wa* trial. In addition to publishing a book and several articles narrativizing historical evidence of Gitxsan territorial claims, Sterritt had also published an award-winning memoir and genealogical history shortly before his death (Sterritt 1998, 2016; Sterritt et al. 1998). When I first met him in 2013, he had already received honorary doctorates from several of Canada's most prestigious universities. Initially, perhaps not unlike the journalists who lionized the man after his death, I had approached Sterritt primarily to learn about the historical experiences that had led to his accolades. As Sterritt and I became friends during my first trips to British Columbia, and as we continued to visit with one another in the years that followed, though, it soon became clear that he was far more eager to talk about his new mapmaking and writing endeavors, the individual genealogical studies he was undertaking on behalf of other Gitxsan, and the many other research projects he had started in recent years that as yet remained unfinished.

Like the myriad research projects that Sterritt had initiated over the course of his career, the social and professional ties that the man accrued through this work were at once dynamic and far-ranging. After the conclusion of the original *Delgamuukw and Gisday'wa* trial, Sterritt had moved to Ottawa to serve on the Canada-wide Assembly of First Nations, where he also worked as an official mediator in several high-profile conflicts, including the 1990 Oka Crisis. In the years that followed, Sterritt worked as an independent researcher and private consultant on behalf of First Nations and other Indigenous governments involved in land claims research and development disputes throughout the world. Most of the posthumous news coverage of Sterritt's life, however, effectively cast him as a figure from an earlier era. It had been Sterritt, my Gitxsan interlocutors liked to remind me, who had played the leading role in assembling all of the depositions and interview data collected for the original *Delgamuukw and Gisday'wa* trial into a single, spectacular paper map (Sparke 1998). It had also been Sterritt and his complex career path, national prominence, and incredible dexterity with cartographic techniques that had caused the provincial government's legal counsel to aggressively undermine his authenticity as a Gitxsan person during the original trial, when he was cross-examined for thirty-three days (Monet and Skanu'u 1992; Özden-Schilling 2020).

Unlike many other researchers I came to know in northwest British Columbia who framed their expertise as a product of place, Sterritt explicitly acknowledged the ways that his sense of the region as home had shifted as his research into Gitxsan and other territorial histories grew more complex. This sense of place had also transformed, he readily acknowledged in our conversations, each time he moved away from the Gitxsan territories, and each time he responded to new compulsions to return. Sterritt's first return to northwest British Columbia took place in the early 1970s, after he had completed a certificate as a mining technician and spent a decade moving between mineral exploration projects in northern Canada, Latin America, the United States, and Ireland. Originally recruited to run the 'Ksan campground and Gitxsan history museum only to be enrolled into budding land claims research efforts shortly thereafter in the wake of the epochal *Calder* decision, Sterritt saw the opportunity as a chance to raise his two sons on the Gitxsan territories, in the company of the same family members with whom Sterritt himself had learned to hunt, fish, and trap as a young boy.

Reflecting in his memoir on the farm where they lived then at Temlaham, "the prairie place . . . on the right bank of the Skeena River a few kilometers below Hazelton" (2016, 25), Sterritt emphasizes the urge he felt to articulate his own life within the ancestral traces he found in the landscape. Sterritt also highlights how his sense of the dynamism underlying these ancestral traces informed this engagement, foreshadowing more detailed discussions of his own oral historical and archival research covered in later chapters of the memoir. "It [Temlaham] is said to have been a village of hundreds of people, the ancestral home of many Tsimshian, Nisga'a, and Gitxsan until they abandoned it and scattered throughout the northwest. For . . . thirty-five years we lived in this mythic space, envisioning ancient events as depicted in the stories of our peoples. Barbara [Sterritt's wife] and I have spent more of our lives at Temlaham than anywhere else—and raised our sons there. Regardless of where we may be, Temlaham is home" (25).

Temlaham had become home for Sterritt, it seemed to me, because he had learned to inhabit it through research, and to carry it with him in language (see Cassin 2016, 41–64). Reflecting in his memoir on the initial exchanges with Gitxsan elders that first led him into a life of research, Sterritt explicitly underscores how the sense of place, purpose, and competence he attached to his work emerged through sustained conversation with other researchers:

At the outset of my initial mapping research in 1975, I interviewed Luus/ Chris Harris, a leading chief from Kispiox. He had been gathering place names, hunting and fishing sites and House boundaries from other chiefs since the late 1960s and showing them on a map of Gitxsan territory. He had the assistance of anthropologist Wilson Duff, linguist Bruce Rigsby, the National Museum's anthropologist, Marie Françoise Guedon, and my brother Art Sterritt. He showed me his map, and, assuming I spoke Gitxsan, liberally sprinkled his part of our conversation with Gitxsan words. I told Chris that speaking Gitxsan was a challenge for me, and he optimistically said, you can learn to speak our language by mapping Gitxsan territory. Chris was right. By the time the *Delgamuukw* case got to court in 1987, I could, after working with fluent speakers for years, name hundreds of geographic features in Gitxsan.[4] (Sterritt 2016, 304)

The exchanges through which Sterritt assembled the main *Delgamuukw and Gisday'wa* map drew him into a geographically dispersed and multigenerational web of relationships. But it was a web that relied for much of its form on the sharing and storage of artifacts. Even as he was still struggling to inhabit the Gitxsanimx language, he was already assuming new responsibilities for gathering and distributing elder mapmakers' knowledge and ambitions so that he could one day pass them along to others.

When Sterritt returned to live in British Columbia again after several years living in Ottawa—initially back to his farm at Temlaham, then later to 150 Mile House, a small town in the center of the province where one of his sons and other family members lived—the archive he had begun building through his mapmaking work for the *Delgamuukw and Gisday'wa* trials and subsequently expanded through independent projects had come to occupy an entire floor of his house. During my last in-person visit with Sterritt, in 2017, we spent most of our time eating banana bread, drinking tea, and sifting through sections of this archive together. Notes from meetings with well-known land claims negotiators during a recent trip to Australia; helicopter photographs of the Gitxsan territories taken and annotated during preparations for the *Delgamuukw and Gisday'wa* trials; genealogical charts tracing out more than half a dozen generations of his mother's Scottish ancestry; self-made exercise sheets he had constructed during his early years studying the Gitxsanimx language: each artifact prompted musings about an old project that he hoped to expand and refine.

As in all of our earlier meetings, he seemed optimistic that many years of research still awaited him. He had not yet been diagnosed with cancer.

Plans for the upcoming 104th birthday celebration of his father, Wiik̲'aax (Neil B. Sterritt), were underway.⁵ Despite his energetic outlook and his ever-expanding sense of his own authorial agency, though, Sterritt nevertheless made it clear that his primary tasks increasingly focused on preparing his archive for others. As we sat together, many of his stories drifted back to his recent and ongoing efforts to find a new home for his many research materials in the event of his untimely passing. He recounted conversations with longtime collaborators in Smithers about establishing a trust and finding resources for digitization. He described the progress of negotiations with museum archives in the provincial capital where he had conducted research throughout his career. Even for a renowned and well-connected researcher, each of these operations underscored the precariousness of his archive and the myriad uncertainties surrounding its future uses.

As he listed divergent scenarios for how the steps involved in securing the archive might eventually come together, Sterritt acknowledged that most of his projects would not be finished within his lifetime. What he was seeking was an imperfect sense of assurance—that his tens of thousands of documents would be safe and accessible to future land claims researchers, historians, and other Gitxsan eager to know more about their territories and ancestors, whatever new conflicts might arise. "Of course, nobody can promise you that kind of thing, especially nowadays," Sterritt admitted with a laugh. "Libraries and things like that go under all the time. A lot of their stuff just gets thrown out." The knowledge that he would spend the rest of his life seeking this assurance and recruiting other researchers and archivists to his cause nevertheless helped him to approach the end of his career in peace. Temlaham had become home for him through a life of research; in time, this labor might yet inflect the homecomings of others.

Convergence and Duration

For both White and First Nations researchers who began building careers in northwest British Columbia at the end of the twentieth century, the original War in the Woods was a period of convergence. Throughout the 1990s, many different kinds of political actors in British Columbia had argued that long-term scientific research and technical capacity building would revolutionize land governance in the province by providing a foundation for new forms of consensus. As I have shown throughout this book, the government programs launched in the wake of these earlier blockades found only limited success in achieving their original aims. Socially and politically, however, the rural towns and reserve villages that played host to these initiatives remain profoundly changed. Parts of northwest British Columbia have become substantially Whiter and wealthier (Chipeniuk 2004; Özden-Schilling 2019a). Accusations of "sellout" and "radical" lobbed between activists and their collectives—terms that were already in wide circulation well before the blockades of the 1990s—have garnered new connotations (White 1995; Satterfield 2002; see also Seymour 2018). Across this spectrum of practical and ideological orientations, locally organized research projects have continued to ground criticisms of centralized management practices and government interventions, even as routes for sustaining these projects have grown more complex. First Nations–led mapping projects, long-term ecological experiments, and other collaborative research endeavors have become anchors for senses of place and consequential processes of social reproduction, even if their impacts on policy may seem modest.

Long-term research, in other words, persists as forms of life. Yet what this persistence portends for Indigenous and settler colonial contests over stewardship is far from clear. Calls for bureaucratic "consultation" over resource development proposals long ago gave way to pleas for more thoroughgoing and historically engaged "reconciliation" on the Gitxsan, Wet'suwet'en, and Gitanyow territories, as they have across Canada as a whole. In much the same way that the term *consultation* quickly came to ring hollow for Vegh and her SWAT colleagues, though, Wet'suwet'en land defenders and other prominent spokespersons have loudly criticized the liberal sentiments and suspect motives that appear to undergird the reconciliation-themed initiatives already proliferating across the country (see Coulthard 2014; M.-A. Murphy 2020; Niezen 2017). More than three decades after War in the Woods–era initiatives and reforms emerged and began to unravel, the sense that researchers' work might yet contribute to a shared emancipatory project continues to feel frustratingly out of reach. Taken together, the previous chapters reflect the broad range of attitudes with which White and First Nations researchers regard the likelihood of future convergences. As the institutional landscape of northwest British Columbia grows more diverse with the ongoing transition toward contract-based research, however, the ways that White and First Nations researchers have come to understand the shared and parallel histories underlying their work will only become more important.

As the legacies and afterlives of the *Delgamuukw and Gisday'wa* trials, the Bulkley Land and Resource Management Plan, SWAT, the Date Creek

Research Forest, and other multifaceted architectures of research continue to unfold in the present, the duration of individual researchers' investments and entanglements in these processes must be given considered attention. Read and retemporalized together, these investments will continue to reveal patterns of constructive interference, as well as evidence of persistent gaps. As I was beginning my fieldwork in Smithers in early 2013, some younger White scientists asked me outright why I seemed to be more interested in conflicts that had transpired decades ago than in the confrontations that were unfolding all around me. Particularly that winter, when the confluence of the Idle No More movement and mounting protests against the Enbridge Northern Gateway pipeline continually shaped everyday conversations, such skepticism was understandable. These expressions, though, also underscored how particular temporal scales within the lives and careers of my interlocutors affected their sense of the ways their own research might be embedded within historical processes.

Many of the non-Indigenous researchers who became my friends and interlocutors in northwest British Columbia had been children during the original *Delgamuukw and Gisday'wa* trials. Most had moved to the region as adults with postgraduate degrees. Several had grown up outside Canada. To these researchers, my stakes in the region's politics and the circumstances of my arrival sometimes seemed little different from theirs. Occasionally, they asked me if I had considered leaving academia and permanently relocating to Smithers. The years that many of these researchers had spent learning to navigate the vagaries of philanthropic funding, corporate projects, and other forms of contract-based work had given them confidence in their skills and agility. For some, these experiences had also helped them to cultivate a wariness of more durable institutional attachments. Finding remunerative work as a researcher in the rural northwest simply demanded patience and creativity, they sometimes offered encouragingly. Making and maintaining a sense of meaning through this work, their stories suggested, was inseparable from the work of making neighbors. Yet as more researchers continue to move to the region and set about crafting strategies for sustaining their lives there, the senses of meaning—and of neighborly history—that they draw on in these efforts will inevitably continue to change.

The War in the Woods was not the first moment of convergence for White and First Nations researchers in northwest British Columbia. For at least a decade, the establishment of camps and checkpoints on Wet'suwet'en territory has already effected another period of convergence; the raids and arrests in early 2020 may well initiate yet another. For all of their structural similarities and differences, each of these moments of convergence will endure in part through the movements and investments of specific individuals. As was the case in the 1980s and '90s, future convergences will likely be set into motion as individual researchers and activists begin to articulate their labor through particular conceptualizations of home. In the early 1990s, numerous First Nations men and women upended the lives that they were beginning to build in Vancouver and other urban centers to devote their skills and energies to an unfolding political movement. Reflecting on her own movements through the region three decades later, Freda Huson, a representative of the Unist'ot'en Clan and a founder of the long-running Unist'ot'en Camp, referred to the structures that she and other activists were building on the territories as a "permanent home" (Spice 2019, 211). Keeping track of the activities of mineral exploration technicians, pipeline surveyors, and other prospective resource developers required a continual presence on the Unist'ot'en territories, Huson argued. Like many of my interlocutors, she effectively defined her role as a form of survivance—of taking up the work of the many Wet'suwet'en who had actively resisted colonial incursions since the nineteenth century, and of leaving things in place to assist new arrivals after she eventually departed. The presence of permanent structures and institutional support systems will no doubt cause future activists to experience their arrival on the Unist'ot'en and Gidimt'en territories with new kinds of horizons in mind. What senses of home these future activists might cultivate as they devote their lives and careers to the region, then, will ultimately be for them to decide.

NOTES

Preface

1   The Anglicized spelling of inherited names, place-names, and broader First Nations
     group names have all varied historically. Differences in spellings can be conten-
     tious, since they occasionally reflect disagreements over the legitimacy of spe-
     cific bureaucratic bodies and legal decisions. Some scholars use *Gitxsan* and
     Wet'suwet'en to remain in keeping with how each group referred to themselves
     during the *Delgamuukw and Gisday'wa* trials, but use *Gitxsan* (or *Gitẕsan*) and
     Witsuwit'en in other contexts to reflect the spellings that some linguists from each
     group have deemed more phonetically appropriate. The Office of the Wet'suwet'en,
     a treaty organization that represents the hereditary leaders of the Wet'suwet'en
     house groups, has retained this spelling to keep congruence with their legal case
     for Aboriginal title. Popular media accounts of recent direct action protests have
     almost exclusively used the term *Wet'suwet'en* to refer to the territories and people
     involved. To avoid confusion and to underscore the continuing connection between
     my interlocutors and contemporary protests, I have decided to use the spellings of
     Gitxsan and *Wet'suwet'en* throughout the book.

2   Each of the terms used to refer generally to the original inhabitants of Canada and
     their descendants is problematic in different ways. The term *Aboriginal* is defined
     in the Canadian constitution and refers to all Inuit, Métis, and First Nations people
     in Canada. *Aboriginal* and *Indian* remain common in bureaucratic use (e.g., the

federally run Department of Indian Affairs and Northern Development, now known as Indigenous and Northern Affairs Canada, has for decades administered to all of Canada's band reserves in accordance with the federal Indian Act, as well as managed the national government's engagements with the Inuit-run territory Nunavut). *First Nations*, a term that refers to all non-Inuit, non-Métis Indigenous groups in Canada, was brought into common usage as a political term in the second half of the twentieth century, although it is not defined in Canadian law. Official band membership is typically referred to as *Indian status*, although the term *First Nations* has begun appearing more frequently in these contexts as federally registered "Indian bands" change their official names. In practice, many of the Gitxsan, Gitanyow, and Wet'suwet'en men and women I worked with used the terms *Indian*, *Native*, and *Aboriginal* interchangeably, a fact that I reflect in direct quotations throughout the book. While very few of my interlocutors used the term *Indigenous* to refer to themselves, this term was frequently used by some activists as a means of articulating their work with other globally distributed networks of Indigenous activism. Beyond these problematic terminologies, the technicalities of formal band membership have also long been a source of tension for Indigenous people in North America, particularly for those with parents from different recognized groups. Some individuals living on the Gitxsan territories may be recognized by their peers as a member of a particular Gitxsan house group, for instance, but have their federally recognized status associated with a Gitanyow band office (or vice versa) due to where their parents were born. For attention to the myriad tensions and jurisdictional ambiguities associated with membership claims in the contemporary era, see TallBear 2013; Simpson 2014.

3   Critical discussions of the original 1991 provincial decision in the *Delgamuukw and Gisday'wa* case have occupied dozens, if not hundreds, of scholarly books and articles. For a comprehensive overview of the case, its precedents, and the immediate responses of anthropologists, see Culhane 1998. For more recent perspectives on the aftermath of the decision and its appeals, see McCreary 2014; Napoleon 2013. Many Gitxsan, including all of my Gitxsan interlocutors and nearly all of my non-Indigenous interlocutors in British Columbia as well, refer to the Gitxsan and Wet'suwet'en land claims trials simply as "Delgamuukw," rather than including the first named Wet'suwet'en chief in the title. Rather than mirror this usage myself, I have chosen throughout this book to use *Delgamuukw and Gisday'wa* for all references to these trials in order to keep Wet'suwet'en involvement in view.

4   The confrontations that followed the 1988 blockades at Kispiox Bridge were hardly Gitxsan people's first experiences disrupting travel and transport through their territories to protest colonial rule. In 1872, Gitxsan people blocked fur traders and other settlers from traversing the Skeena River after a campfire abandoned by White traders and mining prospectors destroyed Kitsegulka village (Galois 1992). Two years before the Kispiox blockade, federal Canadian fisheries officials and officers of the Royal Canadian Mounted Police attempted to shut down a Gitxsan fishing camp and were pelted with marshmallows until they retreated (Sterritt 1989). In the summer of 1990, Gitxsan men and women, like people from many First Nations,

established numerous additional blockades in support of Kanehsatà:ke First Nations living on the Oka reserve in Quebec, whose protests against the construction of a golf course on their traditional territories had led to an armed standoff with police and military forces. While the original Kanehsatà:ke protests were concerned with the disruption of grave sites rather than with the destruction of old-growth forests, many subsequent journalists and scholars have cited the resulting standoff as a major inflection point in the War in the Woods. See Blomley 1996; Davey 2019.

Introduction

1   All of the people identified in this book by their first names only have been given pseudonyms. People identified by first and last names have asked that I use their real names.

2   On the origins, diversification, and continuing unfolding of Idle No More, see Dhillon 2017.

3   Darlene's exasperation with the many ways that Canadian journalists erase Indigenous histories and conflicts in much contemporary coverage of resource conflicts is a frustration that she shares with numerous critical media scholars. See in particular Callison and Young 2020.

4   Yielding as many as ninety million cubic meters of hemlock, spruce, pine, and cedar for foreign and domestic markets each year, the interior of British Columbia has for decades been the single largest source of lumber sold in the United States, and an increasingly major supplier for East Asia as well (Government of British Columbia 2017).

5   Since 1982, the government of Canada has been engaged in a series of lawsuits with the United States government over the methods that provincial governments employed for pricing timber harvested on public land, a saga collectively referenced in popular media as the "Softwood Lumber Dispute" (Zhang 2007). Canadian companies who exported timber to the United States, US trade officials argued, effectively benefited from unfair "subsidies" unavailable to US-based companies, the majority of which operated on private lands and sold timber on unprotected markets. While a tariff agreement was put into place in 2006, the expiration of this agreement in 2015 has initiated yet another phase of diplomatic conflict.

6   Both White- and First Nations–organized civil society groups have become increasingly central to resource management disputes throughout British Columbia in recent years. For a general overview of these shifts within the context of community forests, see McCarthy 2006. For the Gitxsan experience, see McCreary 2014.

7   While the 1997 Supreme Court of Canada decision in *Delgamuukw and Gisday'wa v. The Queen* nominally established the government's obligation to consult First Nations on *recognized* Aboriginal title lands, the obligation to consult on *claimed* lands was not established until the *Haida Nation* decision in 2004. For this reason, I use the term *negotiate* throughout most of the book to refer to the administrative

encounters that took place between First Nations representatives and provincial government officials, outside the ambit of formal recognition, between 1997 and 2004.

8 Within the forests of northwest British Columbia, the expansion of private expertise has been perhaps most visible in the transition away from state-directed, or "prescriptive" land use planning programs, toward a range of industry self-reporting practices initiated in 2002 as part of the provincial government's "results-based" management regulatory regime (Thielmann and Tollefson 2009).

9 While the Campbell government's earnest attempt to pass a Recognition and Reconciliation Act failed to gain substantial support from either First Nations representative groups or business leaders throughout the province, the increasingly severe warnings of the courts gradually convinced developers and government officials alike that their long-standing strategies of deferral and nonengagement would no longer protect them from future legal action from First Nations with outstanding land claims. See Wood and Rossiter 2011.

10 During the 1990s, the BC Forest Service supported several collaborative research projects between First Nations people and government scientists, including several multiyear studies of postfire succession dynamics in berry gathering areas and other Gitxsan harvesting sites. As I show in chapter 2, Gitxsan berry harvesting sites have been subject to a range of published studies. See, e.g., C. Burton 1999; P. J. Burton 1998; Trusler and L. M. Johnson 2008.

11 These numbers warrant some explanation. While provincial governments are the largest single landholders in several Canadian provinces, the federal government remains the largest landholder in the country as a whole thanks to its sprawling tenures in Yukon, Nunavut, and Northwest Territories. (For a more detailed breakdown of Canadian land ownership statistics, see the "Statistical Data" page on the Government of Canada website, https://cfs.nrcan.gc.ca/statsprofile.) By comparison, only the state governments of New York and Alaska own more than 15 percent of the lands within their borders.

12 Prior to the proclamation of British colonial rule over the region in the nineteenth century, visitors intending to travel or hunt in Gitxsan house territories were expected to seek permission from the chiefs of each house (Sterritt et al. 1998, 98–131). The complicated legal history of Canada's Crown land, including the procedures required to develop it, the "rights" of early Euro-Canadian settlers to preempt it, and the challenges First Nations groups have faced while attempting to use and reclaim it, is the subject of numerous books and articles. For a detailed discussion of the historical roots of the "free entry" system, see Dickerson 1992. For a discussion of the links between free entry and other historical developments in property law and expropriation in former British colonies, see Overstall 2005.

13 Increased attention to the violence done to First Nations groups and other Indigenous communities by bureaucratic categories—violence often enacted by anthropologists themselves (Kuper 2003; Simpson 2007; Starn 2011; see also V. Deloria 1988,

78–100)—has of late precipitated a resurgence of activism deliberately pitched out-side the ambit of legal and bureaucratic legibility (Coulthard 2014; Simpson 2014).

14 Three separate treaties have been implemented through the BCTC process, includ-ing the Maa-nulth First Nations Treaty, which encompasses five separate First Nations. This number does not include the Nisga'a Final Agreement, which was ne-gotiated outside the BCTC framework.

15 While treaty negotiations based on the land selection model have been carried out by provincially appointed officials, the actual process of extinguishing Aboriginal claims can only be administered by the federal government, through federal legis-lative processes. The 1997 *Delgamuukw and Gisday'wa* decision explicitly affirmed that the provincial government could not extinguish claims on its own.

16 Initially positioned by my interlocutors as a cheerfully naive American observer, I was often encouraged to view the unraveling of provincial support for research in the early 2000s as complementary to the "war on science" playing out during my main research period, a new "war" led by then prime minister Stephen Harper and his Conservative federal government of Canada. See, e.g., Peyton and Franks 2016.

17 Riles's typical usage of "technocracy" is considerably narrower than the one I am de-veloping in this book. In *Collateral Knowledge*, Riles (2011) uses the term to describe the centralized, prescriptive regulatory system through which cohorts of govern-ment experts governed finance and banking in Japan up until the introduction of liberalizing reforms in the 1990s. "State knowledge—what I will call 'technocratic knowledge,'" she argues, "is indeed different from . . . private technical expertise" (85). Within Riles's framing, expert identities are much more closely aligned with in-stitutional positions; while the relative authority exerted by different kinds of experts underwent radical changes during the period Riles investigates, she presents the nominal boundaries between public and private institutions as remaining discrete.

18 For a broader look at the constitutive roles played by rumor and violence in the manifestation of authority within other supposedly marginal practices and spaces, see Das and Poole 2004.

19 Even as the trials and related blockades were unfolding, some Gitxsan were actively experimenting with selective logging on their own territories (A. Mills 1994, 179).

20 In British Columbia and elsewhere, scholars have primarily sought to understand the effects of the neoliberalization of industrial forestry by tracking the rise of cor-porate power within governance processes previously managed by state agencies (see, e.g., McCarthy 2005, 2006; Brockington, Duffy, and Igoe 2008; Heynen et al. 2007; T. M. Li 2014).

21 Numerous scholars have critiqued the tendency of state officials in the United States and Canada to conflate social continuity with "tradition." See, e.g., Dombrowski 2001; Sider 2003; Bell 2016.

22 In recent years, Indigenous-led activism has brought these issues to the attention of broad audiences. Particularly during the still-ongoing Idle No More protests, which began in late 2012 and spanned all of Canada by early 2013, thousands of

First Nations activists in British Columbia and elsewhere questioned the long-term value of job training programs, development consultation procedures, and other government-run initiatives like those established during the War in the Woods (McCreary 2013a; Bell 2017). Since 2015, government-run capacity-building initiatives in Canada have been increasingly framed as official responses to the Government of Canada's Truth and Reconciliation Commission on Indian residential schools. While some Indigenous scholars and political leaders have commended this transition for emphasizing the role of social histories and collective healing in contemporary institution building, others have expressed concern about the ways that these programs have helped to mollify urgent and concrete political demands. In much the same way that government emphases on "recognition" during the 1990s failed to produce lasting economic change for First Nations communities, Dene theorist Glen Coulthard argues, the use of the concept of "reconciliation" as a tool for political dialogue offers "little insight into how to address the more overtly structural and/or economic features of social oppression" (Coulthard 2014, 34).

23 Newspaper articles and blog posts published by dissident chiefs during the office blockade and its aftermath broadcast the breadth of their alliance through a color-coded version of the original *Delgamuukw* map: white-colored house territories were for the GTS; yellow remained opposed (Gitxsan Unity Movement 2012b).

24 In 2013, GTS officials countered dissidents' attempts to dissolve the society by rewriting their bylaws to recruit new members from the remaining loyal house groups (*Spookw v. Gitxsan Treaty Society* [2015] BCCA 77 (Can. LII), J. A. Groberman).

1. Nostalgia

1 Nathan Cullen, Taylor Bachrach, and Irving Fox are all public figures, and thus I am using their real names. All of the other names of my interlocutors used in this chapter are pseudonyms.

2 Yes, the most widely used demonym for residents of Smithers, BC, is indeed *Smithereen*.

3 The BC Liberal Party and the federal Liberal Party are different entities with a long history of antagonism. Whereas BC NDP officials routinely caucus with their federal NDP colleagues, BC and federal Liberals have no such working relationship. On April 12, 2023, the party changed its name to BC United.

4 On the participation of First Nation communities in these reviews and protests, see McCreary and Milligan 2014.

5 This was the same contentious election that saw Stephen Harper and his Conservative Party win another term as leaders of federal parliament. It was also the first time that the NDP overtook the federal Liberal Party in a nationwide election.

6 Several of the fourteen original LRMPs were completed by government planners after community board members failed to reach consensus. Numerous groups saw their meetings devolve into acrimony. See Booth and Halseth 2011.

7   As Victoria-based political scientists Tim Thielmann and Chris Tollefson explain, the Forest and Range Practices Act (FRPA), which took effect in early 2004, transformed the role of ecological scientists in key processes of government assessment. "Under the former legislation," they explain, "[timber] licensees were obliged to conduct an array of site-specific planning and preparatory measures prior to receiving logging authorization. Consistent with the results-oriented approach, the new law, by contrast, allowed licensees to demonstrate that the strategies outlined in their site-specific plans were consistent with the objectives in FRPA or related regulations" (2009, 119). For a critique of the proliferation of "results-based" management programs in international aid programs, see Eyben 2010.

8   Within two years of the implementation of the new regime, even the provincial government's own independent advisory group, the Forest Practices Board, admitted that, as Thielmann and Tollefson (2009, 119) put it, "forest planning documents approved by the Ministry under this model often disclosed few details about how, when, and where logging would occur, and most did not define forestry outcomes or results that were capable of measurement." See also Forest Practices Board 2006.

9   Smithers resident and former University of Northern British Columbia professor of Environmental Planning Ray Chipeniuk's work on "amenity migration" (cf. Chipeniuk 2004) is well known among BVRC affiliates (several of whom thought—incorrectly—that Chipeniuk himself had coined the term), whose reflexivity about their own status as "amenity migrants" helped to make many of them richly provocative, if occasionally awkwardly self-conscious ethnographic interlocutors. (For a local profile on Chipeniuk himself, see *Northword* 2007.) While most North American scholars interested in amenity migration have approached its effects as problem of economic geography, municipal planning, and rural sociology, several ethnographies add texture to these analyses. Anthropologist Leslie Robertson (2005) has explored the social ruptures and ethnic and class conflict and alienation induced through the construction of a ski resort in the historic coal mining town of Fernie, British Columbia. For a broader overview of the geography, sociology, and planning literature on amenity migration, see Gosnell and Abrams 2011.

10   Early settlers apparently described the northwest quarter of British Columbia as a "a territory so vast" it would "never be surveyed" (Shand 1898, 501).

11   Prior to the construction of the Alcan smelter in Kitimat in the 1950s, nearly all of the aluminum production in Canada took place in Quebec. For a glimpse into the federal reaction to the formation of unions in Kitimat, see Lapointe 1994.

12   For a retrospective discussion of this project, see Pojar, Klinka, and Meidinger 1987.

13   Although no longer extant, the Social Credit Party, or SoCred, is widely credited with being the driving force behind the commercial and infrastructural development of the provincial interior during the middle decades of the twentieth century. For more on the Social Credit influence on BC land management and development, see Barman 2007, 286–314.

14   The history of the LRMP process deserves its own book and has already generated a considerable literature among Canadian and non-Canadian policy scholars,

several of whom have written entire dissertations devoted to the early stages of the process (e.g., Giesbrecht 2003; Frame 2002; T. Thornton 2002). The initial design and implementation of LRMP processes across the province (including its government-led predecessor, the Commission on Resources and Environment, or CORE) was eagerly hailed as a spectacular success of "democratization," despite the exclusion of First Nations concerns throughout the 1990s and the communication breakdowns suffered by numerous community resources boards. For some policy scholars, the mere fact that the process was "completed" and that the resultant LRMPs were then incorporated into provincial land use policy was more important than assessing whether the final plans achieved local consensus or not (Jackson and Curry 2004; see also Bernstein and Cashore 2000). A more recent iteration, the Sustainable Resource Management Plan program introduced by the BC Liberal government in 2002 and led by the newly created Ministry of Sustainable Resource Management, has worked to develop land use plans for use by First Nations and other groups (see chapter 4), but has been primarily run by smaller (and less well supported) government planners and analysts with minimal public involvement. As political scientist Jeremy Wilson (2001) has acknowledged, most of these processes were flawed from the outset due to the severe constraints imposed by the government planners ultimately responsible for accepting community-produced plans. Legal scholars Tim Thielmann and Chris Tollefson (2009) are among a group of more recent scholars to look past the decline in direct action protests and other forestry conflicts and recognize the lingering sense of alienation most, if not all, LRMP participants have come to feel toward these documents, and to the widespread frustration with the Liberal government's nonrecognition of these documents' many nonbinding land use recommendations (see also Booth and Halseth 2011; Halseth and Booth 2003; Reed 2003).

15 The local genesis of the Bulkley CRB began in conversations between members of other Smithers-based conservation groups in the late 1970s and early 1980s, long before the provincial government first considered opening up the land management planning process to nonspecialists. After the appointment of the initial CRB group in September 1991, the board's critiques of the Ministry of Forests–driven Forests and Lands Management Plan program pressured the government to develop an alternative process. The LRMP document alludes to some of these antecedents: see Bulkley Valley Community Resources Board 1998, 22–23. See also Giesbrecht 2003.

16 These include the Babine Mountains and Driftwood Canyon Provincial Parks, as well as the Babine River Corridor, a critical salmon spawning site. Like many governments at the time, the government of British Columbia was particularly motivated by the influence of the Bruntland Report, "Our Common Future," a treatise on "sustainable development" that the United Nations issued in 1987 (World Commission on Environment and Development 1987). Thanks to the report, the rather arbitrary argument that 12 percent of a given territory should be protected for ecological conservation was treated (somewhat simplistically) by the incoming NDP government as a mandate for the creation of new provincial parks. As LRMP participants soon discovered, however, ministry planners who facilitated the ap-

proval of these plans were often more concerned with achieving the province-wide 12 percent threshold than with focusing conservation efforts on particularly vulnerable or significant regions (see also Thielmann and Tollefson 2009, 112–13).

17 In some cases, the lack of new data also forestalled the provincial approval of LRMPs that had already achieved consensus among CRB members. Perhaps the most notable example of this is the Morice LRMP, set in the Morice Forest District immediately southeast of the Bulkley District. After the initial LRMP was sent to the provincial government for final approval in the early 2000s, the onset of a spectacular mountain pine beetle epidemic and the subsequent death of a huge portion of the district's mature lodgepole pine was cited as discrediting the Morice planning committee's stipulations of timber harvesting areas and park boundaries. The plan was finally approved nearly a decade later, despite the fact that no additional ground-based inventory data on the tree cover in the district had been assembled during the interim. See Morton, Gunton, and Day 2012.

18 Irving Fox, the architect of the original Bulkley Valley CRB, deliberately eschewed other CORE and LRMP groups' manner of recruiting representatives based from specific businesses or "sectors," believing that individuals elected based on their "values" would be less beholden to the interests of private entities (Booth and Halseth 2011, 900).

19 Arun Agrawal (2005) makes a similar point while discussing the decentralization of forest use law enforcement work in postcolonial India. Whereas the state could mete out harsh fines and prison terms for infractions, community-led councils were more apt to be lenient on rule-breakers "out of the recognition that group members who are punished will remain members" (95) of the council and of the local community.

20 The work of authoring connections to place has required many different residents of British Columbia to lay claim to a sense of time as well. Historian William Turkel (2007) argues that rural groups' claims to authority often require them to narrativize the histories of local landscapes with artifacts ready to hand, be they tables of geophysical data, First Nations–authored oral histories, or contested landmarks of exploration and colonial settlement. Particularly in rural British Columbia, Turkel suggests, historical consciousness and social memory emerge not only through texts and traditions, but through environmental traces of contested events. Assembling archives of these traces, whether through historiography, archaeological excavation, geophysical surveys, or storytelling positions the province's rural resource experts within discordant discursive worlds.

21 Covering an incredible 150,000 square kilometers, the Stikine District was home to roughly twenty thousand people in 2013. Demographic information for each of British Columbia's eighty-five ridings, or electoral districts, is maintained on the "Electoral District Maps" section of the Elections BC website (https://elections.bc.ca/resources/maps/electoral-district-maps/). Given the small populations in the immense north and the tremendous influence of the resource industries and interests active in the region, the provincial northwest has been the target of an unending

series of redistricting proposals by the provincial electoral commission, Elections BC. The current Stikine District has existed only since 2009, and it is quite likely that it will change significantly in size and shape within the next few election cycles. For several of the proposed redistricting plans, see "Part 9—Proposed Single Member Plurality Boundaries" of the official report of Elections BC (http://www.elections .bc.ca/docs/rpt/BCEBC-Prelim/Part%209-TheNorth.pdf).

2. Calling

1 Russell Collier and Darlene Vegh have each asked me to use their real names. Don Ryan is a public figure and published author, so I use his real name throughout this book as well. All other names of my interlocutors in this chapter are pseudonyms.

2 The choice of the name SWAT was indeed meant as a tongue-in-cheek reference to the police-related American usage, which had begun gaining currency in northwest British Columbia in the early 1990s thanks to the reality TV show *Cops*.

3 During the 2016 national census, 5,675 people claimed Gitxsan ancestry (J. V. Powell, Jensen, and Pedersen 2018). Of these, roughly 3,400 had band membership through one of the Gitxsan reserves (see Gitxsan Government Commission 2017).

4 In 1975, immediately after the *Calder* decision, Gitxsan and Wet'suwet'en chiefs (then organized as the Gitksan-Carrier Tribal Council, the predecessor to the later Gitxsan-Wet'suwet'en Alliance) attempted to begin treaty negotiations with the provincial government, but withdrew when they were informed that the maximum extent of the jurisdiction they could hope to achieve through the process were the powers accorded to municipal governments. See Napoleon 2005.

5 Anthropologists who participated in and wrote about the original *Delgamuukw and Gisday'wa* decision have repeatedly criticized the provincial court's unwillingness to acknowledge the epistemic incommensurabilities presented by Gitxsan and Wet'suwet'en performances of their oral histories and legal orders (see, e.g., Cruikshank 1992; Culhane 1998; Sparke 1998; Daly 2005). For an irreverent yet comprehensive Gitxsan take on the original trial and its immediate aftermath, see Monet and Skanu'u 1992.

6 The consultation process for which SWAT was originally established gained considerable teeth in 2004, after the Haida Nation successfully sued the BC minister of forests for allowing a tree farm license on their traditional territories to be transferred between developers without their consent. See Olynyk 2005.

7 Positive examples from both academic and popular literatures, particularly studies of land-based education (see, e.g., Lowan-Trudeau 2012), are far too numerous to count. Several prominent organizations in North America, including the Harvard Project on American Indian Economic Development support, catalog, and promote what they see to be successful examples of these kinds of partnerships, as do numerous other NGOs active in specific regions of the continent.

8   I am profoundly indebted to Renya Ramirez for reminding me of this painful fact during out discussions of an earlier draft of this chapter. While the term *vocation* did not evoke these kinds of associations for my specific interlocutors, it has far too dark a history for other First Nations communities in Canada to escape critical reflection.

9   A small number of residential schools elsewhere in Canada transitioned to First Nations control and continued to run into the 1990s. See Niezen 2017.

10   As cooperative management programs, cultural artifact protection laws, and large-scale Indigenous knowledge databasing projects expanded in scope throughout Indigenous-claimed territories in North America over the course of the 1980s and '90s, most academic discussions of traditional ecological knowledge, or TEK, sharpened epistemic divides between Indigenous and Euro-American institutions by framing traditional governance and land management systems as possessing an idealized, utopian continuity. Arun Agrawal (1995), an early critic of the large-scale Indigenous knowledge databasing projects organized in the 1990s by the World Bank and other international NGOs, explicitly warned against the dangers inherent in focusing on "knowledge" itself rather than on the sites, circumstances, and subjectivities shaping its emergence (see also Warren, Slikkerveer, and Brokensha 1995). And yet in his later work, Agrawal nevertheless periodically brackets and generalizes Indigeneity itself by asking "whether there is anything particularly Indigenous about knowledge that has undergone the sanitisation implicit in the movement from particularisation to generalisation" (Agrawal 2002, 292).

11   Paul Nadasdy (1999, 2003, 2005a, 2007) spent several years working with the Ruby Range Sheep Steering Committee, a wildlife comanagement committee formed by the government of Yukon in the 1990s. As Nadasdy shows, the mundane practical demands of participating in the committee sometimes carried intergenerational consequences for members of the Kluane First Nation. Few of the people who attended the committee's meetings were equally conversant in the languages and affective registers in which government scientists asserted statistical information relevant to sheep populations and in which Kluane elders reflected on their experiences hunting and living near sheep. Several of the young Kluane assistants recruited to perform translational work for the meetings, Nadasdy points out, eventually took on full-time jobs in policy and administration. That the unceasing demands of office work eventually precluded substantial time on the land, Nadasdy lamented, was a particularly bitter irony: even before their elders had died, the "bureaucratization of the younger generation" (2003, 142) had cast doubt on their legitimacy as Kluane spokespersons.

12   Henry Alfred, Wet'suwet'en chief Wah Tah K'eght and final surviving plaintiff from *Delgamuukw and Gisday'wa v. The Queen*, died in the autumn of 2018. See McCreary 2018a.

13   In much of his early work, Clifford explicitly contrasts Indigenous and diaspora experiences of mobility, even as he argues against reifying either category by attending to their "mutually constitutive tension" (Clifford 2001, 470).

14 Several anthropologists have recognized the growing imbrication of professional demands and technical conventions within contemporary scenes of Indigenous articulation by complimenting Clifford's analytic with the questions and techniques of science and technology studies. Kim TallBear (2013) argues that the contrived narratives and other "false promises" produced through genetic ancestry testing and blood-based group membership thresholds have done much to undermine stories, shared histories, and other foundational forms of collective articulation. See also De la Cadena et al. 2015.

15 As of January 2020, only the Nisga'a Final Agreement, the Tsawwassen First Nation Final Agreement, the Maa-nulth First Nation Final Agreement, and the Tla'amin Final Agreement have gone into effect. The Nisga'a Final Agreement, which was signed in 1998 and went into effect in 2000, preceded the BC Treaty Commission framework. Sixth-stage final agreements reached with the Yale and Lheidli T'enneh First Nations were either not ratified or postponed prior to implementation. For more information, see the "Treaties and Agreements" page of the BC Treaty Commission website (http://www.bctreaty.ca/treaties-and-agreements).

16 On the historical antecedents of certain regional divisions among the *huwilp*, see Galois 1993.

17 Gitxsan legal theorist Val Napoleon (2010) has argued that one of the enduring legacies of the original *Delgamuukw and Gisday'wa* trial research team's focus on the testimony of *wilp* chiefs has been the undermining of the democratic structures that had previously kept in check the authority of individual chiefs. The general valorization of representative forms of politics has rarefied decision-making hierarchies and empowered organizations like the GTS to overrule the objections of constituent house groups, Napoleon suggests, a troubling inversion of earlier Gitxsan political and legal orders. See Borrows 2002; Marsden 2002; McCreary, 2014; P. D. Mills 2008; Napoleon 2005, 2013, 2019; Overstall 2005; Usher, Tough, and Galois 1992.

18 The sensitivity surrounding these original documents is the primary reason that I have chosen not to show any SWAT-produced maps in this chapter.

19 Darlene Vegh's and Russell Collier's names frequently grace the acknowledgments sections of books and articles published on disparate research projects conducted throughout the region (see, e.g., Berkes et al. 1998; Gamiet, Ridenour, and Philpot 1998; Johnson 1997, 2010; Sterritt et al. 1998). Leslie Main Johnson, an anthropologist and ethnobotanist at Athabasca University, has collaborated extensively with Vegh and other former SWAT members for her research on Gitxsan plant knowledge, language, and landscape perception (see, in particular, L. M. Johnson 2010, 185–201; L. M. Johnson, Vegh, and Morgan 2019).

20 While the GTS has adopted the name, language, and orthography of the Gitxsanimx-speaking eastern villages (residents of which call themselves "Gitxsan"), speakers from the western villages, populated by those who call themselves "Gitksen," employ the language and orthography of the Gitsenimx language. As Leslie Main Johnson (2010, 1–7, 219) and Tyler McCreary (2013b, x) have both described

in detail, the spellings, terms, and orthography employed in written texts have lately followed the standards set by the GTS.

21 In his own critiques of the BCTC process, former Gitxsan-Wet'suwet'en Alliance leader Neil J. Sterritt, whose research for the original *Delgamuukw and Gisday'wa* trial I discuss elsewhere (Özden-Schilling 2020), has repeatedly called attention to the reluctance of the province to engage with competing claims in a comprehensive manner, particularly regarding the Nisga'a Final Agreement of 1998, which the BCTC and other provincial institutions initially celebrated as an exemplary success of the commission's new reconciliation procedures in spite of the fact that much of the Gitxsan First Nation's and nearly all of the Gitanyow First Nation's territorial claims were subsumed within the region claimed as Nisga'a traditional territory (see Sterritt 1998; Sterritt et al. 1998). During the sustained break between the provincial appeal of the original *Delgamuukw* decision in 1993 and the beginning of the Supreme Court of Canada hearing several years later, Don Ryan (Mas Gaak) initially began to lead the newly formed GTS through the BCTC negotiation process, but ultimately decided to return to court (Eichstaedt and Donaldson 1994).

22 For Don Ryan's personal reflections on these transitions, see Ryan 2005.

23 On the broader consequences of the shift toward digital mapping and data management infrastructures by governments in the late twentieth century, see Bowker 2000; Edwards 2010; Bowker et al. 2010; Rankin 2016.

24 The FRBC program also sponsored a number of comanagement projects, including a study of the effects of forest canopy shade on the growth of berry gathering sites at various locations around the Gitxsan territories, one of which spawned a short-lived berry harvesting cooperative (see P. J. Burton 1998). In interviews for local newspapers, national magazines, and academic publications, Darlene Vegh and her colleagues reflected on their roles in these projects by emphasizing their hopes that expanded control over logging decisions would lead to new business opportunities in ecotourism and local food production (see, e.g., Convis 2000; Trusler and L. M. Johnson 2008).

25 Rather cruelly, the prospect of a death in a First Nations community suddenly disrupting a long-planned meeting was treated almost as a cliché among many of the government and company representatives I met in the region. A number of anthropologists have described the ways in which death suspends quotidian routines in Indigenous communities. Hugh Brody's (1981, 72–84) moving, somewhat absurdist account of a Christian funeral on a Beaver reserve in northeast British Columbia performs a brilliant countermove, displaying how the mixture of sobbing, boredom, drinking, and comings and goings that accompanies the church ceremony renders strange the awkward, dogmatic efficiency and condescending affect of Christian ritual imposed on the daily life of reserve residents.

26 For an early history of the AMN, see B. D. Johnson 1999.

27 Chapin, Lamb, and Threlkeld (2005, 624) have called attention to the near monopoly that "map biography" techniques have assumed in Indigenous countermapping

projects since the development of the technique with the Inuit Land Use and Occupancy Project in the 1970s. See also Usher, Tough, and Galois 1992.

28 Given Collier's status within the countermapping community, even his master's thesis received media attention. See Delisle 2012.

29 Ethnographic treatments of Indigenous countermapping projects typically presume that the technocratic apparatus of the state precedes and enframes the "introduction" or "arrival" of digital mapping technologies and competencies in Indigenous communities (see, e.g., Rundstrom 1995; Fox 2002).

30 "Nathan Cullen's tribute to Russell Collier in the House of Commons," May 26, 2014, YouTube, https://www.youtube.com/watch?v=cJeS43rfyMQ.

31 When Collier received the name in the late 1980s, the invention of new names was a rare event. In recent years, however, the practice of inventing new names has become far more common, although the lack of authority held by these names in the feast hall continues to make them somewhat undesirable for most Gitxsan. On the relationship between feast names and Gitxsan social hierarchy, see Daly 2005, 194–210. On the politics of names among other neighboring First Nations within the broader Tsimshianic language family, see Roth 2001.

3. Inheritance

1 Ethnomethodologists have long explored the use of visual heuristics, ideal-typic models, and learned techniques of differentiation that are central to contemporary field research. As they show for fieldwork in disciplines ranging from geology and astronomy to archaeology and botany, recognizing forms and objects of study, developing authoritative counts, and delimiting spatial and temporal areas of study all depend on a balance of tacit knowledge (Polanyi 1966), formalized techniques (Rudwick 1976; Lynch 1985; Law and Lynch 1990), and embodied and institutionally conditioned forms of sight that Charles Goodwin (1994) refers to as "professional vision."

2 For a schematic illustration of one such "gap," see figure 3.2. Dennis and his group spent months identifying the operational variables that would be imposed on their experiment by the topography of the initial installation. Covering four square kilometers of the Kispiox Valley, the largest experimental plot encompassed the entire research forest itself and included all of the smaller experimental plots within it. Selecting a broad and relatively flat swath of transitional forest that had evaded logging companies working their way north through the Skeena watershed in the 1970s and '80s, the founders proposed to establish a series of sixteen "treatment" units (see figure 3.3). The founders described the structure of the experiment as follows:

> Two levels of partial cutting were used and compared with both undisturbed forests and clearcuts. In the light partial cutting treatment, approximately 30% of the stand volume was removed by cutting either single stems or small gaps (3–10 trees). In the heavy partial cutting experiment, approximately 60% of stand volume was removed. The cutting pattern utilized both large gaps (0.1–0.5

ha [hectare, or 0.01 square kilometers] in size), evenly distributed across the treatment units and either single trees or small gaps in the forest matrix between the large openings. With the exception of scattered residual deciduous trees (most trembling aspen and paper birch), all stems were removed in the clearcut treatment units. There were four replicates of each of the four treatments, organized in a randomized block design; treatment units were approximately 20 hectares in size. The intent was to create four differently structured stands that would provide a wide variety of environmental conditions both between and within treatments. (K. D. Coates et al. 1997, 7)

Dennis and his early collaborators treated the "field" produced through these tree-removal "treatments" as a massive physical simulator, a model of the forested landscapes across all of the province's mapped ICHMC2 climatic zones ("interior cedar-hemlock, moist-cold, second subdivision"; or in the parlance of conventional BC silviculture, site index 20). The biogeoclimatic ecosystem classification (BEC) system was developed in British Columbia between 1950 and 1975 as a means of providing ministry silviculturists and other government and academic environmental scientists with a standardized language for grouping sites and regions across the province according to the kinds of vegetation found there. As I describe in chapter 1, several residents of Smithers participated in these foundational studies prior to moving into forestry consulting or other ministry work. For a historical discussion of the creation of the BEC system, see Pojar, Klinka, and Meidinger 1987.

3   Since 1992, Dennis and his collaborators have put together numerous websites and offline catalogs, although the constant restructuring of the provincial resource industries and the subsequent migration of Forest Service websites to new domain names has rendered almost all of these lists inaccessible.

4   Elsewhere, I examine how Dennis utilized computer modeling tools that he established through his field research at Date Creek as a means of securing and reformatting intergenerational transfers of knowledge, experience, and ambition (see Özden-Schilling 2021). By expanding the meanings an individual scientist might attribute to authorship, collaboration, and individual legacy, I argue, computer models challenge long-standing anthropological theories of succession as mechanisms for ensuring continuity (e.g., Fortes 1970) and raise uneasy questions about how individuals collaborating through contracting institutions might conceptualize a shared future. For a more detailed analysis of succession and contingency within elite settings, see De Pina-Cabral and Pedroso de Lima 2000.

5   Rebecca Lemov (2015) discusses the effects of personnel changes and institutional instability on issues of closure and continuity in large-scale social science research. See also Edwards 2010.

6   Dennis also devoted much of the last decade of his career to developing an elaborate ecological succession model that conveyed uncertainties through broad statistical envelopes. As he and Sanjit explained to me, its distributions continued to broaden as climate change brought increasingly dramatic swings in rainfall and temperature to the Kispiox Valley.

7   While commercial tree harvesting began in the Upper Skeena almost as soon as Euro-Canadian settlers arrived there in the late nineteenth century, the kind of large-scale clear-cutting that powered the timber economies of Vancouver Island and the southern coast had only begun to move into the region in the 1970s. As logging trucks pushed northward through the provincial interior and inland from the coast in the following decades, producers operating throughout the province consolidated. By 2017, only eighty-one lumber mills remained throughout the entire interior, down from a total of well over two hundred less than a century earlier. Their combined annual output of forty million cubic meters, however (despite representing a substantial decline from a decade earlier), had long since made northern British Columbia one of the most prolific timber producers in the world (Government of British Columbia 2017). In the process, the questions used to organize new research trials narrowed. Earlier work on mixed species and age classes was abandoned across the province in favor of research on the issues that mattered to intensively managed silvicultural systems, including genetics, productivity, and sustained yield (see Bernsohn 1981; Barman 2007; Wilson 1998).

8   Exploring the professional identity crises that reshaped various disciplines of field biology between the nineteenth and twentieth centuries, historian Robert Kohler (2002) describes how communities of scientists approached and policed the often ambiguous boundaries between the spaces of laboratories and field science. Kohler draws heavily on the work of sociologist Thomas Gieryn (1983), whose concept of "boundary work" was originally addressed to the long-standing problem in the philosophy of science of distinguishing between "science" and "nonscience." Ultimately, Kohler argues, proponents of ecology and field-based biological studies resigned themselves not to challenging the hegemony of laboratory practice, but to using their work to champion the value of longitudinal studies, "natural" variability, and "real-world" experience. As Kohler and others make plain, of course, each of these "values" bears the mark of historical construction and contingency. See Kohler and Kuklick 1996. For a contemporary analysis of the political stakes of similar demarcation strategies, see Cittadino 2004; Lave 2012. As Philip Pauly (2000) has argued, the design and organization of field research stations was also in many cases driven by researchers' desires to maximize their access to summer holiday destinations and various middle-class leisure pursuits. By essentially taking at face value what each community defined as an "experiment," however, Kohler avoids explaining how the transposition of laboratory practices from bench tops to forests implicates field biologists in broader dialogues on the worth and meaning of these evolving experimental spaces. In the seventh chapter of the book *Nature's Experiments*, Kohler (2002, 212–51) does discuss how the emergence of glaciology and other disciplines provoked debates over the accuracy of existing observational practices, but he says little about the broader political roles played by the scientists engaged in this work.

9   Leandra Swanner (2017) has discussed the uneven reception of similarly oriented "outreach" projects organized around controversial telescope projects built or planned for contested mountaintops in Hawai'i and northern Arizona.

10 Anthropologists and historians of science have called attention to the ways in which the haptic dimensions of field-based scientific work cause researchers to obsess over learned strategies of bodily comportment as a means not merely of navigating, but of making foreign terrain feel more familiar (Messeri 2017; Myers and Dumit 2011). The influence of these techniques is particularly profound in the work of imperial cartographers, especially in places where techniques of "self-discipline" were often equated with proxies of physical infrastructure (see Burnett 2000). More recently, scholars have extended their discussions to cover related questions regarding the computer-assisted navigation of virtual worlds and the robot-led exploration of inhospitable environments like the surface of Mars or the bottom of the ocean. See Daston and Galison 2007, 363–416; Helmreich 2009; Messeri 2016; Turkle 2009.

11 For a more detailed discussion of one of the earliest studies of historical health indicators at Date Creek see Goward, Diederich, and Rosentreter 1994.

12 Dennis occasionally reminded me of the scale of this transformation when our conversations drifted to the vulnerability of intensively managed, even-aged stands to fire and disease. After hemlock trees recolonized immense areas once filled by the many western red cedar trees killed in these fires, much of the resulting forest was left vulnerable to large-scale fires and pest outbreaks. The fact that so much forested land had been effectively cleared and refertilized all at once by the great fires of the mid-1800s created a fire-prone forest, leading eventually to the establishment of obsessive fire-suppression policies during the early years of the provincial Forest Service (see Agee 1993; Arno 1980).

13 Speaking before an academic audience in California in 1993, Derrida used figures and phrases from *Hamlet* to work through a series of bluntly empirical problems. The recent collapse of the Eastern Bloc was the ostensible premise of the meeting "Whither Marxism?," but a rising tide of violence against Black South Africans following the lifting of apartheid weighed heavily on him. He prefaced his remarks with a dedication to Chris Hani, the leader of a communist offshoot of Nelson Mandela's African National Congress party, who had been murdered two weeks before Derrida's address. Apartheid's myriad legacies would be inherited not only by the residents of South Africa, he suggested, but by countless others who had tacitly tolerated its violence. "At once part, cause, effect, example, what is happening [in South Africa] translates what takes place here, always here, wherever one is and wherever one looks, closest to home. Infinite responsibility, therefore, no rest allowed for any form of good conscience" (Derrida 1994, xiv). The timing of Hani's death, he urged, was also a reminder that the violence attending the political and economic transitions then taking place would be inherited by other generations as impossible commitments to justice, as well.

14 The prospect of treating historicity as a kind of "haunting" has provided some anthropologists with a means of analyzing the hegemonic authority that can come to inhere in formations of collective memory. See Good 2012; Fischer 2012, 2015; Cantero 2017.

15 Drawing on a different genealogy routed primarily though the ethnographic work of Claude Lévi-Strauss and of Veena Das (2007), Andrew Brandel makes a similar argument for treating both the object and practice of anthropology as "thought grounded in conviviality, in life lived with others with whom we share an intimacy that allows our forms of thought, the very conditions of our experience of the world, to be challenged" (2016, 324).

16 Technologies of forgetting are not limited to the landscapes of scientific fieldwork, of course. As Simon Harrison explains through the gradual erasure of place-based stories in the shifting riverine landscapes in Papua New Guinea, "A society's material technologies of memory are always also its technologies of forgetting, though some societies seem to acknowledge the truth of this more readily than others" (2004, 135).

17 Writing on the material culture of fieldwork and experimentation characteristic of nineteenth-century geology, Martin Rudwick (1996) suggests that scientists working in temperate regions benefited from long, winter-induced pauses between summer exploration seasons, arguing that geologists forced to spend months indoors used the time to develop more sophisticated theories to guide their summer prospecting work.

4. Consignment

Portions of chapter 4 were published as an article in *Anthropological Quarterly* (Özden-Schilling 2019b).

1 Other than Darlene Vegh, all other names of my interlocutors in this chapter are pseudonyms.

2 As Gitxsan researcher Neil J. Sterritt (1998) reminded the readers of the journal *BC Studies* shortly after the Nisga'a Final Agreement was signed, the initial provincial announcement of the agreement contained mention of an even larger area—38,000 square kilometers—for these traditional territories. Government officials' public references to these impressive figures after over a century of explicit nonrecognition, Sterritt argues, represented deliberate attempts to reassure White British Columbians that the scale of the actual land transfers effected through treaty negotiations would be minuscule compared to each participating First Nation's claims.

3 The historical arc of activists' responses to the land selection model for treaty negotiation bears some resemblance to the aftermath of the "termination" movement that the United States Congress initiated in the mid-twentieth century with the aim of reducing the federal government's fiduciary responsibilities to American Indian tribes by dissolving the federally recognized governments and reservations of dozens of apparently "economically independent" tribes (see Cattelino 2010). While the termination process eventually galvanized the Red Power movement, the most significant pan-Indigenous political movement in the United States in the twen-

tieth century, the BCTC's land selection model—and its promise of limited, if still potentially lucrative title—has proven to be a more polarizing force among claimants and activists in British Columbia. For a discussion of how the consultation processes developed following the establishment of the BCTC model inflamed tensions between Indigenous activists and community members involved in protests against the construction of the Sun Peaks ski resort near Kamloops, for instance, see S. Robertson 2017.

4   In March 2019, the federal government announced that it would forgive all outstanding loan debts that First Nations had accumulated in order to participate in treaty negotiations (Stueck 2019). While some commentators initially assumed that this would lead dozens of groups back into active negotiations (e.g., Palmer 2019), relatively few groups have reinitiated talks with the BCTC in the years since, and the broader impact of the loan forgiveness plan remains to be seen.

5   Vegh explicitly reflects on the kinds of continuity produced through her mapwork in her recent writings on contemporary food sovereignty practices. See L. M. Johnson, Vegh, and Morgan 2019.

6   I am indebted to Bryce Peake for first proposing the concept of *consignment* that I develop here based on his careful reading of an earlier version of this chapter.

7   The Enbridge Northern Gateway pipeline project, by far the most controversial development proposal in the region in 2013, was put on indefinite hiatus after tanker traffic through northwest British Columbia's interior passage was formally banned in late 2015.

8   At the time, all members of the GTS were self-appointed. Membership has since been extended to the chiefs of all Gitxsan house groups, although many house chiefs have refused to take up these positions as a means of boycotting the GTS.

9   In 2014, GTS executives publicly evicted all TCP surveyors from the Gitxsan traditional territories, although they subsequently signed agreements with other prospective pipeline developers. Several people who attended the Kispiox meeting told me that news coverage of unauthorized incursions by TCP surveyors into protected grizzly bear habitat nearby had helped to generate high turnout for the meeting (see Constantineau 2013). For an extended discussion of conflicts between specific Gitxsan chiefs and members of the GTS over several different proposed pipelines, see Jang 2017.

10 Prince Rupert Gas Transmission Project map, TC Energy (formerly known as TransCanada Pipeline Corporation), https://www.tcenergy.com/siteassets/pdfs /natural-gas/prince-rupert-gas-transmission/transcanada-prince-rupert-gas -transmission-project-map.pdf.

11 The seven Indian Reserves (which all now identify as First Nations) Brody identified as Beaver Indian groups in 1978 now use multiple different spellings (Dunneza, Dunne Tsaa, etc.) to designate their collectivity. The term *First Nations*, a consciously adopted term referring to all non-Inuit, non-Métis Indigenous groups in Canada, was not in common usage at the time of Brody's fieldwork.

12 For a genealogy of use and occupancy mapping methods that emerged from the Inuit project, see Chapin, Lamb, and Threlkeld 2005.

13 The only First Nations groups within British Columbia covered by the numbered federal treaties of the nineteenth and twentieth centuries, the Dane-zaa and their neighbors northeast of the Rocky Mountains have not taken part in BCTC-led treaty negotiations that have dominated provincial interactions with other First Nations groups for the past three decades.

14 The proposed Alaska gas pipeline that originally brought Brody into contact with the Beaver has been abandoned and reimagined multiple times since the late 1970s as contracts changed hands, sources and markets reconfigured, and different prospective routes encountered new forms of opposition. The route along the Alaska Highway, in discussions for over forty years by this point, has also faced opposition from proposed routes through the Mackenzie River Valley in the Northwest Territories and through the Alaskan Range mountains to Valdez, Alaska, the current endpoint of the trans-Alaskan oil pipeline. In its most recent iteration, TCP, the proposal's latest proponents, put forth yet another set of plans for a route along the Alaska Highway to a distribution station in Calgary, Alberta, before a drop in gas prices in 2014 led the company to suspend its bid.

15 Thanks to the development of hydraulic fracturing techniques and other shale gas extraction methods, natural gas development within the Peace region expanded so quickly in the first years of the twenty-first century that in 2013, the provincial government created an entirely new ministry, the Ministry of Natural Gas Development, to manage the legal and bureaucratic consequences of its growth. See M. Lee and Klein 2020.

5. Resilience

Portions of chapter 5 were published as an article in *American Anthropologist* (Özden-Schilling 2022).

1 Prior to being taken up as a rallying call by displaced government researchers in British Columbia, the term *cumulative effects analysis* first came into use in critiques of the EIA process (Sinclair, Doelle, and Duinker 2017). Almost since the inception of environmental assessment legislation with the passage of the National Environmental Policy Act of 1970 in the United States and its subsequent adoption in Canada with the establishment of the federal Environmental Assessment and Review Process in 1973, academic researchers, prospective developers, and the technical consultants who typically compile the EIA reports themselves have continually taken issue with the way each group has defined *impacts*. Nominally, attention to cumulative impacts has been a component of the federal and most provincial EIA processes for several decades (Hegmann et al. 1999). Within British Columbia, however, attempts to broaden the purview of EIA reviews to include attention to other projects happening nearby were repeatedly overruled, frequently

in terms that delimited the regulatory jurisdictions of specific government ministries. Even after the federal review process was replaced by the expanded Canadian Environmental Assessment Act in 1995 and explicit requirements to include attention to cumulative effects were adopted into EIA review policies in British Columbia and other provinces, the actual scope of the analyses included in individual reports, particularly their attention to future projections, has varied tremendously. According to several of the ecologists who first formulated the version of cumulative effects research that was nominally adopted into Canadian federal policy in the 1990s, the pervasive failure of cumulative effects analysis projects across the country is a symptom less of impoverished data sets than of an indiscriminate approach to defining objects of study (Duinker and Greig 2006).

2   Jeremy Walker and Melinda Cooper (2011) go further still, provocatively comparing Holling's strategic institution-building work (including his role in founding the journal *Conservation Ecology*, now renamed *Ecology and Society*, as well as the Resilience Alliance research network) to the free market triumphalism of Friedrich Hayek (see also Bakker 2010).

3   For a general discussion of scenario planning workshops in environmental policy-making, see Peterson, Cumming, and Carpenter 2003.

4   By 2019, interim reports for four values were posted online. According to CEF planning documents, this initial list is designed to grow as reports on existing values are completed (Government of British Columbia 2016).

5   The Skeena watershed was divided into fifty-three conservation units in 2005 by the BC government's Wild Salmon Policy. See M. Price et al. 2017.

Epilogue

1   The visibility of police uses of force at the camps had become an issue during an RCMP-led sweep at the Gidimt'en camp in 2019, when documents uncovered by investigating academics revealed that police had been prepared to use lethal force if Wet'suwet'en activists resisted arrest (see Dhillon and Parrish 2019).

2   For a much more nuanced discussion of these groups, their members' personal histories, and the complex interests at play, see Baker 2020.

3   Prior to assuming the name Smogelgem, Naziel's Likhts'amisyu name was Toghestiy.

4   Most non-Wet'suwet'en people omit the name Gisday'wa when referring to the Gitxsan and Wet'suwet'en land claims trials. See preface, note 3.

5   Sadly, Neil B. Sterritt died at the age of 106, six months before his son passed away. In many other sources, including Gitxsan Treaty Society–authored publications related to the Gitxsan hereditary chiefs and the *huwilp*, Neil B. Sterritt's Gitxsan name is spelled Wii Gaak. Here, I am using the spelling that Neil J. Sterritt and his father both used for this name during the last decades of their lives.

REFERENCES

Aboriginal Affairs and Northern Development Canada. 2008. "BC Treaty Commission: Annual Report." http://www.aadnc-aandc.gc.ca/eng/1100100022305/1100100022489.

Adams, Vincanne. 2016. *Metrics: What Counts in Global Health*. Durham, NC: Duke University Press.

Agee, James K. 1993. *Fire Ecology of Pacific Northwest Forests*. Washington, DC: Island Press.

Agrawal, Arun. 1995. "Dismantling the Divide between Indigenous and Scientific Knowledge." *Development and Change* 26 (3): 413–39.

Agrawal, Arun. 2002. "Indigenous Knowledge and the Politics of Classification." *International Social Science Journal* 54 (173): 287–97.

Agrawal, Arun. 2005. *Environmentality: Technologies of Government and the Making of Subjects*. Durham, NC: Duke University Press.

Alcantara, Christopher. 2013. *Negotiating the Deal: Comprehensive Land Claims Agreements in Canada*. Toronto: University of Toronto Press.

Aleza Lake Research Forest. 1935. *Ex. Plot 106 with humus and moss trenched*. Photograph. Aleza Lake Research Forest fonds. Northern BC Archives, University of Northern British Columbia, Prince George. https://search.nbca.unbc.ca/index.php/2007-1-45-27-3.

Aleza Lake Research Forest. 1936a. *View of Aleza Lake camp after electrical service installed by Young Men's Forestry Training Program (YMFTP) crew*. Photograph. Aleza Lake Research Forest fonds. Northern BC Archives, University of Northern

British Columbia, Prince George. https://search.nbca.unbc.ca/index.php/2007-1
-25-7-31.

Aleza Lake Research Forest. 1936b. *Young Men's Forestry Training Program (YMFTP)
crew digging pipeline trench to take water from dam to reservoir*. Photograph. Aleza
Lake Research Forest fonds. Northern BC Archives, University of Northern British
Columbia, Prince George. https://search.nbca.unbc.ca/index.php/2007-1-25-7-18.

Aleza Lake Research Forest. 1969. *Tamarack Larch wildling transplanted 1965 on the
East side of E.P. 646.1*. Photograph. Aleza Lake Research Forest fonds. Northern
BC Archives, University of Northern British Columbia, Prince George. https://
search.nbca.unbc.ca/index.php/2007-1-30-2-141.

Aleza Lake Research Forest. 1976. *Spruce stand at Aleza Lake Research Forest*. Photograph. Aleza Lake Research Forest fonds. Northern BC Archives, University of
Northern British Columbia, Prince George. https://search.nbca.unbc.ca/index.php
/2007-1-25-6-16.

Anand, Nikhil. 2017. *Hydraulic City: Water and the Infrastructures of Citizenship in
Mumbai*. Durham, NC: Duke University Press.

Anderson, Ben. 2015. "What Kind of Thing Is Resilience?" *Politics* 35 (1): 60–66.

Anderson, William. 2017. "How Scientists and Scientific Information Influence Public
Forest Policy." PhD diss., University of New Brunswick, Fredericton.

Aporta, Claudio, and Eric Higgs. 2005. "Satellite Culture: Global Positioning Systems,
Inuit Wayfinding, and the Need for a New Account of Technology." *Current Anthropology* 46 (5): 729–53.

Armitage, Derek. 2005. "Adaptive Capacity and Community-Based Natural Resource
Management." *Environmental Management* 35 (6): 703–15.

Armitage, Derek, Fikret Berkes, and Nancy Doubleday, eds. 2007. *Adaptive Co-
management: Collaboration, Learning, and Multi-level Governance*. Vancouver:
University of British Columbia Press.

Arno, Stephen F. 1980. "Forest Fire History in the Northern Rockies." *Journal of Forestry* 78 (8): 460–65.

Auditor General of British Columbia. 2015. "Managing the Cumulative Effects of Resource Development in B.C." Victoria, BC: Office of the Auditor General.

Austen, Ian. 2020. "Canadian Police Move against Pipeline Blockades, Arresting Dozens." *New York Times*, February 10, 2020. https://www.nytimes.com/2020/02/10
/world/canada/gas-pipeline-protests.html.

Babül, Elif M. 2017. *Bureaucratic Intimacies: Translating Human Rights in Turkey*.
Stanford, CA: Stanford University Press.

Bains, Jessy. 2020. "The Financial Fallout of the Railroad Blocking Wet'suwet'en Protests." *Yahoo Finance*, February 13, 2020. https://sg.news.yahoo.com/the-financial
-fallout-of-the-railroad-blocking-wetsuweten-pipeline-protests-195530969.html.

Baker, Rafferty. 2020. "A Who's Who of the Wet'suwet'en Pipeline Conflict." *CBC News*,
February 26, 2020. https://www.cbc.ca/news/canada/british-columbia/wetsuweten
-whos-who-guide-1.5471898.

Bakker, Karen. 2010. "The Limits of 'Neoliberal Natures': Debating Green Neoliberalism." *Progress in Human Geography* 34 (6): 715–35.

Barker, Adam. 2009. "The Contemporary Reality of Canadian Imperialism: Settler Colonialism and the Hybrid Colonial State." *American Indian Quarterly* 33 (3): 325–51.

Barker, Joanne, ed. 2017. *Critically Sovereign: Indigenous Gender, Sexuality, and Feminist Studies*. Durham, NC: Duke University Press.

Barman, Jean. 2007. *The West beyond the West: A History of British Columbia*. Toronto: University of Toronto Press.

Barrios, Roberto. 2014. "'Here, I'm Not at Ease': Anthropological Perspectives on
Community Resilience." *Disasters* 38 (2): 329–50.

Barry, Janice. 2012. "Indigenous State Planning as Inter-institutional Capacity Development: The Evolution of 'Government-to-Government' Relations in Coastal British Columbia, Canada." *Planning Theory and Practice* 13 (2): 213–31.

Basso, Keith. 1996. *Wisdom Sits in Places: Landscape and Language among the Western Apache*. Albuquerque: University of New Mexico Press.

Bateson, Gregory. 1972. *Steps to an Ecology of Mind*. Chicago: University of Chicago
Press.

BBC News. 2020. "Indigenous Pipeline Blockades Spark Canada-Wide Protests." *BBC
News*, February 11, 2020. https://www.bbc.com/news/world-us-canada-51452217.

BC Treaty Commission. 2021. "Negotiations Update." http://www.bctreaty.ca
/negotiation-update.

Beese, William J., John Deal, B. Glen Dunsworth, Stephen J. Mitchell, and Timothy J.
Philpott. 2019. "Two Decades of Variable Retention in British Columbia: A Review
of Its Implementation and Effectiveness for Biodiversity Conservation." *Ecological
Processes* 8 (1): 1–22.

Bell, Lindsay. 2016. "Longing for Evidence-Based Traditions: Addiction Treatment in
Canada's Northwest Territories." *Medicine Anthropology Theory* 3 (1): 55–67.

Bell, Lindsay. 2017. "Soft Skills, Hard Rocks: Making Diamonds Ethical in Canada's
Northwest Territories." *Focaal*, no. 79, 74–88.

Bell, Lindsay. 2023. *Under Pressure: Diamond Mining and Everyday Life in Northern
Canada*. Toronto: University of Toronto Press.

Bellrichard, Chantelle, and Yvette Brand. 2020. "6 Arrested at Wet'suwet'en Antipipeline Camp." *CBC News*, February 6, 2020. https://www.cbc.ca/news/canada
/british-columbia/wetsuweten-arrests-coastal-gaslink-pipeline-1.5454007.

Berger, Thomas R. 1978. "The Mackenzie Valley Pipeline Inquiry." *Osgoode Hall Law
Journal* 16:639–48.

Berkes, Fikret, Carl Folke, and Johan Colding, eds. 2000. *Linking Social and Ecological Systems: Management Practices and Social Mechanisms for Building Resilience*.
Cambridge: Cambridge University Press.

Berkes, Fikret, Mina Kislalioglu, Carl Folke, and Madhav Gadgil. 1998. "Minireviews:
Exploring the Basic Ecological Unit: Ecosystem-Like Concepts in Traditional Societies." *Ecosystems* 1 (5): 409–15.

Bernsohn, Ken. 1981. *Cutting Up the North: The History of the Forest Industry in the
Northern Interior*. North Vancouver, BC: Hancock House.

Bernstein, Steven, and Benjamin Cashore. 2000. "Globalization, Four Paths of Inter-
nationalization and Domestic Policy Change: The Case of Ecoforestry in British

Columbia, Canada." *Canadian Journal of Political Science/Revue canadienne de science politique* 33 (1): 67–99.

Blackburn, Carole. 2005. "Searching for Guarantees in the Midst of Uncertainty: Negotiating Aboriginal Rights and Title in British Columbia." *American Anthropologist* 107 (4): 586–96.

Blackburn, Carole. 2009. "Differentiating Indigenous Citizenship: Seeking Multiplicity in Rights, Identity, and Sovereignty in Canada." *American Ethnologist* 36 (1): 66–78.

Blackhawk, Ned. 2006. *Violence over the Land: Indians and Empires in the Early American West*. Cambridge, MA: Harvard University Press.

Blackman, Margaret. 1982. *During My Time: Florence Edenshaw Davidson, a Haida Woman*. Vancouver, BC: Douglas and McIntyre.

Blomley, Nicholas. 1996. "'Shut the Province Down': First Nations Blockades in British Columbia, 1984–1995." *BC Studies: The British Columbian Quarterly*, no. 111, 5–35.

Booth, Annie, and Greg Halseth. 2011. "Why the Public Thinks Natural Resources Public Participation Processes Fail: A Case Study of British Columbia Communities." *Land Use Policy* 28 (4): 898–906.

Borrows, John. 2002. *Recovering Canada: The Resurgence of Indigenous Law*. Toronto: University of Toronto Press.

Borrows, John. 2015. "The Durability of *Terra Nullius: Tsilhqot'in Nation v. British Columbia*." *University of British Columbia Law Review* 48 (3): 701–42.

Bowker, Geoffrey C. 2000. "Biodiversity, Datadiversity." *Social Studies of Science* 30 (5): 643–83.

Bowker, Geoffrey C., Karen Baker, Florence Millerand, and David Ribes. 2010. "Toward Information Infrastructure Studies: Ways of Knowing in a Networked Environment." In *International Handbook of Internet Research*, edited by Jeremy Hunsinger, Lisbeth Klastrup, and Matthew Allen, 97–117. Amsterdam: Springer Netherlands.

Boym, Svetlana. 2001. *The Future of Nostalgia*. New York: Basic Books.

Bracken, Amber, and Leyland Cecco. 2020. "Canada: Protests Go Mainstream as Support for Wet'suwet'en Pipeline Fight Widens." *Guardian*, February 14, 2020. https://www.theguardian.com/world/2020/feb/14/wetsuweten-coastal-gaslink-pipeline-allies.

Brand, Fridolin Simon, and Kurt Jax. 2007. "Focusing the Meaning(s) of Resilience: Resilience as a Descriptive Concept and a Boundary Object." *Ecology and Society* 12 (1): 1–16.

Brandel, Andrew. 2016. "The Art of Conviviality." *HAU: Journal of Ethnographic Theory* 6 (2): 323–43.

Braun, Bruce. 2002. *The Intemperate Rainforest: Nature, Culture, and Power on Canada's West Coast*. Minneapolis: University of Minnesota Press.

Brockington, Dan, Rosaleen Duffy, and Jim Igoe. 2008. *Nature Unbound: Conservation, Capitalism and the Future of Protected Areas*. London: Earthscan.

Brody, Hugh. 1976. "Inuit Land Use in North Baffin Island and Northern Foxe Basin." In *Inuit Land Use and Occupancy Project: A Report*, 153–71. Milton Freeman Research Limited and Department of Indian Affairs and Northern Development. Ottawa: Ministry of Supply and Services, Canada.

Brody, Hugh. 1981. *Maps and Dreams*. New York: Pantheon Books.

Brown, Katrina. 2014. "Global Environmental Change I: A Social Turn for Resilience?" *Progress in Human Geography* 38 (1): 107–17.

Bryan, Joe. 2011. "Walking the Line: Participatory Mapping, Indigenous Rights, and Neoliberalism." *Geoforum* 42 (1): 40–50.

Buck-Morss, Susan. 2002. *Dreamworld and Catastrophe: The Passing of Mass Utopia in East and West*. Cambridge, MA: MIT Press.

Bulkley Valley Community Resources Board. 1998. *Bulkley Land and Resource Management Plan*. Victoria: BC Ministry of Environment. http://bvcrb.ca/lrmp/.

Burda, Cheri, Russell Collier, and Bryan Evans. 1999. *The Gitksan Model: An Alternative to the Destruction of Forests, Salmon and Gitksan Land*. Victoria, BC: The Eco-Research Chair of Environmental Law and Policy.

Burnett, D. Graham. 2000. *Masters of All They Surveyed: Exploration, Geography, and a British El Dorado*. Chicago: University of Chicago Press.

Burton, Carla. 1999. "The Wilp Sa Maa'y Harvesting Co-operative." *Ecoforestry* (Winter): 20–23.

Burton, Philip J. 1998. "Inferring the Response of Berry Producing Shrubs to Different Light Environments in the ICHmc." Project number SB96030-RE. Unpublished report. Victoria: Forest Renewal BC.

Bustard, David, and Chris Shell. 2002. *Conserving Morice Watershed Fish Populations and Their Habitat: Stage II Biophysical Profile*. Smithers, BC: David Bustard and Associates.

Callison, Candis. 2014. *How Climate Change Comes to Matter: The Communal Facts of Life*. Durham, NC: Duke University Press.

Callison, Candis. 2020. "The Twelve-Year Warning." *Isis* 111 (1): 129–37.

Callison, Candis, and Mary Lynn Young. 2020. *Reckoning: Journalism's Limits and Possibilities*. Oxford: Oxford University Press.

Campbell, Ken. 1989. "The Skeena War." *The Beaver* 69 (4): 34–40.

Canadian Press. 2012. "Six-Month Occupation of Gitxsan Treaty Office Ends Peacefully in Hazelton." *Vancouver Sun*, June 11, 2012.

Canadian Press. 2020. "First Case of COVID-19 in B.C. Has Fully Recovered, Health Officer Says." *Abbotsford News*, February 19, 2020. https://www.abbynews.com/news/first-case-of-covid-19-in-b-c-has-fully-recovered-health-officer-says/.

Canham, Charles D., K. Dave Coates, Paula Bartemucci, and Stefan Quaglia. 1999. "Measurement and Modeling of Spatially Explicit Variation in Light Transmission through Interior Cedar-Hemlock Forests of British Columbia." *Canadian Journal of Forest Research* 29 (11): 1775–83.

Cantero, Lucia. 2017. "Sociocultural Anthropology in 2016: In Dark Times: Hauntologies and Other Ghosts of Production." *American Anthropologist* 119 (2): 308–18.

Cassin, Barbara. 2016. *Nostalgia: When Are We Ever at Home?* Translated by Pascale-Anne Brault. New York: Fordham University Press.

Cattelino, Jessica. 2010. "The Double Bind of American Indian Need-Based Sovereignty." *Cultural Anthropology* 25 (2): 235–62.

Cattelino, Jessica. 2019. "From Green to Green: The Environmentalization of Agriculture." *Journal for the Anthropology of North America* 22 (2): 135–38.

CBC News. 2020. "Indigenous Rights Activist, Award Winning Author Neil Sterritt Dead at 79." April 14, 2020. https://www.cbc.ca/news/canada/british-columbia/neil-sterritt-dies-79-1.5532059.

Cecco, Leyland. 2020. "Canada: Wet'suwet'en Sign Historic Deal to Negotiate Land Rights." *Guardian*, May 15, 2020. https://www.theguardian.com/world/2020/may/15/canada-wetsuweten-historic-deal-land-rights-pipeline.

Chandler, David. 2014. *Resilience: The Governance of Complexity*. London: Routledge.

Chandler, David. 2018. *Ontopolitics in the Anthropocene: An Introduction to Mapping, Sensing and Hacking*. Abingdon, UK: Routledge.

Chapin, Mac, Zachary Lamb, and Bill Threlkeld. 2005. "Mapping Indigenous Lands." *Annual Review of Anthropology* 34:619–38.

Chipeniuk, Raymond. 2004. "Planning for Amenity Migration in Canada: Current Capacities of Interior British Columbian Mountain Communities." *Mountain Research and Development* 24 (4): 327–35.

Choy, Tim. 2011. *Ecologies of Comparison: An Ethnography of Endangerment in Hong Kong*. Durham, NC: Duke University Press.

Cittadino, Eugene. 2004. "Borderline Science: Expert Testimony and the Red River Dispute." *Isis* 95 (2): 183–219.

Clarke, Lee. 1999. *Mission Improbable: Using Fantasy Documents to Tame Disaster*. Chicago: University of Chicago Press.

Clifford, James. 2001. "Indigenous Articulations." *Contemporary Pacific* 13 (2): 467–90.

Clifford, James. 2004. "Looking Several Ways: Anthropology and Native Heritage in Alaska." *Current Anthropology* 45 (1): 5–30.

Clifford, James. 2007. "Varieties of Indigenous Experience: Diasporas, Homelands, Sovereignties." In *Indigenous Experience Today*, edited by Marisol de la Cadena and Orin Starn, 197–224. New York: Berg.

Clifford, James. 2013. *Returns: Becoming Indigenous in the Twenty-First Century*. Cambridge, MA: Harvard University Press.

Clogg, Jessica. 2012. "Upholding the Law, Protecting the Land, Sharing the Wealth: The Gitanyow Huwilp Recognition and Reconciliation Agreement." West Coast Environmental Law, October 10, 2012. https://www.wcel.org/blog/upholding-law-protecting-land-sharing-wealth.

Coates, K. Dave, Allen Banner, J. Douglas Steventon, Phil LePage, and Paula Bartemucci. 1997. *The Date Creek Silvicultural Systems Study in the Interior Cedar-Hemlock Forests of Northwestern British Columbia: Overview and Treatment Summaries*. Victoria: BC Ministry of Forests.

Coates, Ken. 2020. "Don't Confuse Support for the Wet'suwet'en Chiefs with the Spirit of Idle No More." *Globe and Mail*, February 13, 2020. https://www.theglobeandmail.com/opinion/article-dont-confuse-support-for-the-wetsuweten-hereditary-chiefs-with-the/.

Collier, Russell. 2012. "Dances with Words: Ecosystem Terminology and the Gitxsan Language." Master's thesis, Royal Roads University, Victoria, BC.

Collier, Russell, and Tom Hobby. 2010. "It's All about Relationships: First Nations and Non-timber Resource Management in British Columbia." *BC Journal of Ecosystems and Management* 11 (1–2): 1–8.

Collier, Stephen J. 2011. *Post-Soviet Social: Neoliberalism, Social Modernity, Biopolitics*. Princeton, NJ: Princeton University Press.

Collier, Stephen J. 2017. "Neoliberalism and Rule by Experts." In *Assembling Neoliberalism: Expertise, Practices, Subjects*, edited by Vaughan Higgins and Wendy Larner, 23–44. New York: Palgrave MacMillan.

Cons, Jason. 2018. "Staging Climate Security: Resilience and Heterodystopia in the Bangladesh Borderlands." *Cultural Anthropology* 33 (2): 266–94.

Constantineau, Bruce. 2013. "Possible B.C. Pipeline Route Crosses Grizzly Bear Sanctuary." *Vancouver Sun*, September 7, 2013.

Convis, Charles. 2000. "The Gitxsan Model: A Vision for the Land and the People." *Native Geography: Annual Magazine of the ESRI Native American/First Nations Program*. http://www.conservationgis.org/native/native2.html.

Cooke, Martin, and Erin O'Sullivan. 2015. "The Impact of Migration on the First Nations Community Well-Being Index." *Social Indicators Research* 122 (2): 371–89.

Coulthard, Glen. 2014. *Red Skin, White Masks: Rejecting the Colonial Politics of Recognition*. Minneapolis: University of Minnesota Press.

Cowen, Deborah. 2014. *The Deadly Life of Logistics: Mapping Violence in Global Trade*. Minneapolis: University of Minnesota Press.

Cruikshank, Julie. 1992. "The Invention of Anthropology in British Columbia's Supreme Court: Oral Tradition as Evidence in *Delgamuukw v. B.C.*" *BC Studies: The British Columbian Quarterly*, no. 95, 25–42.

Cruikshank, Julie. 2005. *Do Glaciers Listen? Local Knowledge, Colonial Encounters, and Social Imagination*. Vancouver: University of British Columbia Press.

Culhane, Dara. 1998. *The Pleasure of the Crown: Anthropology, Law and First Nations*. Vancouver, BC: Talon.

Daly, Richard. 2005. *Our Box Was Full: An Ethnography for the Delgamuukw Plaintiffs*. Vancouver: University of British Columbia Press.

Daly, Richard, and Val Napoleon. 2003. "A Dialogue on the Effects of Aboriginal Rights Litigation and Activism on Aboriginal Communities in Northwestern British Columbia." *Social Analysis* 47 (3): 108–29.

D'Arcus, Bruce. 2010. "The Urban Geography of Red Power: The American Indian Movement in Minneapolis–Saint Paul, 1968–70." *Urban Studies* 47 (6): 1241–55.

Das, Veena. 1995. *Critical Events: An Anthropological Perspective on Contemporary India*. Delhi: Oxford University Press.

Das, Veena. 1997. "Sufferings, Theodicies, Disciplinary Practices, Appropriations." *International Social Science Journal* 49 (154): 563–72.

Das, Veena. 2007. *Life and Words: Violence and the Descent into the Ordinary*. Berkeley: University of California Press.

Das, Veena, and Deborah Poole. 2004. "Anthropology in the Margins of the State." *PoLAR: Political and Legal Anthropology Review* 30 (1): 140–44.

Daston, Lorraine, ed. 2000. *Biographies of Scientific Objects*. Chicago: University of Chicago Press.

Daston, Lorraine, and Peter Galison. 2007. *Objectivity*. New York: Zone Books.

Davey, James. 2019. "A Bridge to Nowhere: British Columbia's Capitalist Nature and the Carmanah Walbran War in the Woods (1988–1994)." PhD diss., University of Victoria, Victoria, BC.

Davis, Emily Jane. 2009. "The Rise and Fall of a Model Forest." *BC Studies: The British Columbian Quarterly*, no. 161, 35–57.

De la Cadena, Marisol. 2015. *Earth Beings: Ecologies of Practice across Andean Worlds*. Durham, NC: Duke University Press.

De la Cadena, Marisol, Marianne E. Lien, Mario Blaser, Casper Bruun Jensen, Tess Lea, Atsuro Morita, Heather Anne Swanson, Gro B. Ween, Paige West, and Margaret J. Wiener. 2015. "Anthropology and STS: Generative Interfaces, Multiple Locations." *HAU: Journal of Ethnographic Theory* 5 (1): 437–75.

Delisle, Raina. 2012. "Connecting through Language." Royal Roads University, July 11, 2012. Accessed February 11, 2015. http://www.royalroads.ca/news/connecting -through-language.

Deloria, Philip J. 2004. *Indians in Unexpected Places*. Lawrence: University Press of Kansas.

Deloria, Philip J. 2019. *Becoming Mary Sully: Toward an American Indian Abstract*. Seattle: University of Washington Press.

Deloria, Vine, Jr. 1988. *Custer Died for Your Sins: An Indian Manifesto*. Norman: University of Oklahoma Press.

De Pina-Cabral, João, and Antónia Pedroso de Lima. 2000. *Elites: Choice, Leadership and Succession*. Lisbon: Etnográfica Press.

Derrida, Jacques. 1988. *Limited, Inc*. Translated by Alan Bass. Evanston, IL: Northwestern University Press.

Derrida, Jacques. 1994. *Specters of Marx*. Translated by Peggy Kamuf. Abingdon, UK: Routledge.

Derrida, Jacques. 1998. *Archive Fever: A Freudian Impression*. Translated by Eric Prenowitz. Chicago: University of Chicago Press.

Derrida, Jacques. 2005a. *The Politics of Friendship*. Translated by George Collins. New York: Verso.

Derrida, Jacques. 2005b. *Rogues: Two Essays on Reason*. Translated by Pascale-Anne Brault and Michael Nass. Stanford, CA: Stanford University Press.

Devlin, Christopher. 2009. "Deep Consultation at a Higher Level: *Wii'litswx v. British Columbia (Minister of Forests)*." *The Advocate* 67 (1): 25–32.

Dhillon, Jaskiran. 2017. *Prairie Rising: Indigenous Youth, Decolonization, and the Politics of Intervention*. Toronto: University of Toronto Press.

Dhillon, Jaskiran, and Will Parrish. 2019. "Exclusive: Canada Police Prepared to Shoot Indigenous Activists, Documents Show." *Guardian*, December 20, 2019. https:// www.theguardian.com/world/2019/dec/20/canada-indigenous-land-defenders -police-documents.

Dickerson, Mark O. 1992. *Whose North? Political Change, Political Development, and Self-Government in the Northwest Territories*. Vancouver: University of British Columbia Press.

Dinwoodie, David W. 2002. *Reserve Memories: The Power of the Past in a Chilcotin Community*. Lincoln: University of Nebraska Press.

Dombrowski, Kirk. 2001. *Against Culture: Development, Politics, and Religion in Indian Alaska*. Lincoln: University of Nebraska Press.

Dorries, Heather, Robert Henry, David Hugill, Tyler McCreary, and Julie Tomiak, eds. 2019. *Settler City Limits: Indigenous Resurgence and Colonial Violence in the Urban Prairie West*. Winnipeg: University of Manitoba Press.

Dove, Michael. 2006. "Indigenous People and Environmental Politics." *Annual Review of Anthropology* 35:191–208.

Duffield, Mark. 2012. "Challenging Environments: Danger, Resilience and the Aid Industry." *Security Dialogue* 43 (5): 475–92.

Duinker, Peter, and Lorne Greig. 2006. "The Impotence of Cumulative Effects Assessment in Canada: Ailments and Ideas for Redeployment." *Environmental Management* 37 (2): 153–61.

Dumit, Joseph. 2004. *Picturing Personhood: Brain Scans and Biomedical Identity*. Princeton, NJ: Princeton University Press.

Edwards, Paul N. 2010. *A Vast Machine: Computer Models, Climate Data, and the Politics of Global Warming*. Cambridge, MA: MIT Press.

Egan, Brian. 2013. "Towards Shared Ownership: Property, Geography, and Treaty Making in British Columbia." *Geografiska Annaler: Series B, Human Geography* 95 (1): 33–50.

Eichstaedt, Carol, and Doug Donaldson. 1994. "Gitxsan, Wet'suwet'en Suspend Suit in Favor of Treaty Negotiations." *Windspeaker* 12 (18): 2.

Estes, Nick. 2019. *Our History Is the Future: Standing Rock versus the Dakota Access Pipeline, and the Long Tradition of Indigenous Resistance*. New York: Verso.

Eyben, Rosalind. 2010. "Hiding Relations: The Irony of 'Effective Aid.'" *European Journal of Development Research* 22 (3): 382–97.

Fabian, Johannes. 1983. *Time and the Other: How Anthropology Makes Its Object*. New York: Columbia University Press.

Fearnley, Lyle. 2020. *Virulent Zones: Animal Disease and Global Health at China's Pandemic Epicenter*. Durham, NC: Duke University Press.

Fee, Bill. 2015. "TransCanada, Gitanyow Reach Pipeline Agreement." *CFNR Network*, April 22, 2015. Accessed July 15, 2015. http://cfnrfm.ca/transcanada-gitanyow -reach-pipeline-agreement/.

Ferguson, James. 1990. *The Anti-politics Machine: "Development," Depoliticization and Bureaucratic Power in Lesotho*. Cambridge: Cambridge University Press.

Fienup-Riordan, Ann. 2000. *Hunting Tradition in a Changing World: Yup'ik Lives in Alaska Today*. New Brunswick, NJ: Rutgers University Press.

Fischer, Michael M. J. 2003. *Emergent Forms of Life and the Anthropological Voice*. Durham, NC: Duke University Press.

Fischer, Michael M. J. 2009. *Anthropological Futures*. Durham, NC: Duke University Press.

Fischer, Michael M. J. 2012. "On Metaphor: Reciprocity and Immunity." *Cultural Anthropology* 27 (1): 144–52.

Fischer, Michael M. J. 2015. "Ethnography for Aging Societies: Dignity, Cultural Genres, and Singapore's Imagined Futures." *American Ethnologist* 42 (2): 207–29.

Forest Practices Board. 2006. "New Forest Stewardship Plans Need More Details, Improved Accountability." May 1, 2006. https://www.bcfpb.ca/news-resources /news-releases/new-forest-stewardship-plans-need-more-details-improved -accountability/.

Forest Practices Board. 2008. "Provincial Land Use Planning: Which Way from Here?" November 1, 2008. https://www.bcfpb.ca/release-publications/releases/provincial -land-use-planning-which-way-from-here/.

Fortes, Meyer. 1970. *Kinship and the Social Order: The Legacy of Lewis Henry Morgan*. Chicago: Aldine.

Fox, Jefferson. 2002. "Siam Mapped and Mapping in Cambodia: Boundaries, Sovereignty, and Indigenous Conceptions of Space." *Society and Natural Resources* 15 (1): 65–78.

Frame, Tanis M. 2002. "Shared Decision Making and Sustainability: An Evaluation of Land and Resource Management Planning in British Columbia." Master's thesis, Simon Fraser University, Burnaby, BC.

Franklin, Jerry F. 1989. "Toward a New Forestry." *American Forests* 95 (November/ December): 37–44.

Furniss, Elizabeth. 1999. *The Burden of History: Colonialism and the Frontier Myth in a Rural Canadian Community*. Vancouver: University of British Columbia Press.

Galison, Peter. 1987. *How Experiments End*. Chicago: University of Chicago Press.

Galois, Robert M. 1992. "The Burning of Kitsegulka, 1872." *BC Studies: The British Columbian Quarterly*, no. 94, 59–81.

Galois, Robert M. 1993. "The History of the Upper Skeena Region, 1850 to 1927." *Native Studies Review* 9 (2): 113–83.

Galois, Robert M. 2007. "Gitxsan Law and Settler Disorder: The Skeena 'Uprising' of 1888." In *New Histories for Old: Changing Perspectives on Canada's Native Pasts*, edited by Theodore Binnema and Susan Neylan, 220–49. Vancouver: University of British Columbia Press.

Gamiet, Sharmin, Holly Ridenour, and Fred Philpot. 1998. "An Overview of Pine Mushrooms in the Skeena-Bulkley Region." Unpublished report. Smithers, BC: The Northwest Institute for Bioregional Research.

Garcia, Angela. 2014. "Regeneration: Love, Drugs and the Remaking of Hispano Inheritance." *Social Anthropology* 22 (2): 200–212.

Gershon, Ilana. 2011. "Neoliberal Agency." *Current Anthropology* 52 (4): 537–55.

Gibson-Graham, Julie Katherine. 2006. *A Postcapitalist Politics*. Minneapolis: University of Minnesota Press.

Gieryn, Thomas F. 1983. "Boundary-Work and the Demarcation of Science from Nonscience: Strains and Interests in Professional Ideologies of Scientists." *American Sociological Review* 48 (6): 781–95.

Giesbrecht, Kelly. 2003. "Public Participation in Natural Resource Management: The Bulkley Valley Community Resources Board." Master's thesis, University of Northern British Columbia, Prince George.

Gitanyow Hereditary Chiefs. 2009. *The Gitanyow Ayookxw: The Constitution of the Gitanyow Nation.* http://www.gitanyowchiefs.com/media/constitution/.

Gitanyow Hereditary Chiefs. n.d. "File Downloads." Accessed February 20, 2015. http://www.gitanyowchiefs.com/media/.

Gitxsan Government Commission. 2017. "Local Population Stats." http://www.gitxsangc.com/membership/membership-statistics/local-population-stats/.

Gitxsan Hereditary Chiefs. n.d. "Statement of Intent: Traditional Territory Boundary." British Columbia Treaty Commission. Accessed May 5, 2023. https://www.bctreaty.ca/sites/default/files/Gitxsan_SOI_Map.pdf.

Gitxsan Unity Movement. 2012a. "Gitxsan Chiefs Threatened by Imprisonment." *Kitimat Daily Online*, May 8, 2012. Accessed October 31, 2014. http://www.kitimatdaily.ca/go5980a/gitxsan_chiefs_threatened-by-imprisonment.

Gitxsan Unity Movement. 2012b. "Gitxsan Nation in Talks to Resolve Treaty Society Crisis." *Kitimat Daily Online*, July 17, 2012. Accessed October 31, 2014. http://www.mwpr.ca/go10018a/gitxsan_nation_in_talks_to_resolve_society_crisis.

Gitxsan Watershed Authorities. 2004. "Gitxsan Watershed Areas." Scale 1:350k.

Glavin, Terry. 1988. "Natives Say Wilderness Now a Rotting Heritage." *Vancouver Sun*, June 14, 1988.

Glavin, Terry. 1990. *A Death Feast in Dimlahamid.* Vancouver, BC: New Star Books.

Goeman, Mishuana. 2009. "Notes toward a Native Feminism's Spatial Practice." *Wicazo Sa Review* 24 (2): 169–87.

Goeman, Mishuana. 2013. *Mark My Words: Native Women Mapping Our Nations.* Minneapolis: University of Minnesota Press.

Good, Byron J. 2012. "Phenomenology, Psychoanalysis, and Subjectivity in Java." *Ethos* 40 (2): 24–36.

Goodwin, Charles. 1994. "Professional Vision." *American Anthropologist* 96 (3): 606–33.

Gordon and Betty Moore Foundation. 2013. "North Pacific Wild Salmon Organizational Resilience Project 2." Accessed May 5, 2023. https://www.moore.org/grant-detail?grantId=GBMF3314.01.

Gordon and Betty Moore Foundation. 2017. "Wild Salmon Ecosystems Initiative." https://www.moore.org/initiative-strategy-detail?initiativeId=wild-salmon-ecosystems-initiative.

Gosnell, Hannah, and Jesse Abrams. 2011. "Amenity Migration: Diverse Conceptualizations of Drivers, Socioeconomic Dimensions, and Emerging Challenges." *GeoJournal* 76 (4): 303–22.

Government of British Columbia. 2006. *A New Direction for Strategic Land Use Planning in BC: Synopsis.* Ministry of Agriculture and Lands. https://www2.gov.bc.ca/assets/gov/farming-natural-resources-and-industry/natural-resource-use/land-water-use/crown-land/land-use-plans-and-objectives/policies-guides/new_direction_synopsis.pdf.

Government of British Columbia. 2016. "Cumulative Effects Framework: Frequently Asked Questions." Accessed December 29, 2018. https://www2.gov.bc.ca/assets /gov/environment/natural-resource-stewardship/cumulative-effects/cumulative _effects_faq_5_may_2016.pdf.

Government of British Columbia. 2017. *Major Primary Timber Processing Facilities in British Columbia*. Victoria: British Columbia Ministry of Forests, Lands, Natural Resource Operations and Rural Development. https://www2.gov.bc.ca/assets /gov/farming-natural-resources-and-industry/forestry/fibre-mills/2017_mill_list _report_final.pdf.

Government of British Columbia. n.d. "Bulkley Valley Sustainable Resource Management Plan." Land Use Plans and Legal Direction by Region. Accessed May 5, 2023. https://www2.gov.bc.ca/gov/content/industry/crown-land-water/land-use -planning/regions/skeena/bulkley-lrmp/bulkleyvalley-srmp.

Government of Canada. 2022a. "Download Geographical Names Data." Accessed May 5, 2023. https://www.nrcan.gc.ca/earth-sciences/geography/download -geographical-names-data/9245.

Government of Canada. 2022b. "National Road Network—NRN—GeoBase Series." Accessed May 5, 2023. https://open.canada.ca/data/en/dataset/3d282116-e556-400c -9306-ca1a3cada77f.

Goward, Trevor, Paul Diederich, and Roger Rosentreter. 1994. "Notes on the Lichens and Allied Fungi of British Columbia II." *Bryologist* 97 (1): 56–62.

Grossman, Zoltán. 2017. *Unlikely Alliances: Native Nations and White Communities Join to Defend Rural Lands*. Seattle: University of Washington Press.

Grove, Kevin. 2018. *Resilience*. Abingdon, UK: Routledge.

Grove, Kevin, and David Chandler. 2017. "Resilience and the Anthropocene: The Stakes of 'Renaturalising' Politics." *Resilience* 5 (2): 79–91.

Gusterson, Hugh. 2005. "A Pedagogy of Diminishing Returns: Scientific Involution across Three Generations of Nuclear Weapons Science." In *Pedagogy and the Practice of Science: Historical and Contemporary Perspectives*, edited by David Kaiser, 75–109. Cambridge, MA: MIT Press.

Haddad, Samir. 2013. *Derrida and the Inheritance of Democracy*. Bloomington: Indiana University Press.

Hall, Stuart. 1986. "The Problem of Ideology: Marxism without Guarantees." *Journal of Communication Inquiry* 10 (2): 28–44.

Halseth, Greg, and Annie Booth. 2003. "'What Works Well; What Needs Improvement': Lessons in Public Consultation from British Columbia's Resource Planning Processes." *Local Environment* 8 (4): 437–55.

Han, Clara. 2020. *Seeing Like a Child: Inheriting the Korean War*. New York: Fordham University Press.

Han, Clara, and Andrew Brandel. 2020. "Genres of Witnessing: Narrative, Violence, Generations." *Ethnos* 85 (4): 629–46.

Hann, Chris. 2008. "Reproduction and Inheritance: Goody Revisited." *Annual Review of Anthropology* 37:145–58.

Hansen, Andrew J., Steven L. Garman, James F. Weigand, Dean L. Urban, William C. McComb, and Martin G. Raphael. 1995. "Alternative Silvicultural Regimes in the Pacific Northwest: Simulations of Ecological and Economic Effects." *Ecological Applications* 5 (3): 535–54.

Haraway, Donna J. 1997. *Modest_Witness@Second_Millenium.FemaleMan©_Meets_OncoMouse™*. Abingdon, UK: Routledge.

Harris, Cole. 2002. *Making Native Space: Colonialism, Resistance, and Reserves in British Columbia*. Vancouver: University of British Columbia Press.

Harrison, Simon. 2004. "Forgetful and Memorious Landscapes." *Social Anthropology* 12 (2): 135–51.

Hayter, Roger. 2003. "'The War in the Woods': Post-Fordist Restructuring, Globalization, and the Contested Remapping of British Columbia's Forest Economy." *Annals of the Association of American Geographers* 93 (3): 706–29.

Hébert, Karen. 2015. "Enduring Capitalism: Instability, Precariousness, and Cycles of Change in an Alaskan Salmon Fishery." *American Anthropologist* 117 (1): 32–46.

Hegmann, G., C. Cocklin, R. Creasey, S. Dupuis, A. Kennedy, L. Kingsley, W. Ross, H. Spaling, and D. Stalker. 1999. *Cumulative Effects Assessment Practitioners Guide*. Hull, QC: AXYS Environmental Consulting and the CEA Working Group for the Canadian Environmental Assessment Agency.

Helmreich, Stefan. 2009. *Alien Ocean: Anthropological Voyages on Microbial Seas*. Berkeley: University of California Press.

Heynen, Nik, James McCarthy, Scott Prudham, and Paul Robbins, eds. 2007. *Neoliberal Environments: False Promises and Unnatural Consequences*. Abingdon, UK: Routledge.

Hillier, Cathlene, Yujiro Sano, David Zarifa, and Michael Haan. 2020. "Will They Stay or Will They Go? Examining the Brain Drain in Canada's Provincial North." *Canadian Review of Sociology/Revue canadienne de sociologie* 57 (2): 174–96.

Hirsch, Eric. 2017. "Investment's Rituals: 'Grassroots' Extractivism and the Making of an Indigenous Gold Mine in the Peruvian Andes." *Geoforum* 82:259–67.

Hirtz, Frank. 2003. "It Takes Modern Means to Be Traditional: On Recognizing Indigenous Cultural Communities in the Philippines." *Development and Change* 34 (5): 887–914.

Hoag, Colin. 2011. "Assembling Partial Perspectives: Thoughts on the Anthropology of Bureaucracy." *PoLAR: Political and Legal Anthropology Review* 34 (1): 81–94.

Hobart, Hiʻilei Julia. 2019. "At Home on the Mauna: Ecological Violence and Fantasies of Terra Nullius on Maunakea's Summit." *Native American and Indigenous Studies* 6 (2): 30–50.

Hodgson, Dorothy, and Richard Schroeder. 2002. "Dilemmas of Counter-mapping Community Resources in Tanzania." *Development and Change* 33 (1): 79–100.

Hoffman, Ross. 2019. *Song of the Earth: The Life of Alfred Joseph*. Smithers, BC: Creekstone Press.

Holling, Crawford S. 1973. "Resilience and Stability of Ecological Systems." *Annual Review of Ecology and Systematics* 4 (1): 1–23.

Holling, Crawford S. 1978. *Adaptive Environmental Assessment and Management*. New York: Wiley and Sons.

Holyk, Travis John. 1999. "From Colonization to Globalization: The Gitxsan Nation's Struggle for Jurisdiction within Their Traditional Territories." Master's thesis, University of Northern British Columbia, Prince George.

Houde, Nicolas. 2007. "The Six Faces of Traditional Ecological Knowledge: Challenges and Opportunities for Canadian Co-management Arrangements." *Ecology and Society* 12 (2): 34.

Ingold, Tim. 2000. *The Perception of the Environment: Essays on Livelihood, Dwelling and Skill*. New York: Psychology Press.

Ingold, Tim. 2007. *Lines: A Brief History*. Abingdon, UK: Routledge.

Ingold, Tim. 2008. "Bindings against Boundaries: Entanglements of Life in an Open World." *Environment and Planning A: Economy and Space* 40 (8): 1796–810.

Ingold, Tim. 2011. *Being Alive: Essays on Movement, Knowledge and Description*. New York: Taylor and Francis.

Innes, John L. 2003. "The Incorporation of Research into Attempts to Improve Forest Policy in British Columbia." *Forest Policy and Economics* 5 (4): 349–59.

Jackson, Tony, and John Curry. 2004. "Peace in the Woods: Sustainability and the Democratization of Land Use Planning and Resource Management on Crown Lands in British Columbia." *International Planning Studies* 9 (1): 27–42.

Jacoby, Karl. 2001. *Crimes against Nature: Squatters, Poachers, Thieves, and the Hidden History of American Conservation*. Berkeley: University of California Press.

Jang, Trevor. 2017. "Twenty Years after Historic Delgamuukw Land Claims Case, Pipeline Divides Gitxsan Nation." *Discourse*, February 7, 2017. https://thediscourse .ca/urban-nation/twenty-years-historic-delgamuukw-land-claims-case-pipeline -divides-gitxsan-nation.

Johnson, Benjamin David. 1999. "The Aboriginal Mapping Network: A Case Study in the Democratization of Mapping." Master's thesis, University of British Columbia, Vancouver.

Johnson, Leslie Main. 1997. "Health, Wholeness, and the Land: Gitksan Traditional Plant Use and Healing." PhD diss., University of Alberta, Edmonton.

Johnson, Leslie Main. 2000. "'A Place That's Good': Gitksan Landscape Perception and Ethnoecology." *Human Ecology* 28:301–25.

Johnson, Leslie Main. 2010. *Trail of Story, Traveller's Path: Reflections on Ethnoecology and Landscape*. Edmonton, AB: Athabasca University Press.

Johnson, Leslie Main, Darlene Vegh, and Ruby E. Morgan. 2019. "Huckleberries, Food Sovereignty, Cumulative Impact and Community Health: Reflections from Northern British Columbia, Canada." In *Wisdom Engaged: Traditional Knowledge for Northern Community Well-Being*, edited by Leslie Main Johnson, 143–74. Edmonton: University of Alberta Press.

Joly, Tara L., Hereward Longley, Carmen Wells, and Jenny Gerbrandt. 2018. "Ethnographic Refusal in Traditional Land Use Mapping: Consultation, Impact Assessment, and Sovereignty in the Athabasca Oil Sands Region." *Extractive Industries and Society* 5 (2): 335–43.

Joseph, Jonathan. 2013. "Resilience as Embedded Neoliberalism: A Governmentality Approach." *Resilience* 1 (1): 38–52.

Keele, Svenja. 2019. "Consultants and the Business of Climate Services: Implications of Shifting from Public to Private Science." *Climatic Change* 157 (1): 9–26.

Kelm, Mary-Ellen, and Keith D. Smith. 2018. *Talking Back to the Indian Act: Critical Readings in Settler Colonial Histories*. Toronto: University of Toronto Press.

Kestler-D'Amours, Jillian. 2020. "Understanding the Wet'suwet'en Struggle in Canada." *Al Jazeera*, March 1, 2020. https://www.aljazeera.com/news/2020/3/1/understanding-the-wetsuweten-struggle-in-canada.

Khalfan, Amani. 2015. "Indigenous Sovereignty Fuels Pipeline Resistance: An Interview with Freda Huson and Toghestiy of the Unist'ot'en Camp." *Upping the Anti*, no. 17, 46–59.

Klassen, Michael A., Rick Budhwa, and Rudy Reimer/Yumks. 2009. "First Nations, Forestry, and the Transformation of Archaeological Practice in British Columbia, Canada." *Heritage Management* 2 (2): 199–238.

Kohlbry, Paul. 2018. "Owning the Homeland: Property, Markets, and Formations of Land Defense in the West Bank." *Journal of Palestine Studies* 47 (4): 30–45.

Kohler, Robert. 2002. *Landscapes and Labscapes: Exploring the Lab-Field Border in Biology*. Chicago: University of Chicago Press.

Kohler, Robert. 2011. "History of Field Science: New Trends and Prospects." In *Knowing Global Environments: New Historical Perspectives on the Field Sciences*, edited by Jeremy Vetter, 212–40. New Brunswick, NJ: Rutgers University Press.

Kohler, Robert, and Henrika Kuklick, eds. 1996. "Science in the Field." Special issue, *Osiris,* no. 11.

Kolopenuk, Jessica. 2020. "Miskâsowin: Indigenous Science, Technology, and Society." *Genealogy* 4 (1): 21.

Kosek, Jake. 2006. *Understories: The Political Life of Forests in Northern New Mexico*. Durham, NC: Duke University Press.

Krehbiel, Richard. 2004. "Common Visions: Influences of the Nisga'a Final Agreement on Lheidli T'enneh Negotiations in the BC Treaty Process." *International Journal on Minority and Group Rights* 11 (3): 279–88.

Kuhn, Thomas. 1962. *The Structure of Scientific Revolutions*. Chicago: University of Chicago Press.

Kuin, Frank. 1998. "Gitxsan Indianen winnen slag bij strijd om land in westelijk Canada." http://frankkuin.com/nl/1998/08/01/gitxsan-eigendomsrechten-land/.

Kulchyski, Peter. 2005. *Like the Sound of a Drum: Aboriginal Cultural Politics in Denendeh and Nunavut*. Winnipeg: University of Manitoba Press.

Kuper, Adam. 2003. "The Return of the Native." *Current Anthropology* 44 (3): 389–402.

Kurjata, Andrew. 2020. "Why Coastal GasLink Says It Rejected a Pipeline Route Endorsed by Wet'suwet'en Hereditary Chiefs." *CBC News*, February 16, 2020. https://www.cbc.ca/news/canada/british-columbia/wetsuweten-coastal-gaslink-pipeline-alternative-path-1.5464945.

Lakatos, Imre. 1976. *Proofs and Refutations: The Logic of Mathematical Discovery*. Cambridge: Cambridge University Press.

Lakoff, Andrew. 2007. "Preparing for the Next Emergency." *Public Culture* 19 (2): 247–71.

Lapointe, Paul-Andre. 1994. "Quebec: Aluminum Valley or Aluminum Republic?" In *States, Firms, and Raw Materials: The World Economy and Ecology of Aluminum*, edited by Bradford Barnham, Stephen G. Bunker, and Denis O'Hearn, 215–37. Madison: University of Wisconsin Press.

Latour, Bruno. 1990. "Drawing Things Together." In *Representation in Scientific Practice*, edited by Michael Lynch and Steve Woolgar, 19–68. Cambridge, MA: MIT Press.

Latour, Bruno. 1996. *Aramis, or The Love of Technology*. Translated by Catherine Porter. Cambridge, MA: Harvard University Press.

Lave, Rebecca. 2012. *Fields and Streams: Stream Restoration, Neoliberalism, and the Future of Environmental Science*. Athens: University of Georgia Press.

Lave, Rebecca. 2015. "The Future of Environmental Expertise." *Annals of the Association of American Geographers* 105 (2): 244–52.

Law, John, and Michael Lynch. 1990. "Lists, Field Guides, and the Descriptive Organization of Seeing: Bird-Watching as an Exemplary Observational Activity." In *Representation in Scientific Practice*, edited by Michael Lynch and Steve Woolgar, 267–99. Cambridge, MA: MIT Press.

Lee, Kai. 1999. "Appraising Adaptive Management." *Conservation Ecology* 3 (2): 3. http://www.consecol.org/vol3/iss2/art3/.

Lee, Marc, and Seth Klein. 2020. "Why Now Is the Time to Reform BC's Oil and Gas Royalties." *Policy Note*, December 8, 2020. https://www.policynote.ca/royalties-and-wind-down/.

Lemov, Rebecca. 2015. *Database of Dreams: The Lost Quest to Catalog Humanity*. New Haven, CT: Yale University Press.

Lewis, John. 2000. "GIS and the Visualization of First Nations Resource Management." In *From Science to Management and Back: A Science Forum for Southern Interior Ecosystems of British Columbia*, edited by Chris Hollstedy, Karyn Sutherland, and Trina Innes, 63–64. Kamloops, BC: Southern Interior Forest Extension and Research Partnership.

Li, Fabiana. 2015. *Unearthing Conflict: Corporate Mining, Activism, and Expertise in Peru*. Durham, NC: Duke University Press.

Li, Tania Murray. 2005. "Beyond 'the State' and Failed Schemes." *American Anthropologist* 107 (3): 383–94.

Li, Tania Murray. 2014. *Land's End: Capitalist Relations on an Indigenous Frontier*. Durham, NC: Duke University Press.

Liboiron, Max. 2021. *Pollution Is Colonialism*. Durham, NC: Duke University Press.

Liboiron, Max, Manuel Tironi, and Nerea Calvillo. 2018. "Toxic Politics: Acting in a Permanently Polluted World." *Social Studies of Science* 48 (3): 331–49.

Little, Simon. 2020. "Port of Vancouver Faces 'Backlog' with More than 40 Ships at Anchor amid Protests, Blockades." *Global News*, February 17, 2020. https://globalnews.ca/news/6561313/port-of-vancouver-wetsuweten-blockade-2/.

Lowan-Trudeau, Greg. 2012. "Methodological Métissage: An Interpretive Indigenous Approach to Environmental Education Research." *Canadian Journal of Environmental Education* 17:113–30.

Luckert, M. K., and Peter Boxall. 2009. "Institutional Vacuums in Canadian Forest Policy: Can Criteria and Indicators and Certification of Sustainable Forest Management Fill the Void?" *Forestry Chronicle* 85 (2): 277–84.

Lynch, Michael. 1985. "Discipline and the Material Form of Images: An Analysis of Scientific Visibility." *Social Studies of Science* 15 (1): 37–66.

Mackenzie, A. Fiona, and Simon Dalby. 2003. "Moving Mountains: Community and Resistance in the Isle of Harris, Scotland, and Cape Breton, Canada." *Antipode* 35 (2): 309–33.

Mancell, Garry, Jeff Waatainen, and Erin Hunter. 2014. "The Supreme Court of Canada's Decision in *Tsilhqot'in Nation v. British Columbia*: Implications for the Application of the Forest Act in BC." *DLA Piper*, July 4, 2014. https://www.mondaq.com /canada/land-law-agriculture/327342/the-supreme-court-of-canada39s-decision -in-tsilhqot39in-nation-v-british-columbia-implications-for-the-application-of -the-forest-act-in-bc.

Manuel, Arthur, and Grand Chief Ronald Derrickson. 2015. *Unsettling Canada: A National Wake-Up Call*. Toronto: Between the Lines.

Marsden, Susan. 2002. "Adawx, Spanaxnox, and the Geopolitics of the Tsimshian." *BC Studies: The British Columbian Quarterly*, no. 135, 101–35.

Mason, Arthur. 2002. "The Rise of an Alaskan Native Bourgeoisie." *Études/Inuit/ Studies* 26 (2): 5–22.

Mason, Arthur. 2013. "Forms of Time in Alaska Natural Gas Development." *Polar Record* 49 (1): 42–49.

Mathews, Andrew. 2011. *Instituting Nature: Authority, Expertise, and Power in Mexican Forests*. Cambridge, MA: MIT Press.

Mavhunga, Clapperton Chakanetsa, ed. 2017. *What Do Science, Technology, and Innovation Mean from Africa?* Cambridge, MA: MIT Press.

McCarthy, James. 2005. "Devolution in the Woods: Community Forestry as Hybrid Neoliberalism." *Environment and Planning A: Economy and Space* 37 (6): 995–1014.

McCarthy, James. 2006. "Neoliberalism and the Politics of Alternatives: Community Forestry in British Columbia and the United States." *Annals of the Association of American Geographers* 96 (1): 84–104.

McClellan, Michael, Douglas Swanston, Paul Hennon, Robert Deal, Toni DeSanto, and Mark Wipfli. 2000. "Alternatives to Clearcutting in the Old-Growth Forests of Southeast Alaska: Study Plan and Establishment Report." *General Technical Report*. PNW-GTR-494. Pacific Northwest Research Station. USDA Forest Service.

McCreary, Tyler. 2013a. "Mining Aboriginal Success: The Politics of Difference in Continuing Education for Industry Needs." *Canadian Geographer/Le Géographe canadien* 57 (3): 280–88.

McCreary, Tyler. 2013b. "New Relationships on the Northwest Frontier: Episodes in the Gitxsan and Witsuwit'en Encounter with Colonial Power." PhD diss., York University, Toronto.

McCreary, Tyler. 2014. "The Burden of Sovereignty: Court Configurations of Indigenous and State Authority in Aboriginal Title Litigation in Canada." *North American Dialogue* 17 (2): 64–78.

McCreary, Tyler. 2016. "Historicizing the Encounter between State, Corporate, and Indigenous Authorities on Gitxsan Lands." *Windsor Yearbook of Access to Justice* 33 (3): 163–97.

McCreary. Tyler. 2018a. "Plaintiff Helped Win a Major Victory for Canada's Native People." *Globe and Mail*, October 10, 2018. https://www.theglobeandmail.com /canada/british-columbia/article-plaintiff-helped-win-a-major-victory-for-canadas -native-people/.

McCreary, Tyler. 2018b. *Shared Histories: Witsuwit'en-Settler Relations in Smithers, British Columbia, 1913–1973*. Smithers, BC: Creekstone Press.

McCreary, Tyler, and Richard Milligan. 2014. "Pipelines, Permits, and Protests: Carrier Sekani Encounters with the Enbridge Northern Gateway Project." *Cultural Geographies* 21 (1): 115–29.

McCreary, Tyler, and Jerome Turner. 2018. "The Contested Scales of Indigenous and Settler Jurisdiction: Unist'ot'en Struggles with Canadian Pipeline Governance." *Studies in Political Economy* 99 (3): 223–45.

McIntosh, Emma. 2020. "RCMP Breach Final Wet'suwet'en Camp in the Path of Coastal GasLink Pipeline." *Canada's National Observer*, May 10, 2020. https://www .nationalobserver.com/2020/02/10/news/rcmp-breach-final-wetsuweten-camp -path-coastal-gaslink-pipeline.

Medina, Eden, Ivan da Costa Marques, and Christina Holmes. 2014. *Beyond Imported Magic: Essays on Science, Technology, and Society in Latin America*. Cambridge, MA: MIT Press.

Meissner, Dirk. 2012. "Land-and-Cash Deal with First Nation Seen as Treaty Precursor." *Globe and Mail*, November 16, 2012. https://www.theglobeandmail.com/news /british-columbia/land-and-cash-deal-with-first-nation-seen-as-treaty-precursor /article5394257/.

Messeri, Lisa. 2016. *Placing Outer Space: An Earthly Ethnography of Other Worlds*. Durham, NC: Duke University Press.

Messeri, Lisa. 2017. "Resonant Worlds: Cultivating Proximal Encounters in Planetary Science." *American Ethnologist* 44 (1): 131–42.

Million, Dian. 2008. "Felt Theory." *American Quarterly* 60 (2): 267–72.

Million, Dian. 2009. "Felt Theory: An Indigenous Feminist Approach to Affect and History." *Wicazo Sa Review* 24 (2): 53–76.

Million, Dian. 2011. "Intense Dreaming: Theories, Narratives, and Our Search for Home." *American Indian Quarterly* 35 (3): 313–33.

Million, Dian. 2013. *Therapeutic Nations: Healing in an Age of Indigenous Human Rights*. Tucson: University of Arizona Press.

Mills, Antonia. 1994. *Eagle Down Is Our Law: Witsuwit'en Law, Feasts, and Land Claims*. Vancouver: University of British Columbia Press.

Mills, Antonia. 2005. *"Hang onto These Words": Johnny David's Delgamuukw Evidence*. Toronto: University of Toronto Press.

Mills, P. Dawn. 2008. *For Future Generations: Reconciling Gitxsan and Canadian Law*. Saskatoon, SK: Purich.

Mitchell, Timothy. 2002. *Rule of Experts: Egypt, Techno-Politics, Modernity*. Berkeley: University of California Press.

Monet, Don, and Skanu'u (Ardythe Wilson). 1992. *Colonialism on Trial: Indigenous Land Rights and the Gitksan and Wet'suwet'en Sovereignty Case*. Philadelphia, PA: New Society.

Morton, Cedar, Thomas I. Gunton, and J. C. Day. 2012. "Engaging Aboriginal Populations in Collaborative Planning: An Evaluation of a Two-Tiered Collaborative Planning Model for Land and Resource Management." *Journal of Environmental Planning and Management* 55 (4): 507–23.

Murphy, Margaret-Anne. 2020. "'Reconciliation Is Dead': Unist'ot'en Camp, Land Back and How the Movements Can Inform Settler Responsibilities and Indigenous-Settler Relationships Going Forward." PhD diss., University of Alberta, Edmonton.

Murphy, Michelle. 2015. "Unsettling Care: Troubling Transnational Itineraries of Care in Feminist Health Practices." *Social Studies of Science* 45 (5): 717–37.

Myers, Natasha, and Joe Dumit. 2011. "Haptic Creativity and the Mid-embodiments of Experimental Life." In *A Companion to the Anthropology of the Body and Embodiment*, edited by Frances E. Mascia-Lees, 239–61. Malden, MA: Wiley-Blackwell.

Nadasdy, Paul. 1999. "The Politics of TEK: Power and the 'Integration' of Knowledge." *Arctic Anthropology* 36 (1–2): 1–18.

Nadasdy, Paul. 2003. *Hunters and Bureaucrats: Power, Knowledge, and Aboriginal-State Relations in the Southwest Yukon*. Vancouver: University of British Columbia Press.

Nadasdy, Paul. 2005a. "The Anti-politics of TEK: The Institutionalization of Co-management Discourse and Practice." *Anthropologica* 47 (2): 215–32.

Nadasdy, Paul. 2005b. "Transcending the Debate over the Ecologically Noble Indian: Indigenous Peoples and Environmentalism." *Ethnohistory* 52 (2): 291–331.

Nadasdy, Paul. 2007. "Adaptive Co-management and the Gospel of Resilience." In *Adaptive Co-management: Collaboration, Learning and Multi-level Governance*, edited by Derek Armitage, Fikret Berkes, and Nancy Doubleday, 208–27. Vancouver: University of British Columbia Press.

Nadasdy, Paul. 2010. "Resilience and Truth: A Response to Berkes." *Maritime Studies (MAST)* 9 (1): 41–45.

Nadasdy, Paul. 2017. *Sovereignty's Entailments: First Nation State Formation in the Yukon*. Toronto: University of Toronto Press.

Napoleon, Val. 2001. "Extinction by Number: Colonialism Made Easy." *Canadian Journal of Law and Society* 16 (1): 113–45.

Napoleon, Val. 2005. "*Delgamuukw*: A Legal Straightjacket for Oral Histories?" *Canadian Journal of Law and Society/La Revue Canadienne Droit et Société* 20 (2): 123–55.

Napoleon, Val. 2010. "Ayook: Gitksan Legal Order, Law, and Legal Theory." PhD diss., University of Victoria, Victoria, BC.

Napoleon, Val. 2013. "Thinking about Indigenous Legal Orders." In *Dialogues on Human Rights and Legal Pluralism*, edited by René Provost and Colleen Sheppard, 229–45. Amsterdam: Springer.

Napoleon, Val. 2019. "Did I Break It? Recording Indigenous (Customary) Law." *PER: Potchefstroomse Elektroniese Regsblad* 22 (1): 1–35.

Natcher, David C. 2001. "Land Use Research and the Duty to Consult: A Misrepresentation of the Aboriginal Landscape." *Land Use Policy* 18 (2): 113–22.

Neale, Timothy, and Eve Vincent. 2017. "Mining, Indigeneity, Alterity: Or, Mining Indigenous Alterity?" *Cultural Studies* 31 (2–3): 417–39.

Nesper, Larry. 2002. *The Walleye War: The Struggle for Ojibwe Spearfishing and Treaty Rights*. Lincoln: University of Nebraska Press.

Nicholas, George. 2006. "Decolonizing the Archaeological Landscape: The Practice and Politics of Archaeology in British Columbia." *American Indian Quarterly* 30 (3): 350–80.

Niezen, Ronald. 2017. *Truth and Indignation: Canada's Truth and Reconciliation Commission on Indian Residential Schools*. Toronto: University of Toronto Press.

Noakes, Taylor C. 2020. "The Pandemic Is Slicing Away Indigenous Sovereignty in Canada." *Foreign Policy*, April 20, 2020. https://foreignpolicy.com/2020/04/20/gas-pipeline-wetsuweten-coronavirus-pandemic-indigenous-sovereignty-canada-oil/.

Northword. 2007. "Amenity Man." November 19, 2007. http://northword.ca/december-2007/amenity-man.

Office of the Wet'suwet'en. 2014. *Submission to: British Columbia Environmental Assessment Office regarding the TransCanada Coastal GasLink Application*. http://www.wetsuweten.com/files/EAO_Process_Report_for_Coastal_GasLink_pipeline_application_2014.pdf.

Office of the Wet'suwet'en. n.d. *Wet'suwet'en Territory* (map). Accessed September 19, 2022. http://www.wetsuweten.com/images/uploads/article_photos/wetsu_territory_map.jpg.

Olynyk, John. 2005. "The Haida Nation and Taku River Tlingit Decisions: Clarifying Roles and Responsibilities for Aboriginal Consultation and Accommodation." *The Negotiator: The Magazine of the Canadian Association of the Petroleum Landman*, April 2005, 2–7.

Orchard, C. D. 1953. "Sustained Yield Forest Management in British Columbia." *Forestry Chronicle* 29 (1): 45–54.

Overstall, Richard. 2005. "Encountering the Spirit in the Land: 'Property' in a Kinship-Based Legal Order." In *Despotic Dominion: Property Rights in British Settler Societies,* edited by John McLaren, A. R. Buck, and Nancy E. Wright, 196–212. Vancouver: University of British Columbia Press.

Overstall, Richard. 2008. "The Law Is Opened: The Constitutional Role of Tangible and Intangible Property in Gitanyow." In *First Nations Cultural Heritage and Law*, edited by Catherine Bell and Val Napoleon, 92–113. Vancouver: University of British Columbia Press.

Özden-Schilling, Tom. 2019a. "Amenity Migration Revisited." *Journal for the Anthropology of North America* 22 (2): 131–34.

Özden-Schilling, Tom. 2019b. "Cartographies of Consignment: First Nations and Mapwork in the Neoliberal Era." *Anthropological Quarterly* 92 (2): 541–73.

Özden-Schilling, Tom. 2020. "Technopolitics in the Archive: Sovereignty, Research, and Everyday Life." *History and Theory* 59 (3): 394–402.

Özden-Schilling, Tom. 2021. "Aging in Digital: Simulation and Succession in Canadian Forestry Research." *American Ethnologist* 48 (1): 37–50.

Özden-Schilling, Tom. 2022. "Promising Resilience: Systems and Survival after Forestry's Ends." *American Anthropologist* 124 (1): 64–76.

Özden-Schilling, Tom. Forthcoming. "Authors of Misfortune: Interpretation and Expertise in a Model Disaster." *Journal of the Royal Anthropological Society* 30 (1).

Palmer, Vaughn. 2019. "Feds Forgive Treaty Loans, but Will It Revive Painfully Slow Process?" *Vancouver Sun*, March 22, 2019.

Parker, John, and Beatrice Crona. 2012. "On Being All Things to All People: Boundary Organizations and the Contemporary Research University." *Social Studies of Science* 42 (2): 262–89.

Parkins, John R., Michael Dunn, Maureen G. Reed, and A. John Sinclair. 2016. "Forest Governance as Neoliberal Strategy: A Comparative Case Study of the Model Forest Program in Canada." *Journal of Rural Studies* 45:270–78.

Parminter, John. 1983. "Fire History and Fire Ecology in the Prince Rupert Forest Region." In *Prescribed Fire—Forest Soils Symposium Proceedings*, edited by R. L. Trowbridge and A. Macadam, 1–36. Victoria: British Columbia Ministry of Forests.

Parreñas, Juno Salazar. 2018. *Decolonizing Extinction: The Work of Care in Orangutan Rehabilitation*. Durham, NC: Duke University Press.

Pasternak, Shiri. 2015. "How Capitalism Will Save Colonialism: The Privatization of Reserve Lands in Canada." *Antipode* 47 (1): 179–96.

Pasternak, Shiri. 2017. *Grounded Authority: The Algonquins of Barriere Lake against the State*. Minneapolis: University of Minnesota Press.

Pauly, Philip J. 2000. *Biologists and the Promise of American Life: From Meriwether Lewis to Alfred Kinsey*. Princeton, NJ: Princeton University Press.

Peeling, Albert. 2004. *Traditional Governance and Constitution Making among the Gitanyow*. First Nations Governance Centre. https://fngovernance.org/wp-content/uploads/2020/06/Constitution_Making_Among_the_Gitanyow.pdf.

Penikett, Tony. 2006. *Reconciliation: First Nations Treaty Making in British Columbia*. Toronto: Douglas and McIntyre.

Peterson, Garry, Graeme Cumming, and Stephen Carpenter. 2003. "Scenario Planning: A Tool for Conservation in an Uncertain World." *Conservation Biology* 17 (2): 358–66.

Peyton, Jonathan. 2017. *Unbuilt Environments: Tracing Postwar Development in Northwest British Columbia*. Vancouver: University of British Columbia Press.

Peyton, Jonathan, and Aaron Franks. 2016. "The New Nature of Things? Canada's Conservative Government and the Design of the New Environmental Subject." *Antipode* 48 (2): 453–73.

Pojar, James, Karel Klinka, and Del V. Meidinger. 1987. "Biogeoclimatic Ecosystem Classification in British Columbia." *Forest Ecology and Management* 22 (1): 119–54.

Polanyi, Michael. 1966. "The Logic of Tacit Inference." *Philosophy* 41 (155): 1–18.

Posadzki, Alexandra. 2014. "CN Railway and Gitxsan First Nation Discuss Eviction Notices." *Globe and Mail*, August 4, 2014. https://www.theglobeandmail.com/news /british-columbia/cn-railway-and-gitxsan-first-nation-discuss-eviction-notices /article19910432/.

Powell, Dana E. 2018. *Landscapes of Power: Politics of Energy in the Navajo Nation*. Durham, NC: Duke University Press.

Powell, J. V., Vickie D. Jensen, and Anne-Marie Pedersen. 2018. "Gitxsan." *The Canadian Encyclopedia*. https://www.thecanadianencyclopedia.ca/en/article/gitksan.

Price, Karen, and Dave Daust. 2009. "Making Monitoring Manageable: A Framework to Guide Learning." *Canadian Journal of Forest Research* 39 (10): 1881–92.

Price, Michael, Karl English, Andrew G. Rosenberger, Misty MacDuffee, and John D. Reynolds. 2017. "Canada's Wild Salmon Policy: An Assessment of Conservation Progress in British Columbia." *Canadian Journal of Fisheries and Aquatic Sciences* 74 (10): 1507–18.

Prudham, W. Scott. 2005. *Knock on Wood: Nature as Commodity in Douglas-Fir Country*. London: Routledge.

Prudham, W. Scott. 2007. "Sustaining Sustained Yield: Class, Politics, and Post-war Forest Regulation in British Columbia." *Environment and Planning D: Society and Space* 25 (2): 258–83.

Rabinow, Paul. 1996. *Making PCR: A Story of Biotechnology*. Chicago: University of Chicago Press.

Ramirez, Renya K. 2007. *Native Hubs: Culture, Community, and Belonging in Silicon Valley and Beyond*. Durham, NC: Duke University Press.

Ramirez, Renya K. 2009. "Henry Roe Cloud: A Granddaughter's Native Feminist Biographical Account." *Wicazo Sa Review* 24 (2): 77–103.

Ramirez, Renya K. 2018. *Standing Up to Colonial Power: The Lives of Henry Roe and Elizabeth Bender Cloud*. Lincoln: University of Nebraska Press.

Rankin, William. 2016. *After the Map: Cartography, Navigation, and the Transformation of Territory in the Twentieth Century*. Chicago: University of Chicago Press.

Rankin, William. 2017. "Zombie Projects, Negative Networks, and Multigenerational Science: The Temporality of the International Map of the World." *Social Studies of Science* 47 (3): 353–75.

Reardon, Jenny, and Kim TallBear. 2012. "'Your DNA Is Our History': Genomics, Anthropology, and the Construction of Whiteness as Property." *Current Anthropology* 53 (S5): S233–45.

Reed, Maureen G. 2003. *Taking Stands: Gender and the Sustainability of Rural Communities*. Vancouver: University of British Columbia Press.

Reid, Julian. 2012. "The Disastrous and Politically Debased Subject of Resilience." *Development Dialogue* 58:67–79.

Revel, John. 2007. *Devil's Club, Black Flies, and Snowshoes: A History of the Aleza Lake Forest Experiment Station*. Prince George: Aleza Lake Research Forest Society and the University of Northern British Columbia Press.

Rheinberger, Hans-Jörg. 1993. "Experiment and Orientation: Early Systems of In Vitro Protein Synthesis." *Journal of the History of Biology* 26 (3): 443–71.

Rheinberger, Hans-Jörg. 1994. "Experimental Systems: Historiality, Narration, and Deconstruction." *Science in Context* 7 (1): 65–81.

Rheinberger, Hans-Jörg. 1997. *Toward a History of Epistemic Things: Synthesizing Proteins in the Test Tube*. Stanford, CA: Stanford University Press.

Rheinberger, Hans-Jörg. 2000. "Cytoplasmic Particles: The Trajectory of a Scientific Object." In *Biographies of Scientific Objects*, edited by Lorraine Daston, 270–94. Chicago: University of Chicago Press.

Rheinberger, Hans-Jörg. 2010. *An Epistemology of the Concrete: Twentieth-Century Histories of Life*. Durham, NC: Duke University Press.

Riles, Annelise. 2011. *Collateral Knowledge: Legal Reasoning in the Global Financial Markets*. Chicago: University of Chicago Press.

Robertson, Leslie A. 2005. *Imagining Difference: Legend, Curse, and Spectacle in a Canadian Mining Town*. Vancouver: University of British Columbia Press.

Robertson, Sean. 2017. "'Thinking of the Land in That Way': Indigenous Sovereignty and the Spatial Politics of Attentiveness at Skwelkwek'welt." *Social and Cultural Geography* 18 (2): 178–200.

Rosaldo, Renato. 1989. "Imperialist Nostalgia." *Representations* 26:107–22.

Rossiter, David, and Patricia Wood. 2005. "Fantastic Topographies: Neo-liberal Responses to Aboriginal Land Claims in British Columbia." *Canadian Geographer/Le Géographe canadien* 49 (4): 352–66.

Roth, Christopher. 2001. "'The Names Spread in All Directions': Hereditary Titles in Tsimshian Social and Political Life." *BC Studies: The British Columbian Quarterly*, no. 130, 69–92.

Rudwick, Martin J. S. 1976. "The Emergence of a Visual Language for Geological Science 1760–1840." *History of Science* 14 (3): 149–95.

Rudwick, Martin J. S. 1996. "Geological Travel and Theoretical Innovation: The Role of 'Liminal' Experience." *Social Studies of Science* 26 (1): 143–59.

Rundstrom, Robert. 1995. "GIS, Indigenous Peoples, and Epistemological Diversity." *Cartography and Geographic Information Systems* 22 (1): 45–57.

Ryan, Don. 2005. "Afterword: Back to the Future." In *Our Box Was Full: An Ethnography for the Delgamuukw Plaintiffs*, edited by Richard Daly, 299–304. Vancouver: University of British Columbia Press.

Satterfield, Terre. 2002. *Anatomy of a Conflict: Identity, Knowledge, and Emotion in Old-Growth Forests*. Vancouver: University of British Columbia Press.

Scott, James. 1985. *Weapons of the Weak: Everyday Forms of Peasant Resistance*. New Haven, CT: Yale University Press.

Scott, James. 1998. *Seeing Like a State: How Certain Schemes to Improve the Human Condition Have Failed*. New Haven, CT: Yale University Press.

Seymour, Nicole. 2018. *Bad Environmentalism: Irony and Irreverence in the Ecological Age*. Minneapolis: University of Minnesota Press.

Shand, A. Innes. 1898. "Romance of the Fur Trade: The Companies." *Blackwood's Edinburgh Magazine* 164:495–508.

Sheenan, Carol, and Joseph David Gallant. 2019. "Walter Harris." *The Canadian Encyclopedia*. https://www.thecanadianencyclopedia.ca/en/article/walter-harris.

Sider, Gerald. 2003. *Between History and Tomorrow: Making and Breaking Everyday Life in Rural Newfoundland*. Toronto: University of Toronto Press.

Sillitoe, Paul. 1998. "The Development of Indigenous Knowledge: A New Applied Anthropology." *Current Anthropology* 39 (2): 223–52.

Simon, Stephanie, and Samuel Randalls. 2016. "Geography, Ontological Politics and the Resilient Future." *Dialogues in Human Geography* 6 (1): 3–18.

Simpson, Audra. 2007. "On Ethnographic Refusal: Indigeneity, 'Voice' and Colonial Citizenship." *Junctures: The Journal for Thematic Dialogue*, no. 9, 67–80.

Simpson, Audra. 2014. *Mohawk Interruptus: Political Life across the Borders of Settler States*. Durham, NC: Duke University Press.

Sinclair, A. John, Meinhard Doelle, and Peter Duinker. 2017. "Looking Up, Down, and Sideways: Reconceiving Cumulative Effects Assessment as a Mindset." *Environmental Impact Assessment Review* 62:183–94.

Sivaramakrishnan, Kalyanakrishnan. 1999. *Modern Forests: Statemaking and Environmental Change in Colonial Eastern India*. Stanford, CA: Stanford University Press.

Smith, Jen Rose. 2021. "'Exceeding Beringia': Upending Universal Human Events and Wayward Transits in Arctic Spaces." *Environment and Planning D: Society and Space* 39 (1): 158–75.

Smith, Neil. 1984. *Uneven Development: Nature, Capital, and the Production of Space*. Athens: University of Georgia Press.

Sparke, Matthew. 1998. "A Map That Roared and an Original Atlas: Canada, Cartography, and the Narration of Nation." *Annals of the Association of American Geographers* 88 (3): 463–95.

Spice, Anne. 2018. "Fighting Invasive Infrastructures: Indigenous Relations against Pipelines." *Environment and Society* 9 (1): 40–56.

Spice, Anne. 2019. "Heal the People, Heal the Land: An Interview with Freda Huson." In *Standing with Standing Rock: Voices from the #NODAPL Movement*, edited by Nick Estes and Jaskiran Dhillon, 211–21. Minneapolis: University of Minnesota Press.

Starn, Orin. 2011. "Here Come the Anthros (Again): The Strange Marriage of Anthropology and Native America." *Cultural Anthropology* 26 (2): 179–204.

Stem, Caroline, Richard Margoluis, Nick Salafsky, and Marcia Brown. 2005. "Monitoring and Evaluation in Conservation: A Review of Trends and Approaches." *Conservation Biology* 19 (2): 295–309.

Sterritt, Neil J. 1989. "Unflinching Resistance to an Implacable Invader." In *Drumbeat: Anger and Renewal in Indian Country*, edited by Boyce Richardson, 267–94. Toronto: Summerhill.

Sterritt, Neil J. 1998. "The Nisga'a Treaty: Competing Claims Ignored!" *BC Studies: The British Columbian Quarterly*, no. 120, 73–98.

Sterritt, Neil J. 2016. *Mapping My Way Home: A Gitxsan History*. Smithers, BC: Creekstone Press.

Sterritt, Neil J., Susan Marsden, Robert Galois, Peter R. Grant, and Richard Overstall. 1998. *Tribal Boundaries in the Nass Watershed*. Vancouver: University of British Columbia Press.

Stoler, Ann Laura. 2016. *Duress: Imperial Durabilities in Our Times*. Durham, NC: Duke University Press.

Stueck, Wendy. 2019. "B.C. Indigenous Leaders Praise Ottawa's Loan Forgiveness Plan." *Globe and Mail*, April 10, 2019. https://www.theglobeandmail.com/canada/article-bc-indigenous-leaders-praise-ottawas-loan-forgiveness-plan/.

Sutherland, Callum C. J. 2021. "Sockeye at the Boundary: Controversial and Contested Salmon in the Cohen Commission, 2009–2012." PhD diss., York University, Toronto.

Swanner, Leandra. 2017. "Instruments of Science or Conquest? Neocolonialism and Modern American Astronomy." *Historical Studies in the Natural Sciences* 47 (3): 293–319.

Talaga, Tanya. 2017. *Seven Fallen Feathers: Racism, Death, and Hard Truths in a Northern City*. Toronto: House of Anansi Press.

Talaga, Tanya. 2018. *All Our Relations: Finding the Path Forward*. Toronto: House of Anansi Press.

TallBear, Kim. 2013. *Native American DNA: Tribal Belonging and the False Promise of Genetic Science*. Minneapolis: University of Minnesota Press.

Thielmann, Tim, and Chris Tollefson. 2009. "Tears from an Onion: Layering, Exhaustion and Conversion in British Columbia Land Use Planning Policy." *Policy and Society* 28 (2): 111–24.

Thom, Brian. 2009. "The Paradox of Boundaries in Coast Salish Territories." *Cultural Geographies* 16 (2): 179–205.

Thornton, Thomas F. 2008. *Being and Place among the Tlingit*. Seattle: University of Washington Press.

Thornton, Tracy. 2002. "Women's Participation in Land Use Planning: A Case Study of the Cariboo-Chilcotin Land Use Plan (CCLUP)." Master's thesis, University of Northern British Columbia, Prince George.

Todd, Loretta, dir. 1994. *The Hands of History*. Film. National Film Board of Canada. https://www.nfb.ca/film/hands_of_history/.

Todd, Zoe. 2014. "Fish Pluralities: Human-Animal Relations and Sites of Engagement in Paulatuuq, Arctic Canada." *Études/Inuit/Studies* 38 (1–2): 217–38.

Todd, Zoe. 2016. "From Classroom to River's Edge: Tending to Reciprocal Duties beyond the Academy." *Aboriginal Policy Studies* 6 (1): 90–97.

Tollefson, Chris, ed. 1998. *The Wealth of Forests: Markets, Regulation, and Sustainable Forestry*. Vancouver: University of British Columbia Press.

Traweek, Sharon. 1988. *Beamtimes and Lifetimes: The World of High Energy Physicists*. Cambridge, MA: Harvard University Press.

Trusler, Scott, and Leslie Main Johnson. 2008. "'Berry Patch' as a Kind of Place: The Ethnoecology of Black Huckleberry in Northwestern Canada." *Human Ecology* 36 (4): 553–68.

Tuck, Eve. 2009. "Suspending Damage: A Letter to Communities." *Harvard Educational Review* 79 (3): 409–27.

Tuhiwai Smith, Linda. 1999. *Decolonizing Methodologies: Research and Indigenous Peoples*. London: Zed Books.

Turkel, William. 2007. *The Archive of Place: Unearthing the Pasts of the Chilcotin Plateau*. Vancouver: University of British Columbia Press.

Turkle, Sherry. 2009. "Simulation and Its Discontents." In *Simulation and Its Discontents*, edited by Sherry Turkle, 1–102. Cambridge, MA: MIT Press.

United States Geological Survey. 2021. "USGSShadedReliefOnly (Map Server)." https://basemap.nationalmap.gov/arcgis/rest/services/USGSShadedReliefOnly/MapServer/.

United States Geological Survey. 2022. "North America Rivers and Lakes." ScienceBase-Catalog. https://www.sciencebase.gov/catalog/item/4fb55df0e4b04cb937751e02.

Usher, Peter J., Frank J. Tough, and Robert M. Galois. 1992. "Reclaiming the Land: Aboriginal Title, Treaty Rights and Land Claims in Canada." *Applied Geography* 12 (2): 109–32.

Veltmeyer, Henry, and Paul Bowles. 2014. "Extractivist Resistance: The Case of the Enbridge Oil Pipeline Project in Northern British Columbia." *Extractive Industries and Society* 1 (1): 59–68.

Vizenor, Gerald. 1990. *Bearheart: The Heirship Chronicles*. Minneapolis: University of Minnesota Press.

Vizenor, Gerald. 1994. *Manifest Manners: Postindian Warriors of Survivance*. Middletown, CT: Wesleyan University Press.

Vizenor, Gerald. 2008. "Aesthetics of Survivance: Literary Theory and Practice." In *Survivance: Narratives of Native Presence*, edited by Gerald Vizenor, 1–24. Lincoln: University of Nebraska Press.

Walker, Brian, Crawford S. Holling, Stephen Carpenter, and Ann Kinzig. 2004. "Resilience, Adaptability and Transformability in Social-Ecological Systems." *Ecology and Society* 9 (2): 5–14.

Walker, Jeremy, and Melinda Cooper. 2011. "Genealogies of Resilience: From Systems Ecology to the Political Economy of Crisis Adaptation." *Security Dialogue* 42 (2): 143–60.

Walley, Christine J. 2004. *Rough Waters: Nature and Development in an East African Marine Park*. Princeton, NJ: Princeton University Press.

Warren, D. Michael, L. Jan Slikkerveer, and David Brokensha, eds. 1995. *The Cultural Dimensions of Development: Indigenous Knowledge Systems*. London: Intermediate Technology.

Watts, Michael. 2011. "On Confluences and Divergences." *Dialogues in Human Geography* 1 (1): 84–89.

Weber, Marian, Naomi Krogman, and Terry Antoniuk. 2012. "Cumulative Effects Assessment: Linking Social, Ecological, and Governance Dimensions." *Ecology and Society* 17 (2): 22.

Weber, Max. 1958. "Science as a Vocation." Translated by Philip Rieff. *Daedalus* 87 (1): 111–34.

Weber, Max. 1961. *General Economic History*. Translated by Frank H. Knight. New York: Collier Books.

Webmoor, Timothy. 2005. "Mediational Techniques and Conceptual Frameworks in Archaeology: A Model in 'Mapwork' at Teotihuacán, Mexico." *Journal of Social Archaeology* 5 (1): 52–84.

Weiss, Joseph. 2018. *Shaping the Future on Haida Gwaii: Life beyond Settler Colonialism*. Vancouver: University of British Columbia Press.

West, Paige. 2006. *Conservation Is Our Government Now: The Politics of Ecology in Papua New Guinea*. Durham, NC: Duke University Press.

White, Richard. 1995. "'Are You an Environmentalist or Do You Work for a Living?': Work and Nature." In *Uncommon Ground: Rethinking the Human Place in Nature*, edited by William Cronon, 171–85. New York: W. W. Norton.

Whyte, Kyle Powys. 2013. "On the Role of Traditional Ecological Knowledge as a Collaborative Concept: A Philosophical Study." *Ecological Processes* 2 (1): 1–12.

Whyte, Kyle Powys. 2014. "Indigenous Women, Climate Change Impacts, and Collective Action." *Hypatia* 29 (3): 599–616.

Whyte, Kyle Powys. 2018. "Indigenous Science (Fiction) for the Anthropocene: Ancestral Dystopias and Fantasies of Climate Change Crises." *Environment and Planning E: Nature and Space* 1 (1–2): 224–42.

Wilson, Jeremy. 1998. *Talk and Log: Wilderness Politics in British Columbia, 1965–1996*. Vancouver: University of British Columbia Press.

Wilson, Jeremy. 2001. "Experimentation on a Leash: Forest Land Use Planning in the 1990s." In *In Search of Sustainability: British Columbia Forest Policy in the 1990s*, edited by Benjamin Cashore, Michael Howlett, Jeremy Wilson, George Hoberg, and Jeremy Rayner, 31–60. Vancouver: University of British Columbia Press.

Wood, Patricia, and David Rossiter. 2011. "Unstable Properties: British Columbia, Aboriginal Title, and the 'New Relationship.'" *Canadian Geographer/Le Géographe canadien* 55 (4): 407–25.

World Commission on Environment and Development. 1987. *Our Common Future*. Oxford: Oxford University Press.

Yurchak, Alexei. 2006. *Everything Was Forever, Until It Was No More: The Last Soviet Generation*. Princeton, NJ: Princeton University Press.

Zhang, Daowei. 2007. *The Softwood Lumber War: Politics, Economics, and the Long US-Canadian Trade Dispute*. Washington, DC: Earthscan.

INDEX

Note: Page numbers in italics refer to figures, photos, and maps.

"Aboriginal," as term, 237n2

Aboriginal Mapping Network (AMN), 100, 249n26

adaptive management: Bulkley Land and Resource Management Plan and, 201–2; Gitxsan First Nation and, 71; meaning of, 201; in Yukon, 203

Agrawal, Arun, 70, 245n19, 247n10

Alaska gas pipeline, 177–78, 256n14

Aleza Lake Forest Experiment Station, 127–28, *145–48*

Alfred, Henry, 247n12

Alternative Silvicultural Systems, 129

amenity migrants, 12, 50, 67, 243n9

Anderson, Ben, 204–5

Aporta, Claudio, 160

Armstrong, David, 83

artifacts: displacement and, 11, 21–27, 32, 43, 232; of Gitxsan Strategic Watershed Analysis Team (SWAT), 5, 75; history and, xvi, 18, 31, 46, 84, 245n20; as objects of inheritance, 31, 45, 66, 88; sense of belonging and, 18, 43, 44, 60, 75, 84; technical, 18, 33, 49, 65, 124

Assembly of First Nations, 10, 155, 230

autobiographies, Indigenous, 105

Bachrach, Taylor, 40, 242n1

band membership in First Nations, 238n2; meaning of, 89

Bateson, Gregory, 195

BC Cumulative Effects Framework (CEF), 192–93, 205, 211–12

BC Forest Service: deregulation and, 9, 48, 208; fire-suppression policies of, 253n12; industrial planting and, 126, 129; leadership of, 4, 120–21, 130, 139; logging regulation and, 8; office closure in Smithers, 36, 48, 55–56; research forests and, 8; Watershed Restoration Research program, 128. *See also* Aleza Lake Forest Experiment Station; Date Creek Research Forest

BC Liberal Party: conservation policies of, 9–10, 41, 45, 130, 208, 244n16; provincial versus federal, 242n3. *See also* Campbell, Gordon; Legislative Assembly of British Columbia; New Relationship

BC Ministry of Environment: "dirt ministries" and, 47; reorganization of, 56; research forests and, 8

BC Ministry of Forests: "dirt ministries" and, 47; financial support for First Nations, 99; Forests and Lands Management Plan and, 244n15; reorganization of, 8

BC Ministry of Mines, "dirt ministries" and, 47

BC Ministry of Natural Gas Development, 256n15

BC Ministry of Sustainable Resource Management, 243n14

BC United, 242n3

Beaver Indian: and Hugh Brody, 177–78; as term, 255n11

belonging: artifacts in, 18, 43, 44, 60, 75, 84; in collective life, 27; displacement and, 43–44, 66; in Indigenous research, 79; in research forest, 126; Smithers researchers and, 40, 42–43, 50

berry harvesting, 11, 240n10, 249n24

biographies: Indigenous, 105; map, 100–101, 249

Boym, Svetlana, 44, 45, 65–66

Brandel, Andrew, 119, 254n15

British Columbia Treaty Commission (BCTC), 9, 156, 248n15; countermapping and corporate funding, 6, 152, 158, 165, 171; establishment of, 91, 155; land selection model and, 155, 157, 255n3; treaty negotiation process of, 241n14, 249n21

Brody, Hugh, 177–78, 249n25

Bulkley Community Resources Board, 57–63, 68, 244n15, 245n18

Bulkley Land and Resource Management Plan (LRMP): adaptive management in, 201–2; boundaries of, ix; development of, 57–63, 242n6, 243n14; disenchantment with, 244n14; dismantling of, 41, 64, 66, 67; land use designations of, 58–59, *59*, 244n16; map of, *38*; proponents of, 40–41, 60, 64–66, 244n14

Bulkley Valley Research Centre (BVRC): collaborations with First Nations people, 70; independent research and, 36, 38, 50, 67, 120, 207; as space for interaction, 52

Calder, Frank, 14, 155

Callison, Candis, 27

Calvillo, Nerea, 164

Campbell, Gordon, 9–10; conservation policies, 45; New Relationship and, 10, 32, 41, 45; reelection of, 41. *See also* BC Liberal Party; Legislative Assembly of British Columbia

Canadian Association of Smelters and Allied Workers, 53

Canadian Boreal Forest Agreement, 100

Canadian Geographical Names Database, ix

Chandler, David, 197

Chipeniuk, Ray, 243n9

Choy, Tim, 65

Clarke, Lee, 45–46

Clifford, James, 84, 247n13, 248n14

climate change, effects of, 21, 23, 123, 195, 198, 203–4, 251n6

Cloud, Henry, 105

Coastal GasLink pipeline project, 168, 224, 227. *See also* TransCanada Pipelines (TCP) Corporation

Cohen Commission, 192

Collier, Lori, 73, 96, 246n1

Collier, Russell: Aboriginal Mapping Network and, 100; Canadian Boreal Forest Agreement and, 100; career of, 74, 76, 87–89, 96, 99–101, 102–3, 248n19; countermapping movement and, 74, 77, 87, 88, 99–101, 250n28; as "cultural entrepreneur," 74, 78; death of, 107–9, 250n30; Ecotrust Canada and, 100; feast name of, 250n31; Gitxsan Treaty Society, 74, 97; Mikisew Cree First Nation and, 74, 96, 107

Collier, Russell, and Gitxsan Strategic Watershed Analysis Team (SWAT): cofounding of, 23, 74–75; digital mapping and, 97–98; dissolution of SWAT, 99; division of labor, 94; negotiations with chiefs, 96–97. *See also* Vegh, Darlene

First Nations: artists hub, 90–91; Assembly of, 10, 155, 230; Bulkley Valley Research Centre and, 70; loan debts and, 255n4; politics of names, 250n31; protests against pipelines, 4, 6, 29, 86, 152–53, 168–69, 177–79, 224–29, 235; residential schools, 80, 247n9; as term, 238n2, 255n11; treaty negotiations of, 8–9, 12, 17, 84–85, 155–57, 165–68, 241n15, 246n4, 254n2. *See also* land selection model; *and individual First Nation names*

First Nations Fisheries Council of British Columbia, 211

First Nations Summit, 155

Fischer, Michael, 47

forest: fire, 133–34, 253n12; old growth, 7, 8, 90, 152, 167, 194, 212, 238n4; second growth, 2, 140, 154, 173, 175, *184*, 194, 197

Forest and Range Practices Act (FRPA), 48, 243n7

Forest Practices Board, 243n8

Forest Renewal BC (FRBC), 93, 249n24

Forestry Canada, 129

Forest Service Research Branch, 9. *See also* BC Forest Service

forms of life, 18, 22, 44, 160; collaboration and, 122, 134–35; future of rural research as, 207, 223; long-term research and, 196, 234. *See also* Fischer, Michael

Fox, Irving, 60, 242n1, 245n18

Frank Calder v. British Columbia, effects of, 14, 91, 154–55

Fraser River watershed, 192

Galison, Peter, 124

Garcia, Angela, 119, 136

gender: discrepancies among researchers, 51, 81, 87; issues in Indigenous policy-making, 105

geographic information systems (GIS): databases, 93; training in, 77, 94, 100, 108, 172, 228

Gidimt'en Clan, 193, 224

Gieryn, Thomas, 252n8

Gitanyow First Nation: countermapping, 33, 153–56, 167–71, 179–80; interim treaty agreement, 166–67; land selection

model and, 155; map of, *xi*; Office of Hereditary Chiefs (GHC), 89, 152–53; Recognition and Reconciliation Agreement, 166, 167; Strategic Land and Resource Plan (SLRP), 153, 167, 169, 179; territorial borders of, ix–x. *See also* Vegh, Darlene

Gitksan: Carrier Tribal Council, 90, 246n4; spelling of, 237n1

Gitxsan Education Society, 91, 94, 97

Gitxsan First Nation: ancestry of, 74, 86, 231, 246n3; artists, 91; blockades and, xiii–xiv, 6, 19–20, 29, 34, 86–87, 168–69; feast (potlatch) of, 14, 82, 83, 86, 95, 107; feast names of, 86, 250n31; Kispiox Bridge blockade and, xiv, 3, 238n4; map of, *xi*; residential schools, 80; sovereignty project, xiv, 26, 78–79, 80, 81, 84, 101, 106, 168; spelling of, 237n1; territorial borders of, ix–x; TransCanada Pipelines and, 6, 152–53, 168–69, 171, 179, 255n9

Gitxsanimx language, 89, 248n20

Gitxsan Strategic Watershed Analysis Team (SWAT): artifacts of, 5, 75; as calling, 88; collapse of, 23, 78, 99, 106; consulting, 5, 77–78, 88, 91–96, 169, 234, 246n6; countermapping and, 5–6, 74–75, 77, 80, 92–95, 97–98; former members of, 85–86, 95, 99, 101–2, 104, 106; founding of, 5, 23, 74–75, 77, 91–92, 96, 97–98, 246n6; naming of, 246n2; negotiations with chiefs, 96–97; teaching GIS analysis and mapping, 94–95. *See also* Collier, Russell; Vegh, Darlene

Gitxsan Territorial Management program, 90

Gitxsan Treaty Society (GTS): countermapping and, 8–9, 91–92, 97–98; formation of, 91; pipeline disputes and, 168–69, 255n9; tensions with house groups and, 29, 86–87, 242n24, 248n17, 255n8

Gitxsan-Wet'suwet'en land claims. See *Delgamuukw and Gisday'wa v. The Queen*

Global Positioning System (GPS), 31, 98, *188*; in trail mapping, 152, 173; training in, 100, 172

Goodwin, Charles, 131, 250n1

Gordon and Betty Moore Foundation, 192; Wild Salmon Ecosystems Initiative and, 210

Greenpeace, 100, 114

Grossman, Zoltán, 27

ground truthing, 98, 152–53, 173

Grove, Kevin, 197

Haddad, Samir, 136

Haida First Nation, 83; *v. British Columbia* decision, 10, 15, 137–38, 157, 239n7, 246n6

Hall, Stuart, 162, 164

Han, Clara, 119, 136

Hani, Chris, 253n13

Harcourt, Mike, 8, 17

Harper, Stephen, 242n5

Harris, Walter, 91

Harrison, Simon, 254n16

Harvard Project on American Indian Economic Development, 246n7

haunting, 253n14. *See also* Derrida, Jacques

Hayek, Friedrich, 257n2

Higgs, Eric, 160

"historiality," as term, 136

history and artifacts, xvi, 18, 31, 46, 84, 245n20

Holling, Crawford S. "Buzz," 200–201, 205, 257n2

Hudson Bay Mountain, *37*

Huson, Freda, 228, 236

hydrology, 19, 62, 194–95, 216

Idle No More, 4, 235, 241n22

"Indian," as term, 237n2

Indian Act (1951), 14, 238n2

Indian residential schools, 80, 247n9

"Indian status," as term, 237n2

indicators: biodiversity, 49, 67, 211, 212, 217, 253n11; risk, 192, 207, 212, 215, 216, 217; social, 209

Indigenous, as term, 238n2

Indigenous biographies, 105

Indigenous elites, 83–84, 105

Indigenous-led mapmaking, 228–29, 250n29; and corporate support, xvi, 158, 165, 167, 169, 222, 235; Gitanyow and, 13, 161–62; Gitxsan and, 13–14, 71, 85–86, 88, 103, 106; technology and, 158, 160; Wet'suwet'en and, 30. *See also* Collier, Russell; countermapping movement; Smogelgem; transect mapping; Vegh, Darlene

Indigenous legal orders, 85, 106, 227, 246n5, 248n17. *See also* land claims

Indigenous mobilities, 82–84, 247n13

Indigenous researchers: anthropologists and, 159–60; "the calling," 79–80, 81, 84, 88; oral histories and, 160; sense of belonging for, 79

Ingold, Tim, 160–61

inheritance: government downsizing and, 119–21; intergenerational relationships and, 128; objects of, 31, 45, 66, 88; silviculture and, 115–23, 130, 141–42. *See also* succession

intergenerational relationships: inheritance and, 128; as sources of empowerment, 80; tensions of, 120, 178; transfers of knowledge and, 118, 135, 136, 251n4

Inuit Land Use and Occupancy Project, 250n27

Inuit territory, 177, 237n2

Jensen, Doreen, 91

Johnson, Leslie Main, 248nn19–20

Joseph, Alfred, 91

Joseph, Jonathan, 202

journalists: at blockade camps, 225; erasing Indigenous histories, 239n3; Unist'ot'en Clan and, 228; War in the Woods and, xiv, 6, 16, 238n4

Kispiox Bridge blockade, xiv, 3, 238n4. *See also* Gitxsan First Nation

Kispiox Valley fire, 133–34, 253n12

Kitimat, 53, 243n11

Kitwanga, 75, *112*, 151, 172

Kluane First Nation, 247n11

knowledge trusts, 29

Kohler, Robert, 252n8

'Ksan village, 90–91

land claims, 76; map biographies and, 100–101, 249; oral histories and, 15, 159, 160, 231, 245; trials, 14–15, 76–77, 138–39, 156–57, 238n3, 239n7, 241n15. See also *Delgamuukw and Gisday'wa v. The Queen*

Resilience Alliance, 202, 257n2

resilience theory: meaning of, 192–93; proponents of, 203, 205–6, 221–23; rhetoric of, 202–3; and survival of researchers, 195–99, 205–6, 208–9, 222–23

Rheinberger, Hans-Jörg, 47, 123–25, 136–37

Robertson, Leslie, 243n9

Rosaldo, Renato, 43

Rudwick, Martin, 254n17

Ryan, Don, 91, 246n1, 249n21

salmon fishing: health of, 39, 192, 218; study of, 209–13, 213–14

second-growth forests: clear-cutting sites and, 2, 154, 175, *184*, 194, 197; research in, 140, 173

Sierra Club, 100, 114

silviculture: criticisms of, 114, 129; gap dynamics in, *115*, *143*, 173, 250n2; genetics and, 126; inheritance and, 115–21, 122–23, 130, 141–42; mensuration and, 4, 112–14, 131–32, *133*, 140; prism plot in, 133; research forests and, 126–29; secondary structure and, 114, 120, 131; timber cruising and, 90. *See also* Aleza Lake Forest Experiment Station; Date Creek Research Forest

Simon, Stephanie, 202

Simpson, Audra, 84

Skeena River watershed, *11*, 28, 75, *138*, 257n5; fishing and, 39, 142, 215, 219, 257n5; logging and, 76, 141, 250n2, 252n7; 1988 blockades on, xiii, 238n4; zones of, 215

"slow activism," as term, 164

Smithers: closure of Forest Service office in, 36, 48, 55–56; consultants in, 10, 30, 42, 51, 53, *55*; contract work in, 3, 46–47, 68, 199, 209; history of, 50–51; as hub for researchers, 12–13, 36, 42, 49–53; map of, *38*; sense of belonging in, 40, 42–43, 50

Smogelgem, 228–29, 257n3

Social Credit Party, 56, 243n13

soil, science and ecology of, 113, 120, 140, 210

sovereignty: British, 156; burdens of seeking, 87, 88; conflicts over, 7; Gitxsan project

of, xiv, 26, 77, 78–79, 80, 81, 84, 101, 106, 168; paradoxes of, 79, 84

Sparrow, Robert, 15

Stegyawden (Hagwilget Peak), 2, *72*

Sterritt, Neil J., 90–91, 230–33, 249n21, 254n2, 257n5

Stikine electoral district, 96, 245n21

Stoler, Ann Laura, 44

Strategic Land and Resource Plan (SLRP), 60, 68; Gitanyow, 153, 167, 169, 179

succession: forest, 1, 71, 89, 123, 125, 129–30, 134, 141, 251n6; hereditary, 26, 95; institutional, 24, 114, 118–20, 125, 131, 191, 251n4. *See also* inheritance

Supreme Court of Canada, 10, 14–15, 137, 155, 211; in *Delgamuukw and Gisday'wa* decision, 76, 239n7, 249n21

survivance, meaning of, xvii, 164

Sustainable Resource Management Plan, 243n14

Swanner, Leandra, 252n9

Taku River Tlingit First Nation, 10, 157

TallBear, Kim, 248n14

TCP Energy. *See* TransCanada Pipelines (TCP) Corporation

technocracy, 24, 31, 42–49, 58, 203, 204, 213, 250; as term, 241n17; traditional governance and, 102

Thielmann, Tim, 243nn7–8, 244n14

timber cruising, 90

timber trade. *See* logging industry

Tironi, Manuel, 164

Tla'amin Final Agreement, 248n15

Tollefson, Chris, 243nn7–8, 244n14

traditional ecological knowledge (TEK), 159, 247n10

trail mapping, 5, 89, 92, 94–95, 108; with Global Positioning System (GPS), 152, 173

TransCanada Pipelines (TCP) Corporation, 6, 158, 224, 256n14; eviction of surveyors, 168, 255n9; funding of research, 171; Gitxsan and, 6, 152–53, 168–69, 171, 179, 255n9; negotiations with Wet'suwet'en, 168–69, 224–29; pipeline plan in Gitanyow territories, 152–53, 168–71

transect mapping, 33, 152–53, 161–62, *163*,
165, 173, 179
Treaty 8, 14, 177
trusts: data-sharing, 210; knowledge, 29
Truth and Reconciliation Commission, 105
Tsawwassen First Nation Final Agreement,
248n15
Tsilhqot' First Nation, 211; *v. British
Columbia*, 137–38
Tsimshianic language family, 250n31
Tuck, Eve, 81
Turkel, William, 245n20

Union of British Columbia Indian Chiefs,
177
United Nations Rio Declaration on
Environment and Development, 159
University of British Columbia, 54, 91,
94
University of Northern British Columbia, 51,
127–28, 243n9
US Geological Survey (USGS), ix

Vegh, Darlene: career of, 89–95, 246n1,
248n19; countermapping movement
and, 11, 13, 77, 99, *150*, 157, 169–70, 172,
179; Gitanyow countermapping and, 6,
89, 152–54, 156, 157, 167, 171–76,
179–80; Gitxsan Strategic Watershed

Analysis Team and, 5–6, 75, 78, 87,
91–95, 169, 172. *See also* Collier, Russell
Victoria versus Smithers, BC, 51
Vizenor, Gerald, xvii, 164
vocation, 79, 80, 247n8

Wah Tah K'eght, 247n12
Walker, Jeremy, 257n2
War in the Woods: blockades during,
xiii–xiv, 92, 114; as historical term, 2–3;
legacy of, xvi, 8, 12, 17–20, 128–29, 196,
225; migrants during, 50
Watts, Michael, 203
Weber, Max, 79, 103–4, 106
Weiss, Joseph, 83
Wet'suwet'en First Nation: antilogging
blockades and, xiii–xiv; map of, *xi*;
Office of the Wet'suwet'en, 168, 193, 218;
pipeline blockades and, 4, 6, 168,
224–29, 257n1; spelling of, 237n1;
territorial borders of, ix–x. See also
Delgamuukw and Gisday'wa v. The Queen
Whyte, Kyle Powys, 25
Wild Salmon Ecosystems Initiative, 210
Wilson, Jeremy, 244n14

Yale First Nation, 248n15
Yukon Umbrella Final Agreement, 166
Yurchak, Alexei, 46